Research and Development in
Intelligent Systems XX

Springer

London
Berlin
Heidelberg
New York
Hong Kong
Milan
Paris
Tokyo

Frans Coenen, Alun Preece and
Ann Macintosh (Eds)

Research and Development in Intelligent Systems XX

Proceedings of AI2003, the Twenty-third SGAI International Conference on Innovative Techniques and Applications of Artificial Intelligence

Springer

Dr Frans Coenen
Department of Computer Science, University of Liverpool, Liverpool, UK

Dr Alun Preece
University of Aberdeen, Dept of Computer Science, Aberdeen, UK

Dr Ann Macintosh, BSc, CEng
Napier University, International Teledemocracy Centre, Edinburgh, EH10 5DT, UK

British Library Cataloguing in Publication Data
A catalogue record for this book is available from the British Library

Library of Congress Cataloging-in-Publication Data
A catalog record for this book is available from the Library of Congress

ISBN 1-85233-780-X Springer-Verlag London Berlin Heidelberg
Springer-Verlag is part of Springer Science+Business Media GmbH
springeronline.com

Typesetting: Camera-ready by editors
Printed and bound at the Athenæum Press Ltd., Gateshead, Tyne & Wear
34/3830-543210 Printed on acid-free paper SPIN 10951484

TECHNICAL PROGRAMME CHAIRMAN'S INTRODUCTION

Frans Coenen
University of Liverpool, UK

This volume comprises the refereed technical papers presented at AI2003, the Twenty-third SGAI International Conference on the theory, practice and application of Artificial Intelligence, held in Cambridge in December 2003. The conference was organised by SGAI, the British Computer Society Specialist Group on Artificial Intelligence (previously known as SGES).

The papers in this volume present new and innovative developments in the field, divided into sections on Machine Learning, Knowledge Representation and Reasoning, Knowledge Acquisition, Constraint Satisfaction, Scheduling and Natural Language Processing.

This year's prize for the best refereed technical paper was won by a paper entitled *An Improved Hybrid Genetic Algorithm: New Results for the Quadratic Assignment Problem* by A. Misevicius (Department of Practical Informatics, Kaunas University of Technology, Lithuania). SGAI gratefully acknowledges the long-term sponsorship of Hewlett-Packard Laboratories (Bristol) for this prize, which goes back to the 1980s.

This is the twentieth volume in the *Research and Development* series. The Application Stream papers are published as a companion volume under the title *Applications and Innovations in Intelligent Systems XI*.

On behalf of the conference organising committee I should like to thank all those who contributed to the organisation of this year's technical programme, in particular the programme committee members, the referees and our administrator Fiona Hartree and Linsay Turbert.

Frans Coenen Technical Programme Chairman,
AI2003

ACKNOWLEDGEMENTS

AI2003 CONFERENCE COMMITTEE

Prof. Ann Macintosh, Napier University (Conference Chair)
Dr Robert Milne, Sermatech Intelligent Applications (Deputy Conference Chair, Finance and Publicity)
Dr Frans Coenen, University of Liverpool (Technical Programme Chair)
Dr. Alun Preece, University of Aberdeen (Deputy Technical Programme Chair)
Professor Max Bramer, University of Portsmouth (Application Programme Chair)
Mr Richard Ellis, Stratum (Deputy Application Programme Chair)
Prof. Adrian Hopgood, Nottingham Trent University (Tutorial Organiser)
Dr. Nirmalie Wiratunga, Robert Gordon University (Poster Session Organiser)
Bob Howlett, University of Brighton (Exhibition Organiser)
Rosemary Gilligan, University of Hertfordshire (Research Student Liaison)

TECHNICAL PROGRAMME COMMITTEE

Dr. Frans Coenen, University of Liverpool (Chair)
Dr. Alun Preece, University of Aberdeen (Vice-Chair)
Prof. Adrian Hopgood, Nottingham Trent University
Mr. John Kingston, University of Edinburgh
Dr. Peter Lucas, University of Nijmegen (The Netherlands)
Dr. Nirmalie Wiratunga, Robert Gordon University, Aberdeen

TECHNICAL STREAM REFEREES

Samir Aknine (University of Paris 6)
Andreas Albrecht (University of Hertfordshire)
Daniel Allsopp (University of Portsmouth)
Yaxin Bi (Queen's University Belfast)
Arkady Borisov (Riga Technical University)
Keith Bradley (University College Dublin)
Frans Coenen (University of Liverpool)
Bruno Cremilleux (University of Caen)
John Debenham (University of Technology, Sydney)
Stefan Diaconescu (Romainia)
Nicolas Durand (France Telecom)

Adriana Giret (Universidad Politecnica de Valencia)
Mercedes Gomez-Albarran (University Complutense, Madrid)
Anne Håkansson (Uppsala University, Sweden)
Mark Hall (University of Waikato)
Eveline M. Helsper (Utrecht University, The Netherlands)
Ray Hickey (University of Ulster)
Adrian Hopgood (Nottingham Trent University)
Bo Hu (University of Southampton)
John Kingston (University of Edinburgh)
T. K. Satish Kumar (Stanford University)
Alvin C. M. Kwan (University of Hong Kong)
Brian Lees (University of Paisley)
Peter Lucas (University of Nijmegen)
Angeles Manjarres (Madrid)
David McSherry (University of Ulster)
Daniel Manrique (Campus de Montegancedo, Madrid)
Lars Nolle (Nottingham Trent University)
Fernando Sáenz Pérez (Universidad Complutense de Madrid)
Alun Preece (University of Aberdeen)
Gerrit Renker (Robert Gordon University, Aberdeen)
María Dolores Rodríguez-Moreno (Universidad de Alcalá, Madrid)
Debbie Richards (Macquarie University, Australia)
Miguel A. Salido (Universidad Politecnica de Valencia, Spain)
Barry Smyth (University College, Dublin)
Kilian Stoffel (University of Neuchatel)
Jonathan Timmis (University of Kent)
Kai Ming Ting (Monash University, Australia)
Marina de Vos (University of Bath)
Jan Willemson (Tartu University, Estonia)
Graham Winstanley (University of Brighton)
Nirmalie Wiratunga (Robert Gordon University, Aberdeen)
Mercedes Gomez-Albarran (Univ. Complutense de Madrid)

CONTENTS

SESSION 4: KNOWLEDGE ORGANISATION, REPRESENTATION, V&V AND REFINEMENT

SESSION 5: MULTI-AGENT SYSTEMS AND RECOMMENDER SYSTEMS

BEST REFEREED TECHNICAL PAPER

An Improved Hybrid Genetic Algorithm: New Results for the Quadratic Assignment Problem

Alfonsas Misevicius

Department of Practical Informatics, Kaunas University of Technology,
Studentų St. 50–400a, LT–3031 Kaunas, Lithuania
alfonsas.misevicius@ktu.lt

Abstract

Genetic algorithms (GAs) have been proven to be among the most powerful intelligent techniques in various areas of the computer science, including difficult optimization problems. In this paper, we propose an improved hybrid genetic algorithm (IHGA). It uses a robust local improvement procedure (a limited iterated tabu search (LITS)) as well as an effective restart (diversification) mechanism that is based on so-called "shift mutations". IHGA has been applied to the well-known combinatorial optimization problem, the quadratic assignment problem (QAP). The results obtained from the numerous experiments on different QAP instances from the instances library QAPLIB show that the proposed algorithm appears to be superior to other modern heuristic approaches that are among the best algorithms for the QAP. The high efficiency of our algorithm is also corroborated by the fact that the new, record-breaking solutions were obtained for a number of large real-life instances.

1 Introduction

Genetic algorithms (GAs) are population based heuristic approaches. They have been applied successfully in various domains of artificial intelligence, search, and optimization. The promising results were obtained for many difficult optimization problems, for example, continuous optimization [1], graph partitioning [2], network design problem [3], scheduling problems [4 & 5], set covering problem [6], traveling salesman problem [7]. (GAs for the quadratic assignment problem are discussed in Section 3.)

The principles of genetic algorithms were developed by Holland [8]. Very briefly, GAs can be characterized by the following features: a) a mechanism for selecting individuals (corresponding to solutions of the optimization problem) from the population; b) an operator for creating new individuals, i.e. offsprings by combining the information contained in the previous individuals; c) a procedure for generating new solution by random perturbations of the single previous solutions; d) a rule for updating the population (culling solutions from the current population). These features are referred to as selection, crossover (recombination), mutation, and culling (updating), respectively.

There exists a great variety in the choice of how select, cross, mutate, and cull the individuals (for various modifications, see, for example, [9, 10 & 11]). Regarding QAP, the detailed implementations of selection, crossover, mutation, and culling procedures are described in Section 3.2.

The remaining part of this paper is organized as follows. In Section 2, basic ideas of a hybrid genetic approach are outlined. Section 3 describes the improved hybrid genetic algorithm to the quadratic assignment problem (QAP). Also, the results of computational experiments are presented. Section 4 completes the paper with concluding remarks.

2 An Improved Hybrid Genetic Algorithm: Basic Concepts

In contrast to the classical GAs that rely on the concept of biological evolution, the modern GAs, known as hybrid GAs (or memetic algorithms), are based rather on ideas evolution [12]. In the context of optimization, a GA is called hybrid if solutions of a given problem are improved by a local optimization (local search) algorithm – like the ideas are modified by the person before passing to the next generation. This means that populations consist solely of locally optimal solutions.

The hybrid genetic algorithm succeeds in search only if it disposes of an efficient local optimization procedure. We propose to use an iterated local search (ILS) technique [13] (very similar to a variable neighbourhood search (VNS) [14] and ruin and recreate (R&R) approach [15]). The central idea of the ILS method is to obtain high quality results by reconstruction (destruction) of an existing solution and a following improving procedure, i.e. ILS can be thought of as an iterative process of reconstructions and improvements applied to solutions. This technique appears to be superior to the well-known random multistart method in most cases. The advantage is that, instead of generating new solutions, a better idea is to reconstruct (a part of) the current solution: for the same computation time, many more reconstruction improvements can be done than when starting from purely random solutions, because the reconstruction improvement requires only a few steps to reach the next local optimum; a new local optimum can be found very quickly – usually faster than when starting from a randomly generated solution.

The favourable feature of the iterated search is that it includes reconstructions that can be viewed as mutations. This helps considerably when incorporating ILS into the hybrid GA: there is no need in mutation operator within GA itself (excepting only the case discussed below) since each individual already undergoes some transformations in the ILS procedure. Another important aspect is related to the size of population. As long as the ILS procedure is distinguished for the outstanding performance, the large populations of solutions are not necessary at all: the small size of the population is fully compensated by the ILS procedure. So, this feature allows to save the computation (CPU) time when comparing to other population-based algorithms.

It should also be noted that, in the hybrid GA proposed, a so-called restart mechanism [16] is used; this means that, if the fact of a premature convergence of the algorithm is determined, then a specific procedure ("cold restart") takes place. In fact, this restart consists of a special type mutations (referred to as "shift mutations") to be applied to all the individuals but the best. (The shift mutation procedure is described in Section 3.2.)

Returning to improvement of solutions within ILS, the different improving procedures can be used, for example, hill climbing (HC), simulated annealing (SA) or tabu search (TS). The last one seems to be the best candidate for the role of the local improvement: the power of TS has been demonstrated for a variety of optimization problems [17]. This is due to the robustness, efficacy and quickness of the TS procedure. (The basic principles of TS will briefly be considered in Section 3.2.) Note that, as a rule, we use exclusively short runs of the tabu search – we call this approach a limited iterated tabu search (LITS). Many simulations have demonstrated that these limited iterations allow saving the CPU time; on the other hand, LITS in combination with other genetic operators is quite enough to seek for near-optimal solutions.

The basic flowchart of the resulting hybrid GA – improved hybrid GA (IHGA) – is presented in Figure 1. More thoroughly, we discuss the components of this algorithm in the next section in the context of the quadratic assignment problem.

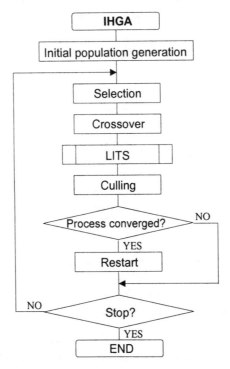

Figure 1 Basic flowchart of the improved hybrid genetic algorithm

3 New Results for the Quadratic Assignment Problem

3.1 The Quadratic Assignment Problem

The quadratic assignment problem is formulated as follows. Given two matrices $A = (a_{ij})_{n \times n}$ and $B = (b_{kl})_{n \times n}$ and the set Π of permutations of the integers from 1 to n, find a permutation $\pi = (\pi(1), \pi(2), ..., \pi(n)) \in \Pi$ that minimizes

$$z(\pi) = \sum_{i=1}^{n} \sum_{j=1}^{n} a_{ij} b_{\pi(i)\pi(j)} .$$

The important areas of the application of the QAP are: campus planning [18], computer-aided design (CAD) (placement of electronic components) [19], image processing (design of grey patterns) [20], ranking of archaeological data [21], typewriter keyboard design [22], etc [23]. For example, in the design of grey patterns (frames) [20], in order to get a grey frame of density m/n, one can generate a grid containing n ($n = n_1 * n_2$) square cases with m black cases and $n-m$ white cases. By juxtaposing many of these grids, one gets a grey surface of density m/n. To get the finest frame, the black cases have to be spread as regularly as possible. (Some examples of grey frames will be presented in Section 3.3.)

It has been proved that the QAP is NP-hard [24], therefore heuristic approaches have to be used for solving medium- and large-scale QAPs: ant algorithms [25], simulated annealing [26], tabu search [27]. Starting from 1994, several authors applied genetic algorithms to the QAP, first of all, [28, 29, 30, 31, 32, 33 & 34].

3.2 An Improved Hybrid Genetic Algorithm for the Quadratic Assignment Problem

The template of the improved hybrid genetic algorithm (IHGA) for the QAP (in an algorithmic language form) is shown in Figure 2. The details are described below in this section.

The initial population P ($P \subset \Pi$) is obtained by generating PS ($PS \leq n$) random permutations that are improved by the LITS procedure (see below).

For the parents selection, we apply a rank based selection rule [34]. This means that the better the individual, the larger probability of selecting it for the crossover.

The crossover operator used is based upon a uniform like crossover (ULX) [34]. It works as follows. First, all items assigned to the same position in both parents are copied to this position in the child. Second, the unassigned positions of a permutation are scanned from left to right: for the unassigned position, an item is chosen randomly, uniformly from those in the parents if they are not yet included in the child. Third, remaining items are assigned at random. In IHGA, we have slightly improved this classic scheme to get a so-called optimized crossover (OX). An optimized crossover is a crossover that (a) is ULX, and (b) produces a child that has the smallest objective function among the children created by M runs of ULX. So, only the best (elite) child among M children is passed through the subsequent improvement procedure. Usually, the value of M is between $0.5n$ and $2n$ (n is the problem size). The number of optimized crossovers, i.e. elite offsprings per one generation can be controlled by a parameter, Q_{cross}. Typically, the value of Q_{cross} depends on the size of a population.

---

procedure *improved_hybrid_genetic_algorithm*
  generate initial population $P \subset \Pi$ // the population size is equal to PS, where $PS \leq n$ //
  $P^\bullet := \varnothing$ // $P^\bullet$ – the population containing the improved (optimized) permutations //
  foreach $\pi \in P$ **do begin**
    $\pi^\bullet := lits(\pi)$ // *lits* – the function that performs the limited iterated tabu search on π //
    $P^\bullet := P^\bullet \cup \{\pi^\bullet\}$
  end // foreach //
  $\pi^* := \operatorname*{argmin}_{\pi \in P^\bullet} z(\pi)$ // π^* – the best permutation found //
  repeat // main cycle of the genetic algorithm: generations cycle //
    sort the members of the population $P^\bullet$ according the ascending order of the fitness
    for $i := 1$ **to** Q_{cross} **do begin** // cycle of offsprings generation and improvement //
      select $\pi', \pi'' \in P^\bullet$
      apply optimized crossover to π' and π'', get offspring π_{offspr}
      $\pi^\bullet := lits(\pi_{offspr})$ // improvement of the offspring //
      $P^\bullet := P^\bullet \cup \{\pi^\bullet\}$
      if $z(\pi^\bullet) < z(\pi^*)$ **then** $\pi^* := \pi^\bullet$
    end // for //
    remove $k = Q_{cross}$ worst individuals from population $P^\bullet$ // culling of the population //
    if population $P^\bullet$ converged **then begin**
      $P := P^\bullet, P^\bullet := \varnothing$
      foreach $\pi \in P \setminus \text{bestof}(P)$ **do begin**
        $\tilde{\pi} := shift\text{-}mutation(\pi), P^\bullet := P^\bullet \cup \{lits(\tilde{\pi})\}$
      end // foreach //
    end // if //
  until maximum generation number is reached
end // *improved_hybrid_genetic_algorithm* //

Figure 2 Template of the improved hybrid genetic algorithm for the QAP

---

function *lits*(π) // *limited_iterated_tabu_search* //
  set τ to the number of steps of tabu search procedure
  apply tabu search procedure to π, get the resulting permutation π^*, set π to π^*
  for $q := 1$ **to** Q_{lits} **do begin** // main cycle consisting of Q_{lits} iterations //
    set μ to the current reconstruction (mutation) level
    apply reconstruction procedure to π, get the resulting permutation $\tilde{\pi}$
    apply tabu search procedure to $\tilde{\pi}$, get the resulting permutation π^*
    if π^* is better than π **then** $\pi := \pi^*$
  end // for //
  return π
end // *lits* //

Figure 3 Template of the limited iterated tabu search procedure for the QAP

The limited iterated tabu search procedure (presented in Figure 3) contains two main components: a tabu search based local search procedure, and a solution reconstruction procedure.

Before describing the TS procedure for the QAP, we give some very basic definitions. Let $N_2: \Pi \to 2^{\Pi}$ be a 2-exchange neighbourhood function that defines for each $\pi \in \Pi$ a set of neighbouring solutions of π, $N_2(\pi) = \{\pi' \mid \pi' \in \Pi, d(\pi, \pi') \le 2\}$ ($d(\pi, \pi')$ is the "distance" between solutions π and π': $d(\pi, \pi') = \sum_{i=1}^{n} \text{sgn} \mid \pi(i) - \pi'(i) \mid$). A move (transformation) from the current solution π to the neighbouring one $\pi' \in N_2(\pi)$ can formally be defined by using a special operator, p_{ij} ($i,j = 1, 2, ..., n$): $\Pi \to \Pi$, which exchanges ith and jth elements in the current permutation (see Figure 4). (Notation $\pi' = \pi \oplus p_{ij}$ means that π' is obtained from π by applying p_{ij}.) The TS algorithm can then be outlined as follows (for the detailed template, see [35]). Initialize tabu list, T, and start from an initial permutation π. Then, continue the following process until a predetermined number of steps, τ, have been performed:

i) find a neighbour π'' of the current permutation π in such a way that
$\pi'' = \arg\min_{\pi' \in N_2'(\pi)} z(\pi')$, where $N_2'(\pi) = \{\hat{\pi} \mid \hat{\pi} \in N_2(\pi), \hat{\pi} = \pi \oplus p_{ij}$ and p_{ij} is not tabu$\}$;

ii) replace the current permutation π by the neighbour π'', and use as a starting point for the next step;

iii) update the tabu list T.

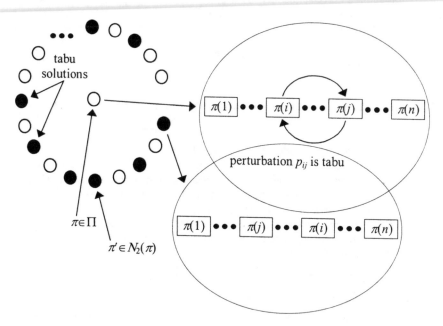

Figure 4 Illustration of the 2-exchange neighbourhood and tabu search

A reconstruction (a random pairwise interchanges based mutation) of the current solution can simply be achieved by performing some number, say μ ($\mu > 1$), random elementary perturbations, like p_{ij}. Here, the parameter μ is referred to as a reconstruction (mutation) level. For the sake of robustness, we let the parameter μ vary within some interval, say $[\mu_{min}, \mu_{max}] \subseteq [2, n]$. The values of μ_{min}, μ_{max} can be related to the problem size, n, i.e. $\mu_{min} = \max(2, \lfloor \rho_1 n \rfloor)$ and $\mu_{max} = \max(2, \lfloor \rho_2 n \rfloor)$, where ρ_1, ρ_2 ($0 < \rho_1 \le \rho_2 \le 1$) are user-defined coefficients (reconstruction factors). In our implementation, μ varies in the following way: at the beginning, μ is equal to μ_{min}; once the maximum value μ_{max} has been reached (or a better locally optimal solution has been found), the value of μ is immediately dropped to the minimum value μ_{min}, and so on.

In the limited iterated tabu search algorithm, we accept the best locally optimal solution as the only candidate for the reconstruction.

The parameter Q_{lits} (the number of iterations) plays the role of the termination criterion for the LITS procedure. Note that the increased value of Q_{lits} is used in two cases: first, when the initial population is being generated; second, when the restart of the algorithm is being performed.

The culling (updating) of the population takes place every time before going to the next generation. After k ($k = Q_{cross}$) offsprings have been added to the population, it is sorted according to the increasing values of the objective function. Solutions with the greatest objective function value are then removed away from the population to keep the size of the population constant. A special kind of updating is performed when convergence of the algorithm is observed, i.e. further improvements of the individuals are unlikely. As the convergence criterion, a threshold of entropy of the population is used. (For the definition of the entropy the reader is addressed to [30].) So, if the entropy, E, is close enough to zero ($E \le 0.1$), the population is updated in the following way: all the individuals but the best undergo a special mutation – shift mutation (SM); the mutated individuals are then improved by the LITS procedure; after this, IHGA proceeds with the new population in an ordinary way.

---

function *shift-mutation*(π, μ) // shift mutation procedure for the QAP //
    save μ elements of the permutation π starting from the location $n - \mu + 1$
    shift $n - \mu$ elements to right starting from the location μ
    replace μ elements by the elements previously saved starting from the location 1
    return π
end // *shift-mutation* //

Figure 5 Template of the shift mutation procedure

Regarding the shift mutation, this mutation was used in [35], in an efficient tabu search algorithm. It has been proven to be a highly effective diversification tool. The idea of SM is, nevertheless, very simple: having a permutation just shift all the items to right (left) (in a wrap-around fashion) by a predefined number of positions, μ ($0 < \mu < n$, n is the size of the permutation). SM distinguishes itself for the important property: as long as the population size, *PS*, is less than the problem size, *n*, the following equality holds $d(\pi_i, \pi_j) = n$, $\forall \pi_i, \pi_j \in P$, where *P* is the current population, π_i, π_j are the mutated permutations, and *d* is the "distance" between permutations (see above). The template of the SM procedure is presented in Figure 5. An example is shown Figure 6.

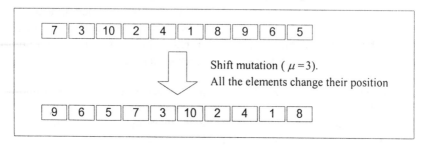

Figure 6 Example of shift mutation

The run time of IHGA is controlled by a special parameter – the total number of generations, Q_{gen}, i.e. the algorithm is continued until exactly Q_{gen} generations have been executed.

3.3 Computational Results

A large number of computational experiments were carried out in order to test the performance of the proposed algorithm. We used a wide range of the QAP instances from the quadratic assignment problem library QAPLIB [36]. The types of the QAP instances are as follows:

(a) randomly generated instances (these instances are randomly generated according to a uniform distribution; in QAPLIB, they are denoted by tai20a, tai25a, tai30a, tai35a, tai40a, tai50a, tai60a, tai80a, tai100a);

(b) real-life instances (instances of this class are real world instances from practical applications, among them: chr25a, els19, esc32a, esc64a, esc128, kra30a, kra30b, ste36a, ste36b, ste36c, tai64c, tai256c (also known as grey_16_16_92); for example, the instances tai64c, tai256 occur in the generation of grey patterns (see Section 3.1));

(c) real-life like instances (they are generated in such a way that the entries of the data matrices resemble a distribution from real-life problems; the instances are denoted by tai20b, tai25b, tai30b, tai35b, tai40b, tai50b, tai60b, tai80b, tai100b, tai150b).

For the comparison, we used robust tabu search (RTS) algorithm [27], genetic hybrid (GH) algorithm [30], fast ant system (FANT) [25], and genetic algorithm hybridized with R&R procedure (GAHRR) [33]. These algorithms belong to the most powerful algorithms for the QAP. As a main performance measure, the average deviation from the best known solution is chosen. The average deviation, θ_{avg}, is defined according to the formula $\theta_{avg} = 100(z_{avg} - z_b)/z_b$ [%], where z_{avg} is the average objective function value over *W* (*W*=1, 2, ...) restarts (i.e. single applications of the algorithm to a problem instance), and z_b is the best known value (BKV) of the objective function. (BKVs are from [36].)

The results of the comparison, i.e. the average deviations from BKV, as well as the approximated CPU times per restart (in seconds) are presented in Tables 2–4. The deviations are averaged over 10 restarts. CPU times are given for the x86 Family 6 processor. The best values are printed in bold face (in addition, in parenthesis, we give the number of times that BKV is found (if $\theta_{avg}>0$)). The values of the parameters of the algorithm IHGA for the different problem types are presented below.

Table 1 Values of the parameters for the algorithm IHGA.
The meaning of the notations used in the table is as follows: PS – the population size, Q_{gen} – # of generations, Q_{cross} – # of crossovers per generation, Q_{lits} – # of LITS iterations, τ – # of TS steps, SF – the selection factor, (ρ_1,ρ_2) – the reconstruction factors, n – the size of the instance. Regarding Q_{gen} for the instance types (b), (c), it varies from $0.1n$ and n

Problem type	PS	Q_{gen}	Q_{cross}	Q_{lits}	τ	SF	(ρ_1,ρ_2)
(a)	$3\sqrt{n}$	$\frac{1}{3}n$	$\frac{2}{3}PS$	3	$\frac{1}{2}n$	1.3	depends on problem
(b)	$3\sqrt{n}$	depends on problem	$\frac{1}{3}PS$	depends on problem	n	1.7	(0.35,0.45)
(c)	$2\sqrt{n}$	----"----	$\frac{1}{2}PS$	----"----	n	1.7	(0.35,0.45)

The values of the control parameters of the remaining algorithms were chosen in such a way that all the algorithms use approximately the same CPU time. Some differences in run time are, in most cases, negligible and cannot influence the results significantly.

Table 2 Comparison of the algorithms on randomly generated instances (type (a)).
Note. IHGA was run in two variants, first using $(\rho_1,\rho_2)=(0.3,0.4)$, and second using $(\rho_1,\rho_2)=(0.4,0.5)$. The results for the best of two variants are displayed in the column IHGA

Instance name	n	BKV	θ_{avg}					t
			RTS	GH	FANT	GAHRR	IHGA	
tai20a	20	703482	0.061 (8)	0.411 (2)	0.857 (0)	0.061 (8)	**0**	2.5
tai25a	25	1167256	0.125 (7)	0.382 (2)	1.100 (1)	0.088 (7)	**0**	6.0
tai30a	30	1818146	0.058 (7)	0.362 (4)	0.940 (1)	0.019 (8)	**0**	16
tai35a	35	2422002	0.184 (4)	0.643 (0)	1.271 (0)	0.126 (6)	**0**	36
tai40a	40	3139370	0.436 (0)	0.618 (0)	1.394 (0)	0.338 (0)	**0.209** (1)	85
tai50a	50	4941410	0.736 (0)	0.871 (0)	1.645 (0)	0.567 (0)	**0.424** (1)	300
tai60a	60	7208572	0.816 (0)	1.009 (0)	1.596 (0)	0.590 (0)	**0.547** (0)	720
tai80a	80	13557864	0.611 (0)	0.593 (0)	1.249 (0)	**0.271** (0)	0.320 (0)	3200
tai100a	100	21125314	0.582 (0)	0.493 (0)	1.160 (0)	0.296 (0)	**0.259** (0)	12000

Table 3 Comparison of the algorithms on real-life instances (type (b)).
Note. IHGA was run in three variants, first using Q_{lits}=5, second using Q_{lits}=7, and third with Q_{lits}=10. The results for the best of three variants are displayed in the column IHGA

Instance name	n	BKV	θ_{avg}					t
			RTS	GH	FANT	GAHRR	IHGA	
chr25a	25	3796	5.148 (1)	3.825 (1)	6.033 (3)	0.232 (9)	**0**	1.9
els19	19	17212548	3.076 (2)	0.421 (9)	0.421 (9)	**0**	**0**	0.1
esc32a	32	130	1.231 (3)	0.769 (6)	2.615 (3)	0.154 (9)	**0**	2.5
esc64a	64	116	0.862 (6)	**0**	**0**	**0**	**0**	4.0
esc128	128	64	16.562 (1)	**0**	**0**	**0**	**0**	24
kra30a	30	88900	0.403 (7)	**0**	1.380 (2)	0.224 (8)	**0**	1.8
kra30b	30	91420	0.023 (7)	0.031 (6)	0.071 (7)	0.028 (7)	**0**	2.3
ste36a	36	9526	0.063 (6)	0.086 (6)	0.355 (2)	0.061 (7)	**0**	9.8
ste36b	36	15852	0.106 (8)	0.025 (9)	0.426 (5)	**0**	**0**	2.4
ste36c	36	8239.11	0.022 (7)	0.051 (5)	0.139 (4)	0.001 (9)	**0**	3.8
tai64c	64	1855928	0.015 (4)	**0**	**0**	**0**	**0**	0.3
tai256c	256	44759294 [a]	0.086 (0)	0.078 (0)	0.121 (0)	0.053 (1)	**0.021** (5)	1280

[a] comes from [37].

Table 4 Comparison of the algorithms on real-life like instances (type (c)).
Note. IHGA was run in two variants, first using Q_{lits}=5, and second using Q_{lits}=7.
The results for the best of two variants are displayed in the column IHGA

Instance name	n	BKV	θ_{avg}					t
			RTS	GH	FANT	GAHRR	IHGA	
tai20b	20	122455319	**0**	0.045 (9)	0.091 (8)	**0**	**0**	0.4
tai25b	25	344355646	0.044 (8)	**0**	0.007 (9)	0.007 (9)	**0**	0.9
tai30b	30	637117113	0.408 (3)	0.000 (9)	0.029 (7)	**0**	**0**	1.8
tai35b	35	283315445	0.233 (5)	0.132 (4)	0.198 (1)	0.059 (7)	**0**	3.0
tai40b	40	637250948	0.204 (6)	**0**	**0**	**0**	**0**	7.0
tai50b	50	458821517	0.239 (0)	0.035 (7)	0.222 (0)	0.002 (8)	**0**	20
tai60b	60	608215054	0.291 (0)	0.018 (6)	0.179 (3)	0.000 (9)	**0**	40
tai80b	80	818415043	0.270 (0)	0.354 (2)	0.312 (0)	0.003 (2)	**0**	150
tai100b	100	1185996137	0.186 (0)	0.045 (3)	0.096 (0)	0.014 (3)	**0**	440
tai150b	150	498896643 [a]	0.392 (0)	0.394 (0)	0.514 (0)	0.200 (0)	**0.111** (2)	2300

[a] comes from [38].

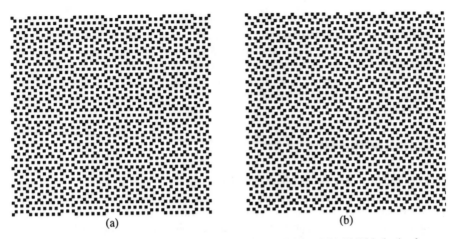

(a)   (b)

Figure 7 Examples of grey frames of density (a) 71/256 and (b) 72/256 obtained
by solving QAP by IHGA

Table 5 New best known solutions for grey patterns problems. Problems of this type are
described in [20 & 38] under the name grey_n_1_n_2_m, where m is the density of the grey
$(0 \leq m \leq n = n_1 * n_2)$, and $n_1 * n_2$ is the size of a frame

Instance name	n	Previous best known value	New best known value
grey_16_16_71	256	24742496[a]	24693608
grey_16_16_72	256	25570996[a]	25529984
grey_16_16_73	256	26423856[a]	26382310
grey_16_16_74	256	27276468[a]	27235240
grey_16_16_75	256	28154258[a]	28114952
grey_16_16_76	256	29001308[a]	29000908
grey_16_16_77	256	29895152[b]	29894452
grey_16_16_78	256	30820660[a]	30797954
grey_16_16_79	256	31736576[a]	31702182
grey_16_16_80	256	32658876[a]	32593088

[a] comes from [38], [b] comes from [33].

It can be seen from Tables 2–4 that the algorithm IHGA appears to be superior to
other efficient algorithms. Our algorithm obtained the best known solutions for all
the instances tested, excepting the large difficult random instances tai60a, tai80a
and tai100a. Nevertheless, the results obtained for these instances are considerably
better than those of FANT and RTS due to Taillard [25 & 27] or GH due to
Fleurent and Ferland [30]. Moreover, for almost all (excepting the largest
available) real-life and real-life like instances, the average deviation of the

objective function is equal to zero – this indicates that these instances are most probably solved to pseudo-optimality. It is important that IHGA finds the pseudo-optimal solutions surprisingly quickly; for example, for the instance tai100b, approximately 400 seconds are enough (see Table 4). It should also be stressed that IHGA discovered new best known solutions for several large grey patterns problems. New solutions are presented in Table 5. Some visual examples are shown in Figure 7.

4 Concluding Remarks

The method that has been widely applied to many fields of computer science, among them optimization problems, is the genetic approach. In this paper, we introduce an improved hybrid genetic algorithm (IHGA) for the difficult combinatorial optimization problem, the quadratic assignment problem.

In contrast to standard GAs that rely on the concept of biological evolution, the hybrid GAs are based rather on cultural evolution. In hybrid GAs, the individuals (solutions) are improved by using efficient local optimization techniques. In some sense, this is similar to ideas' lifetime – human ideas usually undergo many transformations before passing to the future generations.

The success of a hybrid GA depends, in a high degree, on the efficiency of a local optimization algorithm. In this paper, we propose a very promising procedure based upon so-called limited iterated tabu search (LITS) approach that, in turn, rely on the tabu search (TS) and the iterated local search (ILS) principle. The robustness of LITS is achieved by applying a proper diversification mechanism, i.e. one tries to obtain better optimization results by reconstruction of a locally optimal solution and a following TS-relying improvement procedure.

It is important that the LITS procedure includes the reconstructions of solutions: these reconstructions can be viewed as mutations, so this helps greatly in the case of incorporating LITS into the hybrid GA. In our improved HGA, the populations are typically very compact – this is due to the high performance of the LITS procedure. Therefore, a lot of computations can be saved when comparing to other GAs. Another favourable feature of our genetic algorithm is related to a restart mechanism. This mechanism is distinguished for a special sort of mutations, so-called shift mutations, which have been proven to be extremely robust and effective.

All these features coupled with additional refinements furthered the development of a powerful hybrid genetic algorithm for the QAP. The results from the experiments show that this algorithm appears to be superior to other intelligent optimization techniques, as well as the genetic algorithm that was presented by the author at ES2002 (Cambridge, UK, 2002). For many QAP instances from QAPLIB (especially, for the real life and real-life like instances), a few seconds are enough for our algorithm to find the best known (pseudo-optimal) solutions. Moreover, for several grey patterns problems (that are special QAP cases), record-breaking solutions were obtained.

Acknowledgements

Author is grateful to Prof. E. Taillard for providing the codes of the robust tabu search and fast ant algorithms. He also would like to thank Prof. C. Fleurent for the paper that helped coding the hybrid genetic algorithm.

References

1. Chelouah R, Siarry P. A continuous genetic algorithm designed for the global optimization of multimodal functions. J Heurist 2000; 6:191–213
2. Bui TN, Moon BR. Genetic algorithm and graph partitioning. IEEE Trans Comput 1996; 45:841–855
3. Drezner Z, Salhi S. Using metaheuristics for the one-way and two-way network design problem. Nav Res Logist 2002; 49:449–463
4. Miller DM, Chen HC, Matson J, Liu Q. A hybrid genetic algorithm for the single machine scheduling problem. J Heurist 1999; 5:437–454
5. Yagiura M, Ibaraki T. Genetic and local search algorithms as robust and simple optimization tools. In: Osman IH (ed) Meta-heuristics: theory & applications, Kluwer, Dordrecht, 1996, pp 63–82
6. Beasley JE, Chu PC. A genetic algorithm for the set covering problem. Eur J Oper Res 1996; 94:392–404
7. Merz P, Freisleben B. Genetic local search for the TSP: new results. Proceedings of the 1997 IEEE international conference on evolutionary computation, 1997, pp 159–164
8. Holland JH. Adaptation in natural and artificial systems, University of Michigan Press, Ann Arbor, MI, 1975
9. Davis L. Handbook of genetic algorithms, Van Nostrand, New York, 1991
10. Goldberg DE. Genetic algorithms in search, optimization and machine learning, Addison-Wesley, Reading, MA, 1989
11. Mühlenbein H. Genetic algorithms. In: Aarts E, Lenstra JK (eds) Local search in combinatorial optimization, Wiley, Chichester, 1997, pp 137–171
12. Moscato P. Memetic algorithms: a short introduction. In: Corne D, Dorigo M, Glover F (eds) New ideas in optimization, McGraw-Hill, London, 1999, pp 219–234
13. Lourenco HR, Martin O, Stützle T. Iterated local search. In: Glover F, Kochenberger G (eds) Handbook of metaheuristics, Kluwer, Norwell, 2002, pp 321–353
14. Mladenović N, Hansen P. Variable neighbourhood search. Comput Oper Res 1997; 24:1097–1100
15. Schrimpf G, Schneider K, Stamm-Wilbrandt H, Dueck V. Record breaking optimization results using the ruin and recreate principle. J Comput Phys 2000; 159:139–171
16. Eshelman L. The CHC adaptive search algorithm: how to have safe search when engaging in nontraditional genetic recombination. In: Rowlings GJE (ed) Foundations of genetic algorithms, Morgan Kaufmann, 1991, pp 265–283
17. Glover F, Laguna M. Tabu search, Kluwer, Dordrecht, 1997
18. Dickey JW, Hopkins JW. Campus building arrangement using TOPAZ. Transp Res 1972; 6:59–68
19. Hu TC, Kuh ES (ed). VLSI circuit layout: theory and design, IEEE Press, New York, 1985
20. Taillard E. Comparison of iterative searches for the quadratic assignment problem. Location Sci 1995; 3: 87–105
21. Krarup J, Pruzan PM. Computer-aided layout design. Math Program Study 1978; 9:75–94

22. Burkard RE, Offermann J. Entwurf von schreibmaschinentastaturen mittels quadratischer zuordnungsprobleme. Z Oper Res 1977; 21:121–132
23. Burkard RE, Çela E, Pardalos PM, Pitsoulis L. The quadratic assignment problem. In: Du DZ, Pardalos PM (eds) Handbook of combinatorial optimization, Vol.3, Kluwer, Dordrecht, 1998, pp 241–337
24. Sahni S, Gonzalez T. P-complete approximation problems. J ACM 1976; 23:555–565
25. Taillard E. FANT: fast ant system. Tech. report IDSIA-46-98, Lugano, Switzerland, 1998
26. Bölte A, Thonemann UW. Optimizing simulated annealing schedules with genetic programming. Eur J Oper Res 1996; 92:402–416
27. Taillard E. Robust taboo search for the QAP. Parallel Comput 1991; 17:443–455
28. Ahuja RK, Orlin JB, Tiwari A. A greedy genetic algorithm for the quadratic assignment problem. Comput Oper Res 2000; 27:917–934
29. Drezner Z. A new genetic algorithm for the quadratic assignment problem. INFORMS J Comput 2003 (in press)
30. Fleurent C, Ferland JA. Genetic hybrids for the quadratic assignment problem. In: Pardalos PM, Wolkowicz H (eds) Quadratic assignment and related problems. DIMACS series in discrete mathematics and theoretical computer science, Vol.16, AMS, Providence, 1994, pp 173–188
31. Lim MH, Yuan Y, Omatu S. Efficient genetic algorithms using simple genes exchange local search policy for the quadratic assignment problem. Comput Optim Appl 2000; 15:249–268
32. Merz P, Freisleben B. Fitness landscape analysis and memetic algorithms for the quadratic assignment problem. IEEE Trans Evolut Comput 2000; 4:337–352
33. Misevicius A. Genetic algorithm hybridized with ruin and recreate procedure: application to the quadratic assignment problem. In: Bramer M, Preece A, Coenen F (eds) Research and development in intelligent systems XIX. Proceedings of 22nd SGAI international conference on knowledge based systems and applied artificial intelligence (Cambridge, UK), Springer, London, 2002, pp 163–176
34. Tate DM, Smith AE. A genetic approach to the quadratic assignment problem. Comput Oper Res 1995; 1:73–83
35. Misevicius A. A tabu search algorithm for the quadratic assignment problem. Working paper, Kaunas University of Technology, Lithuania, 2002 (under review)
36. Burkard RE, Karisch S, Rendl F. QAPLIB – a quadratic assignment problem library. J Glob Optim 1997; 10:391–403
37. Stützle T. MAX-MIN ant system for quadratic assignment problems. Res. report AIDA-97-04, Darmstadt University of Technology, Germany, 1997
38. Taillard E, Gambardella LM. Adaptive memories for the quadratic assignment problem. Tech. report IDSIA-87-97, Lugano, Switzerland, 1997

SESSION 1A:

ALGORITHMS AND A1 (GAS, HIDDEN MARKOV MODELS, SIMULATED ANNEALING AND PERCEPTRONS

Adaptive Mutation Using Statistics Mechanism for Genetic Algorithms

Shengxiang Yang

Department of Computer Science

University of Leicester

University Road, Leicester LE1 7RH, UK

Email: s.yang@mcs.le.ac.uk

Abstract

It has long been recognized that mutation is a key ingredient in genetic algorithms (GAs) and the choice of suitable mutation probability will have a significant effect on the performance of genetic search. In this paper, a statistics-based adaptive non-uniform mutation (SANUM) is presented within which the probability that each gene will subject to mutation is learnt adaptively over time and over the loci. As a search algorithm based on mechanisms abstracted from population genetics, GAs implicitly maintain the statistics about the search space through the population. SANUM explicitly makes use of the statistics information of the allele distribution in each gene locus to adaptively adjust the mutation probability of that locus. To test the performance of SANUM, it is compared to traditional bit mutation operator with a number of "standard" fixed mutation probabilities suggested by other researchers over a range of typical test problems. The results demonstrate that SANUM performs persistently well over the range of test problems while the performance of traditional mutation operators with fixed mutation probabilities greatly depends on the problem under consideration. SANUM represents a robust adaptive mutation operator that needs no prior knowledge about the fitness landscape of the problem being solved.

1   Introduction

The genetic algorithm (GA), as one kind of generation-based evolutionary algorithm, maintains a population of candidate solutions to a given problem, which are evaluated according to a problem-specific fitness function that defines the environment for the evolution. New populations are created by selecting relatively fitter members of the present population and evolving them through recombination and mutation operations [12]. The performance of a GA depends on many factors, such as the encoding scheme, the selection method, the population size, the crossover and mutation operators. This makes it difficult, if not impossible, to choose operators and relevant parameters for optimal performance. In this paper we focus on the mutation operator.

Holland [15] introduced the mutation operator as a "background operator" that changes bits of individuals only occasionally, with a rather small mutation probability $p_m \in [0, 1]$ per bit. Mutation is used to ensure that all possible alleles can enter the population and provide variation in a GA population. This is done by having one allele replaced by another. For example, in a binary string representation, mutation on a parent to produce a child is done by flipping each bit randomly according to a mutation probability. Based on Holland's simple GA, there has been much work, both practically [20] and theoretically [23] on the relative merits of mutation as a search mechanism. Much of the work has been concerned with finding globally "optimal" mutation probability for GAs. Common settings of static mutation probability recommended by researchers are as follows: $p_m = 0.001$ by De Jong [7], $p_m = 0.01$ by Grefenstette [11], and $p_m \in [0.005, 0.001]$ by Schaffer $et\ al$ [20]. Based on the result of Schaffer $et\ al$ [20], Bäck [3] proposed an expression of $p_m = 1.75/(N * L^{1/2})$ where N is the population size and L denotes the string length. Mühlenbein [19] derived that $p_m = 1/L$ should be generally 'optimal', which was further verified by Smith and Fogarty [22]. These settings were obtained by experimental investigations and are consistent with Holland's proposal of using mutation as a background operator. However, there is an increasing body of both empirical [10] and theoretical [3] evidence showing that the optimal mutation probability will not only depend on the problem being solved but also vary with the progress of evolutionary searching.

In this paper, a statistics-based adaptive non-uniform mutation (SANUM) is proposed for GAs. As a search algorithm based on mechanisms abstracted from population genetics, GAs implicitly maintain the statistics about the search space through the population. GAs use the selection, crossover and mutation operations to extract the implicit statistics from the population to reach the next set of points in the search space. This implicit statistics can be used explicitly to enhance GA's performance. SANUM explicitly makes use of the statistics information of the distribution of alleles in a gene locus over the population to adjust the mutation probability for that locus adaptively with the progress of the GA.

In the rest of this paper, we first briefly review relevant work, next describe SANUM in detail, and then present our experiment study that compares SANUM over traditional bit mutation based on a typical set of test problems, finally give out our conclusions as well as discussions on potential future work relevant to SANUM.

2 Adapting the Mutation in GAs

The adaptation of genetic operators and relevant parameters was first introduced into Evolutionary Strategies (ESs) where the mutation step size is successfully controlled by self-adaptation, e.g., see Schwefel [21]. In recent years with the interaction between the GA and the ES communities, there has been an increasing interest in the use of adaptive operators within the GA to enhance GA's performance [9]. Based on how the strategy parameters are changed adaptation in GAs can be classified into three categories: *deterministic mechanism* where the value of a strategy parameter is altered according to some deterministic rule, *adaptive mechanism* where there is some form of feedback information from the search process that is used to direct the change of a strategy parameter, and *self-adaptive mechanism* where the parameter to be adapted is encoded into the chromosomes and undergoes genetic operations (hence, also called *co-evolution*).

There has been much work on adaptation in mutation for GAs [4]. Generally speaking, adaptation in mutation happens at two levels. At the top level, the ratio between mutation and crossover is adapted during the run of a GA. Davis [6] proposed that the GA can select from a set of operators to perform on a chosen parent, each with a fixed probability. Julstrom [16] adaptively adapted the ratio between mutation and crossover based on their performance. Corne *et al.* [5] devised the COst Based operator Rate Adaptation (COBRA) method where the GA periodically swaps given k fixed probabilities between k operators by giving the highest probability to the operator that has been producing the most gains in fitness. Tuson and Ross [24] extended the COBRA method by co-evolving the mutation and crossover probabilities (one-normalized real numbers) with each individual.

At the bottom level, the probability of mutation is adapted during the run of a GA, uniformly or non-uniformly over the loci. Bäck [3] proposed a self-adaptation scheme by adding a probability vector $\vec{p} = \{p_1, \ldots, p_n\}$ (n is the number of object variables) for each individual. The mutation scheme first mutates the mutation probability p_i with p_i itself and then uses the resulting p_i to mutate the ith object variable. Hesser and Männer [14] derived a general expression that deterministically varies the mutation probability with time by

$$p_m(t) = (\alpha/\beta)^{1/2} \times exp(-\gamma t/2)/(N \times L^{1/2})$$

where α, β, γ are constants, N is the population size, L is the string length, and t is the time (generation counter). Fogarty [10] used a deterministic scheme that decreases p_m over time exponentially, such that $lim_{t \to \infty} P_m(t) = 0$. Fogarty [10] also used a scheme that decreases the mutation probability over bit representation and gives bits of different significance different schedules. In this paper a new mechanism is proposed that adapts the mutation probability over the loci but needs no knowledge in advance about the bit representation of the problem, such as the significance of a bit position as in Fogarty's scheme [10].

3   Statistics-based Adaptive Non-Uniform Mutation

For the convenience of description and analysis, we introduce the concepts of intrinsic attribute and extrinsic tendency of allele valuing for a gene locus. In the binary-encoded optimal solution(s) of a given problem, a gene locus is called *1-intrinsic* if its allele is 1, *0-intrinsic* if its allele is 0, or *neutral* if its allele can be either 0 or 1. Whether a locus is 1-intrinsic, 0-intrinsic, or neutral depends on the problem under consideration and encoding scheme, e.g., whether introns are inserted [17]. During the running of a GA, a gene locus is called *1-inclined* if the frequency of 1s in its alleles over the population tends to increase (to the limit of 1.0) with time (generation), *0-inclined* if the frequency of 1s tends to decrease (to the limit of 0.0), or *non-inclined* if there is no tendency of increasing or decreasing. Whether a locus is 1-inclined, 0-inclined, or non-inclined depends on the problem under consideration, encoding scheme, genetic operators and initial conditions.

Usually with the progress of the GA, those gene loci that are 1-intrinsic (or 0-intrinsic) will appear to be 1-inclined (or 0-inclined), i.e., the frequency of 1s in the alleles of these loci will eventually converge to 1 (or 0). SANUM makes use of this convergence information as feedback information to control the mutation by adjusting the mutation probability for each locus.

We use the frequency of 1s in the alleles in a locus over the population (equivalently we can use the frequency of 0s as the argument) to calculate corresponding mutation probability of that locus. The frequency of 1s in a locus's alleles can be looked as the degree of convergence to "1" for that locus. Let $f_1(i, t)$ $(i = 1, \ldots, L)$ denote the frequency of 1s in the alleles in locus i over the population at time (generation) t and $p_m(i, t)$ $(i = 1, \ldots, L)$ denote the mutation probability of locus i at time t. Then, as shown in Figure 1, $p_m(i, t)$ can be calculated from $f_1(i, t)$ as follows:

$$p_m(i, t) = P_{max} - 2 * |f_1(i, t) - 0.5| * (P_{max} - P_{min}) \tag{1}$$

where $|x|$ denotes the absolute value of x, P_{max} and P_{min} are the maximum and minimum allowable mutation probabilities for a locus respectively, e.g., $P_{max} = 1/L$ and $P_{min} = 10^{-4}$.

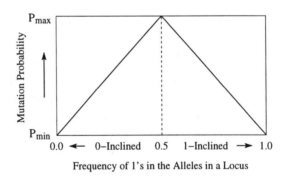

Figure 1: Triangular function used for calculating the mutation probability for a gene locus.

Now during the evolution of the GA, after a new population t has been generated, we first calculate the distribution of 1s $f_1(i, t)$ for each locus i over the population and from this obtain the mutation probability $p_m(i, t)$ for gene locus i. Then we can perform SANUM operations similarly as traditional bit mutation except that SANUM uses $p_m(i, t)$ for each locus i instead of a global p_m for all the loci.

According to the classification of adaptation for GAs reviewed in section 2, the goal of adaptive mechanism is to use the knowledge dynamically acquired about the search space to adjust the GA suitably to the problem. SANUM belongs to the class of adaptive mechanism that occurs at the bottom-level of mutation. It uses the statistics of allele distribution as feedback information to adaptively adjust the mutation probability non-uniformly over the loci, hence the name Statistics-based Adaptive Non-Uniform Mutation (SANUM).

SANUM is simpler than those mechanisms that add one extra value per bit and co-evolve these values with each individual, such as Bäck's self-adaptation scheme [3]. With SANUM, what we add to traditional bit mutation are spatially only one real vector of L-dimension that records the frequency of ones for each locus, and computationally only one statistics per generation that calculates the frequency of ones over the population (hence the mutation probability) for each locus. This simple statistics added is well rewarded as discussed below.

The motivation behind SANUM lies in the fact that with the progress of genetic search SANUM helps protecting building blocks found so far while still exploiting new building blocks. To formally analyze the behavior of GAs, Holland [15] first introduced the concept of *schema* to describe a subset of binary strings of fixed length that have similarities at certain positions. For example, the schema $S = 1****0$ (where "*" denotes a "don't care" bit) represents the set of all 6-bit strings that begin with 1 and end with 0. Given a schema S, its *order o(S)* is the number of fixed positions within S and its *defining length l(S)* is the distance between the outermost fixed bits of S. Building blocks are short, low-order, better than average schemas. Holland's *schema theorem* states that building blocks receive an exponentially increasing number of trials in the subsequent generations.

In fact building blocks can be looked as the combination of non-neutral (1-intrinsic or 0-intrinsic) genes. When the population is randomly initialized, the frequency of 1s in the alleles in each locus is statistically about 0.5 and hence $p_m(i,t) = P_{max}$ for all the loci. However, with the progress of the GA, when building blocks are partially found, that is, some 1-intrinsic and 0-intrinsic loci tend to converge to 1 and 0 respectively, SANUM decreases the mutation probabilities of these loci according to Equation (1). In this way, SANUM can protect building blocks found so far that are located on these partially or totally converged loci. While on the other hand, for those unconverged loci the mutation probabilities are remained to be high within SANUM. This is useful because there may be building blocks not expressed on these loci yet. From these discussions, it can be seen that SANUM strikes to balance the construction of new building blocks and protection of found building blocks over the loci with time adaptively.

Traditional bit mutation keeps a constant mutation probability over all the loci. As the population converges, with traditional bit mutation, in fact fewer and fewer offsprings generated by mutating those converged loci will survive in the next generation. That is, many mutation operations are wasted on those converged loci. Most of these wasted mutation operations and hence wasted fitness evaluations are saved by SANUM through adaptively decreasing $p_m(i,t)$

to P_{min} for those converged loci.

4   The Test Problems

In order to compare the performance of SANUM, a wide range of typical benchmark problems is selected as the test set. These problems represent different difficulty levels for GAs. They are described as follows.

4.1   The One-Max Problem

The One-Max problem [1] simply counts the ones contained in a binary string as the fitness of that string. The aim is to obtain a string containing all ones, that is, to maximize ones in a string. A string length of 100 bits was used for our study.

4.2   The Royal Road Functions

The Royal Road functions R_1 and R_2 were devised by Mitchell, Forrest and Holland [18] to investigate GA's performance with respect to schema processing and recombination in an idealized form. Royal Road functions contain tailor-made building blocks (schemas) based on 64-bit binary strings. They are defined using a list of schemas. Each schema s_i is given a coefficient c_i which is equal to its order $o(s_i)$ (a schema's order is the number of fixed positions within that schema). R_1 consists of 8 disjunctive order-8 schemas of which each has 8 adjacent ones. R_2 consists of four levels of schemas: level 0 (bottom level) is the same as R_1, level 1 has 4 order-16 schemas of which each combines two adjacent schemas in level 0, level 2 contains 2 order-32 schemas each combining two adjacent schemas in level 1, and finally level 3 (the optimal schema) combines the 2 schemas in level 2. The fitness of a bit string x for $R_1(x)$ and $R_2(x)$ is computed by summing the coefficients c_i corresponding to each of the given schema s_i of which x is an instance. That is, $R_1(x)$ and $R_2(x)$ are defined as follows:

$$R_1(x) = \sum_{i=1}^{i=8} c_i \delta_i(x) \text{ and } R_2(x) = \sum_{i=1}^{i=14} c_i \delta_i(x)$$

where $\delta_i(x) = \{1, \text{if } x \in s_i; 0, \text{otherwise}\}$. The optimal solutions for R_1 and R_2 are given as: $R_1(111...1) = 64$ and $R_2(111...1) = 192$.

4.3   The L-SAT Problem Generator

The random L-SAT problem generator devised by De Jong, Potter and Spears [8] is a boolean satisfiability problem generator devised to investigate the effects of epistasis on the performance of GAs. It generates random boolean expressions in conjunctive normal form of clauses subject to three parameters v (number of boolean variables), c (number of disjunctive or conjunctive clauses) and l (the length of the clauses). Each clause is created by selecting l

of v variables uniformly randomly and negating each variable with probability 0.5. For each generated boolean expression, the aim is to find an assignment of truth values to the v variables that makes the entire expression true. Since the boolean expression is randomly generated, there is no guarantee that such an assignment exists. The difficulty and complexity of the problem varies with the parameters v, c and l. For example, increasing the number of clauses increases the epistasis. The fitness function for the L-SAT problem is as follows:

$$f(chrom) = \frac{1}{c} \sum_{i=1}^{c} f(clause_i)$$

Where $chrom$ consists of c clauses and the fitness contribution of clause i, $f(clause_i)$, is 1 if the clause is satisfied or 0 otherwise.

In our experiments we will use the same parameters as in [8]. We fixed the number of variables v to 100 and the length of the clauses l to 3. The number of clauses c was varied from 200 (low epistasis) to 1200 (medium epistasis) to 2400 (high epistasis).

4.4 Deceptive Functions

Deceptive functions are those functions where the low-order building blocks do not combine to form higher-order building blocks: instead they form building blocks resulting in a sub-optimal solution. Deceptive functions are developed as difficult test functions for comparing different implementations of GAs. Goldberg, Korb and Deb [13] have devised an order-3 minimum fully deceptive problem as follows:

```
f(000) = 28   f(001) = 26   f(010) = 22   f(011) = 0
f(100) = 14   f(101) = 0    f(110) = 0    f(111) = 30
```

where all the order-1 and order-2 building blocks (e.g., "0**" and "*00" where the wildcard "*" matches both 0 and 1) in the search space are deceptive and will lead the genetic search away from the global optimum "111" and toward the deceptive local optimum "000" instead.

Based on an algorithm of constructing fully deceptive functions, Whitley [25] has also developed an order-4 fully deceptive problem as follows:

```
f(0000) = 28   f(0001) = 26   f(0010) = 24   f(0011) = 18
f(0100) = 22   f(0101) = 16   f(0110) = 14   f(0111) = 0
f(1000) = 20   f(1001) = 12   f(1010) = 10   f(1011) = 2
f(1100) = 8    f(1101) = 4    f(1110) = 6    f(1111) = 30
```

In this paper, we constructed two 60 bit deceptive functions: one contains 20 copies of Goldberg, Korb and Deb's 3-bit fully deceptive subfunction (called Deceptive Function DF_1) and another contains 15 copies of Whitley's 4-bit fully deceptive subfunction (called Deceptive Function DF_2). The optimal solutions for DF_1 and DF_2 have a fitness of 600 and 450 respectively.

5 Experimental Study

5.1 Design of Experiment

In order to test SANUM, in this experimental study it is compared with traditional bit mutation with a series of recommended "standard" fixed probabilities: $1/L$ by Mühlenbein [19], 0.01 by Grefenstette [11], $1.75/(N*L^{1/2})$ by Bäck [3], and 0.001 by De Jong [7]. Note that for L-SAT and One-Max problems, $1/L = 0.01$. For SANUM, the mutation probability $p_m(i,t)$ for each locus i $(i = 1, \ldots, L)$ varied adaptively with time (generation counter t) between $P_{max} = 1/L$ and $P_{min} = 10^{-4}$ according to equation (1). For each experiment of combining different mutation (traditional bit flip mutation with different mutation rate or SANUM) and test problem, 100 independent runs were executed. In all the experiments, the fitness proportionate selection with the stochastic universal sampling [2], 2-point crossover, and elitist model [7] were used in the GA. The crossover probability was fixed to the typical value of 0.6, and the population size was set to 100 for each run. In order to have a strict comparison the same 100 different random seeds were used to generate initial populations for the 100 runs of each experiment. For each run, the initial population is randomly created using a technique that generates exactly equal number of 0s and 1s for each locus[1], that is, $f_1(i,0) = 0.5$ for each locus i $(i = 1, \ldots, L)$ in the initial population. In this way the random sampling bias in the initial population (for example for some locus j, $f_1(j,0) = 0.8$ or 0.2) that may mislead SANUM is cancelled.

For each run, the best-so-far fitness was recorded every 100 evaluations. Here, only those chromosomes changed by crossover and mutation operations were evaluated and counted into the number of evaluations. For each run, the maximum allowable number of evaluations varies with the test problem and is suitably set to let all the mutation operators have the chance to express their power. Each experiment result was averaged over 100 independent runs.

5.2 Experimental Results

The experimental results on different test problems are shown in Figure 2 to Figure 5 respectively. From these figures, the following observations can be seen.

First, SANUM performs persistently well on the test problems. In fact, SANUM performs better than traditional mutation operators with different "standard" fixed rates on all the test problems except the deceptive functions DF_1 and DF_2. On the deceptive functions, SANUM is beaten by traditional mutation operators with $p_m = 0.001$ and $p_m = 1.75/(N*L^{1/2})$. However, it also performs better than bit mutation with $p_m = 1/L$ and as well as bit mutation with $p_m = 0.01$.

Second, $p_m = 0.001$ suggested by De Jong [7] seems to be a good choice for bit mutation. It performs better than other fixed probabilities on most of the

---

[1]It is possible because the population size is set to an even number, 100.

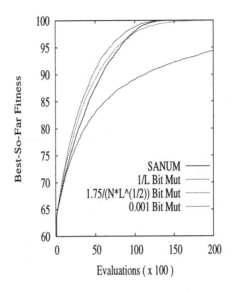

Figure 2: Experiment results with respect to best-so-far fitness against evaluations of GAs with different mutation operators on One-Max problem. The data were averaged over 100 runs.

test problems. However, its performance is seriously the worst on royal road functions R_1 and R_2. This happens because of its worst construction power for building blocks. This example shows that the performance of traditional bit mutation with fixed mutation probability heavily depends on the problem fitness landscape.

Third, SANUM performs much better than traditional mutation operators on royal road functions R_1 and R_2 (see Figure 3). This is due to the strong building blocks built in the royal road functions. During the early stage of searching GAs with traditional bit mutation perform better than the GA with SANUM. However, after certain evaluations, when some useful building blocks has been built up the GA with SANUM greatly outperforms GAs with traditional bit mutation because SANUM efficiently avoids mutating those converged loci where building blocks already found so far reside. Similar results can be observed on L-SAT problems (see Figure 4) as on royal road functions. The GA with SANUM is beaten by GAs with traditional bit mutation with $p_m = 0.001$ and $p_m = 1.75/(N * L^{1/2})$ during the early stage of searching. However, after certain evaluations the GA with SANUM outperforms GAs with traditional bit mutation.

Finally, as recognized by other researchers, the choice of mutation operators and proper probabilities in genetic algorithms really has a significant effect on the performance of genetic search. Hence, developing mutation operators that

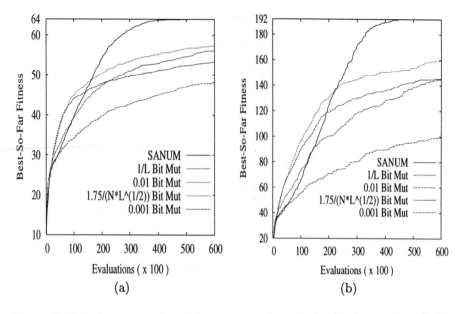

Figure 3: Experiment results with respect to best-so-far fitness against evaluations of GAs with different mutation operators on Royal Road Functions (a) R_1 and (b) R_2. The data were averaged over 100 runs.

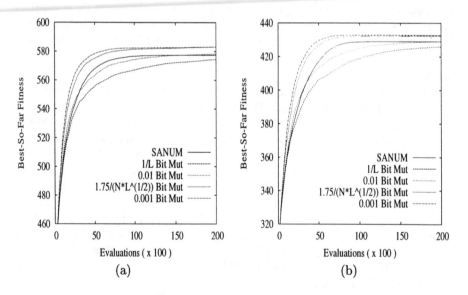

Figure 4: Experiment results with respect to best-so-far fitness against evaluations of GAs with different mutation operators on Deceptive Functions (a) DF_1 and (b) DF_2. The data were averaged over 100 runs.

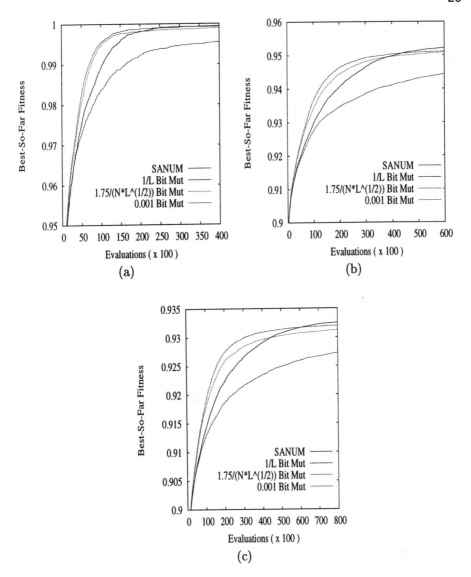

Figure 5: Experiment results with respect to best-so-far fitness against evaluations of GAs with different mutation operators on L-SAT problems with $v = 100$, $l = 3$ and (a) low epistasis $c = 200$, (b) medium epistasis $c = 1200$, and (c) high epistasis $c = 2400$. The data were averaged over 100 runs.

can adjust the mutation probability adaptively with the problem fitness landscape and with the progress of genetic searching is really meaningful for improving GA's performance. SANUM is obviously a good attempt to this direction.

6 Conclusions

In this paper a statistics-based adaptive non-uniform mutation, SANUM, is proposed for genetic algorithms The motivation of SANUM is to make use of the statistics information implicitly contained in the population explicitly to guide the mutation operation. SANUM achieves this by using the allele distribution in the current population to adjust the mutation probability for each gene locus adaptively during the progress of the GA. Through decreasing the mutation probabilities on those converged loci SANUM can save mutation operations wasted on them.

The experimental results of this study demonstrate that the GA with SANUM performs persistently well over a wide range of test problems while the performance of GAs with traditional bit mutation with different fixed mutation probabilities greatly depends on the problem under consideration. The experiment results indicate that SANUM represents a robust adaptive mutation operator that needs no prior knowledge about the problem fitness landscape and that it is a good candidate mutation operator for GAs.

Since SANUM works at the bottom-level of mutation, it can be easily combined with other adaptation techniques for mutation and can act as the basis for analyzing and designing new related algorithms. In this study, a simple triangular function is used to calculate the mutation probability for each locus. Other functions such as exponential functions instead may further improve GA's performance, which is one future work about SANUM. Comparing obtained SANUM with other adaptation techniques for mutation is another future work about SANUM.

References

[1] D. H. Ackley (1987). *A Connectionist Machine for Genetic Hillclimbing.* Boston, MA: Kluwer Academic Publishers.

[2] J. E. Baker (1987). Reducing bias and inefficiency in the selection algorithms. In J. J. Grefenstelle (ed.), *Proc. 2nd Int. Conf. on Genetic Algorithms,* 14-21. Lawrence Erlbaum Associates.

[3] T. Bäck (1992). Self-Adaptation in Genetic Algorithms. In F. J. Varela and P. Bourgine (eds.), *Proc. of the 1st European Conf. on Artificial Life,* 263-271. MIT Press.

[4] T. Bäck (1997). Mutation Parameters. In T. Bäck, D. B. Fogel, and Z. Michalewicz (eds.), *Handbook of Evolutionary Computation,* E1.2.1-E1.2.7. Oxford University Press.

[5] D. Corne, P. Ross and H.-L. Fang (1994). GA Research Note 7: Fast Practical Evolutionary Timetabling. *Technical Report,* Department of Artificial Intelligence, University of Edinburgh, UK.

[6] L. Davis (1989). Adapting operator probabilities in genetic algorithms. In D. Schaffer (ed.), *Proc. of the 3rd Int. Conf. on Genetic Algorithms*, 60-69. San Mateo CA: Morgan Kaufmann Publishers.

[7] K. A. De Jong (1975). *An Analysis of the Behavior of a Class of Genetic Adaptive Systems*. PhD Thesis, Department of Computer and Communication Sciences, University of Michigan, Ann Abor.

[8] K. A. De Jong, M. A. Potter and W. M. Spears (1997). Using problem generators to explore the effects of epistasis. In T. Bäck (ed.), *Proc. of the 7th Int. Conf. on Genetic Algorithms*, 338-345. San Mateo, CA: Morgan Kaufmann Publishers.

[9] A. E. Eiben, R. Hinterding and Z. Michalewicz (1999). Parameter control in evolutionary algorithms. *IEEE Trans. on Evolutionary Computation* 3(2):124-141.

[10] T. C. Fogarty (1989). Varying the Probability of Mutation in the Genetic Algorithm. In J. D. Schaffer (ed.), *Proc. of the 3rd Int. Conf. on Genetic Algorithms*, 104-109. San Mateo, CA: Morgan Kaufmann Publishers.

[11] J. J. Grefenstette (1986). Optimization of Control Parameters for Genetic Algorithms. *IEEE Trans. on Systems, Man and Cybernetics*, 16(1): 122-128.

[12] D. E. Goldberg (1989). *Genetic Algorithms in Search, Optimization, and Machine Learning*. Reading, MA: Addison-Wesley.

[13] D. E. Goldberg, B. Korb and K. Deb (1989). Messy Genetic Algorithms: Motivation, Analysis, and First Results. *Complex Systems*, 4: 415-444.

[14] J. Hesser and R. Männer (1991). Towards an Optimal Mutation Probability in Genetic Algorithms. In H.-P. Schwefel, R. Männer (eds.), *Proc. of the 1st Conf. on Parallel Problem Solving from Nature*, 23-32.

[15] J. H. Holland (1975). *Adaptation in Natural and Artificial Systems*. Ann Arbor, University of Michigan Press.

[16] B. Julstrom (1995). What have you done for me lately? adapting operator probabilities in a steady-state genetic algorithm. In L. J. Eshelman (ed.), *Proc. of the 6th Int. Conf. on Genetic Algorithms*, 81-87. San Mateo, CA: Morgan Kaufmann Publishers.

[17] J. Levenick (1995). Metabits: Genetic Endogenous Crossover Control. In L. J. Eshelman (ed.), *Proc. of the 6th Int. Conf. on Genetic Algorithms*, 88-95. San Mateo, CA: Morgan Kaufmann Publishers.

[18] M. Mitchell, S. Forrest and J. H. Holland (1992). The Royal Road for Genetic Algorithms: Fitness Landscapes and GA Performance. In F. J. Varela and P. Bourgine (eds.), *Proc. of the 1st European Conference on Artificial Life*, 245-254. Cambridge, MA: MIT Press.

[19] H. Mühlenbein (1992). How Genetic Algorithms Really Work: I. Mutation and Hillclimbing. In R. Männer and B. Manderick (eds.), *Proc. of the 2nd Conf. on Parallel Problem Solving from Nature*, 15-29.

[20] J. D. Schaffer, R. A. Caruana, L. J. Eshelman, and R. Das (1989). A Study of Control Parameters Affecting Online Performance of Genetic Algorithms for Function Optimization. In J. D. Schaffer (ed.), *Proc. of the 3rd Int. Conf. on Genetic Algorithms*, 51-60. San Mateo, CA: Morgan Kaufmann Publishers.

[21] H-P. Schwefel (1981). Numerical Optimization of Computer Models. Wiley, Chichester.

[22] J. E. Smith and T. C. Fogarty (1996). Self-adaptation of Mutation Rates in a Steady-State Genetic Algorithm. In *Proc. of the 3rd IEEE Conf. on Evolutionary Computation*, 318-323. IEEE Press.

[23] W. Spears (1992). Crossover or Mutation. In L. D. Whitley (ed.), *Foundations of Genetic Algorithms 2*. San Mateo, CA: Morgan Kaufmann Publishers.

[24] A. Tuson and P. Ross (1998). Adapting Operator Settings in Genetic Algorithms. *Evolutionary Computation*, 6(2): 161-184.

[25] L. D. Whitley (1991). Fundamental Principles of Deception in Genetic Search. In G. J. E. Rawlins (ed.), *Foundations of Genetic Algorithms 1*, 221-241. San Mateo, CA: Morgan Kaufmann Publishers.

Off-line Recognition of Handwritten Arabic Words Using Multiple Hidden Markov Models

Somaya Alma'adeed, Colin Higgins, and Dave Elliman
University of Nottingham
Nottingham NG8 1BB, UK
sxa@cs.nott.ac.uk, cah@cs.nott.ac.uk, dge@cs.nott.ac.uk

Abstract

Hidden Markov Models (HMM) have been used with some success in recognising printed Arabic words. In this paper, a complete scheme for unconstrained Arabic handwritten word recognition based on a Multiple discriminant Hidden Markov Models is presented and discussed. The overall engine of this combination of a global feature scheme with an HMM module, is a system able to classify Arabic-Handwritten words and has been tested on one hundred different writers. The system first attempts to remove some of the variation in the images that do not affect the identity of the handwritten word. Next, the system codes the skeleton and edge of the word such that feature information about the strokes in the skeleton is extracted. Then, a classification process based on a rule-based classifier is used as that a global recognition engine to classify words into eight groups. Finally, for each group, the HMM approach is used for trial classification. The output is a word in the lexicon. A detailed experiment has been carried out, and successful recognition results are reported.

1 Introduction

Off-line handwriting recognition is the automatic transcription by computer, where only the image of that handwriting is available. Much work has been done on the recognition of Latin characters, both separated and in cursive script. The case of recognizing Arabic characters has received much less attention. Recognizing Arabic characters is also important for non-Arabic speaking countries such as Farsi, Curds, Persians, and Urdu-speakers who use the Arabic characters in writing although the pronunciation is different. Significant previous work has been carried out by: Abuhaiba et al. This dealt with some problems in the processing of binary images of handwritten text documents [1]. Almuallim and Yamaguchi proposed a structural recognition technique for Arabic handwritten words [2]. A look-up table can be used for the recognition of isolated hand-written Arabic characters [3]. Amin and others proposed a technique for the recognition of hand-printed Arabic characters using a neural network [4]. Obaid introduced Arabic handwritten character recognition by neural networks [5]. Saleh et al. describe an efficient algorithm for coding handwritten Arabic characters [6]. It is noted that most of this work was done assuming that the Arabic handwritten word is already segmented into separated characters before recognition. This paper deals with the segmentation step, as well as the recognition step of offline handwritten Arabic words, since off-line Arabic character recognition operations involve many inter-related steps that cannot be separated from each other, as a simple sequence of operations.

In this paper, the Arabic handwritten word recognition problem is modelled within the framework of multiple Hidden Markov Models (HMMs). The states of the HMM are identified with the letters of the alphabet. Once the models are established the Viterbi algorithm is used to recognize the sequence of letters composing the word.

Because writers of Arabic write the same handwritten word in different fonts and styles (figure 1), it is difficult to device one classifier or one set of features that gives a reasonable recognition rate. For example two or more different words can have the same meaning. By training and testing we found that some words in the database are clearly distinguished by a single set of features. We can have close to 100% recognition rate for words that are written in only one kind of writing style. So we develop two substantially different recognition engines, both based on a segmentation-free approach. Our first engine is a global feature scheme [7,8] using some ascender and descender features and making use of a rule-based classification engine. The second scheme is based on a set of features using a HMM classifier.

Some researchers seem to agree that the future of reliable recognition systems lies in the combination of multiple classifiers [9]. As such, we incorporate those two different recognition engines into one hybrid system. The engine with global features is first used to dynamically reduce the original lexicon to a restricted number of possible choices for each input word. We then make use of our second engine to recognise accurately the handwritten data.

(a)

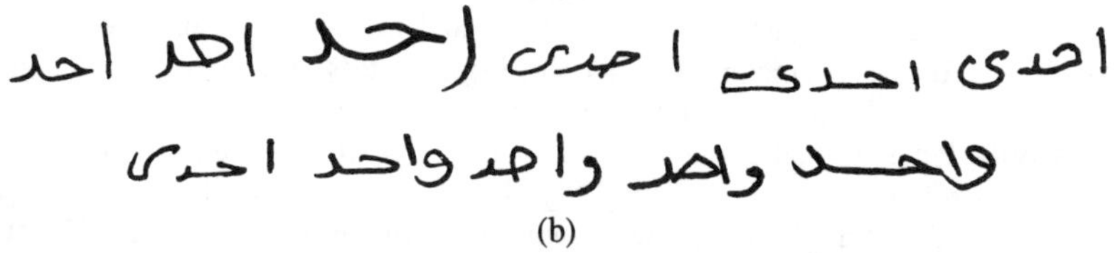

(b)

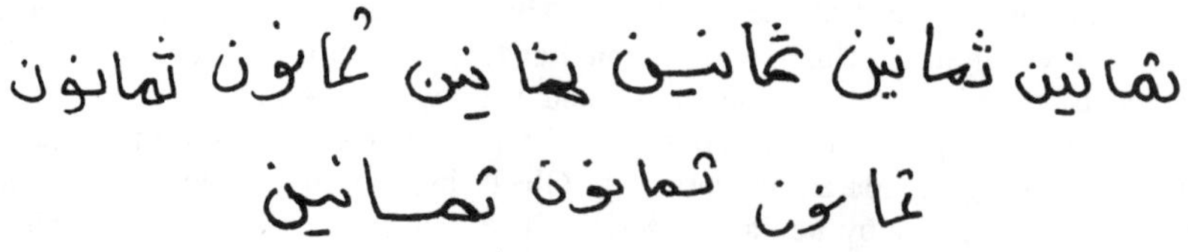

(c)

figure 1: Examples of Arabic words written in different fonts and styles. (a) nine (b) one or part eleven, and (c) eighty.

2 System Overview

This paper describes the operation of the complete classification process for a handwriting recognition system for single Arabic words, from the handwritten Image of the Arabic script to the output of the recognized word. Any word recognition system can be divided into sections: pre-processing, recognition, and post-processing. The handwritten word is normalized so as to be presented in a more reliable manner by the stage of pre-processing. Then recognition is carried out to identify the word. First using the global feature engine to reduce the original lexicon. The HMM recogniser [10] is then applied to that reduced lexicon. Then the data likelihoods for each frame of data in the representation, are estimated using a vector quantization (VQ) method. The proposed system has two main advantages. Firstly, it deals with similar Arabic words with different meaning. Secondly, it takes advantage of the position of features in the character or sub character, to be used by the VQ and HMM classifier. The following sections describe the pre-processing operation. They also discuss the features used in such a system. In section four, the HMM classifier, which classifies the features captured from the word image, is discussed. Finally, experimental results are included in section five. Figure 2 illustrates the recognition system, which is based on the combination of rather different segmentation-free engines based, respectively, on global features and HMM schemes.

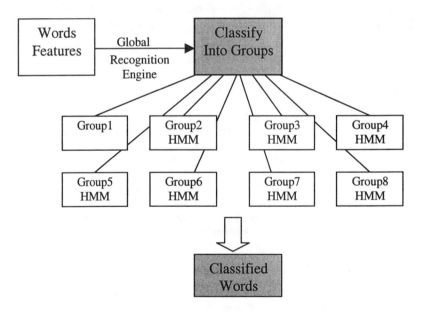

Figure 2: Recognition of Off-Line Handwritten Arabic Words Using Multiple Hidden Markov Models

3 Preprocessing

The main advantage in pre-processing the handwritten word image is to organize the information so as to make the subsequent task of recognition simpler and more accurate. The most significant operation in the pre-processing stage is normalization. This attempts to remove some variation in the images, which do not affect the identity of the word. This system incorporates normalization for each of the following factors: the stroke width, the slope, and the height of the letters. The normalization task will reduce each word image to one consisting of vertical letters of uniform height on a horizontal base line made of one-pixel-wide strokes. In this system, the word image is loaded and cropped. Then the slant and slope of the word is corrected and thinned. Features are calculated to represent the useful information contained in the image of the word [7]. Finally, the word is segmented into frames, so the previous features in these frames could be distributed.

4 Global Word features

In our classification scheme, we differentiate between global features and local features. For the global classifier that separated the data into groups of words, the global features are used, while for the HMM local feature are used. In [10] we found that the recognition rate was low because some words conflict with other words. The words that were confused with other words, can be differentiated from each other, by three main features: the number of upper dots, the number of lower dots, and the number of segments. Using these three features and noting the existing of each feature by a one or zero we generate 2^3, that is 8 groups. Figure 3 describes the relation between words and groups in the training phase.

5 Local classifier

The local classifier classifies the groups into words using a different HMM for each group as described in [10]. However, in the new system each group will have a different set of parameters: the number of states, the number of symbols and the stopping criteria. These parameters are chosen depending on the result of training and testing. The set of parameters that gives higher recognition rate were selected. Also, each HMM used a different set of features. The author of [11] mentioned that classifier that depend on time like HMM training and testing using the most suitable features is the best way of feature selection. Table 3 describes the set of parameters that gave the best recognition rate for each group.

6 Local Grammar

In Arabic handwriting the same word can be written in different ways. The forty-seven words in the lexicon are actually twenty-five words that have the same meaning but are written in a slightly different way (see the examples in figure 2). So a local grammar is used to find the words that are missclassified as words that have the same meaning.

Table 1: The recognition rate for the global Word Feature Recognition Engine

Feature used	Recognition rate into groups (chossing the best rate)	Recognition rate into groups (choosing the best two rates)	Recognition rate into groups (choosing all rates)
1,2,3	94.86%	98.46%	99.10%

7 Experimental Results

The system described in this paper has been applied to a database of handwritten words produced by one hundred writers. It was created especially for this application since there is no previous publicly available database of Arabic handwritten characters available to use as a standard test bed, in contrast to the case in Latin characters [8] where many standard data sets exist. Samples of about 4700 Arabic words for the lexicon used in cheque filling were gathered and stored in separate files.

About 10% of the data was excluded from the testing and training data because of errors in baseline detection and preprocessing, which presents an interesting area for future research. Also feature classification must be optimal in order to extract the distinct primitives and correctly identify the characters. However, the hand-printed characters tended to have "hairs" which created problems in generalizing the primitives. Another problem encountered with feature extraction was that of establishing the direction of curves.

For the global features at first we used seven features which were the number of loops, the position of ascenders (ra "ر" , and waw "و"), and descenders (alef "ا"), the number of "Alef", lower dots, upper dots, and the number of segments. By testing the data on the database, the last three features were found to give the best recognition rate as illustrated in table 2.

The database was seperated into training and testing data. In the training phase the words were segmented into characters or sub-characters. Feature extraction then transformed the segmented images into quantity feature vectors, which were then partitioned into several groups by the clustering algorithm. The cluster centroid (or codebook) from this part of the training is kept for further use. For each word, the (quantized) observation sequences are then used to train an HMM for this word, using the Forward-Backward re-estimation algorithm. In the testing phase, a frame-based analysis (pre-processing, feature extraction, and segmentation) is performed to give observation vectors, which are then vector quantized into the possible codebook vectors. The code book size was chosen after empirical testing, and selected to be 90 for the first group, 100 for the next group, 80 for group three, 90 for group four, 120 for group 5, and 120 for group 8. The resulting observation sequence and the probability measures for all the HMMs, given by $\lambda = \{\Pi, A, B\}$, are then used to calculate the log-likelihoods for each HMM. The word associated with the HMM of highest log-likelihood is declared to be the recognized word, and the index is returned. Two thirds of the data were used for training and the rest for testing. By training and testing the system on the database of handwritten Arabic

38

words, the system has obtained a near 60% recognition rate (without using post-processing). (Table 3 gives the recognition rate for each group). The first group which contains one word has 97% recognition rate, and according to [12] this word has the highest use in cheque-filling applications.

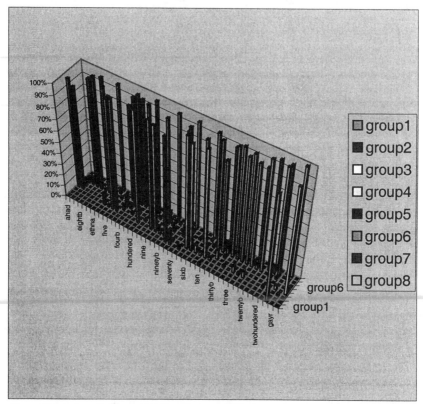

Figure 3 The relation between words, groups, and the percentage of each word in the each group for global classifier.

The prototype system described here is promising. However, there remains much room for improvement in terms of early use of the lexicon. Comparison of the results obtained in this research with other research is difficult because of differences in experimental details, the actual handwriting used, the method of data collection, and dealing with real Arabic off-line handwritten words. If this work is compared to an Arabic thesis [1-6, 12-15] on recognition of handwritten Arabic words, it is the first one that uses a multiple HMM to recognize Arabic handwritten words. This also means that it uses different sets of features and segmentation techniques. Comparing this work with [13] which has 32% recognition rate, and [10] which achieves 45%, both using HMM (implemented on unconstrained Arabic handwritten). Our approach has been much more successful.

Table 2: The relation between words, groups, and the percentge of each word in each group for some words in the dictionary

Word	group1	group2	group3	group4	group5	group6	group7	group8
ahad	0.00%	0.00%	0.00%	96.67%	1.67%	1.67%	0.00%	0.00%
ahda	0.00%	0.00%	0.00%	91.53%	1.69%	5.08%	1.69%	0.00%
eight	0.00%	0.00%	0.00%	0.00%	0.00%	6.35%	92.06%	1.59%
eightb	0.00%	0.00%	0.00%	0.00%	0.00%	96.77%	3.23%	0.00%
eightyb	0.00%	0.00%	0.00%	0.00%	0.00%	1.52%	98.48%	0.00%
ethna	0.00%	0.00%	0.00%	0.00%	0.00%	94.74%	5.26%	0.00%
fifty	0.00%	0.00%	11.11%	0.00%	0.00%	88.89%	0.00%	0.00%
fiftyb	0.00%	0.00%	1.56%	0.00%	0.00%	0.00%	3.13%	95.31%
four	0.00%	0.00%	0.00%	2.86%	11.43%	0.00%	85.71%	0.00%

Table 3: The recognition rate for the global Word Feature Recognition Engine

Feature used	Recognition rate into group
Group1	97
Group2	55
Group3	55
Group4	78
Group5	100
Group6	56
Group7	59
Group8	57
Recognition rate	60
Recognition rate with simple grammar	69

8 Conclusion and Future work

The system described in this thesis has been applied to a database of handwritten words written by one hundred different writers, and each word can be written in different fonts. Some fonts are common in writing styles while other are rare. For this reason, we don't have enough patterns for training the system, and it is clear that the system needs more patterns from the rare writing styles. Also more features might be used in future work. Adding a simple statistical diagram approach to adjust the likelihood of each word using data from a sample of cheques would produce a high percentege of correctly recognition sentences.

40

References

1. Abuhaiba, S.Mahmoud, and R.Green, Recognition of Handwritten Cursive Arabic Characters, IEEE Trans. Pattern Analysis and Machine Intelligence, June, 1994, 16(6):664-672

2. H. Almuallim and S. Yamaguchi, A method of recognition of Arabic cursive handwriting,, IEEE Trans. Pattern Anal. Machine Intell., 1987, T-PAMI(9):715-722.

3. S. Saadallah and S. Yacu, Design of an Arabic character reading machine, Proc. Of computer Processing of Arabic language, Kuwait, 1985.

4. Amin, H.Al-Sadoun and S.Fischer, Hand printed character recognition system using artificial network, Pattern recognition, 1996, 29(4):663-675.

5. A.M. Obaid, Arabic handwritten character recognition by neural nets, Journal on communications, , July-Aug, 1994, 45(i):90-91.

6. A. Saleh, A method of coding Arabic characters and it's application to context free grammar, Pattern recognition letters, 1994, 15(12)1265-1271.

7. S. Almaadeed, C. Higgens, and D. Elliman, A New Preprocessing System for the Recognition of Off-line Handwritten Arabic Words, IEEE International Symposium on Signal Processing and Information Technology, December, 2001.

8. S. Almaadeed, C. Higgens, and D. Elliman, a Database for Arabic Handwritten Text Recognition Research, Proc. 8th IWFHR, Ontario, Canada, 2000, (8):130-135.

9. D. Guillevic and C. Y. Suen, Recognition of Legal Amount on Bank Cheques, Pattern Analysis & Applic, 1998, 1(1):485-489.

10. Somaya Alma'adeed, Colin Higgins, and Dave Elliman, Recognition of Off-Line Handwritten Arabic Words Using Hidden Marcov Model Approach, ICPR 2002, Quebec City, August 2002.

11. Pavel Pudil, Petr Somol, and Josef Kittler, Feature Selection in Statistical Pattern Recognition, ICPR 2002 Tutorial, Quebec City, August 2002.

12. Y. Al-Ohali, M. Cheriet and C. Y. Suen, Databases for Recognition of Handwritten Arabic Cheques, Proc. 7th IWFHR, Amsterdam, the Netherlands, 2000, (7):601-606.

13. M. Dehghan, K. Faez, M. Ahmadi, M. shridhar, Handwritten Farsi word recognition: a holistic approach using discrete HMMM, Pattern Recognition, 2001, 34(5):1057-1065.

14. S. Snoussi Maddouri, H. Amiri, Combination of LocalandGlobal Vision Modelling for Arabic Handwritten Words Recognition, Proc. 8th IWFHR, Ontario, Canada, the Netherlands, 2000, 130-135.

15. M. Khorsheed, A dissertation for the degree of Doctor of philosophy, University of Cambridge, UK, 2002.

On a new Stepwidth Adaptation Scheme for Simulated Annealing and its Practical Application

Lars Nolle

School of Computing and Mathematics
The Nottingham Trent University
Burton Street, Nottingham, NG1 4BU, UK
lars.nolle@ntu.ac.uk

Abstract

Simulated Annealing is a general optimisation algorithm, based on hill-climbing. As in hill-climbing, new candidate solutions are selected from the 'neighbourhood' of a current solution and then processed. For continuous parameter optimisation, it is practically impossible to choose direct neighbours, because of the vast number of points in the search space. In this case, it is necessary to choose new candidate solutions from a wider neighbourhood, i.e. from some distance of the current solution, for performance reasons. The right choice of this distance is often crucial for the success of the algorithm, especially in real-world applications where the number of fitness evaluations is limited. This paper introduces a new neighbourhood selection scheme for Simulated Annealing, based on a simplified measurement of the mean distance between particles of the population. This new algorithm is refereed to as Differential Annealing. The performance of the new algorithm is compared with standard Simulated Annealing and Stepwidth Adapting Simulated Annealing for on-line Langmuir probe tuning.

1. Black Box Optimisation in Engineering Applications

Many black-box optimisation algorithms have been developed and studied extensively over the recent years. However, these studies were mostly carried out on artificial test functions or simulations rather than on real systems. Optimisation algorithms for engineering applications have different demands compared to artificial test functions, because they often work on real systems, are often confronted with noisy and incomplete data, and they must not only be effective but also be efficient. This is because in real-time applications, the number of fitness evaluations is often strictly limited. One of these optimisation algorithms is Simulated Annealing (SA), which will be briefly introduced in the next section.

2. Simulated Annealing

Simulated Annealing (SA) is a robust general optimisation method that was first introduced by Kirkpatrick et. al. [1], based on the work of Metropolis et. al. [2]. It simulates the annealing of a metal, in which the metal is heated-up to a temperature near its melting point and then slowly cooled to allow the particles to move towards an optimum energy state. This results in a more uniform crystalline structure and so the process allows some control over the microstructure. SA has been demonstrated to be robust and capable of dealing with noisy and incomplete real-world data [3,4]. This makes SA suitable for engineering applications.

2.1 Basic Simulated Annealing

Simulated annealing is actually a variation of the hill-climbing algorithm. Both start off from a randomly selected point within the search space. Unlike in hill-climbing, if the fitness of a new candidate solution is less than the fitness of the current solution, the new candidate solution is not automatically rejected. Instead, it becomes the current solution with a certain transition probability p(T). This transition probability depends on the difference in fitness ΔE between the current solution and the candidate solution, and the temperature T. Here, 'temperature' is an abstract control parameter for the algorithm rather than a real physical measure. The algorithm starts with a high temperature, which is subsequently reduced slowly, usually in steps. At each step, the temperature must be held constant for an appropriate period of time (i.e. number of iterations) in order to allow the algorithm to settle in a 'thermal equilibrium', i.e. in a balanced state. If this time is too short, the algorithm is likely to converge to a local minimum. The combination of temperature steps and cooling times is known as the annealing schedule, which is usually selected empirically. Figure 1 shows a typical run of a SA algorithm, optimising a real-world system [4]. It documents the development of the fitness during a search. It can be observed that the algorithm initially explores the search space (large differences in fitness), while later on (after approximately 400 iterations in this example) it exploits the most promising region. Hence, the behaviour of the algorithm at the beginning of the search is similar to a random walk, while towards the end it performs like ordinary hill climbing. Simulated Annealing may also work on a population of particles, i.e. solutions, rather than on just one particle.

2.2 Simulated Annealing and Continuous Parameter Optimisation

For engineering applications with continuous parameter optimisation, it is practically impossible to choose direct neighbours of the current solution as new candidate solutions, simply because of the vast number of points in the search space. In this case, it is necessary to choose new candidate solutions from some distance in a random direction of the current solution in order to travel in an acceptable time through the search space. In such a case, a neighbourhood selection scheme needs to be applied [5].

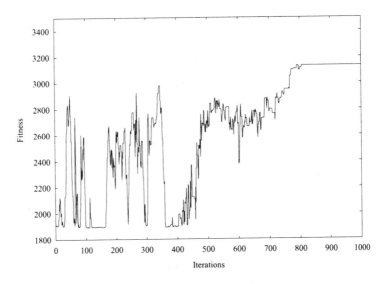

Figure 1: Typical run of a SA algorithm; at the beginning of the search the algorithm explores the search space, while it is exploiting the most promising region of the search space after the algorithm has been 'frozen'.

2.2.1 Neighbourhood Selection

This distance could either be a fixed step width s or it could be chosen randomly with an upper limit s_{max}. In the first case, the neighbourhood would be defined as the surface of a hypersphere around the current solution, in the second case the neighbourhood would be defined as the volume of the hypersphere. In the latter case, new candidate solutions might be generated by adding small, equally distributed random numbers from the interval $[-s_{max}, s_{max}]$ to each component of the current solution vector.

2.2.2 Need for Step Width Variation

The maximum step width s_{max} is crucial to the success of SA. If s_{max} is chosen to be too small and the start point for a search run is too far away from the global optimum (Figure 2), the algorithm might not be able to get near that optimum before the algorithm 'freezes', i.e. the temperature becomes so small that $p(T)$ is virtually zero and the algorithm starts to perform only hill climbing. In that case, it will get stuck in the nearest local optimum. If, on the other hand, the step width has been chosen to be too large, and the peak of the optimum is very narrow (Figure 3), the algorithm might well get near the global optimum before the algorithm 'freezes', but never reaches the top, because most of the steps are simply too large so that new candidate solutions 'fall off' the peak. Hence, there is always a trade-off between accuracy and robustness in selecting an appropriate maximum step width. If s_{max} is too small, SA has the potential to reach the peak of the 'frozen-in' optimum, but it cannot be guaranteed that this optimum is the global one. On the other hand, if s_{max} is too large, SA has the potential to get near the global optimum, but it might never reach the top of it.

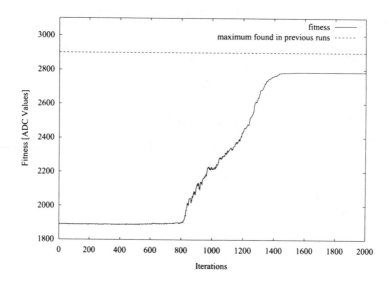

Figure 2: The step width has been chosen too small; the algorithm failed to reach the region containing the maximum peak during the exploration phase of the search.

A solution could be to use small steps and to adjust the cooling schedule to increase the length of the Markov chains, i.e. to allow for a longer search. This is not always be possible in real-world optimisation problems with time constrains, i.e. a limited number of possible fitness evaluations.

Another solution is to adapt the maximum step width s_{max} to the search process itself [5]. In general, there are two possible approaches. Firstly, s_{max} may be adapted to an SA parameter, like current iteration, temperature, etc. The search starts with a large value for s_{max} and is subsequently decreased towards the end. Secondly, s_{max} can be adapted to the fitness landscape, e.g. ΔE or p(T). The proposed new adaptation scheme, which is inspired by Differential Evolution [6], uses information about the fitness landscape.

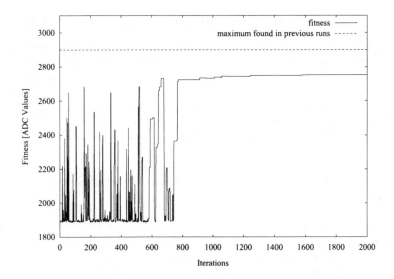

Figure 3: The maximum step width has been chosen too large; the algorithm failed to find the maximum peak during the exploitation phase of the search run.

For Simulated Annealing, it was mentioned above that, for continuous parameter optimisation, solutions from some distance s_{max} in a random direction of the current solution have to be chosen in order to travel in an acceptable time through the search space. The right choice for the maximum step width s_{max} is crucial to the success of SA. The fact that it should not be limited at the beginning of the search, whereas it should be sufficiently small towards the end of the search, has lead to the development of SWASA, a step width adaptation scheme, in previous research [5]. SWASA only used information about the elapsed time, i.e. the current number of generations. Although the scheme has been shown to increase the performance of SA, it did not use information from the fitness landscape itself. This would clearly be of benefit for the search process. In this work, a new adaptation scheme, based on the mean distance between the individuals (here referred to as particles), in one generation (iteration), is presented.

3. Differential Annealing

In this new adaptation scheme, referred to as Differential Annealing (DA) throughout this article, the neighbourhood of a particle x_i is either determined by the mean distance of the population or by the distance between two (randomly) selected particles of the population: At the beginning of a search this distance would be relatively large, because the initial population is equally distributed over the search space. If the search has progressed, the particles would be attracted by the global optimum and hence would be closer together. In turn, their mean distance would be much smaller than in the initial population. As a result, the maximum step width s_{max} would be sufficiently small to yield into the global optimum. There are two variations of the algorithm, DA with random selection (DA/r) and DA with fitness related selection (DA/f).

3.1 Differential Annealing with Random Selection (DA/r)

For large populations, it might be impractical to calculate the mean distance between all the particles of a generation on-line. Therefore, the mean distance has to be estimated. In the first variant of DA, this is done by the random selection of two particles. The distance between these two particles is used to define the maximum step width s_{max} for every component of a candidate solution x_i. This method would be cheap in computation terms, but would probably not adapt fast enough for on-line applications.

3.2 Differential Annealing with Fitness Related Selection (DA/f)

Another promising approach is to select the two particles for distance estimation not randomly but according to the fitness of the individuals in the population. Fitness related selection is commonly used in Genetic Algorithms [7]. Using a fitness related selection should have the advantage that it would take the fitter particles into account for mean distance estimation. This would be an advantage, because some of the particles can easily get stuck in a local optimum and hence would distort the estimation process, whereas the best individuals would aim for the global optimum, and hence, these should be used for estimating the mean distance. Using Genetic Selection, e.g. fitness proportional selection or rank based selection, should therefore result in faster convergence.

4. Comparison of Algorithms

Although DA was initially proposed in [8], it has not actually been applied to any problem yet. Therefore, in this research DA/r was applied to a challenging engineering application, the automated tuning of a Langmuir probe [4].

4.1 The Test Problem

In this experiments, SA, SWASA and DA have been employed to deduce fourteen Fourier terms in a radio-frequency (RF) waveform in real-time for a simulated Langmuir probe compensation system [4].

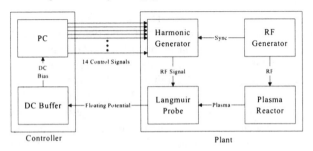

Figure 4: Closed optimisation loop.

Figure 4 shows the closed optimisation loop: 14 parameters need to be tuned on-line in order to achieve a maximum Floating Potential. Each of the digital inputs and the digital output of the system to be optimised had a resolution of 12 bits, hence the search space consisted of approximately 3.7×10^{50} search points. The search time is limited to approximately one minute.

Simulated Annealing has been applied to this problem successfully in the past, therefore, in order to allow a fair comparison of the algorithms, the parameter settings for SA, SWASA and DA, have been chosen to be identical as in [4], except for s_{max}.

4.2 Selection of the Maximum Step Width s_{max} for SA

In order to make a fair comparison between the algorithms, the optimum setting for s_{max} had to be found for SA.. For this, the optimum maximum step width s_{max} was experimentally determined: s_{max} was changed from 10 to 1500 for SA and applied 50 times for each s_{max}. The results can be seen in Figure 5:

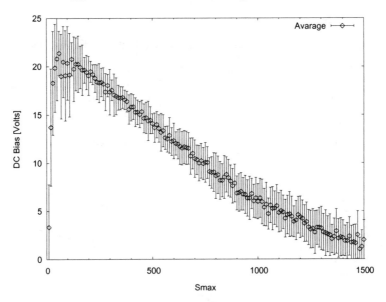

Figure 5: Average fitness and standard deviation versus s_{max}.

The dots represent the average fitness for this maximum step width over the 50 runs and the error bars represent the standard deviation of the fitness achieved. All the experiments were run on a Pentium 4 2.53 GHz PC with 256 MB RAM running the Linux operating system. It took approximately 19 hours to run the simulations. In order to make the results more clear, a moving average was taken from the data to produce Figure 6. Here, it can be seen that a maximum average fitness was achieved for a maximum step width s_{max}=70 whereas a minimum standard deviation was achieved for s_{max}=400.

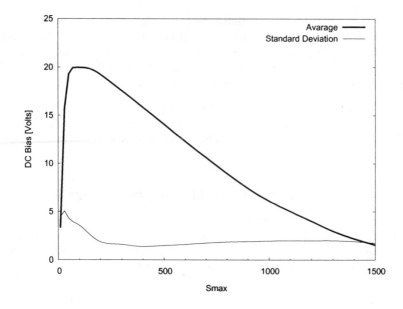

Figure 6: Smoothed average fitness and standard deviation versus s_{max}.

Figure 7 shows the fitness over generations for the best run for s_{max}=10. It can be seen that the algorithm failed to reach the region containing the maximum peak during the exploration phase of the search and hence got stuck in a local optimum.

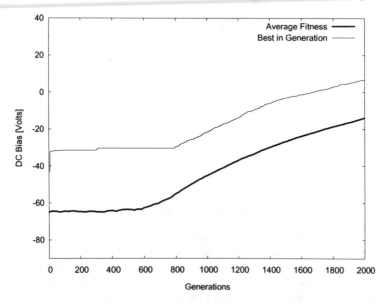

Figure 7: The maximum step width has been chosen to be 10. It can be seen that the algorithm failed to reach the region containing the maximum peak during the exploration phase of the search.

Figure 8 shows the results for the best run with s_{max}=1500. It can be seen that the algorithm, although it came close to the global optimum, failed to reach the maximum peak during the exploitation phase of the search run, because most of the new candidate solutions are simply 'falling off' the peak.

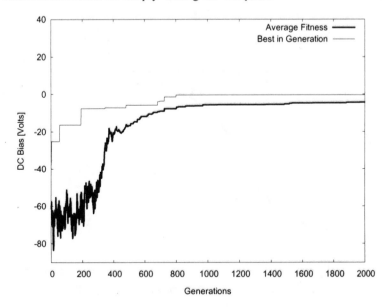

Figure 8: The maximum step width was chosen to be 1500. It can be seen that the algorithm failed to find the maximum peak during the exploitation phase of the search run.

4.3 Experimental Results

Each algorithm was finally applied 50 times. For SA, s_{max} has been chosen to be 70, according to Figure 6. All other SA parameters settings were chosen from [4]. Table 1 shows the results of the experiments.

Algorithm	Average Fitness [Volts]	Standard Deviation
SA	18.99	4.37119
SWASA	23.39	2.13100
DA/r	25.26	0.00069

Table 1: Comparison of results.

As it can be seen from Table 1, the average fitness has increased for DA by 33.02% compared to SA and 7.99% compared to SWASA. The standard deviation achieved by DA was reduced by 99.98% compared to SA and 99.97% compared to SWASA! Therefore, DA not only has improved the average fitness for the system; it has also improved the reproducibility of the results significantly, which is of great importance for industrial applications.

5.   Discussion

Figure 9 shows the development of the fitness over time for the best run of SA, Figure 10 and Figure 11 show the same for SWASA and DA.

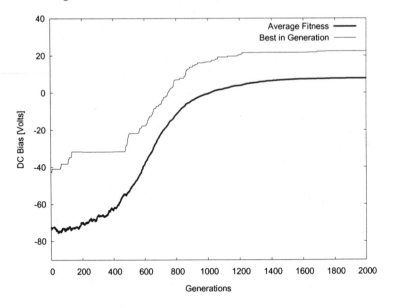

Figure 9: Development of fitness over time for best run of SA.

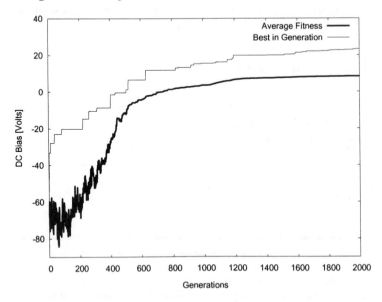

Figure 10: Development of fitness over time for best run of SWASA.

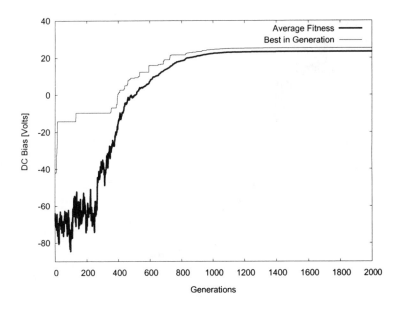

Figure 11: Development of fitness over time for best run of DA.

It can be seen that for all three algorithms the fitness achieved is almost the same in this cases, whereas the average fitness of the whole population for SA is much lower than the average fitness for SWASA, which in turn is much lower than the average fitness achieved by DA.

This indicates that most of the particles in SA and SWASA have settled on local optima and only a small number has actually reached the top of the global one. In contrast, the average fitness of the population for DA is quite close to the best fitness, i.e. most of the particles seem to have reached the top of the global optimum.

Figure 12 also shows that DA has converged towards the optimum after approximately 1100 generations, in contrast to SA needed approximately 1700 generations and SWASA has reached the optimum after approximately 1950 generations. This shows that the convergence speed for DA is higher than the convergence speed of two other algorithms.

Another interesting finding is the actual development of s_{max} over time for DA (Figure 12). As it can be seen, s_{max} in DA behaves for this application very similar to s_{max} in SWASA [5] (Figure 13). The scaling function for SWASA was originally found empirically during a large number of experiments on the Langmuir probe system, whereas DA found a very similar function automatically during the search, i.e. DA has adapted to the system to be optimised.

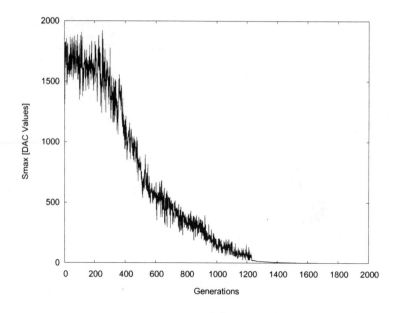

Figure 12: Development of s_{max} over time for Differential Annealing.

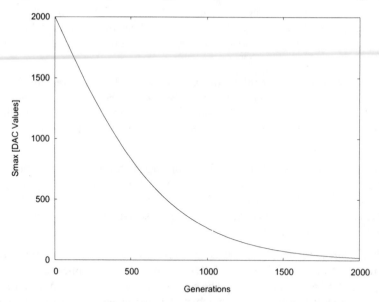

Figure 13: Originally scaling function for s_{max} for SWASA.

6. Conclusions and Future Work

Simulated Annealing is a black-box optimisation algorithm, which is robust and capable of dealing with noisy and incomplete real-world data. This makes it particularly suitable for on-line optimisation for real-world engineering problems. However, for continuous parameter optimisation, selecting an appropriate maximum step width s_{max} for simulated annealing is always a compromise between accuracy and robustness. If it is too small, SA has good exploitation capabilities but reduced chances of reaching the global optimum to exploit it. If s_{max} is too large, the algorithm has good exploration capabilities, and hence is likely to find the region of the search space containing the global optimum, but it then performs badly in the exploitation of this region. A solution to this problem is the on-line adaptation of the maximum step width to either a SA parameter, like temperature or iteration, as in SWASA, or to the fitness landscape.

In this research, the performance of SA in the optimisation of a Langmuir probe system has been dramatically improved by adapting the maximum step width to the fitness landscape, i.e. the estimated average distance between particles in the population. This has not only improved the average fitness achieved, it has also improved the reproducibility of the results, which is of great importance for industrial applications.

The next step will be to compare the performance of DA with standard SA and SWASA, not only for this industrial application, but also for a number of standard test problems. It might also be worthwhile to combine DA with more advanced cooling schedules, like Very Fast Simulated Re-annealing [9], which should further increase the performance of the resulting algorithm in terms of convergence speed.

References

1. Kirkpatrick, S., Gelatt Jr, C. D., Vecchi, M. P.: Optimization by Simulated Annealing, Science, 13 May 1983, Vol. 220, No. 4598, pp 671-680
2. Metropolis, A., Rosenbluth, W., Rosenbluth, M. N., Teller, H., Teller, E.: Equation of State Calculations by Fast Computing Machines, The Journal of Chemical Physics, Vol. 21, No. 6, June 1953, pp 1087-1092
3. Nolle, L., Armstrong, D.A., Hopgood, A.A. and Ware, A.: Simulated annealing and genetic algorithms applied to finishing mill optimisation for hot rolling of wide steel strip, International Journal of Knowledge-Based Intelligent Engineering Systems, 6 (2002),pp 104-110
4. Nolle, L., Goodyear, A., Hopgood, A.A., Picton, P.D. and Braithwaite, N.S.: Automated control of an actively compensated Langmuir probe system using simulated annealing, Knowledge-Based Systems, 15 (2002), pp 349-354
5. Nolle, L., Goodyear, A., Hopgood, A.A., Picton, P.D. and Braithwaite, N.S.: On step width adaptation in simulated annealing for continuous parameter optimisation, Lecture Notes in Computer Science, Vol. 2206 (2001), pp 589-598
6. Storn, R., Price, K.: Differential evolution - a simple and efficient adaptive scheme for global optimization over continuous spaces, Technical Report TR-95-012, ICSI, Berkeley, March 1995
7. Hopgood, A.A.: Intelligent System for Engineers and Scientists, Second Edition, CRC Press, 2001
8. Nolle, L.: Differential Annealing: a new adaptation scheme for simulated annealing based on Differential Evolution, Proceedings of the 9th International MENDEL Conference on Soft Computing, Brno, CZ, 4-6 June 2003, pp 53-58
9. Ingber, L.: Very fast simulated re-annealing, Journal of Mathematical Computer Modelling, Vol. 12, No. 8, 1989, pp 967-973

An Approximate Algorithm for Reverse Engineering of Multi-layer Perceptrons

Wojtek Kowalczyk

Free University Amsterdam, Department of Artificial Intelligence,
De Boelelaan 1081A, 1081HV Amsterdam, The Netherlands

wojtek@cs.vu.nl

Abstract

We present an approximate algorithm for reconstructing internals of multi-layer perceptrons from membership queries. The key component of the algorithm is a procedure for reconstructing weights of a single linear threshold unit. We prove that the approximation error, measured as the distance between the original and the reconstructed weights, is dropping exponentially fast with the number of queries.

The procedure is combined with a labelling strategy that involves solving multiple Linear Programming problems. This combination results in an algorithm that extracts internals of multi-layer perceptrons: the number of units in the first hidden layer, their weights, and a boolean function that is computed by the remaining nodes. In practice, networks that compute boolean combinations of 10-15 hyperplanes can be reconstructed in several minutes.

1   Introduction

In this paper we consider the following problem. Suppose that we are given a "black-box" multi-layer perceptron[1] that calculates a function f over the d-dimensional cube $[-1, 1]^d$. We are interested in finding the "internals" of this perceptron by asking a sequence of questions in the form: *what is the value of $f(x)$ on the given x from $[-1, 1]^d$?* In particular, we are interested in finding the number of hyperplanes that are computed by units from the first hidden layer, their parameters (weights), and a "labelling function" that determines which intersections of halfspaces are labelled as "positive" and which as "negative".

The main result of this paper is an algorithm that automatically finds all these items. As we impose no restrictions on the precision of perceptron's weights, our algorithm returns an *approximate* model of the original perceptron.

An almost identical problem has been addressed by Baum, [4], who considered learning with examples and queries. He provided an algorithm that learns the "black-box" perceptron (in PAC sense, [11]) in polynomial time, provided the number of units in the first hidden layer is ≤ 4. The algorithm was also tested on more complicated, randomly generated problems (with up to 200

---

[1]By perceptron we mean in this paper a network of linear threshold units. Such units compute halfspaces and a multi-layer perceptron computes a boolean combinations of halfspaces that are determined by nodes of the first hidden layer.

hidden units with 200 inputs). Compared to Baum's original results, we provide another procedure that finds coefficients of hyperplanes (called *orthogonal bracketing*) and present a simple proof that it converges exponentially fast (in the number of queries) to true weights. Moreover, we propose an algorithm for finding the boolean combination of the underlying halfspaces, represented by a lookup table, with help of Linear Programming.

We will start with discussing two algorithms for extracting weights from a single perceptron: random and orthogonal bracketing.

The orthogonal bracketing algorithm is next used as the main component of an algorithm that can handle arbitrary perceptrons. This algorithm generates random queries to discover inconsistencies between the perceptron and its current model. Whenever an inconsistency is spotted, the bracketing procedure locates a new hyperplane that is responsible for it. Next, a number of Linear Programming problems are generated and solved in order to find all non-empty intersections of detected halfspaces and their labels.

The actual implementation of the above algorithm can handle perceptrons with 10-15 nodes in the first hidden layer in a matter of minutes. The overall complexity of the algorithm is shown to be exponential in the number of such nodes, so reversing bigger networks might be practically intractable.

Our work is related to research in the areas of computational learning theory, learning with queries, and active learning. The problem of learning intersections of two homogeneous halfspaces was addressed by Baum, [3] who later generalized it to intersections of an arbitrary number of halfspaces, [4]. His results were further generalized and improved in a sequence of papers; Goldberg and Kwek, [7], present an extensive overview of these papers. They also tackle the problem of exact learning of convex polytopes under assumption of limited precision of weight representations. The discrete case of learning single halfspaces with membership queries was addressed by Schevchenko, [9]. The literature on the subject of learning with queries is very extensive, [1], but it is mostly focused on learning in discrete spaces. Finally, a good survey of active learning literature (in the context of neural networks) can be found in [8].

2 Extracting weights from a single perceptron

Let us consider a single perceptron with d inputs, i.e., a device that calculates a function $f : [-1, 1]^d \to \{-1, 1\}$ which is given by:

$$f(x) = sign(\sum_{i=1}^{d} w_i x_i + b).$$

Traditionally, the elements of vector $\mathbf{w} = (w_1, \ldots, w_d)$ are called *weights* and the parameter b is called the *bias*. Because the linear equation $\mathbf{w}^T x + b = 0$ determines a $(d-1)$-dimensional hyperplane H in R^d, the perceptron returns 1 on points that are above H and -1 on points that are below H. We will denote both halfspaces by H^+ and H^-, respectively. To make sure that the parameters $(\mathbf{w}, b)$ are uniquely determined by H we will assume that $\|\mathbf{w}\| = 1$.

Then **w** is known to be normal to H and $|b|$ is the distance between the origin and H, [5].

We are interested in an algorithm that asks a sequence of questions in the form: *what is the value of $f(x)$ on the given x from $[-1,1]^d$?* and returns a vector $(\mathbf{v}, c)$ that closely approximates $(\mathbf{w}, b)$. Clearly, we would like our algorithm to ask as few questions as possible, while returning good approximations of true weights.

We will present two algorithms for extracting parameters from a single perceptron: Random Bracketing and Orthogonal Bracketing. Both algorithms are based on a simple observation: to find parameters of a hyperplane H one only needs to find d linearly independent points that are on (or very close to) H. When such points are found, say, $p_1, \ldots, p_d$, all the weights can be calculated by solving the system of d linear equations $\mathbf{v}^T p_i + 1 = 0$, in $\mathbf{v} = (v_1, \ldots, v_d)$, and setting $c = 1/\|\mathbf{v}\|$ and $\mathbf{v} = \mathbf{v}/\|\mathbf{v}\|$. To find a point that is close to H it is enough to find a pair of points, p and q, that are on the opposite sides of H. We will call such a pair of points a *bracket*. Given a bracket (p, q) of size $\delta = \|p - q\|$ we can squeeze it exponentially fast by iterating the bisection operation:

```
r=(p+q)/2; if f(r)==f(p) then p=r; else q=r;
```

Clearly, after k iterations (what costs k queries) the resulting bracket has the size $\delta/2^k$.

2.1 Random Bracketing Algorithm

Random bracketing algorithm is very simple: it generates questions at random until d different brackets can be formed. Then the bisection operation is applied to every bracket until all the brackets have size smaller than $1/2^k$, where k is a program parameter. Finally, a hyperplane that passes through centers of all the brackets is found. (As the initial brackets are generated at random, the centers of the squeezed brackets are, with probability 1, linearly independent.)

Let us note that during the squeezing phase the algorithm makes at most $kd \log_2 d$ queries (the distance between two furthest points within $[-1,1]^d$ is $2\sqrt{d}$). The number of random queries made during the initial phase strongly depends on the distance of H from the origin–the smaller the distance the smaller (expected) number of queries. In case H is homogeneous ($b = 0$) about $2\sqrt{2d}$ queries should be sufficient (their labels are distributed 50:50, so the number of brackets that could be formed from them is about $\sqrt{2d}\sqrt{2d}/2 = d$). In the non-homogeneous case the algorithm might not terminate at all (when $|b| > \sqrt{d}$). To avoid such a situation, the algorithm counts the number of queries and when the counter reaches a pre-specified value (without finding a bracket), e.g., 1000, it terminates returning a perceptron that calculates a constant function. Clearly, when the tested perceptron returns in a row 1000 times the same value, then the true probability of returning the opposite value is very small: the 99.99% confidence interval for this probability is $[0, 0.0007]$.

Thus the constant peceptron that is returned by our algorithm imitates almost perfectly the behavior of the original one. As we are not interested (at least not in this paper) in placing our results within the PAC framework we will not investigate the "$\epsilon - \delta - n$" relation any further.

The presented algorithm has several drawbacks. First, the d points that are used for finding the hyperplane might be positioned in such a way that the corresponding system of linear equations is ill-conditioned (they might be either too close to each other or almost linearly dependent). In such situations the approximation error might be relatively big. Second, when two brackets are relatively close to each other, i.e., when the ratio "bracket size":"distance" is big, there is a lot of "uncertainty" about the position of the true hyperplane, which may lead to big errors. Finally, it is very difficult to quantify the relation between the parameter k and the possible error, measured, for example, by $\|\mathbf{w} - \mathbf{v}\|$. Our next algorihtm provides a remedy to all these problems.

2.2 Orthogonal Bracketing Algorithm

The Orthogonal Bracketing Algorithm mimics the classical Gram-Schmidt orthogonalization process, [10]. Brackets are constructed sequentially in such a way that their centers form an orthonormal system.

Let us assume for a while that the hyperplane H is homogeneous, i.e., that the origin O belongs to H. Let $k > 0$ be an integer. We will construct $(d - 1)$ points $p_1, p_2, \ldots, p_{d-1}$ in such a way that their distance to H is at most $1/2^k$, their distance to O is 1, and vectors $p_1, \ldots, p_{d-1}$ are orthogonal to each other. (Whenever there is no risk of confusion we slightly misuse the notation using the same symbols to denote points and vectors.) The construction of p_i's is inductive.

2.2.1 Initialization

Let p be an arbitrary vector of length 1. Due to symmetry (H passes through O) points p and $-p$ have different labels, i.e, $f(p) \neq f(-p)$. Let q be any vector of length 1 that is orthogonal to p. Clearly, $f(q) \neq f(p)$ or $f(q) \neq f(-p)$, so (p, q) or $(-p, q)$ is a bracket. Let us squeeze this bracket by iterating k times the spherical bisection operation:

```
r=(p+q)/2; r=r/||r||; if f(r)==f(p) then p=r; else q=r;
```

(here we assumed that $f(p) \neq f(q)$), and let p_1 denote its normalized center (after squeezing). Let us note that the distance between p_1 and H is smaller than $1/2^k$. Indeed, all the vectors that are produced by the squeezing procedure are on the unit circle that is located in a two dimensional space spanned by vectors p and q. The angular distance between p and q is $2\pi/4 < 2$ and it is divided by 2 with every bisection (k times), so the final bracket has the size smaller than $2/2^k$ and H must pass between its center (p_1) and one of its ends.

2.2.2 Inductive step

Let us suppose that we already have points $p_1, \ldots, p_i$, where $i < d - 1$, that satisfy our constraints. To construct p_{i+1} let us consider an arbitrary vector p of length 1 that is orthogonal to vectors $p_1, \ldots, p_i$. Such a vector can be easily generated: take at random any vector x, define p as

$$x - p_1 < x, p_1 > - \ldots - p_i < x, p_i >$$

and normalize it. (Since $i < d - 1$ vector x is with probability 1 linearly independent from $p_1, \ldots, p_i$, so $\|p\| \neq 0$.) Let q be any vector of length 1 that is orthogonal to $p, p_1, \ldots, p_i$. By the same argument as used in the initialization step, one of the pairs: (p, q) or $(-p, q)$ must be a bracket. To be precise, because p_i's are not exactly on H it may happen that p and $-p$ are on the same side of H. In such a case we repeat the whole operation (picking another x) until p and $-p$ are on the opposite sides of H. Note that in the light of Theorem 1 (below), the chance of such a pathological choice of p is converging to 0 exponentially fast with k. Once we have a bracket we squeeze it by k-fold bisection and define p_{i+1} to be its normalized center. Moreover, by the same argument as before, the distance between p_{i+1} and H is smaller than $1/2^k$.

The fact that vectors $p_1, \ldots, p_{d-1}$ are orthonormal is crucial in the proof of the following theorem.

Theorem 1.

Suppose that H is given by $\mathbf{w}^T x = 0$, $\|\mathbf{w}\| = 1$. Let G denote a hyperplane $\mathbf{v}^T x = 0$, $\|\mathbf{v}\| = 1$, that passes through the points $O, p_1, \ldots, p_{d-1}$ that are determined by the above algorithm. Then we have:

1. *For every $x \in G$ s.t. $\|x\| = 1$ there is $y \in H$ s.t. $\|x - y\| \leq \sqrt{d-1}/2^k$,*

2. *If $\sqrt{d-1}/2^k < \sqrt{3}/2$ then $\|\mathbf{w} - \mathbf{v}\| < \frac{2}{\sqrt{3}}\sqrt{d-1}/2^k$.*

Proof Let $x \in G$ be such that $\|x\| = 1$. Because vectors $p_1, \ldots, p_{d-1}$ form an orthonormal basis in G there exist $\alpha_1, \ldots, \alpha_{d-1}$ such that

$$x = \sum_{i=1}^{d-1} \alpha_i p_i \quad \text{and} \quad \sum_{i=1}^{d-1} \alpha_i^2 = 1.$$

Let $q_1, \ldots, q_{d-1} \in H$ be such that $\|p_i - q_i\| \leq 1/2^k$, for $i = 1, \ldots, d-1$, and let $y = \sum_{i=1}^{d-1} \alpha_i q_i$. Then, using Cauchy-Schwarz inequality, we have:

$$\|x - y\|^2 = \left(\sum_{i=1}^{d-1} \alpha_i (p_i - q_i)\right)^2 \leq \left(\sum_{i=1}^{d-1} |\alpha_i| \|p_i - q_i\|\right)^2 \leq \left(\sum_{i=1}^{d-1} \alpha_i^2\right)\left(\sum_{i=1}^{d-1} \|p_i - q_i\|^2\right).$$

Thus $\|x - y\| \leq \sqrt{d-1}/2^k$.

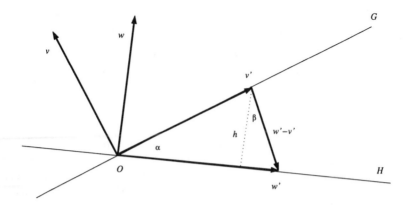

Figure 1: The intersection of P with G and H. Note that vectors v' and w' have the same, fixed length and that decreasing α leads to decrease of β. Therefore, when h tends to 0 the ratio $\|w' - v'\|/h$ tends to 1.

To prove the second part let us consider a two-dimensional plane P that contains vectors v and w. Let $v' \in G \cap P$ and $w' \in H \cap P$ denote unit vectors that are orthogonal to v and w, respectively. Clearly, as v and w are normal to G and H, v' and w' do exit, see Figure 1. Let h denote the height of the triangle $w'Ov'$ and let α denote the angle $v'Ow'$ and β the angle $Ov'w'$. From the first part of our theorem we have $h < \sqrt{d-1}/2^k$, and we assumed that $\sqrt{d-1}/2^k < \sqrt{3}/2$, therefore $h < \sqrt{3}/2$. Let us notice that for $h = \sqrt{3}/2$ the triangle $w'Ov'$ is equilateral, $\alpha = \pi/3$, and $\beta = \pi/6$. Moreover, when h is getting smaller, so does β. But $\|v' - w'\| = h/\cos\beta$ and $\sqrt{3}/2 < \cos\beta < 1$ for $0 < \beta < \pi/6$. Therefore $\|v - w\| = \|v' - w'\| < \frac{2}{\sqrt{3}}\sqrt{d-1}/2^k$.

The bounds derived above, especially the second one, are very useful: they provide information about the value of k under which the error is guaranteed to be smaller than a pre-specified value. As we can see, for a fixed k the error $\|v - w\|$ is bounded by $c\sqrt{d}$. However, the norm definition involves summation over d dimensions. Therefore the error bound "per dimension" (i.e., per weight) is limited by $c\sqrt{d}/d = c/\sqrt{d}$.

Let us return to the homogeneity assumption that we have made at the beginning of this section. When H is not homogeneous we have to make two modifications. First, the initial bracket (or a point that plays the role of the origin) has to be found. Here we apply the same trick as with the random bracketing algorithm: just make at most, say, 1000 random queries, until a bracket is found. If after 1000 queries no bracket is found we have a trivial case of a constant function. Otherwise, as soon as a bracket is found we squeeze it to a point (using a suitably large k) – let us call it p_0. Next, let us consider a ball with center in p_0 and radius r being the smallest coordinate of $|p_0|$, so

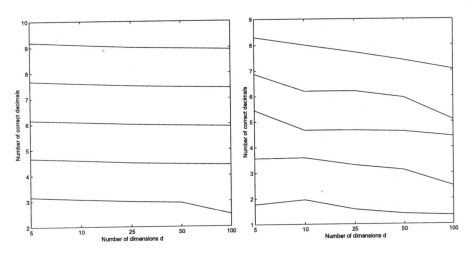

Figure 2: Accuracy of the Orthogonal Bracketing (left) and Random Bracketing (right) for $k = 10, 15, 20, 25, 30$ (bottom-up) and d ranging between 5 and 100. The accuracy measure, $-\log_{10} \|\mathbf{w} - \mathbf{v}\|$ can be interpreted as the number decimals.

the ball is fully included in $[-1, 1]^d$. One can easily verify that the inductive construction of points $p_1, \ldots, p_d - 1$ is still valid: instead of O we use p_0 and instead of a unit ball we work on a ball with radius r. Moreover the bounds of Theorem 1 still hold.

2.3 Experimental results

As we are interested in practical applications of our algorithms we have implemented them and run a number of experiments. For several combinations of d and k we have generated 1000 hyperplanes (i.e., 1000 d-dimensional vectors w of length 1), run both algorithms and measured the difference between the true vector w and the calculated v. We used two error measures: $\|w - v\|$ and $mean(abs(w - v))$. The first measure can be interpreted as the maximal distance between both hyperplanes that is measured on the unit ball, the second one is just the average absolute error on weights. Some results are shown in Figure 2. They are consistent with theoretical analysis of both algorithms and demonstrate that the random bracketing algorithm performs reasonably well. Some irregularities that are present in the plots are caused by few outliers.

3 Extracting internals from a multi-layer perceptron

Let us consider now a multi-layer perceptron with d inputs, i.e., a device that calculates a function $f : [-1, 1]^d \to \{-1, 1\}$. It is well-known that f can be represented as a boolean combination of halfspaces that are determined by linear threshold units from the first layer. Indeed, let these units define h hyperplanes $H_1, \ldots, H_h$, and let $\lambda \in \{-1, 1\}^h$ be a sequence of labels that refer to two possible sides of each hyperplane. Then the value of f on the intersection $\mathbf{H}_\lambda = H_1^{\lambda_1} \cap \ldots \cap H_h^{\lambda_h}$ is constant; let us denote it by f_λ.

In other words, the function f is fully specified by h equations of the hyperplanes H_i

$$\mathbf{w}_i^T \mathbf{x} + b_i = 0, \quad \text{for} \quad i = 1, \ldots, h$$

and at most 2^h labels f_λ, for $\lambda \in \{-1, 1\}^h$ (some $\mathbf{H}_\lambda$'s might be empty).

In the previous section we described the Orthogonal Bracketing algorithm which, after some modifications, can be used for finding H_i's (i.e., vectors $(\mathbf{w}_i, b_i)$). Now we will describe a labelling procedure that for given H_i's finds all labels f_λ.

3.1 Labelling procedure

Let us consider $\lambda \in \{-1, 1\}^h$ and let $\mathbf{H}_\lambda = H_1^{\lambda_1} \cap \ldots \cap H_h^{\lambda_h}$. To find a label for $\mathbf{H}_\lambda$ we only need to find an arbitrary point $x \in \mathbf{H}_\lambda$ and apply f to it. This could be achieved by solving a system of h linear inequalities

$$\mathbf{w}_i^T \mathbf{x} + b_i > 0, \quad \text{or} \quad \mathbf{w}_i^T \mathbf{x} + b_i < 0$$

where choices are made depending on values of λ_i's. However, taking into account that our algorithm works with *approximations* of true H_i's, we would like to find x such that all the inequalities are satisfied by as large margin as possible–this should guarantee that x is in the "safe" region, far from boundaries. Fortunately, this extra requirement can be expressed as a Linear Programming problem that uses $h + 1$ slack variables $z, z_1, \ldots, z_h$. Indeed, let us consider the following LP problem:

Maximize z subject to:

$$\mathbf{w}_i^T \mathbf{x} + b_i - \lambda_i(z + z_i) = 0$$

$$-1 \leq x_i \leq 1$$

$$0 \leq z_i$$

$$0 \leq z$$

$$\text{for} \quad i = 1, \ldots, h$$

We can see that any solution x of this problem lies in $\mathbf{H}_\lambda$ and that the variable z which measures the margin is maximized.

It should be noticed that z doesn't really reflect the Euclidean distance between x and the boundaries of $\mathbf{H}_\lambda$. A direct approach to maximizing this distance would immediately lead to a quadratic optimization problem which is computationally much more expensive than solving a simple LP. This issue is addressed in more depth in [6]. In practice, however, the LP approach is sufficiently powerful and the low computational costs make it very attractive. For

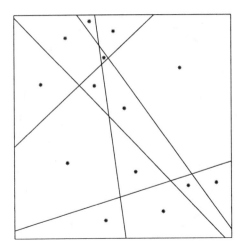

Figure 3: An example solution of the labelling problem. The internal points have been found by solving $2^5 = 32$ Linear Programming problems.

example, using a popular LP solver that implements the interior-point method, LIPSOL, [12], we were able to solve labelling problems for 10 hyperplanes (i.e., generated and solved 1024 instances of LPs) in about 1-2 minutes (for d ranging from 20 to 100) on an ordinary PC with 1GHz processor. An example solution of a 2-dimensional labelling problem for 5 hyperplanes (lines) is shown if Figure 3.

3.2 Main Algorithm

The two procedures described earlier, orthogonal bracketing and labelling procedure, are the key components of the algorithm for extracting internals from multi-layer perceptrons. The algorithm uses two parameters: k, that controls the accuracy, and a threshold t that defines the termination condition.

The algorithm starts with an empty collection of hyperplanes and a constant labelling function that maps all inputs to 1, or -1, depending on the result of the first query, e.g., $f(0)$. Then random queries are made (up to t) to find out any inconsistency between the actual f and the current collection of hyperplanes and the corresponding labelling function. If within t queries no inconsistency is discovered the algorithm terminates. As we argued before, a suitably big value of t, e.g., 1000, is sufficient to provide high confidence in the (approximate) correctness of the result. If an inconsistency is spotted the algorithm switches to the bracketing mode to locate a hyperplane that is responsible for it. After finding approximate weights for this new hyperplane, it is added to the current set of hyperplanes and new labelling is recomputed. The whole process of finding inconsistencies and fixing them is repeated until t consecutive random queries provide answers that are consistent with the current labelling function.

The original bracketing algorithm requires some modifications. First of

64

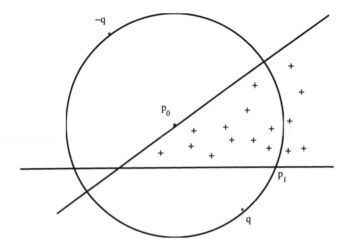

Figure 4: An illustration of two problems that may occur in case of two hyperplanes. Points q and $-q$ have the same labels. Moreover, the bracketing procedure may converge to a point p_1 that is located on another hyperplane than p_0

all, let us notice that an inconsistency is detected when two points x, y are found, such that $f(x) \neq f(y)$, and both x and y belong to the same $\mathbf{H}_\lambda$. In such a situation the pair (x, y) is a bracket for a yet unknown hyperplane. The squeezing procedure can be used for finding a starting point p_0 on this hyperplane, with accuracy $< 1/2^k$. Then the distance r from p_0 to the boundary of $\mathbf{H}_\lambda$ can be found (it is the minimum of the distances to all hyperplanes). Thus the ball with radius r and center in p_0 is fully included in $\mathbf{H}_\lambda$ and the orthogonal bracketing procedure can be started.

Although the orthogonal bracketing procedure always finds a solution in case of a single hyperplane, the possibility of multiple hyperplanes that pass through the ball may complicate things, see Figure 4. Basically, there are two problems that may arise. The first problem is that the search for next bracket may fail: now it is no longer the case that for any q on the ball, q and $-q$ have different labels. The second problem is at first sight even more severe: the procedure may converge and produce points that are on different hyperplanes. In this case, i.e., when the generated points $p_1, \ldots, p_{d-1}$ are located on two or more different hyperplanes, the hyperplane that is determined by these points is irrelevant. Fortunately, the labeling procedure takes care that the new labeling is always consistent with f, so although the new collection of hyperplanes may contain a bogus one, it will have no consequences for the final result. There is, however, a simple method for detecting such pathologies. When p and q belong to the same hyperplane then a small ball with center in $(p+q)/2$ intersects this hyperplane. In turn, testing if a ball intersects a hyperplane is simple: a few random queries on points that are on the ball should produce some alternating labels, otherwise the ball is most likely disjoint with it.

Thus we have two types of problems: the first one is easy to detect (the procedure doesn't converge), the second one, less harmful, can be detected by a heuristic test. In both cases the remedy is simple: divide r by 2 and restart the procedure. By decreasing the size of the ball we decrease the probability of encountering problems.

3.3 Complexity analysis

The presented algorithm detects hyperplanes one after another. Each time a new hyperplane is located the labelling procedure is called. It solves 2^i LPs, where i is the current number of hyperplanes. Therefore, if in total h hyperplanes are detected then $2^{h+1} - 1$ LPs have to be solved. In theory the LP solver works in polynomial time in the number of constraints and the number of variables, but for relatively small values of h and d the execution time may be considered to be constant. The time required by the bracketing procedure is proportional to khd and is so small (when compared to the rest) that it can be neglected.

Every solvable instance of LP generates a query, thus the number of queries that are generated by the labelling procedure is also bounded by 2^{h+1}. Additionally, for each hyperplane at most t random queries are made, followed by k*d queries that are generated by the bracketing procedure (when we ignore pathological cases). Thus the total number of queries is about $h(t + kd) + 2^{h+1}$.

Concluding, both the time complexity and the number of queries are dominated by the 2^h term. Therefore the presented algorithm is applicable only to networks with at most 10-20 nodes in the first layer.

One could ask if the exponential bound could not be improved. We are quite certain that the answer is negative. Namely, while running tests with our labelling procedure, where we were generating at random h hyperplanes in R^d and counting non-empty polytopes $\mathbf{H}_\lambda$, we noticed that for big ratios d/h this count was frequently reaching the maximal value of 2^h.

4 Conclusions

We presented two efficient algorithms for extracting weights from multi-layer perceptrons: the orthogonal bracketing algorithm for single perceptrons and a combined bracketing-labelling procedure for general case. The orthogonal bracketing procedure was proved to produce approximations with error dropping exponentially fast with the number of queries. Experiments with an actual implementation of this procedure demonstrated that when the number of allowed queries is 10 (20 or 30) times the number of inputs, then weights are recovered with accuracy of about 3 (6 or 9, resp.) decimals. The complexity of the general procedure was shown to be bounded exponentially in the number of units in the first hidden layer (or, equivalently, in the number of involved hyperplanes). We believe that this bound is tight.

It would be interesting to compare the speed (measured in terms of queries) and the accuracy of the presented algorithms to the original algorithm of Baum, [4].

We believe that the orthogonal bracketing procedure can be used as a starting point for constructing heuristic strategies for efficient labelling of training examples. This problem, usually called sample selection, is discussed in a wider context of active learning in [2], [8].

Finally, a natural question to ask is the case of "ordinary" feed-forward networks with smooth activation functions (like the logistic sigmoid function). Is the reverse engineering of such networks difficult?

References

[1] D. Angluin. Queries revisited. In T. Z. N. Abe, R. Khardon, editor, *Algorithmic Learning Theory*, 12th International Conference, ALT 2001, Washington, DC, USA, November 25-28, 2001, 12–31. Springer, 2001.

[2] S. Argamon-Engelson and I. Dagan. Committee-based sample selection for probabilistic classifiers. *Journal of Artificial Intelligence Research*, 11:335–360, 1999.

[3] E. Baum. On learning a union of half spaces. *Journal of Complexity*, 6(1):67–101, 1990.

[4] E. Baum. Neural net algorithms that learn in polynomial time from examples and queries. *IEEE Transactions on Neural Networks*, 2(1):5–19, 1991.

[5] C. Bishop. *Neural Newtorks for Pattern Recognition*. Oxford University Press, 1995.

[6] R. Bramley and B. Winnicka. Solving linear inequalities in a least squares sense. *SIAM Journal on Scientific Computing*, 17(1):275–286, 1996.

[7] P. Goldberg and S. Kwek. The precision of query points as a resource for learning convex polytopes with membership queries. In *Proc. 13th Annu. Conference on Comput. Learning Theory*, pages 225–235. Morgan Kaufmann, San Francisco, 2000.

[8] M. Hasenjager and H. Ritter. Active learning in neural networks.

[9] V. Shevchenko. On deciphering a threshold function of many-values logic. *Gorkii State University*, pages 155–166, 1987.

[10] G. Strang. *Linear algebra and its applications*. Third Edition. Harcourt Brace Jovanovich, Publishers, 1988.

[11] L.G. Valiant. A theory of the learnable. *Communications ACM*, vol 27, 11, pp. 1134-1142, 1984.

[12] Y. Zhang. User's guide to LIPSOL, Rice University, 1998.

SESSION 1B:

CONSTRAINT PROGRAMMING 1

A Theoretical Framework for Tradeoff Generation using Soft Constraints

Stefano Bistarelli

Istituto di Informatica e Telematica, CNR, Pisa, Italy

Dipartimento di Scienze
Universitá degli Studi "G. D'annunzio", Pescara, Italy

Barry O'Sullivan

Cork Constraint Computation Centre
Department of Computer Science
University College Cork, Ireland

Abstract

Tradeoffs have been proposed in the literature as an approach to resolving over-constrainedness in interactive constraint-based tools, such as product configurators, that reason about user preferences. It has been reported how tradeoffs can be modeled as additional constraints. This paper presents a formal framework for tradeoff generation based on the semiring approach to soft constraints. In particular, user preferences and tradeoffs are represented as soft constraints and as an entailment operator, respectively. The entailment operator is used to interactively generate new constraints representing tradeoffs. We also introduce a novel definition of substitutability for soft constraints upon which we present a relaxed definition of tradeoffs.

1 Introduction

A typical interactive configuration session is one where a human user articulates preferences for product features to a configurator which ensures consistency between the constraints of the problem and the user's desires. During such a session a point may be reached where all of the user's desires cannot be met. At this point the user could consider "tradeoffs" between his preferences. For example, in configuring a camera, the user may find that it is impossible to have one "*weighting less that 10 ounces with a zoom lens of 10X or more*", but could accept a tradeoff: "*I will increase my weight limit to 14 ounces if I can have a zoom lens of 20X or more.*" Ideally, we would like the configurator to suggest appropriate tradeoffs to the user.

In this paper we extend and formalize previous work on tradeoffs. In [8] tradeoffs are crisp binary constraints that are interactively generated to substitute strict unary crisp constraints representing user desires. In this paper we increase the utility of tradeoff generation since the amount of information gathered from the user is increased using soft constraints to represent preferences. The ability to capture the preferences of the user in a formal way was not addressed in the earlier work in this area. Furthermore, the extended framework presented here is general enough to deal with any arity of preference constraints, not only unary ones as reported in [8].

The task of tradeoff generation is also formalized in this paper. The possible tradeoffs are given as the result of an "entailment" function. A filter function is used to select one of the possible entailed tradeoff constraints. The final generalization in our framework is that tradeoff constraints are not necessarily limited to being binary. This provides us with a richer model of tradeoff. For example, we may wish to add a non-binary tradeoff constraint in certain situations, such as when we are prepared to have a pair of constraints, c_x and c_y, replaced by a ternary constraint, $c'_{(x,y,z)}$. The additional constraining influence on z could be regarded as an imposed constraint.

To handle both of these extensions we use the semiring-based framework [4, 5, 6] that has been shown to be able to represent both crisp and soft constraints in a uniform way. This general framework also gives us the possibility of expressing *approximate* tradeoffs. When it is not possible to find a tradeoff resulting in a solution better than some fixed level of consistency, we can consider the possibility of suggesting to the user solutions that are not worse than a given *degradation* factor. To do this we extend the notion of soft substitutability [2] from domain values to constraints.

Thus, the contributions of this paper are as follows:

1. a formal and general theoretical framework for tradeoff generation for interactive constraint processing that uses soft constraints to represent user preferences and an entailment operator to generate tradeoffs;

2. a notion of substitutability for soft constraints and a relaxed definition of tradeoff based on substitutability and solution degradation.

The remainder of the paper is organized as follows. Section 2 presents the necessary background on the semiring-based approach to handling soft constraints and on the tradeoff generation schema. Section 3 presents our general framework for tradeoff generation. An extension to our approach, for computing approximate tradeoffs, is presented in Section 4. Some concluding remarks are made in Section 5.

2 Background: Tradeoffs and Soft Constraints

Product configuration is becoming a well studied design activity which is often modeled and solved as a constraint satisfaction problem [1, 7, 9, 12]. In this paper we present a formal framework for tradeoff generation in interactive constraint processing. In the existing literature on this topic, a tradeoff is a binary constraint which substitutes a pair of unary preference constraints; the tradeoff constraint representing a satisfactory compromise for the user [8]. For example, consider a set, $U = \{c_1, \ldots, c_k\}$, of user-specified unary preference constraints, and a set P of constraints defining the underlying problem, such that $U \cup P$ is inconsistent. A tradeoff constraint, T_{ij}, is a binary constraint involving a pair of variables, v_i and v_j, on which the user has specified a pair of unary preference constraints, $c_i \in U$ and $c_j \in U$, such that $U \cup T_{ij} - \{c_i, c_j\}$ is consistent and the user's preference on one variable has been strengthened and relaxed on the other. Therefore, currently, a tradeoff is a binary constraint which replaces a pair of unary preference constraints defined over the same pair of variables.

In this paper we regard each constraint in U as a *soft constraint* whose preference levels can be combined accordingly to the specific notion of combination for the problem. Soft constraints associate a qualitative or quantitative value either to the entire constraint or to each assignment of its variables. Such values are interpreted as a level of preference, importance or cost. The levels are usually ordered, reflecting the fact that some levels (constraints) are *better* than others. When using soft constraints it is necessary to specify, via suitable combination operators, how the level of preference of a global solution is obtained from the preferences in the constraints.

Several formalizations of the concept of *soft constraints* are currently available. In the following, we refer to the formalization based on c-semirings [4, 5, 6], which can be shown to generalize and express both crisp and soft constraints [3].

A semiring-based constraint assigns to each instantiation of its variables an associated value from a partially ordered set. When dealing with crisp constraints, the values are the booleans, *true* and *false*, representing the admissible and non-admissible values; when dealing with soft constraints the values are interpreted as preferences.

The framework must also handle the combination of constraints. To do this one must take into account such additional values, and thus the formalism must provide suitable operations for combination ($\times$) and comparison ($+$) of tuples of values and constraints. This is why this formalization is based on the concept of c-semiring. Below we present an overview of semiring-based constraint satisfaction.

Semirings.

A semiring is a tuple $\langle A, +, \times, \mathbf{0}, \mathbf{1} \rangle$ such that:

- A is a set and $\mathbf{0}, \mathbf{1} \in A$;

- $+$ is commutative, associative and $\mathbf{0}$ is its unit element;

- $\times$ is associative, distributes over $+$, $\mathbf{1}$ is its unit element and $\mathbf{0}$ is its absorbing element.

A c-semiring is a semiring $\langle A, +, \times, \mathbf{0}, \mathbf{1} \rangle$ such that: $+$ is idempotent, $\mathbf{1}$ is its absorbing element and $\times$ is commutative. Let us consider the relation $\leq_S$ over A such that $a \leq_S b$ iff $a + b = b$. Then it is possible to prove that (see [5]):

- $\leq_S$ is a partial order;

- $+$ and $\times$ are monotone on $\leq_S$;

- **0** is its minimum and **1** its maximum;

- $\langle A, \leq_S \rangle$ is a complete lattice and, for all $a, b \in A$, $a + b = lub(a, b)$.

Moreover, if $\times$ is idempotent, then: $+$ distribute over $\times$; $\langle A, \leq_S \rangle$ is a complete distributive lattice and $\times$ its glb. Informally, the relation $\leq_S$ gives us a way to compare semiring values and constraints. In fact, when we have $a \leq_S b$, we will say that b *is better than* a. In the following, when the semiring will be clear from the context, $a \leq_S b$ will be often indicated by $a \leq b$.

Constraint Problems.

Given a semiring $S = \langle A, +, \times, \mathbf{0}, \mathbf{1} \rangle$ and an ordered set of variables V over a finite domain D, a *constraint* is a function which, given an assignment $\eta : V \to D$ of the variables, returns a value of the semiring.

By using this notation we define $\mathcal{C} = \eta \to A$ as the set of all possible constraints that can be built starting from S, D and V.

Note that in this *functional* formulation each constraint is a function (as defined in [6]) and not a pair (as defined in [5]). Such a function involves all the variables in V, but it depends on the assignment of only a finite subset of them. We call this subset the *support* of the constraint.

Consider a constraint $c \in \mathcal{C}$. We define its support as $supp(c) = \{v \in V \mid \exists \eta, d_1, d_2.c\eta[v := d_1] \neq c\eta[v := d_2]\}$, where

$$\eta[v := d]v' = \begin{cases} d & \text{if } v = v', \\ \eta v' & \text{otherwise.} \end{cases}$$

Note that $c\eta[v := d_1]$ means $c\eta'$ where η' is η modified with the association $v := d_1$ (that is the operator $[\,]$ has precedence over application).

A *soft constraint satisfaction problem* is a pair $\langle C, con \rangle$ where $con \subseteq V$ and C is a set of constraints: con is the set of variables of interest for the constraint set C, which however may concern also variables not in con.

Note that a classical CSP is a SCSP where the chosen c-semiring is: $S_{CSP} = \langle \{false, true\}, \vee, \wedge, false, true \rangle$. Fuzzy CSPs can instead be modeled in the SCSP framework by choosing the c-semiring $S_{FCSP} = \langle [0, 1], max, min, 0, 1 \rangle$. Many other "soft" CSPs (Probabilistic, weighted, ...) can be modeled by using a suitable semiring structure, such as, $(S_{prob} = \langle [0, 1], max, \times, 0, 1 \rangle$, $S_{weight} = \langle \mathcal{R}, min, +, 0, +\infty \rangle$, ...).

Example 1 Figure 1 shows the graph representation of a fuzzy CSP. Variables X and Y, and constraints are represented, respectively, by nodes and by undirected (unary for c_1 and c_3 and binary for c_2) arcs, and semiring values are written to the right of the corresponding tuples. The variables of interest (that is the set con) are represented with a double circle. Here we assume that the domain D of the variables contains the values a, b and c.

If semiring values represent probability/fuzziness then, for instance, the tuple $\langle a, c \rangle \to 0.2$ in constraint c_2 can be interpreted as the probability/fuzziness of X and Y having values a and c, respectively, is 0.2. $\triangle$

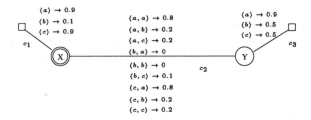

Figure 1: A fuzzy CSP.

Constraints can be defined in both extensional and intensional form. Constraints can be defined extensionally by listing each possible tuple with its preference level. An alternative way is to define constraints in an intensional way (for instance $x \neq y$, or $x \leq y$) and assign a level to each instantiation by using a function. As an example, consider the following fuzzy constraints:

$$c : \{x, y\} \rightarrow \mathcal{R}^2 \rightarrow [0, 1] \qquad \text{s.t.} \ \ c(x, y) = \frac{1}{1 + |x - y|}$$

and

$$c' : \{x\} \rightarrow \mathcal{R} \rightarrow [0, 1] \qquad \text{s.t.} \ \ c'(x) = \begin{cases} 1 & \text{if } x \leq 10, \\ 0 & \text{otherwise.} \end{cases}$$

Notice that the domain of both variables x and y is, in this example, the set of real numbers. As any fuzzy CSP, the definition of the constraints is instead in the interval $[0, 1]$.

Combining constraints.

When there is a set of soft constraints $\mathcal{C}$, the combined weight of the constraints is computed using the operator $\otimes : \mathcal{C} \times \mathcal{C} \rightarrow \mathcal{C}$ defined as $(c_1 \otimes c_2)\eta = c_1\eta \times_S c_2\eta$.

Given a constraint $c \in \mathcal{C}$ and a variable $v \in V$, the *projection* of c over $V - \{v\}$, written $c \Downarrow_{(V - \{v\})}$, is the constraint c' s.t. $c'\eta = \sum_{d \in D} c\eta[v := d]$. Informally, projecting means eliminating some variables from the support. This is done by associating with each tuple over the remaining variables a semiring element which is the sum of the elements associated by the original constraint to all the extensions of this tuple over the eliminated variables. In short, combination is performed via the multiplicative operation of the semiring, and projection via the additive one.

Solutions.

The *solution* of a SCSP, $P = \langle C, con \rangle$, is the constraint $Sol(P) = (\bigotimes C) \Downarrow_{con}$. That is, we combine all constraints, and then project over the variables in *con*. In this way we get the constraint with support (not greater than) *con* which is "induced" by the entire SCSP. Note that when all the variables are of interest we do not need to perform any projection.

Solutions are constraints in themselves and can be ordered by extending the $\leq_S$ order. We say that a constraint c_1 is at least as constraining as constraint c_2 if $c_1 \sqsubseteq c_2$, where for any assignment η of variables then $c_1 \sqsubseteq c_2 \equiv c_1\eta \leq_S c_2\eta$. Notice that using the functional formulation [6] we can easily compare constraints eventhough they have different supports (in [4, 5] only constraints with the same support could be compared).

Example 2 Consider again the solution of the fuzzy CSP of Figure 1. It associates a semiring element with every domain value of variable X. Such an element is obtained by first combining all the constraints together and then projecting the obtained constraint over X.

For instance, for the tuple $\langle a, a \rangle$ (that is, $X = Y = a$), we have to compute the minimum between 0.9 (which is the value assigned to $X = a$ in constraint c_1), 0.8 (which is the value assigned to $\langle X = a, Y = a \rangle$ in c_2) and 0.9 (which is the value for $Y = a$ in c_3). Hence, the resulting value for this tuple is 0.8. We can do the same work for tuple $\langle a, b \rangle \to 0.2$, $\langle a, c \rangle \to 0.2$, $\langle b, a \rangle \to 0$, $\langle b, b \rangle \to 0$, $\langle b, c \rangle \to 0.1$, $\langle c, a \rangle \to 0.8$, $\langle c, b \rangle \to 0.2$ and $\langle c, c \rangle \to 0.2$. The tuples obtained are then projected over variable X, obtaining the solution $\langle a \rangle \to 0.8$, $\langle b \rangle \to 0.1$ and $\langle c \rangle \to 0.8$. △

Sometimes it may be useful to just find the semiring value representing the least upper bound of the values yielded by the solutions. This is called the *best level of consistency* of an SCSP P and it is defined by $blevel(P) = Sol(P) \Downarrow_\emptyset$. We say that P is α-consistent when $blevel(P) = \alpha$.

3   Tradeoff as an Entailment Operator

In this section we define a general notion of tradeoff using the semiring-based framework presented above. We use hard constraints to represent the strict and unmodifiable conditions of the problem (denoted P). We use soft constraints to represent, modifiable, user preferences (denoted U).

While, in general, we may have some constraints in P that are soft, we would regard this softness as a cost that would not be handled in the same way as user-specified preference constraints. In our framework we model softness in the user's desires, U, as preferences. The user makes statements like *"I prefer to have a petrol engine over a diesel one"* in a quantifiable manner by associating semiring values with each option. However, any softness in the physical constraints in the problem, P, represent the costs, or penalties, associated with relaxing them. These costs can be thought of as problem statements such as *"a diesel engine is not normally available for the small chassis, but for an additional cost, we can make the option available"*. Note that these types of softness are semantically different and we would treat them as such. For the remainder of the paper we will simply regard each problem constraints in P as a hard (crisp) constraint.

We model tradeoffs as a special *entailment operator* [13]. As shown in [6], an entailment operator for soft constraints, given a set of constraints C, generates constraints c' s.t. $\bigotimes C \sqsubseteq c'$ (written as $C \vdash c'$).

Tradeoffs specialize entailments in two respects:

- firstly, constraints c' generated by the tradeoff operator are *substituted* for the preference constraints, C, while entailed constraints are usually *added* to the problem.

- secondly, when we add tradeoffs, we do not necessarily obtain a globally better solution, but we may obtain a *Pareto incomparable* one. Specifically, while low preference constraints, $C \in U$, are substituted by c', thus increasing the overall level of preference, c' usually also lowers the preference of some other constraints $\bar{C} \in U$.

So, for instance, if $U = \{c_1, \ldots, c_n\}$, a tradeoff for constraints $C = \{c_1, c_2\}$ could be a constraint c' s.t. $C \vdash c'$ and $supp(c') \supseteq supp(c_1) \cup supp(c_2)$ (usually we have $supp(c') \supset supp(c_1) \cup supp(c_2)$). Formally, we can define the notion of potential tradeoffs as follows:

Definition 1 (Potential Tradeoffs) *Given a configuration problem $\{P \cup U\}$ and a subset of user preference constraints $C \subseteq U$. We say that c' is a* Potential Tradeoff *for C ($c' \in Trades_{\langle P,U \rangle}(C)$) if*

- $supp(\bigotimes C) \subseteq supp(c')$; *let's call $\bar{C} \subseteq U$ the greatest set of preference constraints s.t. $supp(\bigotimes\{C, \bar{C}\}) = supp(c')$;*

- $C \vdash c'$ *(that is $C \sqsubseteq c'$);*

The meaning of this definition is that a potential tradeoff will increase the level of some user preference constraints (those in $C = \{c_1, c_2\}$), and possibly lower some other ones whose support is in $\bar{C}$.

Notice that after the application of the tradeoff operator, we never obtain a best level of consistency worse than before.

Theorem 1 *Given a configuration problem $\{P \cup U\}$ and a subset of user preference constraints $C \subseteq U$. If c' is a* Potential Tradeoff *for C ($c' \in Trades_{\langle P,U \rangle}(C)$) Then, $blevel(P \cup U - C \cup \{c'\}) \not< blevel(P \cup U)$;*

Proof Easily follows from the monotonicity of the $\otimes$ operator and from the hypotheses that $C \sqsubseteq c'$. □

3.1 Computing Tradeoffs

The way the preference constraints $C \subseteq U$ are selected, and the way a specific tradeoff c' is filtered from all the potential ones, and thus, $\bar{C}$ computed, is one of the most important issues when dealing with configuration problems. The potential tradeoffs can be restricted in various ways, which may be problem or context-specific. For example, we may wish to select a tradeoff in a way which could be regarded as "user-friendly". In the context of an interactive constraint-based configuration tool we may need to ensure that the user "trusts" the configurator, which may imply that previously accepted tradeoffs are not revisited. Some possible approaches to selecting preferences and filtering tradeoff constraints are presented in Section 3.2.

Notice that the filtered tradeoff could depend on the presence of a particular (partial) assignment, η, of the variables of the problem whose association has to be maintained[1].

Usually the configuration process first requests preference constraints from the user, and only if a solution better than a threshold α cannot be found with the acquired constraints, then a tradeoff is computed. To perform this check we always compute $blevel(P \cup U) = Sol(P \cup U) \Downarrow_\emptyset$ and compare this value with the semiring level α.

Therefore, tradeoff generation can be characterized in this context as a function:

$$Trades^{\alpha}_{\langle P,U,\eta,!\rangle} : \mathcal{C} \to \mathcal{C}$$

where:

- P is the set of *Problem constraints*;

- U is the set of *User-specified preference constraints*;

- ! is a filter (cut function) that first selects a set of preference constraints, $C \subseteq U$, and then selects one from among the potential tradeoffs giving c' (see Section 3.2).

- η is a (partial) assignment of the variables whose association has to be maintained;

- α represents the minimum best level of consistency we wish to achieve in the SCSP. The level α can be seen as the minimum level of global preference satisfaction we want to achieve;

Definition 2 (Tradeoffs) *Given a configuration problem* $\{P \cup U\}$*, and a subset of the user's preference constraints,* $C \subseteq U$*. We say that* c' *is a* Tradeoff *for* C *using the threshold* α*, the filter* ! *and the partial assignment* η *(*$c' \in Trades^{\alpha}_{\langle P,U,\eta,!\rangle}(C)$*), if the following are satisfied:*

- c' *is a* Potential Tradeoff*, that is:*

  - $supp(\bigotimes C) \subseteq supp(c')$;
  - $C \vdash c'$;

---

[1] In this paper η is fixed and never changes, so in all the definitions it could be omitted. Nevertheless it is important to include it in the notion of preference/tradeoff because in the next step of a configuration problem it will play an important role. After giving the user the opportunity to specify constraint preferences, he will be asked to make some more precise choices. In that phase of the configuration process, η becomes a partial assignment. We plan to address this second phase of the configuration problem as part of our research agenda in this area.

- $blevel(\{P \cup U\}) < \alpha$ (i.e. the problem is no longer α-consistent);

- $blevel(\{P \cup \{U-C\} \cup c'\}) \not< \alpha$ (starting from a solution with an insufficient level of consistency, we want an assignment that gives a solution with a best level of consistency not worse than α).

- ! is used as a filter (see Section 3.2).

3.2 Heuristics for selecting preference and tradeoff constraints

To completely define a tradeoff function we need to specify the selection and filtering heuristic, !, we will use to:

1. select the user preference constraints C to be eliminated – we will denote the selector $!^{out}$), and

2. select a tradeoff, c', from the set of potential tradeoffs computed by the entailment operator – we will denote the filter $!^{in}$; notice that this also implies the selection of the preference constraints $\bar{C}$ whose level of preference could be reduced.

Before presenting some specific examples of the selection heuristic, $!^{out}$, and the filtering heuristic, $!^{in}$, recall that the trigger for generating tradeoff constraints is the detection that there does not exist a solution which is α-consistent, i.e. that $blevel(\{P \cup U\}) < \alpha$. Below, we give here some possible instantiations of $!^{out}$ and $!^{in}$.

Random Selection: Random selection is always a possibility. In this case, the set C containing the preference constraint(s) to remove is randomly selected among those in $!^{out}(U) = \{c_j \in U : P \cup U - \{c_j\}$ is α-consistent$\}$;

Strictly related to P: The preference constraints we want to modify are strictly connected to the problem definition. In this case, the set C containing the preference constraint(s) to remove is randomly selected among those in $!^{out}(U) = \{c_j \in U : P \cup U - \{c_j\}$ is α-consistent $\wedge \exists c_i \in P : supp(c_i) \cap supp(c_j) \neq \emptyset\}$;

Has not appeared in a tradeoff: The preference constraints we want to modify have not already been affected by a tradeoff. In this case, the set C containing the preference constraint(s) to remove is randomly selected among those in $!^{out}(U) = \{c_j \in U : P \cup U - \{c_j\}$ is α-consistent $\wedge \nexists$ a tradeoff $t \in U : supp(t) \supseteq supp(c_j)\}$; this heuristic can be regarded as "user-friendly" since we do not ask the user to consider tradeoffs on variables which have already been involved in a tradeoff.

The tradeoff constraint, c', that we will choose, by filtering using $!^{in}$, has the properties that it will: (a) reflect a relaxation of the user's preference for constraint(s) C (selected by using $!^{out}$, and (b) a strengthening of the user's preference for constraint(s) $\bar{C}$.

Proposition 1 *Given a configuration problem $\{P \cup U\}$, a subset of user preference constraints $C \subseteq U$ and a tradeoff c' for C; let $\bar{C} \subseteq U$ be the greatest set s.t. $supp(\bigotimes\{C, \bar{C}\}) = supp(c')$; Then,*

- $(P \cup \{U - C\} \cup c') \Downarrow_{supp(C)} \sqsupseteq (P \cup U) \Downarrow_{supp(C)};$

- $(P \cup \{U - C\} \cup c') \Downarrow_{supp(\bar{C})} \sqsubseteq (P \cup U) \Downarrow_{supp(\bar{C})}.$

Proof The first item easily follows from the monotonicity of the $\otimes$ operator and from the hypotheses that $C \sqsubseteq c'$. The second follows from the properties of projection and from the fact that $C \cap \bar{C} = \emptyset$. $\qquad\square$

We now give some examples of $!^{in}$ filters that among all possible potential tradeoffs will select one. Some possible approaches we could adopt, based on [8] are:

Maximum viability: c' *is maximal w.r.t. P, U and η (that is for all $c'' \in Trades^{\alpha}_{(P,U,\eta,!)}$ we have $\bigotimes\{P \cup \{U - C\} \cup c''\}\eta \not\succeq \bigotimes\{P \cup \{U - C\} \cup c'\}\eta$;*

Minimum viability: c' *is minimal w.r.t. P, U and η (that is there does not exist $c'' \in Trades^{\alpha}_{(P,U,\eta,!)}$ s.t. $\bigotimes\{P \cup \{U - C\} \cup c''\}\eta \leq \bigotimes\{P \cup \{U - C\} \cup c'\}\eta$.*

Notice that the first approach will be less tasking on the configurator since it always selects the less restrictive tradeoff, i.e. we will have $c' \Downarrow_{supp(C)} = \mathbf{1}$; the tradeoff will give to all domain values of the variables in C the best preference. However, in this way, several preferences made by the user on this assignment are lost.

On the other hand, the second approach will try to always stay as close as possible to the user's preferences, i.e. we will have $c' \Downarrow_{supp(C)} \sqsupseteq C$. The tradeoff will increase the preference on C just sufficiently to reach the prefixed level of consistency α. Therefore, such a minor increment could result in a significant number of tradeoff interactions during the configuration process. In fact, the constraint c' inserted by the configurator could be too strict to be α-consistent when the user will insert new preference constraints in future interactions.

It is worth pointing out at this point that a good user-interface could assist in the detection of preference constraints to restrict and which to relax. An appropriate user-interface could also take care of preference elicitation. For example, we could assume that importance relationships between variables is reflected by the order in which user-choices are made. This is also an issue we are investigating as part of our research agenda in this area.

4 Relaxing Tradeoffs

Sometimes a tradeoff that completely satisfies the user's desires does not exist. This results in a dead-end being reached, where the configurator cannot assist the user to achieve the desired level of consistency. One possibility to resolve this situation is to assist the user in backing-up through the tradeoffs that the user previously accepted and modify one or more of them. In this way, the inserted tradeoffs are considered as user preference constraints that can be removed and substituted during the configuration process. In any case, in our view, a good configurator must to be capable of following a strategy to find a solution for the user without changing tradeoff constraints which have already been accepted by the user. In this way the user may have more trust in the configurator.

Alternatively, a notion of less strict tradeoff is useful. In this section we define a relaxed notion of tradeoffs based on a notion of substitutability for soft constraints which extends a definition of substitutability among domain values [2]. In Section 4.1 we present a generalization of the notion of soft value substitutability to substitutability for soft constraints. We then use this definition in Section 4.2 to relax the earlier notion of tradeoff.

4.1 Substitutability for Soft Constraints

We propose a definition of substitutability among constraints, extending the notions of substitutability among values defined in [2]. Informally, according to the definition of soft value substitutability, a domain value b is substitutable for a domain value a for a variable v if all solutions involving $v := b$ have a level of preference greater than solutions involving $v := a$. We extend this definition to constraints below.

Definition 3 (constraint substitutability/interchangeability) *We say that constraint c_1 is Fully Substitutable for constraint c_2 ($c_1 \in FS(c_2)$) w.r.t. the set of constraints C when $\bigotimes\{C \cup c_2\} \sqsubseteq \bigotimes\{C \cup c_1\}$. When we have $\bigotimes\{C \cup c_2\} = \bigotimes\{C \cup c_1\}$ we say that c_1 and c_2 are Fully Interchangeable ($FI(c_1/c_2)$).*

Note that this definition of substitutability for constraints, when dealing with crisp constraints, is very similar to that defined in [11]. However, the definition above is more general since we are dealing with the soft constraint framework.

As reported in [2] for domain values, the above definition can be relaxed by using degradations. In particular, a constraint $c*$ can be used as a degradation factor.

Definition 4 (Substitutability with degradation) *Consider two constraints c_1 and c_2, the set of constraints C and a degradation constraint $c*$; we say that c_1 is ^{c*}Substitutable for c_2 w.r.t. C if and only if,*

$$\bigotimes\{C \cup c_2 \cup c*\} \sqsubseteq \bigotimes\{C \cup c_1\}$$

4.2 A Relaxed Definition of Tradeoffs

The above notion of degradation can be used to relax the tradeoffs that the configurator proposes to the user. In particular, we will define a notion of *approximate* tradeoff. However, first we will show that tradeoffs and substitutability constraints are strictly related.

Theorem 2 (Substitutability and Potential Tradeoffs) *Consider the sets of constraints P, U, and $C \subseteq U$, and a partial assignment of the variable η. Then, if*

1. *c' is substitutable for $\bigotimes C$ ($c' \in FS(\bigotimes C)$) w.r.t. the set of constraints $\{P \cup U\}$ and the (partial) assignment η, and*

2. *$supp(c') \supseteq supp(C)$,*

then $c' \in Trades_{(P,U)}(C)$.

Proof By definition of substitutability for constraints we have $C \vdash c'$. With the second hypothesis of the theorem we easily have all that is required to say that c' is a potential tradeoff for C ($c' \in Trades_{(P,U)}(C)$). □

We can now relax the definition of tradeoff by using the relaxed version of substitutability.

Definition 5 (Degradation Tradeoffs) *Consider the constraint c', the (set of) constraint $C \in U$, a set of constraints $\{P \cup U\}$, and a degradation constraint $c*$; we say that c' is a Potential tradeoff for C w.r.t. $\{P \cup U\}$ and η with degradation $c*$ ($c' \in {}^{c*}Trades_{(P,U)}(C)$) if and only if, c' is ^{c*}Substitutable for $\bigotimes C$ w.r.t. $\{P \cup U\}$.*

Degradation tradeoffs can be regarded as *approximate* tradeoffs. Notice that by using the notion of degradation, we do not impose the requirement that the configurator has to find a better configuration, but rather a configuration *similar* to that chosen by the user. In this way the solution that the configurator will find will be not too far from the solution proposed by the user in terms of its degree of preference. In this respect the solution is an approximation.

5   Conclusions and Future Work

Tradeoffs have been proposed in the literature as an approach to resolving over-constrainedness in interactive constraint-based tools, such as product configurators, that reason about user preferences. It has already been reported in the literature how tradeoffs can be modeled as additional constraints. This paper presents a formal framework for tradeoff generation based on the semiring approach to handling soft constraints. In particular, we present a formal and general definition of tradeoff generation for interactive constraint processing. We present a novel definition of substitutability for soft constraints upon which we present a relaxed definition of tradeoffs.

Our research agenda in this area involves studying intelligent interfaces for reasoning about the relative importance of the user's preferences. For example, we could assume that importance relationships between variables is reflected by the order in which user-choices are made. We are also working on an empirical evaluation of a number of heuristics for selecting preference constraints to be considered as the basis for generating tradeoffs and strategies for filtering from the set of tradeoffs generated by our entailment operator.

In summary, we have presented a formal framework for studying a very important aspect of interactive constraint processing, the ability to assist users achieve their desires to the maximal degree possible. This framework provides the basis for a research agenda in the area of interactive constraint satisfaction with practical applications in domains such as product configuration, e-commerce, interactive scheduling, negotiation and explanation. As future work we also plan to integrate the notion of tradeoffs into the CHR framework [10].

Acknowledgment

This work has received support from Enterprise Ireland under their Basic Research Grant Scheme (Grant Number SC/02/289) and their International Collaboration Programme (Grant Number IC/2003/88).

References

[1] J. Amilhastre, H. Fargier, and P. Marguis. Consistency restoration and explanations in dynamic CSPs – application to configuration. *Artificial Intelligence*, 135:199–234, 2002.

[2] S. Bistarelli, B. Faltings, and N. Neagu. A definition of interchangeability for soft CSPs. In Barry O'Sullivan, editor, *Recent Advances in Constraints*, volume 2627 of *LNAI*, pages 31–46, 2003.

[3] S. Bistarelli, H. Fargier, U. Montanari, F. Rossi, T. Schiex, and G. Verfaillie. Semiring-based CSPs and Valued CSPs: Frameworks, properties, and comparison. *CONSTRAINTS: An international journal. Kluwer*, 4(3), 1999.

[4] S. Bistarelli, U. Montanari, and F. Rossi. Constraint Solving over Semirings. In *Proc. IJCAI95*, San Francisco, CA, USA, 1995. Morgan Kaufman.

[5] S. Bistarelli, U. Montanari, and F. Rossi. Semiring-based Constraint Solving and Optimization. *Journal of the ACM*, 44(2):201–236, Mar 1997.

[6] S. Bistarelli, U. Montanari, and F. Rossi. Soft concurrent constraint programming. In *Proc. 11th European Symposium on Programming (ESOP)*, Lecture Notes in Computer Science (LNCS), pages 53–67. Springer, 2002.

[7] A. Felfernig, G. Friedrich, D. Jannach, and M. Stumpter. Consistency-based diagnosis of configuration knowledge-bases. In *Proceedings of the 14h European Conference on Artificial Intelligence (ECAI'2000)*, pages 146–150, 2000.

[8] E. C. Freuder and B. O'Sullivan. Generating tradeoffs for interactive constraint-based configuration. In *Proceedings of CP-2001*, pages 590–594, Nov 2001.

[9] E.C. Freuder, C. Likitvivatanavong, M. Moretti, F. Rossi, and R.J. Wallace. Computing explanations and implications in preference-based configurators. In Barry O'Sullivan, editor, *Recent Advances in Constraints*, volume 2627 of *LNAI*, pages 76–92, 2003.

[10] T. Frühwirth. Constraint handling rules. In *Constraint Programming: Basics and Trends*, volume 910 of *Lecture Notes in Computer Science (LNCS)*, pages 90–107. Springer, 1995.

[11] P. Jeavons, D. Cohen, and M. Copper. A substitution operation for constraints. In *Proceedings of the Second International Workshop on Principles and Practice of Constraint Programming – CP-94*, volume 874 of *LNCS*, 1994.

[12] D. Sabin and R. Weigel. Product configuration frameworks – a survey. *IEEE Intelligent Systems and their applications*, 13(4):42–49, July–August 1998. Special Issue on Configuration.

[13] V.A. Saraswat. *Concurrent Constraint Programming*. MIT Press, 1993.

Maximum Partial Assignments for Over-Constrained Problems

Ken Brown

Cork Constraint Computation Centre, Department of Computer Science
University College Cork, Ireland
k.brown@cs.ucc.ie

Abstract

Many real world problems are over-constrained, but with hard constraints which must be satisfied. For such problems we define Max-A-CSP, in which we search for maximal partial assignments which violate no constraints over assigned variables. We develop a branch-and-bound algorithm which interleaves arc consistency maintenance with reasoning about unassigned variables. We show that the unassigned variables make it difficult to find effective lower bounds. Finally, we test the algorithm on random binary constraint problems, comparing it to a version of forward checking, and show that, as for CSPs, the extra consistency maintenance improves performance on hard sparse problems.

1. Introduction

Many real-world problems are over constrained – given the initial formulation as a constraint satisfaction problem, there is no complete assignment which satisfies all the constraints. Instead of returning failure, we may want to find some form of partial solution. Much recent research has focused on *soft constraints*, in which assignments which violate constraints are allowed, at some cost. The aim is then to find an assignment which minimises the total cost over all constraints. This approach, however, does not provide a natural representation for many real world problems which have constraints which cannot or should not be violated. For example, selecting and loading containers on a cargo ship, determining a set of tasks able to be executed by employees, maximising the number of requested features able to be instantiated by a configurator, or deciding which items to bid for in a combinatorial auction, are all problems in which the flexibility lies in the number of sub-tasks able to be completed. As an alternative to soft constraints for modelling and solving such problems, we can generate *partial assignments* which satisfy all constraints on the assigned variables, and in which we gain a reward for each variable we do assign. The aim is then to find a partial assignment which maximises the total reward. In this paper we formalise this notion of partial assignments by defining Max-A-CSP, in which we search for a maximal partial assignment satisfying all constraints. We compare Max-A-CSP to Max-CSP, and show that although they are similar, there are differences which have consequences for solution algorithms and lower bound computation. We present branch-and-bound algorithms for Max-A-CSP, interleaving arc consistency maintenance with reasoning about unassigned variables, and we study their performance on a series of random binary CSPs.

2. Related Research

Freuder and Wallace [1] stated that there were four ways in which a problem could be relaxed – domains could be extended, constraints could be relaxed, constraints could be removed, or variables could be removed. They noted that relaxing constraints by adding tuples could be used to model all four methods of relaxation, and so concentrated on relaxing constraints. They proposed Max-CSP, in which the aim is to find a complete assignment which maximises the number of satisfied constraints (and thus relaxes the other constraints). A number of more sophisticated frameworks have been proposed for handling soft constraints, including *valued* CSPs [2] and *semi-ring* CSPs [3], which associate preferences with the constraints and the constraint tuples respectively, and specify general properties of the operators which aggregate violations. These frameworks encompass a number of other soft constraint formulations. In particular, Max-CSP is a valued CSP with unit violation costs, and the aim is to minimise the sum of the violations.

A number of algorithms have been proposed for Max-CSP, based on branch-and-bound. During a search, the variables are divided into two sets: P, the (past) variables which have been assigned a value, and F, the (future) variables not yet assigned. *distance*(P) is the number of violated constraints over the assigned variables. Each time a value is tried for a variable, *partial forward checking* [1] propagates this choice onto the future variables, but instead of removing an inconsistent value, a, for variable X, it increments its *inconsistency count* (ic_{Xa}), the number of past assignments inconsistent with a. The lower bound at each step is $distance(P) + \sum_{x \in F} (min_a(ic_{Xa}))$. This lower bound can be improved using *directed arc inconsistency counts* and a fixed variable ordering [4]. The directed arc inconsistency count of a value in a domain is the number of future variables it is inconsistent with which appear after it in the ordering. The lower bound is then $distance(P) + \sum_{x \in F} min_a(ic_{Xa} + dac_{Xa})$ [5]. For the unassigned variables, *directed* inconsistency counts are required to avoid double counting of inconsistencies when summing the minima. *Reversible graph-based* DAC [6] maintains the directed arc-inconsistency counts while using a dynamic variable ordering (at the cost of dynamically selecting new directions and reversing the relevant arcs). Individual values for an unassigned variable can also be pruned from domains by summing ic and dac for the value with *distance*(P) and the sum of the minima for the other unassigned variables, and comparing to the upper bound. Further extensions include computing additional contributions to the lower bound from partitions of the unassigned variables [7]. Schiex [8] proposed a general scheme for soft arc consistency which can be applied to many different formulations, and Larrosa [9] has recently proposed an efficient algorithm for achieving arc consistency in a specialisation of this scheme using AC-2001[10].

There has been little previous research on partial assignments. Tsang [11] defined Maximum Utility Problems, although presented no algorithms. Gaspin and Régin [12] define Max$_V$CSP, in which they search for all partial solutions in which all constraints are satisfied for a given set of variables. A preliminary version of Max-A-CSP was presented by Brown [13], including an algorithm which maintained directed arc consistency.

3. Maximal Assignment CSP

A binary Max-A-CSP (X, D, C) is defined as follows: $X = \{X_1, ..., X_n\}$ is a set of *variables*, $D = \{D_1, ..., D_n\}$ is a set of *domains* for each variable, representing their possible values, and C is a set of binary *constraints* $C_{ij} \subseteq D_i \times D_j$ specifying the values pairs of variables can take simultaneously. A *value assignment* for a variable X_i is the selection of a value from D_i. A *partial assignment* is a set of value assignments for a subset of the variables in X. A constraint C_{ij} is *active* for a partial assignment Π if both X_i and X_j have value assignments in Π. A *solution* is a partial assignment which does not violate any active constraints. An *optimal* solution is one of maximal size – i.e. in which the maximum number of variables have been assigned values. There is an obvious similarity to Max-CSP, in which the optimal solution is a complete assignment which satisfies the maximum number of constraints.

Variables:	X	Y	Z	T	
Domains:	{a,b}	{a,b}	{a,b}	{a,b,c}	$\perp$ represents no assignment
Constraints:	C_{XY}: {(a,b), (b,b)}				
(allowable tuples)	C_{XZ}: {(a,a)}				
	C_{XT}: {(a,b)}				
	C_{YZ}: {(a,a), (a,b)}				
	C_{YT}: {(a,b), (a,c), (b,c)}				
	C_{ZT}: {(b,a), (b,c)}				
Max-A-CSP:	X←$\perp$, Y←a, Z←b, T←c (leaves X unassigned)				
Max-CSP:	X←a, Y←a, Z←a, T←b (violates C_{XY} and C_{ZT})				

Figure 1. over-constrained problem, with Max-A-CSP and Max-CSP solutions

Figure 1 shows a simple over-constrained CSP, with optimal solutions for the Max-A-CSP and Max-CSP formulations. Note that there is no obvious mapping between the two solutions. Extending the Max-A-CSP solution to a complete assignment by assigning a value to X will result in at least 3 violations, while removing assignments from the Max-CSP solution would require at least two variables to be unassigned in order to get a satisfying assignment.

For implementing Max-A-CSP, we introduce a new value called *null*, $\perp$, which represents a variable explicitly left unassigned. $\perp$ will be added to each domain, and will be defined to satisfy any constraint. The definition of a solution is then rephrased as an assignment to each variable of a normal value from its domain or the special value ⊥, such that no constraint over the non-null variables is violated. The aim will be to search for solutions with the minimum number of ⊥ assignments. Note that there is a distinction between a variable which has not yet been assigned during a search for a solution, and one which has been explicitly marked (using ⊥) as having no proper assigned value in the eventual solution.

4. Propagation, Lower Bounds and Algorithms

Do we need new algorithms for Max-A-CSP? Clearly, we could represent Max-A-CSP in other frameworks. For example, we could treat it as a variant of Max-CSP in which some constraints are hard and others soft, by adding ⊥ to each domain, and then imposing on each variable a single soft unary constraint associating a cost of 1 with each ⊥ assignment. Although we could now solve the problem using a Max-CSP algorithm, we would have lost the main feature. ⊥ supports every other value, so maintaining consistency counts would have little effect, since there would be no inconsistencies among the future variables. Therefore, in this section we propose lower bounds and develop new algorithms which reason about the ⊥ assignments during search.

4.1 A-FC: Forward Checking for Max-A-CSP

First we describe A-FC, a straightforward extension of forward checking. We extend all domains to include ⊥, as described above. We maintain sets P and F of past and future variables as for Max-CSP. We maintain an upper bound, which is either a preset number of ⊥ assignments which must be improved upon, or the number of ⊥ assignments in the best solution found so far. We select a variable from F, and then try each value in the domain (including ⊥) in turn. For each value, we propagate the constraints over the future variables, removing any values which conflict, and recurse. Since ⊥ satisfies all constraints, we don't need to check ⊥, nor do we need to propagate it. At each step, we can compute *distance*(P), which is simply the number of variables in P assigned ⊥, and *futurenull*(F), the number of variables in F whose domains have been reduced to {⊥}. The lower bound is then *distance*(P) + *futurenull*(F), and whenever that is not less than the upper bound, we backtrack. Compared to PFC for Max-CSP, we can remove values from future domains much earlier (as soon as a constraint is violated), instead of having to wait for an inconsistency count to exceed a bound. We can apply standard dynamic variable ordering heuristics based on domain size, since we reduce the domains of future variables. However, we do introduce extra branches in the search tree by having to consider ⊥ as a possible value.

4.2 Lower Bounds for Max-A-CSP

It is generally accepted that the efficiency of branch-and-bound depends on the quality of the lower bounds. Better lower bounds for Max-A-CSP might be obtained by computing and maintaining arc-inconsistency counts, where we record, for each value, the number of future variables it would force to be left unassigned – i.e. the number of future domains in which ⊥ provides the only support. For a variable x and a value a, denote this by ac_{xa}. However, in the same way that undirected arc consistency for Max-CSP does not allow summing over the counts to produce a lower bound, it also causes a problem for Max-A-CSP.

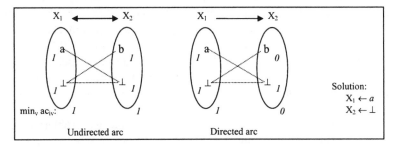

Figure 2. minimum ac_{iv} cannot be summed in Max-A-CSP

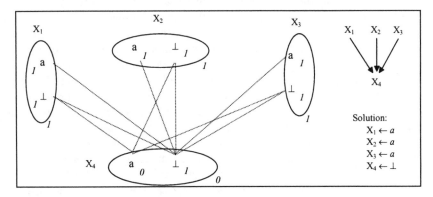

Figure 3. minimum dac_{iv} cannot be summed in Max-A-CSP

Consider the problem in Figure 2 with two future variables X_1 and X_2, domains $D_1 = \{a, \perp\}$ and $D_2 = \{b, \perp\}$ respectively, and a constraint forbidding the pair (a,b). Assigning $X_1 \leftarrow a$ forces X_2 to be ⊥, and assigning $X_1 \leftarrow \perp$ clearly forces X_1 to be ⊥, so the minimum count for X_1 is 1. Similarly, both values for X_2 have a count of 1. We cannot simply add them together and assume there must be two null assignments, since $\{X_1 \leftarrow a, X_2 \leftarrow \perp\}$ would be a solution with just one. We could take the same step as in Max-CSP, assign a direction to each arc, and record directed inconsistency counts (dac_{ia}) with the variables at the start of the arcs only. In the example, if we assume a directed arc from X_1 to X_2, then the count for value b for X_2 will be 0, and so the sum of the minima would be 1, as expected. However, there is a further complication with Max-A-CSP which stops us summing minima even from directed arcs. Consider the problem in Figure 3, where we have directed arcs from X_1, X_2 and X_3 to X_4, the values a for X_1, X_2 and X_3 force X_4 to be ⊥, and there are no other constraints. The minimum counts for X_1, X_2 and X_3 then must each be 1, so summing the minima would give a total of 3. However, we are not forced to have three $\perp$ assignments: assigning $X_4 \leftarrow \perp$ allows X_1, X_2 and X_3 each to take the value a, and so we have a solution with only one $\perp$ assignment. Therefore, even if we restrict inconsistency counts to directed arcs, we still cannot sum the minimum counts for each variable to get a lower bound. Instead of the sum, we could take the maximum of all the minima. We do not expect this to give particularly good results, since in a pure Max-A-CSP, no minimum will ever be greater than 1 (since $\perp$ is in every domain). [13] presented an algorithm A-MDAC which used both the maximum of the minima and the forward checking lower bound. If either $distance(P) + max(max_{x \in F}(min_a(dac_{xa})), futurenull(F))$ is not less than the upper bound, we backtrack. We also prune values for which $distance(P) + dac_{xa}$ is not less than the bound. We fix a variable ordering to correspond to the directed arcs, and then compute the directed arc inconsistency counts while maintaining directed arc consistency.

The reason [13] considered directed arcs was to avoid the problem of double counting when summing the minima. However, if we do not sum the minima, then there is no obvious reason to restrict the algorithm to directed arcs. Therefore, we now use standard arc consistency (i.e. undirected arcs), during which we maintain for each value assignment a count (ac_{ia}) of the number of future variables it would force to be $\perp$. We can obtain a minimum count for each future variable, and then use $distance(P) + max(max_{Xi \in F}(min_a(ac_{ia})), futurenull(F))$ for the lower bound. We can also prune values as before, and we expect more pruning since the counts will be higher for ac_{ia} than for dac_{ia}. The final and perhaps most significant benefit is that we can then use standard variable ordering heuristics to improve search performance. Note that this does not change the classical definition of arc consistency [14], but combines it with reasoning about null counts.

As stated above, we could represent a Max-A-CSP problem as a variant of a Max-CSP problem, by adding $\perp$ to each domain, imposing a soft unary constraint disallowing $\perp$, and making all other constraints hard. PFC-MRDAC [6] is considered a reference algorithm for Max-CSP, and we will assume here an extension PFC-MRDAC' which maintains classical arc consistency on the hard constraints in addition to the arc inconsistency counts. The PFC-MRDAC' lower bound would then be $distance(P) + \sum_{x \in F} min_{a \in Dx}(ic_{xa} + c_{xa} + dac_{xa}(G^F))$, where c_{xa} is 1 if $a = \perp$, 0 otherwise.

Theorem PFC-MRDAC' lower bound $\leq$ Max-A-CSP lower bound

Proof: $distance(P)$ (the number of past variables already assigned null) is the same for both algorithms. Therefore, the theorem statement reduces to

$$\sum_{x \in F} min_{a \in Dx}(ic_{xa} + c_{xa} + dac_{xa}(G^F)) \leq max(max_{x \in F}(min_a(ac_{xa})), futurenull(F))$$

ic_{xa} is 0, since all binary constraints are hard, and so any value in conflict would have been removed. Let x be a variable in F, and let a be a value. Let Y be a variable in F, ordered after x in G^F. If $\perp \in D_Y$, then $dac_{xa}(Y) = 0$. Otherwise, if a has support in D_Y, then $dac_{xa}(Y) = 0$, and if a does not have support, it will be removed. Therefore, $dac_{xa}(Y) = 0$ $\forall$ Y after X in G^F. The left hand side reduces to $\sum_{x \in F} min_{a \in Dx}(c_{xa})$, which is simply *futurenull*(F). $\square$

```
A-AC2001(): boolean
1 wipeout = false
2 while Q is not empty and wipeout is false
3    select and remove Xᵢ from Q
4    for each Xⱼ in F while wipeout is false
5        if cons(Xⱼ,Xᵢ) == true  wipeout = REVISE(Xⱼ,Xᵢ)
6 return wipeout

REVISE(Xⱼ: var, Xᵢ: var): boolean
7  for each v in Dⱼ ≠ ⊥
8      supp == 1
9      if s(Xⱼ,v,Xᵢ) is not in Dᵢ
10         supp = 0
11         u = next(Dᵢ, s(Xⱼ,v,Xᵢ))
12         while supp == 0 and u > -1 and u ≠ ⊥
13             if check(Xⱼ,Xᵢ,v,u)
14                 supp = 1
15                 s(Xⱼ,v,Xᵢ) = u
16             else u = next(Dᵢ,u)
17         if u == ⊥
18             c(Xⱼ,v) = c(Xⱼ,v) + 1
19             supp = 1
20             s(Xⱼ,v,Xᵢ) = ⊥
21     if c(Xⱼ,v) > ub - distance -1 or supp == 0
22         delete v from Dⱼ
23 if Dⱼ is empty return true
24 else if any value removed add Xⱼ to Q
25 return false
```

Figure 4. A-AC2001 – achieving arc consistency and AC-counts in Max-A-CSP

Note that the example in Figure 3 shows that the bounds are not equal, since *futurenull*(F) for that example is 0, but the Max-A-CSP lower bound is 1. In addition, for Max-A-CSP we will be able to maintain counts of the number of times each value has relied on null for support, and prune values with a count higher than the upper bound, while the PFC-MRDAC' counters ic_{xa} and dac_{xa} are both 0.

4.3   A-AC2001: Arc Consistency and Null counts

In Figure 4, we present the algorithm A-AC2001, which is simply the algorithm AC-2001 [10] for establishing arc consistency augmented with facilities to handle ⊥ and to prune values based on the ac_{ia} counts. We assume the following: for each non-⊥ value in a variable's domain, an array recording the first support in the domains of variables it is constrained by, denoted $s(X_i, v_m, X_j)$ and with all cells initialised to −1; for each value in each domain, a count $c(X_i, v_m)$ recording the number of future variables it forces to ⊥, initialised to 0, except for $c(X_i, \perp)$ initialised to 1; a delete queue, Q, initially containing all problem variables; and global variables *ub*, recording an upper bound, and *distance*, recording the incurred cost. The idea of AC2001 is that domains are ordered, constraints are only checked if the first support for a value is removed from the corresponding domain, and then only the values after that support need to be checked. The function *next*(D_i, u)

simply returns the next live value after u in X_i's domain D_i. If $\perp$ is in the domain, it is the last value. The algorithm proceeds as follows. Q contains variables whose domains have changed. A variable X_i is selected from Q, and then the domain of each variable X_j constrained by X_i is revised. To revise the domain of X_j, each live value v is considered in turn. If its support from D_i has been removed or not yet established (line 9), we search on through D_i to find the next supporting value, and update $s(X_j,v,X_i)$ (lines 11-16). If the only supporting value found is $\perp$, we increment the count for (X_j,v) and set $s(X_j,v,X_i)$ to $\perp$ (17-20). If no support was found, or the count is not less than the upper bound minus the distance, we delete v from D_j (21,22). If D_j becomes empty, we return and A-AC2001 reports false. If any value was removed from D_j, we add X_j into Q. The main changes from the AC2001 algorithm are the code to handle $\perp$, the count increment if the first supporting value becomes $\perp$, and the deletion of values when their count exceeds the limit.

4.4 A-MAC: Maintaining Arc Consistency and Null counts

Next we present A-MAC (Figure 5), which maintains arc consistency during search [15], and simultaneously uses the inconsistency counts to prune values and estimate lower bounds. Auxiliary functions are shown in Figure 6. A-MAC is first called with input (-1,-1), and otherwise is called when a value choice has been made for a variable. If it is the last variable, we try to update the best solution (line 1). We then check the lower bound against the upper bound (2). If it is still possible to improve we propagate the choice through the future variables, or establish initial arc consistency and value counts (6,7). If neither of these emptied a domain, we select a new variable, then select a value, and call A-MAC recursively (10-13). Once we have completed the search below that value choice, if there are still other values to choose, we propagate any change to the bound, and select another value (15, 12). When propagating a choice of v for variable X_i (the function PROPAGATE), we first check to see if v is $\perp$. If it is, we need to decrement the count of every future value choice which relied on $\perp$ for support in D_i, since that use of $\perp$ is now included in *distance* (line 19). We then establish how many new domains we are allowed to reduce to $\{\perp\}$ (20). We then apply forward checking to each future variable constrained by X_i (21-26), and check that we haven't exceeded the number of $\perp$ domains (27,28). If any values were removed by forward checking, we prune values with a count not less than the upper bound minus the distance, and then maintain consistency and null-counts by calling A-AC2001 (29-31). To propagate a change in the bound (PROPAGATE_BOUND), we go through a series of bounds checks, value prunings, and consistency and null-count maintenance. Note that if every domain contains $\perp$, and we are simply counting supports of $\perp$, then the best the MAX-MIN() function can return is 1. Better bounds would be obtained if some variables were not allowed to be $\perp$, or if variables had different weights.

```
A-MAC(X_i: var, v: value): boolean
1   if F is empty change = UPDATE-BEST()
2   else if distance + MAX-MIN() >= best return false
3   else
4      start a new entry on restore stack
5      change = false
6      if X ≠ -1 bt = PROPAGATE(X_i,v)
7      else bt = A-AC2001()
8      if bt == false
9         change = false
10        select and remove X_j from F
11        while bt == false and D_j not empty
12           select and remove u from D_j
13           onechange = A-MAC(X_j,u)
14           change = (onechange OR change)
15           if D_j not empty bt = PROPAGATE-BOUND(change)
16     restore all changes at top of stack
17  return change

PROPAGATE(X_i:var, v: value): boolean
18  bt = false
19  if v == ⊥ UPDATE-COUNTS(X_i)
20  nullsallowed = best - distance - 1 - FUTURE-NULL()
21  for each X_j in F such that cons(X_i,X_j) and D_j not empty
22     for each u in D_j
23        if check(X_i,v,X_j,u) == false  delete u from D_j
24     if any values removed from D_j
25        if D_j is empty return true
26        add X_j to Q
27        if D_j == {⊥} nullsallowed = nullsallowed - 1
28        if nullsallowed < 0 return true
29  if any values removed
30     bt = REMOVE-HIGH-VALUES()
31     if bt == false bt = A-AC2001()
32  return bt
```

Figure 5. A-MAC – maintaining arc consistency and AC counts in Max-A-CSP

4.5 Complexity

AC2001 is an optimal arc consistency algorithm for CSPs [10]. A-AC2001 has the same worst-case time and space complexities as AC2001. Let n be the number of variables, e the number of constraints and d the domain size. For each directed constraint (X_i, X_j), we call REVISE at most $d+1$ times. For each value in D_i, over all the calls to REVISE for (X_i, X_j), we do at most d constraint checks, $d+1$ support checks, 1 cost update and 1 deletion. There are d values, giving $O(d^2)$ operations for X_i due to (X_i, X_j). There are $2e$ constraints, giving overall time complexity $O(ed^2)$. Each constraint requires $2d$ support entries (one for each non-$\perp$ value in the domains of its variables), giving $2ed$ supports in total. Each value of each variable also has an inconsistency counter, giving $n(d+1)$ counters. The delete queue is bounded above by n. Thus the overall space complexity is $O(ed)$. In practice, A-MAC will require significantly more time than MAC2001, since it continues to search for an optimal solution in overconstrained problems when MAC2001 simply reports failure.

```
UPDATE-COUNTS(X_i:var)
1   for each X_j in F such that cons(X_i,X_j)
2       for each value u in D_j
3           if s(X_j,u,X_i) == ⊥
4               c(X_j,u) = c(X_j,u)-1

REMOVE-HIGH-VALUES(): boolean
5   limit = best - 1 - distance
6   wipeout = false
7   for each var X_i in F while wipeout == false
8       for each value v in D_i
9           if c(X_i,v) > limit delete v from D_i
10      if D_i is empty wipeout = true
11  return wipeout

PROPAGATE-BOUND(change: boolean): boolean
12  if change == false return false
13  else if distance >= best return true
14  else if REMOVE-HIGH-VALUES() == true return true
15  else if distance + FUTURE-NULL() >= best return true
16  else if A-AC2001() == true return true
17  else if distance + MAX-MIN() >= best return true
18  else return false
```

Fig. 6. Auxiliary functions for A-MAC

5. Experiments

We have tested the algorithms on a set of random binary problems, to get a picture of the nature of Max-A-CSP and to compare the performance of the algorithms. We generate problems characterised by the parameters $<n, m, c, t>$, where n is the number of variables, m is the domain size, c is the number of constraints, and t is the number of forbidden tuples in each constraint. We start by constructing a skeleton ensuring a connected graph. All experiments are the average of 20 problems at each point, and are executed on a 250MHz SPARC. The algorithms are implemented in C. Unless stated otherwise, we use *dom/deg* variable ordering – that is at each stage we choose the variable with the smallest ratio of domain size to original degree [16]. We select variables from the A-AC2001 delete queue in the order of insertion, and we use a fixed lexicographic value ordering.

First, we consider three classes of relatively small problems: $<20,10,180,t>$ (densely connected), $<25,10,150,t>$ (medium) and $<30, 10, 35,t>$ (sparse). In Figure 7 we show graphs of mean cpu time against tightness for A-FC and A-MAC. We compare cpu time instead of constraint checks or nodes for a fairer comparison, because the use of support tables allows A-MAC to avoid constraint checks, at the cost of more work per node. The two algorithms share the same code and data structures wherever possible. On each graph we also show the solubility transition for standard CSPs, and we can see that the hardest problems are in the over-constrained region, where a significant amount of work is required to find and prove the optimal solution. We see that A-MAC is consistently slower on the dense and medium problems, but is significantly faster on the sparse problems at high tightness. Note that the third graph is focused on tight problems, and that cpu time

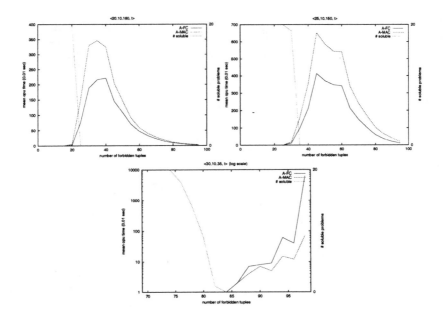

Figure 7. Comparison of A-FC and A-MAC on three small problem classes

is on a log scale. This corresponds to results on standard CSPs, where MAC also performs well on sparse problems ([15]; [16]), but shows little improvement on small problems.

In Figure 8, we compare A-MAC against the earlier A-MDAC on the $<15,10,c,t>$ class at three different densities: c = 21, 63, and 95. This time we compare constraint checks rather than cpu time, since the A-MDAC implementation is noticeably less efficient. For comparison, we include A-MAC with the same static variable ordering as A-MDAC. A-MAC requires significantly fewer checks on the hardest problems, with the greatest improvement again on the sparse problems. By looking at the static curve, we can see that the full (as opposed to directed) consistency contributes a small amount to the improvement, but the main improvement comes from the dynamic variable ordering.

Since the performance of A-MAC appears to vary with the density of the graph, we tested A-MAC against A-FC on a series of $<40,5,c,t>$ problems, gradually increasing the number of constraints. In Figure 9 we plot on the left the mean cpu time (log scale) at the hardest point for each problem class, and on the right the mean cpu time at the tightest point (24 out of 25 forbidden tuples). On the sparsest problems, A-MAC is two orders of magnitude faster, but the two algorithms have become largely comparable by a density of 0.2 (145 constraints).

Finally, we have studied one large sparse problem class ($<100,12,120,t>$, density 0.02) for which [16] had shown MAC on standard CSPs was superior, to see if the same pattern holds for A-MAC. This graph is plotted on a log scale (Figure 10), and we can see that A-MAC is a significant improvement across the tightness

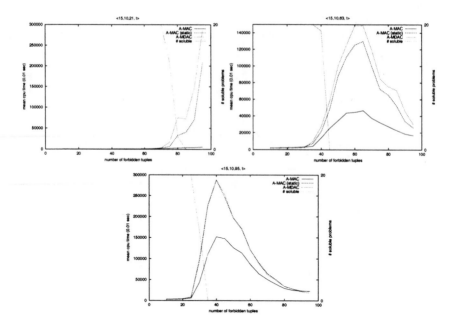

Figure 8. Comparison of A-MAC-dom/deg, A-MAC-static and A-MDAC

range. In addition, there is a limit of 2×10^9 checks for each problem: A-MAC returned within the limit for every instance, but A-FC hits that limit on average three times out of twenty at each point. The graph plots the time to return, and so is favourable to A-FC. For illustration, on the right we plot the mean number of nodes expanded during search, which follows the same pattern. Note that A-MAC is always at least one order of magnitude faster, and frequently multiple orders faster.

6. Future Work

For problems with unit weights (i.e. max-A-CSP), the most pressing requirement is to find better lower bounds: if null is present in every domain then the most the inconsistency counts can contribute to the bound is 1. One possibility would be to identify independent inconsistent subsets of the future variables, which could each contribute to the bound[1]. The algorithms presented here will extend easily to weighted assignment problems, and will benefit from better bounds. The recently proposed soft arc consistency algorithms [9], in which violation counts move from value to value, may also be appropriate, and will be compared to A-MAC. Régin *et al.* [17] have shown how to represent Max-CSP as a global constraint, and a similar treatment should be possible for Max-A-CSP. We will also investigate relaxing the restriction to binary constraints. If we allow global constraints, then the

---

[1] Javier Larrosa, personal communication.

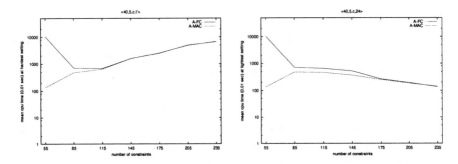

Figure 9. A-MAC vs A-FC for increasing density on hard (left) and tight (right) problems

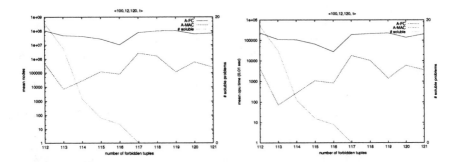

Figure 10. A-MAC vs A-FC on large sparse $<100,12,120,t>$: cpu (right), nodes (left)

interpretation of a constraint on a null-assigned variable must change – for example, an all-different constraint would still have to be satisfied for the remaining variables. We will apply future results for Max-A-CSP to Branching CSP ([18,19]), which models probabilistic changes to CSPs in terms of the addition of new variables to the problem, and searches for contingent partial assignments with maximal expected utility. Finally, we will test the effectiveness of the algorithms on real world problems.

7. Conclusions

Many real-world problems are over-constrained, but require partial solutions without violating constraints. For such problems, we have defined the maximal assignment constraint satisfaction problem, Max-A-CSP, which receives a unit reward for each assigned variable while satisfying all constraints on assigned variables. We have developed two algorithms based on branch and bound: A-FC, using forward checking, and A-MAC, which maintains arc consistency on the hard constraints while checking bounds on unassigned variables. Although Max-A-CSP has obvious similarities to Max-CSP, the fact that variables can be left unassigned in Max-A-CSP makes it harder to obtain effective lower bounds. The A-MAC algorithm with lower bound $distance(P) + \max(\max_{X_i \in F}(\min_a(ac_{ia})), futurenull(F))$ provides significant improvement over A-FC on large, sparse problems.

96

Acknowledgments

Much of this work was carried out at the University of Aberdeen. I thank Javier Larrosa for comments on A-MDAC, Christian Bessière for information on AC-2001, and Nick Murray for assistance with the C programs.

References

1. Freuder, E. and Wallace, R. "Partial Constraint Satisfaction", *Artificial Intelligence* **58**, pp21—70, 1992.
2. Schiex, T., Fargier, H. and Verfaillie, G. "Valued Constraint Satisfaction Problems: hard and easy problems", *Proc. IJCAI'95*, pp631—637, 1995.
3. Bistarelli, S., Montanari, U. and Rossi, F. (1995) "Constraint Solving over Semi-rings", *Proc. IJCAI'95*, pp624--630
4. Wallace, R. "Directed arc consistency pre-processing", *Proc. ECAI-94 Workshop on Constraint Processing* (LNCS 923), Springer, pp121—137, 1994.
5. Larrosa, J. and Meseguer, P. "Exploiting the use of DAC in Max-CSP", *Proc. CP96*, pp308—322, 1996.
6. Larrosa, J., Meseguer, P. and Schiex, T. "Maintaining reversible DAC for Max-CSP", *Artificial Intelligence* **107**, pp149—163, 1999.
7. Larrosa, J. and Meseguer, P. "Partition-based lower bound for Max-CSP", Proc CP99, pp303—315, 1999.
8. Schiex, T. "Arc consistency for soft constraints", *Proc. CP2000*, pp411—424, 2000.
9. Larrosa, J. "Node and Arc Consistency in Weighted CSPs", *Proc AAAI-02*, pp48—53, 2002.
10. Bessière, C. and Régin, J.-C. "Refining the basic constraint propagation algorithm", *Proc IJCAI'01*, pp309—315, 2001.
11. Tsang, E. *Foundations of Constraint Satisfaction*, Academic Press, 1993.
12. Gaspin,C. and Régin, J.-C. "Application of Maximal Constraint Satisfaction Problems to RNA Folding", *CP97 Workshop on Constraints and Bioinformatics/Biocomputing*, 1997.
13. Brown, K. "Searching for Maximal Partial Assignments for Over-Constrained Problems", *Proc Soft'02, 4th Intl Workshop on Soft Constraints*, pp1—10, 2002.
14. Mackworth, A. K. "Consistency in Networks of Relations", *Artificial Intelligence*, **8**, pp99—118, 1977.
15. Sabin, D. and Freuder, E. "Contradicting conventional wisdom in constraint satisfaction", *PPCP'94 :2nd workshop on Principles and Practice of Constraint Programming*, 1994.
16. Bessière, C. and Régin, J.-C. "MAC and Combined Heuristics: two reasons to forsake FC (and CBJ?) on hard problems", *Proc CP'96*, pp61—75, 1996.
17. Régin, J.-C., Petit, T., Bessière, C. and Puget J.-F. (2001) "New Lower Bounds of Constraint Violations for Over-Constrained Problems", Proc. CP2001, pp332—345.
18. Fowler, D. W. and Brown, K. N. "Branching constraint satisfaction problems for solutions robust under likely changes", *Proc CP2000*, pp500—504, 2000.
19. Fowler, D. W. and Brown, K. N. "Branching constraint satisfaction problems and Markov decision problems compared", *Annals of Operations Research*, Vol 118, Issue 1—4, pp85—100, 2003.

Escaping Local Optima in Multi-Agent Oriented Constraint Satisfaction

Muhammed Basharu, Hatem Ahriz, and Inés Arana

School of Computing, The Robert Gordon University, St Andrew Street, Aberdeen, AB25 1HG, U.K.
{mb, ha, ia}@comp.rgu.ac.uk

Abstract

We present a multi-agent approach to constraint satisfaction where feedback and reinforcement are used in order to avoid local optima and, consequently, to improve the overall solution. Our approach, FeReRA, is based on the fact that an agent's local best performance does not necessarily contribute to the system's best performance. Thus, agents may be rewarded for improving the system's performance and penalised for not contributing towards a better solution. Hence, agents may be forced to choose sub-optimal moves when they reach a specified penalty threshold as a consequence of their lack of contribution towards a better overall solution. This may allow other agents to choose better moves and, therefore, to improve the overall performance of the system. FeReRA is tested against its predecessor, ERA, and a comparative evaluation of both approaches is presented.

1. Introduction

A recurring theme with meta-heuristics inspired by the behaviour of social insects is the notion of "emergence from local interaction." In this class of heuristics, control is delegated down to a multitude of simple and unsophisticated agents whose local interactions dynamically drive a process of self-organisation to the emergence of a global solution. Agents are simple because each agent is typically involved in a small aspect of a problem, while the behaviour and interaction between agents are defined by a limited set of reactive rules. These new heuristic approaches have been shown to be successful in solving many hard combinatorial optimisation and constraint satisfaction problems (CSP) in areas such as manufacturing process control [1, 5], frequency planning [2, 10, 13], and network routing [4]. A CSP consists of a set of variables, whose values are taken from finite, discrete domains, and a set of constraints that limit the combination of values some variables may simultaneously take. Solving a CSP is equivalent to finding a consistent assignment of values to all variables such that all constraints are satisfied.

A distributed CSP is a CSP in which variables and constraints are distributed into sub-problems, each of which is to be solved by an agent. Yokoo et al. [14] have made a significant contribution in the area of distributed CSP and have developed a number of algorithms inspired from solutions to the centralised CSP. Recently, Liu et al. [11] developed a new framework called ERA (Environment, Reactive rules and Agents) a self-organising multi-agent algorithm, inspired by swarm models, in which independent agents, representing variables in a CSP, are coupled with their environment to create a recurrent dynamical system that is capable of solving CSPs without much computational overhead. A comparison (in averaged number of cycles) of ERA and Yokoo et al.'s algorithms in solving benchmark n-queen problems is presented in [11] and has shown that ERA is an effective and competitive approach.

In this paper, we propose the FeReRA (Feedback, Reinforcement and Reactive Agents) algorithm, an extension to ERA. The remainder of the paper is organised as follows: Sect. 2 the ERA framework is presented and its strengths and weaknesses discussed; details of our extension to the algorithm are explained in Sect. 3; and a summary of results from empirical tests comparing the performance of ERA and our extension is presented in Sect. 4. Concluding remarks are given in Sect. 5.

2. The ERA Framework

The Environment, Reactive Rules, and Agents (ERA) framework was first introduced as a multi-agent heuristic to solve the n-queen problems [9] and was later extended as a general approach for solving constraint satisfaction problems [11]. ERA is a Swarm-type distributed algorithm, in which a constraint satisfaction problem is divided into smaller problems and each sub-problem is solved by an independent and self-interested agent.

The motivation for this approach is to use the emergent properties of a system, in which agents act locally with respect to local evaluation functions to solve search problems [11]. The algorithm starts with a random initialisation and attempts to improve the solution over a number of discrete time steps. At each time step each agent, representing a single variable, tries to find an assignment within its variable's domain that minimises the number of constraints violated. Decisions of agents are based on a set of locally reactive behaviours, and the resulting interactions create a dynamic system that self-organises itself gradually towards a solution state.

The three components of ERA are:

1. The Environment: It is a two dimensional lattice where a row is dedicated for each variable in the problem, and a column for each possible value of a variable. Each position in the environment holds two values: the domain value and the number of violations for that position if the agent moves there and other agents remain unmoved. The violation values are continuously updated as agents move. By recording violation values within it, the environment extends its role to provide a form of indirect communication between agents. Eliminating the need for message passing to communicate current assignments of variables (as in [14]).

A CSP is given as follows:

    Variables :   { X, Y, Z }

    Domains : $D_X = \{ 1, 2, 3, 4, 5 \}$, $D_Y = \{ 2, 4, 6 \}$, $D_Z = \{ 1, 3, 5, 7 \}$

    Constraints : { $X \neq Y$, $X > Z$ }

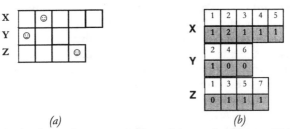

(a)   *(b)*

Figure 1: A schematic representation of the environment within ERA.

Figure 1 is an example of how a CSP can be represented within this framework. For illustration purposes, two rows are used for each agent's local environment to show the two different values held by each position i.e. the domain value and the number of violations (shaded). At initialization, agents are placed in random positions (a). Then, the number of violations is computed for each agent based on the present positions of other agents (b). For example, two violations are recorded in the second position for X because that value would result in violating two constraints; $X \neq Y$ (where $X = 2$ and $Y = 2$) and $X > Z$ (where $X = 2$ and $Z = 7$).

2.   Reactive Rules: at each time step, each agent may choose one of the following behaviours based on a set of behaviour selection probabilities.

    a.   Least move: This is essentially a min-conflicts heuristic and it generally states that the agent is to move to the position with the least number of constraint violations. If more than one such position exists, then it moves to the leftmost one. For example, the least move for the agent Y would take it to the second position (i.e. $Y = 4$).

    b.   Better move: An agent randomly picks a position in its environment and compares its attractiveness with its current position. If that position is better than its current position then the agent moves to that position, otherwise it remains still.

    c.   Random move: With a much smaller selection probability, the agent randomly selects a position that is not its present position and moves there. The random move is introduced for two reasons; first it encourages further exploration of the search space, and secondly, it is a source of internal perturbations that prevents the algorithm from premature convergence on local optima.

3.   Agents: Agents act independently and move locally within their rows. The position of an agent within its environment represents the current value assignment for the variable it represents. The goal for each agent is to find a

position that has the least number of constraint violations for its variable, which ideally should be a zero position.

Two major strengths of ERA have been identified from empirical tests. First, its authors contend that if there is a solution for a problem the algorithm will find it. And if no solution exists the algorithm is capable of finding good approximate solutions. Secondly, it has also been shown that the algorithm is fast and can find good approximate solutions in a few time steps without much computational overhead. For example, in tests carried out on benchmark graph colouring instances, results show that over 80% of variables were assigned consistent values within the first three time steps [11].

For all its strengths, ERA lacks a critical property: consistency (or reliability). This comes out of its reliance on some randomness (i.e. the behaviour selection probabilities and the random move behaviour). This study (and the subsequent extension of ERA) was prompted by this observation from previous work in [2] where ERA was used for the frequency assignment problem. The observed behaviour of the algorithm was a tendency to produce different results for the same problem with different runs. This lack of completeness had also been noted in [9]. Notwithstanding, the randomness is an important aspect of the algorithm especially its role of preventing premature convergence on local optima. To improve the reliability of the algorithm, it is therefore necessary to find alternative deterministic behaviours that preserve this role and at the same time fit into the self-organising structure of the approach.

3. Adding Feedback and Reinforcement to ERA with FeReRA

The min-conflicts heuristic is widely used in distributed constraint satisfaction and it always presents a potential for premature convergence on local optima. A number of strategies have been adopted in the literature to deal with this convergence. One approach has been to simply to try avoid settling on local optimum in the first place. An example of this is the random activation mechanism in [8] in which neighbouring agents were prevented from changing values simultaneously. However, while it did try preventing early convergence, there was still the random likelihood of getting stuck at local optima and there were no apparent mechanisms in algorithm to push it out. In other approaches, such as [7, 16], the adopted strategy have typically gone the down the route of detecting quasi-local optima and applying breakout rules in response, to push the process to another region of the search space. Similar strategies have been suggested with local search algorithms [14, 15], where the objective function is augmented with penalties which change the shape of the fitness landscape as local optimums are detected. Therefore, pushing the search process to another region of the search space.

The work presented here is quite similar to the breakout strategy adopted in [7]. In that work, a counter is incremented while an agent is stuck at a quasi-local optimum and when that counter hits pre-defined threshold the agent is forced to make a non-improving move [7]. However, in this work the emphasis moves from responding to quasi-local optima to real local optima. Emphasis is on self-regulation, whereby the thresholds for which agents are forced to make non-improving moves are defined by the individual structure of the problem. The rest of this section explains our approach where random decisions (including the better move behaviour) have been removed from ERA and are replaced with an explicit feedback mechanism which determines how agents respond to the system's convergence at local optima by taking into consideration the effect of agent behaviours on the global state of the system.

The feedback mechanism applied here by FeReRA is inspired by the pheromone system in the Ant Colony Optimisation algorithm and related work [3]. However, in this instance a 'levy' is introduced into the algorithm as the basis for the reinforcement mechanism and also as a means of providing a form of short-term memory for the system. We must emphasise here that the use of reinforcement in this context is somewhat restrictive; referring to only the "reward" and "punishment" aspect of it and it is not used in the same vein as in machine learning.

The levy system is devised to take into account the particular structure of each problem and is primarily designed to reward or punish agents by increasing or decreasing its levels based on the cumulative effects of particular decisions on the global state of the system. Reinforcement in this context generally serves as individual triggers for agents to make non-improving moves when the individual levies reach a given threshold. The underlying assumption is that the propagation of the fluctuations caused by these non-improving moves will serve as the means by which the system can escape local optimums.

Feedback is established as a combination of positive and negative reinforcement, and it is only applied when agents remain in fixed positions over a few time steps. At initialisation, the lower bounds for the levies are established for each agent. This lower bound and the amount of reinforcement received is determined by a function $f(n, d)$, which in this instance is directly related to the ratio of the number of constraints attached to an agent vis-à-vis the number of constraint for its most constrained neighbour. This also helps to establish a 'pecking order' for the agents, whereby the least constrained agents will tend to have higher levies imposed on them and are therefore likely to move more often.

At each time step, each agent uses the least move behaviour to find the best position in its environment. After all agents have moved, levies are simultaneously updated for all agents whose assignments were unchanged in that time step, as follows:

- Increase the levy if the global solution is either unchanged or has worsened, and the penalties associated with the agent's position have either decreased or stayed unchanged. In this instance, the agent is 'punished' for its improvement at the expense of the system.

- When the global solution improves, agents get a 'refund' by way of a reduction in accumulated levies only if they have not moved in that time step. The rationale for this is that the decision not to move in that time step contributes to an overall improvement in the solution and therefore the agents involved must be rewarded for the decision.

Levies accumulate as agents remain unmoved, increasing at different rates depending on the number of constraints attached to each agent. When an agent's total levy is equal to or greater than a predefined maximum, it is forced to move by applying a break out rule which can be anything from temporal constraint maximisation to picking a slightly worse position. Levies are reset to the initial levels anytime an agent moves to a new position, either as a result of finding a better position or as a result of a forced move. What results is a system whereby the least constrained agents will strive to find consistent assignments with the values picked by more constrained agents. "Backtracking" cascades upwards through the agent hierarchy as levies of more constrained agents hit the upper bounds. In addition, the resulting sub-optimal moves help to periodically push the system away from local optimums to other regions of the search space and hence promote further exploration of the search space.

Given that the feedback mechanism has to mirror the structure of the problem, it gives room for some flexibility in the definition of the lower bounds and the rates of change in levies. With small problems or a direct ratio of the number of constraints between constrained neighbours may be sufficient. However for larger problems, especially those with different magnitudes of constraints, the chosen function has to adequately represent a hierarchy of variables and return values between 0 and 1. Out of empirical tests, it was observed that for the levy-mediated feedback to work a discontinuous step function is required. Although this may result in a situation where groups of agents may change their values in the same time step, it has the advantage of cutting down the number of moves and therefore allows some exploration of the immediate neighbourhood of a solution. The full pseudo-code listing of the FeReRA model can be found in Listing 1.

4. Experimental Results

4.1 The Experimental Set-up

Ten benchmark instances of graph colouring problems from the Center for Discrete Mathematics and Theoretical Computer Science[1] (DIMACS) were used for a comparative evaluation of the performance of FeReRA and the original ERA framework. Graph colouring was chosen as it still remains an important benchmark for the evaluation of the performance of search and constraint satisfaction techniques, and it also provides a basis for comparison with other established techniques. In the graph colouring problem, a graph of n connected nodes is to be coloured using k colours such that no two connected (or neighbouring) nodes are assigned the same colour. This problem is still known to be intractable as there are still no efficient

---

[1] Graph colouring instances from this data set may be found at
http://mat.gsia.cmu.edu/COLOR/instances.html

algorithms for solving it. Two sets of experiments were run for comparison and the results are presented in the following sections. All tests were run in a Java environment on a 1.4GHz machine with 512MB of RAM.

```
1    Sort All Agents by number of attached constraints in descending order

2    For all agentsᵢ
3        Compute initial levy and rate of change for each agent
4        agentsᵢ.position = 1 // starting the algorithm from a
                                    'worst possible scenario'
5    End for

6    repeat
7        For all agentsᵢ
8            sense environmentᵢ
9            select best position i.e. position with least number of violations

10           If best position is same as position at timeₜ₋₁ then
11               If agentᵢ.levy >= upper_bound then
12                   apply breakout rule
13                   agentᵢ.levy = agentᵢ.initial_levy
14               End if
15           End if
16       End for

17       compute current solution solₜ

18       If solₜ is solution then end program and return solution

19       For all agentsᵢ
20           If agentᵢ.positionₜ = agentᵢ.position ₜ₋₁ then
21               If solₜ ≥ solₜ₋₁ then
22                   If agentᵢ.penaltyₜ ≤ agentᵢ.penalty ₜ₋₁ then
                                    increase agentᵢ.levy
23               Else
24                   reduce agentᵢ.levy
25                   If agentᵢ.levy < agentᵢ.initial_ levy then
26                       agentᵢ.levy = agentᵢ.initial_ levy
27                   End if
28               End if
29       End for
30   until ₜ = maximum time steps
```

Listing 1: Pseudo-code listing of FeReRA

4.2 The Step Function

A step function was used by FeReRA to determine the initial levies and the rate of change for reinforcement. These values were computed as follows:

1. For each variable, compute the ratio of its constraints vis-à-vis the number of constraints for its most constrained neighbour:

    $$r(x) = \frac{\text{number of constraints}^2 \text{ for most constrained neighbour of variable } x}{\text{number of constraints for variable } x}$$

2. Normalise $r(x)$ for all variables to ensure that all values fall between 0 and 1:

    $$r'(x) = \frac{r(x) - \mathbf{min}(r(x))}{\mathbf{max}(r(x)) - \mathbf{min}(r(x))}$$

3. Compute the "step" value $r''(x)$ by rounding $r'(x)$ down to one decimal digit.

4. The rate of change for each agent is defined as:

    $$rate\_of\_change(x) = base\_levy \times [\, r''(x) + 0.7 \,]$$

    where $base\_levy = 0.1$

The value of $r''(x)$ ranges from 0 to 1 and the above definition sets a minimum rate of change, which is particularly important for the most constrained agents[3]. The same definition is used to compute the lower bound for each agent. This lower bound is used as the initial levy at the start of the algorithm and is also used to reset levies when agents move to new positions. The value for *base_levy* came out as a result of empirical testing. In theory, it means that under deteriorating conditions an agent with $rate\_of\_change(x) = 1$ is allowed to remain at a particular position for a maximum of nine time steps (i.e. where the threshold is 1). On the other hand, a high *base_levy* value has the tendency to cause the algorithm to settle into a continuous oscillation between two states after a few time steps. Further investigations are still being carried out to explain the reasons behind this and to find optimal values for both *base_levy* and the threshold that trigger the non-improving moves.

In figures 2 and 3 are plots of the rate of change for two problem instances from our test set. These illustrate the structure dependent nature of the levy system. In the plot for the Anna instance (figure 2), the rate of change increases steadily as the node degree decreases. Indicating that a large number of small degree nodes are directly connected to a small number of high degree nodes. In contrast, the plot for the miles500 instance (figure 3) suggests a highly connected graph with a high number of

---

[2] For graph colouring problems, the number of constraints for each node is taken as the number of nodes directly connected to it.

[3] If $r''(x) = 0$ (this is the case for the agents with the largest number of constraints attached to it), agents will not receive any reinforcement and therefore can not be forced to move out of positions that are holding the system at a local optimum.

connections between high degree nodes. It also suggests that the distribution of edges is not particularly skewed to a restricted number of nodes.

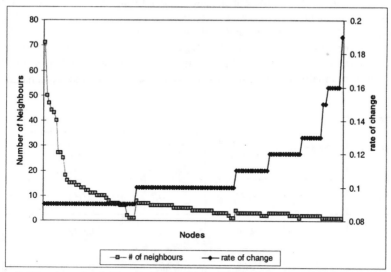

Figure 2: Number of neighbours (left axis) and rate of change (right axis) for the Anna instance.

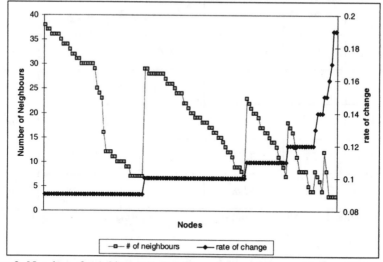

Figure 3: Number of neighbours (left axis) and rate of change (right axis) for the miles500 instance.

4.3 Comparative Results

The first set of experiments were run in order to determine if each algorithm could find a solution for each problem instance and how much time it took to find the solution. On account of its inbuilt randomness, ten runs were made on each problem instance with ERA and the best and worst results are presented in Table 1, along with results for our modified algorithm. FeReRA was expected to be slightly slower than ERA because at each time step all agents use only the least move behaviour which is more computationally intensive than the better move or random move behaviours.

Instance	Nodes	Number of Edges	Time Taken (in seconds)		
			ERA (best time)	ERA (worst time)	FeReRA
Anna	138	493	0.01	0.032	0.015
David	87	406	0.01	0.047	0.01
Huck	74	301	0.01	0.016	0.016
Inithx.I.1	864	18707	0.344	33.437	0.016
Jean	80	254	0.01	0.016	0.01
Miles250	128	387	0.01	0.016	0.015
Miles500	128	1170	0.01	1.922	0.01
Miles750	128	2113	0.953	5.235	0.453
Miles1000	128	3216	2.187	7.438	7.094
Miles1500	128	5198	0.265	1.828	0.015

Table 1: Time taken to find solutions using the optimal number of colours for each instance.

Both algorithms were able to find solutions to all the instances presented[4]. Results show that at its best performance, ERA was able to find solutions quicker in four instances, while FeReRA performed better in three instances and performance was the same with the other problem instances. Compared to ERA's worst performance,

---

[4] In their earlier paper [11], Liu et al had shown that the ERA could find solutions for the all the instances in Table 1

FeReRA outperformed the former in nine out of the ten cases. Overall, FeReRA gave results which were almost as good as the best performance of ERA and substantially better than its worst performance.

Having established that both algorithms were able to find solutions for all instances, further experiments were carried out to find out how well they would perform on a set of over constrained graph colouring instances. The same instances from Table 1 were used for this set of experiments but this time with fewer colours. In these tests, both algorithms were not expected to find solutions for the over constrained instances. Therefore, each algorithm was run for a maximum of 5000 time steps and they were both evaluated on their ability to minimise the number of violated constraints. As with the first set of tests, each over constrained problem instance was run ten times with ERA. Results are shown in Table 2.

Instance	Optimal Colouring	Number of Colours Used	Number of Violations		
			ERA (best)	ERA (worst)	FeReRA
Anna	11	7	4	5	4
Inithx.I.1	54	49	5	6	5
		38	16	18	16
		32	33	36	32
Miles250	8	6	4	5	4
		5	10	12	10
Miles500	20	18	2	3	2
		16	4	5	4
		14	7	9	7
		12	11	15	12
Miles750	31	28	3	4	3
		25	6	8	6
		22	11	13	11
		19	16	20	17
Miles1000	42	38	4	5	4
		34	8	10	8
		29	16	19	16
		25	23	28	24
Miles1500	73	44	29	30	29

Table 2: A comparative evaluation of performance on the same data set from Table 1, using 10%, 20%, 30%, and 40% fewer colours respectively. This table highlights only results where there are performance differences between the ERA best, ERA worst, and FeReRA.

At first glance at the results in table 2, what immediately stands out is the wide performance gap between the best and worst outcomes with ERA. In the worst case, the penalties incurred on the worst result are 50% higher than those incurred with the best result (see Miles500 with 18 colours). Taking the cases where the best and worst outcomes were equal aside, on average the penalties incurred on the worst solutions were 27% higher than those on the best. A similar gap was also observed with results in table 4.1. Although, at its best performance, ERA found slightly better partial solutions than FeReRA in three instances, the latter found substantially better partial solutions than ERA's worst solutions for those same instances. In addition, FeReRA found a better partial solution than ERA's best in one instance, and better solutions than ERA's worst in nineteen instances. Our approach shows higher consistency with better or equal average performance across all instances.

Furthermore, we have to point out here that contrary to Sect. 3 where the need to build the reinforcement mechanism around the individual structure of the problem was mentioned; "default" values were used for all problem instances in these tests. As a result, it is highly probable that this would have had adverse effects on the performance of the FeReRA on some problems. Work is still going on to establish how to determine the optimal set of parameters for each individual problem.

One issue raised in the course of our initial inquiry with ERA was on the ability of the algorithm to minimise the number of colours used in the search for a solution. It was observed from that work that the behaviour of ERA is quite similar to a greedy heuristic, whereby it tries to find a maximum assignment for each colour before using subsequent colours. This is as a result of the least move behaviour which forces an agent to pick its leftmost minimum, if more than one minimum position exists in the environment. This behaviour is still evident with FeReRA. The example in figure 4 shows that 60% of the nodes were assigned the first two colours. The implications of this are particularly important in some application domains such as frequency planning.

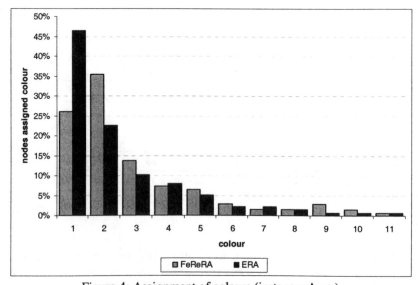

Figure 4: Assignment of colours (instance: Anna)

5. Conclusions

In this paper, we have presented FeReRA, a deterministic and predictable multi-agent meta-heuristic for solving constraint satisfaction problems. FeReRA is an extension to ERA, and introduces a feedback and reinforcement mechanism to replace random decisions as a strategy for escaping local optimums. FeReRA also extends the concept of reactive agents in ERA by allowing the agents take into account the impact of some decisions on the global state of the system when making decisions, rather than relying solely on information from their local environments. This results in a self-regulatory system that decides when these typically self-interested agents have to make non-improving moves necessary to push it out of local optimums.

Preliminary results from our work with graph colouring problems are very encouraging, showing substantial improvement in terms of results and consistency over ERA. We are currently evaluating the performance of FeReRA with different graph structures (sparse, dense and critical) and will consider further improvements to FeReRA for future work; these include possible advances to the present feedback and reinforcement scheme, and a study of the scope of application of FeReRA on various constraint satisfaction and optimisation problems.

6. References

1. Agassounon W., Martinoli A. and Goodman R., A scalable distributed algorithm for allocating workers in embedded systems. *In: Proceedings of the 2001 IEEE Systems, Man and Cybernetics Conference.* October 2001, pp. 3367-3373.

2. Basharu, M.B., *Automatic frequency planning for mixed voice and GPRS systems* MSc Dissertation, University of Sussex, 2002.

3. Bonabeau E., Dorigo M., and Theraulaz G., Inspiration for optimization from social insect behaviour *Nature*, 407, pp. 39-42, July 2000.

4. Bonabeau E., Henaux F., Guérin S., Snyers D., Kuntz P., Routing in telecommunications networks with "smart" ant-like agents. *In: Proceedings of IATA'98, Second International Workshop on Intelligent Agents for Telecommunications Applications.* Lecture Notes in AI vol. 1437, Springer Verlag, 1998.

5. Cicirello V. A. and Smith S. F., Improved routing wasps for distributed factory control. *In: IJCALI-01 Workshop on Artificial Intelligence and Manufacturing: New AI Paradigms for Manufacturing*, August 2001

6. Fabiunke M., A swarm intelligence approach to constraint satisfaction. *In: Proceedings of the Sixth Conference on Integrated Design and Process Technology*, June 2002.

7. Faiunke M. and Kock G., A connectionist method to solve job shop problems. *Cybernetics and Systems: An International Journal*, 31 (5), pp. 491-506, 2000.

8. Fitzpatrick S. and Meertens L., An experimental assessment of a stochastic anytime, decentralized, soft colourer for sparse graphs. *In: Proceedings of the Symposium on Stochastic Algorithms, Foundations and Applications*, Springer, Berlin, pp. 49-64, 2000.

9. Han J., Liu J. and Qingsheng C., From ALIFE agents to a kingdom of n-queens *In:* J. Liu and N. Zhong eds., *Intelligent Agent Technology: Systems, Methodologies, and Tools*, pp. 110-120, The World Scientific Publishing Co. Pte, Ltd., 1999.

10. Lawlor M. and White T., A self organizing social insect model for dynamic frequency allocation in cellular telephone networks. *In: Proceedings of the Second International Joint Conference on Autonomous Agents and Multi-agent Systems (AAMAS 2003)*, to appear.

11. Liu J., Han J. and Tang Y.Y., Multi-agent oriented constraint satisfaction *Artificial Intelligence* 136 (1) pp. 101 – 144, 2002.

12. Swarm Development Group, Swarm simulation system, www.swarm.org

13. Tateson R., Self-organising pattern formation: fruit flies and cell phones. *In: Autonomous Agents and Multi-Agent Systems*, Vol. 3, No. 2, pp. 198-212, 2000.

14. Voudouris, C, Guided local search for combinatorial optimisation problems, PhD Thesis, Department of Computer Science, University of Essex, Colchester, UK, July, 1997

15. Wu, Z. and Wah, B. W. Trap escaping strategies in discrete lagrangian methods for solving hard satisfiability and maximum satisfiability problems. In *AAAI/IAAI*, pp. 673 – 678, 1999.

16. Yokoo M. and Hirayama K., Algorithms for Distributed Constraint Satisfaction. In *Proceedings of the 2nd International Conference on Multi agent systems*, pp. 401 – 408, 1996.

Constraint Acquisition as Semi-Automatic Modeling *

Remi Coletta[1], Christian Bessiere[1], Barry O'Sullivan[2],
Eugene C. Freuder[2], Sarah O'Connell[2], Joel Quinqueton[1]

[1] LIRMM-CNRS (UMR 5506), 161 rue Ada 34392 Montpellier Cedex 5, France
{coletta,bessiere,jq}@lirmm.fr
[2] Cork Constraint Computation Centre, University College Cork, Ireland
{b.osullivan,e.freuder,s.oconnell}@4c.ucc.ie

Abstract

Constraint programming is a technology which is now widely used to solve combinatorial problems in industrial applications. However, using it requires considerable knowledge and expertise in the field of constraint reasoning. This paper introduces a framework for automatically learning constraint networks from sets of instances that are either acceptable solutions or non-desirable assignments of the problem we would like to express. Such an approach has the potential to be of assistance to a novice who is trying to articulate her constraints. By restricting the language of constraints used to build the network, this could also assist an expert to develop an efficient model of a given problem. This paper provides a theoretical framework for a research agenda in the area of interactive constraint acquisition, automated modelling and automated constraint programming.

1   Introduction

Over the last 30 years, considerable progress has been made in the field of Constraint Programming (CP), providing a powerful paradigm for solving complex problems. Applications in many areas such as resource allocation, scheduling, planning and design have been reported in the literature [10]. However, the use of CP still remains limited to specialists in the field. Modelling a problem in the constraint formalism requires significant expertise in constraint programming. This precludes novices from being able to use CP on complex problems without the help of an expert. This has a negative effect on the uptake of constraint technology in the real-world by non-experts [5].

In addition, in many practical applications humans find it difficult to articulate their constraints. While the human user can recognize examples of where their constraints

---

*The collaboration between LIRMM and the Cork Constraint Computation Centre is supported by a Ulysses Travel Grant from Enterprise Ireland, the Royal Irish Academy and CNRS (Grant Number FR/2003/022). This work has also received support from Science Foundation Ireland under Grant 00/PI.1/C075.

should be satisfied or violated, they cannot articulate the constraints themselves. However, by presenting examples of what is acceptable, the human user can be assisted in developing a model of the set of constraints she is trying to articulate. This can be regarded as an instance of constraint acquisition. One of the goals of our work is to assist the, possibly novice, human user by providing semi-automatic methods for acquiring the user's constraints.

Furthermore, even if the user has sufficient experience in CP to encode her problem, a poor model can negate the utility of a good solver based on state-of-the-art filtering techniques. For example, in order to provide support for modelling, some solvers provide facilities for defining constraints extensionally (i.e., by enumerating the set of allowed tuples). Such facilities considerably extend the expressiveness and ease-of-use of the constraints language, thus facilitating the definition of complex relationships between variables. However, a disadvantage of modelling constraints extensionally is that the constraints lose any useful semantics they may have which can have a negative impact on the inference and propagation capabilities of a solver. As a result, the resolution performance of the solver can be significantly deteriorated in the parts of the problem where such constraints are used. Therefore, another goal of our work is to facilitate the expert user who wishes to reformulate her problem (or a part of it that is suspected of slowing down the resolution). Given sets of accepted/forbidden instantiations of the (sub)problem (that can be generated automatically from the initial formulation), the expert will be able, for instance, to test whether an optimised constraint library associated with her solver is able to model the (sub)problem in a way which lends itself to being efficiently solved.

However, constraint acquisition is not only important in an interactive situation involving a human user. Often we may wish to acquire a constraint model from a large set of data. For example, given a large database of tuples defining buyer behaviour in a variety of markets, for a variety of buyer profiles, for a variety of products, we may wish to acquire a constraint network which describes the data in this database. While the nature of the interaction with the source of training data is different, the constraint acquisition problem is fundamentally the same.

The remainder of this paper is organised as follows. Section 2 presents an overview of the related work in this area, Section 3 provides some preliminary definitions on constraint networks. Section 4 briefly presents the machine learning techniques that can be used for our problem. In Section 5, we formulate our problem as a learning problem. Section 6 presents the technique in detail, and proves some properties of the approach that are guaranteed. In Section 7, some of the issues that the approach raises are presented, and their possible effects on the learning process are illustrated by some preliminary experiments. Some concluding remarks are made in Section 8.

2 Related Work

Recently, researchers have become more interested in techniques for solving problems where users have difficulties articulating constraints. In [9], the goal of Rossi and Sperduti is not exactly to help the user learning a constraint network, but to help her learning the valuations of the tuples in a semi-ring constraint network where the constraint structures are already given. Freuder and Wallace have considered suggestion strategies for applications where a user cannot articulate all constraints in advance, but can articulate additional constraints when confronted with something which is unacceptable [3]. Freuder and O'Sullivan have focused on generating constraints which model tradeoffs between variables in problems which have become over-constrained during a interactive configuration session [2]. Version spaces have been reported by O'Connell *et al* for acquiring single constraints, with a focus on acquisition from humans where dialog length is a critical factor [8]. The focus of their work was interactive acquisition of constraints from users of differing abilities.

3   Preliminaries

Definition 1 (Constraint Network) *A constraint network is defined as a triplet* $(\mathcal{X}, \mathcal{D}, \mathcal{C})$ *where:*

- $\mathcal{X} = \{X_1, \ldots, X_n\}$ *is a set of variables.*

- $\mathcal{D} = \{D_{X_1}, \ldots, D_{X_n}\}$ *is the set of their domains: each variable* X_i *takes its values in the domain* D_{X_i}.

- $\mathcal{C} = (C_1, \ldots, C_m)$ *is a sequence of constraints on* $\mathcal{X}$ *and* $\mathcal{D}$, *where a constraint* C_i *is defined by the sequence* $var(C_i)$ *of variables it involves, and the relation* $rel(C_i)$ *specifying the allowed tuples on* $var(C_i)$.

We regard the constraints as a sequence to simplify the forthcoming notations.

Definition 2 (Instance) *Let* $Y = \{Y_1, \cdots, Y_k\}$ *be a subset of* $\mathcal{X}$. *An instance* e_Y *on* Y *is a tuple* $(v_1, \ldots, v_k) \in D_{Y_1} \times \cdots \times D_{Y_k}$. *This instance is partial if* $Y \neq \mathcal{X}$, *complete otherwise (noted e). An instance* e_Y *on* Y *violates the constraint* C_i *iff* $var(C_i) \subseteq Y$ *and* $e_Y[var(C_i)] \notin rel(C_i)$.

Definition 3 (Solution) *A complete instance on the set* $\mathcal{X}$ *of variables is a* solution *of the constraint network* $N = (\mathcal{X}, \mathcal{D}, \mathcal{C})$ *iff it does not violate any constraint. Otherwise it is a* non solution. $Sol(N)$ *denotes the set of solutions of* N.

4   The Fundamental Problem

As a starting point, we assume that the user knows the set of variables of her problem and their domains of possible values. She is also assumed to be able to classify an instance as positive (a solution) or negative (non-solution). Therefore, the available data are the set $\mathcal{X}$ of the variables of the problem, their domains $\mathcal{D}$, a subset E^+ of the solutions of the problem, and a set E^- of non-solutions.

In addition to the "assisting the expert" perspective, the aim is to code the problem efficiently, using only efficient constraint relations between these variables; i.e. a library of constraints with efficient propagation features is assumed to be given. Indications can also be given revealing the possible location of the constraints, by defining variables between which constraints must be found (learned), or by restricting ourselves to binary constraints only. These semantic and structural limitations define the inductive bias:

Definition 4 (Bias) *Given a set $\mathcal{X}$ of variables and the set $\mathcal{D}$ of their domains, a bias $\mathcal{B}$ on $(\mathcal{X}, \mathcal{D})$ is a sequence $(B_1, \ldots, B_m)$ of local biases, where a local bias B_i is defined by a sequence $var(B_i) \subseteq \mathcal{X}$ of variables, and a set $L(B_i)$ of possible relations on $var(B_i)$.*

The set $L(B_i)$ of relations allowed on a set of variables $var(B_i)$ can be any library of constraints of arity $|var(B_i)|$.

Definition 5 (Membership of a Bias) *Given a set $\mathcal{X}$ of variables and the set $\mathcal{D}$ of their domains, a sequence of constraints $C = (C_1, \ldots, C_m)$ belongs to the bias $\mathcal{B} = (B_1, \ldots, B_m)$ on $(\mathcal{X}, \mathcal{D})$ if $\forall C_i \in C, var(C_i) = var(B_i)$ and $rel(C_i) \in L(B_i)$. We note $C \in \mathcal{B}$.*

The problem consists in looking for a sequence of constraints C belonging to a given bias $\mathcal{B}$, and whose solution set is a superset of E^+ containing no element of E^-.

Definition 6 (Constraint Acquisition Problem) *Given a set of variables $\mathcal{X}$, their domains $\mathcal{D}$, two sets E^+ and E^- of instances on $\mathcal{X}$, and a bias $\mathcal{B}$ on $(\mathcal{X}, \mathcal{D})$, the constraint acquisition problem consists in finding a sequence of constraints C such that:*

$C \in \mathcal{B}$,

$\forall e^- \in E^-$, e^- *is a non solution of* $(\mathcal{X}, \mathcal{D}, C)$*, and,*

$\forall e^+ \in E^+$, e^+ *is a solution of* $(\mathcal{X}, \mathcal{D}, C)$*.*

If the sets E^+ and E^-, called the *training data*, are provided by an interaction with the user, then the acquisition problem can be regarded as the modelling phase for the user's problem. Otherwise, it can be regarded as an assistance to the expert for an automatic reformulation of her problem.

We can point out that if $E^+ \cup E^- = D_{X_1} \times \cdots \times D_{X_n}$, and $\mathcal{B}$ is a bias on $(\mathcal{X}, \mathcal{D})$ containing $n(n-1)/2$ local biases such that for each pair of variables (X_i, X_j), $\exists B_i \in \mathcal{B}$ with $var(B_i) = (X_i, X_j)$, and $L(B_i) = \mathcal{P}(D_{X_i} \times D_{X_j})$,[1] then the constraint acquisition problem answers the representability problem of a relation $\rho = E^+$ with a binary constraint network [7].

5 Constraint Acquisition as Concept Learning

Concept induction is a well known paradigm in Machine Learning. The underlying problem can be described the following way: given a set H of hypotheses, two training data sets (E^+ of positive and E^- of negative instances), find an hypothesis h consistent with this training data, i.e., which rejects all the negative instances and accepts all the positive instances. The concept providing the training data is called the target concept.

In our context, this concept is the unknown network that we are looking for that consistently captures all the information given by the user in the training set. So, in our vocabulary:

- An hypothesis h is a sequence of constraints,

---

[1] E being a set, $\mathcal{P}(E)$ is the set of subsets of E.

- H is the set of possible sequences of constraints belonging to $\mathcal{B}$,

- The target concept is the sequence of constraints C we are looking for,

- A positive instance is a solution of $(\mathcal{X}, \mathcal{D}, C)$, a negative one is a non-solution of $(\mathcal{X}, \mathcal{D}, C)$.

There are many techniques from the field of Machine Learning, from decision trees to neural networks or genetic algorithms. We propose here a method based on version spaces [6], which has several nice properties amongst which the most interesting from our perspective are: they provide two approximations of the target concept, an upper bound and a lower bound; their computation is incremental with respect to the training data; and the result does not depend on the order of the instances in the training set (commutativity). This last property is essential in an interactive acquisition process.

We briefly present version spaces, which rely on the partial-order based on inclusion in the set H of hypotheses.

Definition 7 (Generalisation relation $\leq_G$) *Given $(\mathcal{X}, \mathcal{D})$ a set of variables and their domains, an hypothesis h_1 is less general than or equal to an hypothesis h_2 (noted $h_1 \leq_G h_2$) iff the set of solutions of $(\mathcal{X}, \mathcal{D}, h_1)$ is a subset of this of $(\mathcal{X}, \mathcal{D}, h_2)$.*

A version space does not only provide one consistent hypothesis, but the whole subset of H consistent with the training data:

Definition 8 (Version Space) *Given $(\mathcal{X}, \mathcal{D})$ a set of variables and their domains, E^+ and E^- two training data sets , and H a set of hypotheses, the* version space *is the set:*

$$V = \{h \in H/E^+ \subseteq Sol(\mathcal{X}, \mathcal{D}, h), E^- \cap Sol(\mathcal{X}, \mathcal{D}, h) = \emptyset\}$$

Because of its nice property of incrementality with respect to the training data, a version space is learned by incrementally processing the training instances of E^+ and E^-. In addition, due to the $\leq_G$ partial order, a version space V is completely characterised by two boundaries: the specific boundary S of maximally specific (minimal) elements of V (according to $\leq_G$), and the general boundary G of maximally general (maximal) elements.

Property 1 *Given a version space V, and its boundaries S and G, $\forall h \in V, \exists s \in S$ and $\exists g \in G/s \leq_G h \leq_G g$.*

In the general case, V is exponential in the size of the data. So, thanks to Property 1, the constraint acquisition problem is restricted to computing the bounds S and G of the version space consistent with (E^+, E^-).

Given a set of hypotheses H on $(\mathcal{X}, \mathcal{D})$, and the training data (E^+, E^-), if there does not exist any $h \in H$ consistent with (E^+, E^-), then the version space acquisition will finish in a state where there exists $s \in S$ and $g \in G$ such that $s \neq g$ and $g \leq_G s$. This is called the *collapsing* state of the version space.

6 Learning the Constraint Version Space

In this section, we describe the process of learning the version space corresponding to the constraint acquisition problem on $(\mathcal{X}, \mathcal{D})$ with the two training sets (E^+, E^-) of solutions and non-solutions, and bias $\mathcal{B}$ on $(\mathcal{X}, \mathcal{D})$.

Let us first define the concepts that will be used at the single constraint level. We can project the generalisation relation $\leq_G$ at the constraint level. To be completely consistent with version space theory, we define $L^H(B_i) = L(B_i) \cup \{\perp, \top\}$, where $\perp$ is the empty relation $\perp$, and $\top$ the universal relation. Note that without loss of generality, the universal relation can be stated as belonging to any library of constraints. Thus, $\leq_g$ is a partial order on $L^H(B_i)$ such that $\forall r_1, r_2 \in L^H(B_i), r_1 \leq_g r_2 \Leftrightarrow r_1 \subseteq r_2$.

Given $L_1 \subseteq L^H(B_i)$ and $L_2 \subseteq L^H(B_i)$, we note that $L_1 \leq_g L_2$ iff $\forall r_1 \in L_1, \forall r_2 \in L_2, r_1 \leq_g r_2$.

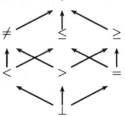

Figure 1: $L^H(B_i)$

Example 1 Let $L(B_i) = \{<, \leq, =, \geq, >, \neq\}$ be a given local bias. Fig. 1 shows the set $(L^H(B_i), \leq_g)$, which in this case is a lattice.

Restricting ourselves to each constraint individually, we introduce a local version space for each local bias. Because $\leq_g$ is, like $\leq_G$, a partial order, each local version space inherits Property 1. Thus, each local version space is completely characterized by its own local specific and general boundaries.

Definition 9 (Local boundaries) $L(S_i)$ (resp. $L(G_i)$) is the set of relations of $L^H(B_i)$ which appear in an element of S (resp. G):

$$L(S_i) = \{r \in L^H(B_i)/\exists s \in S : (var(Bi), r) \in s\}$$
$$L(G_i) = \{r \in L^H(B_i)/\exists g \in G : (var(Bi), r) \in g\}$$

S_i and G_i are the corresponding sets of constraints:

$$S_i = \{(var(B_i), r)\}, \text{ where } r \in L(S_i); \qquad G_i = \{(var(B_i), r)\}, \text{ where } r \in L(G_i)$$

We are now ready to describe the CONACQ algorithm (Algorithm 1), which takes as input two training sets E^+, E^-, and returns the corresponding version space V on the bias $\mathcal{B}$. We present step by step the different scenarios that can occur when a training instance is processed.

6.1 Instances from E^+

A positive instance e^+ must be a solution of all the networks $(\mathcal{X}, \mathcal{D}, h)$ for which $h \in V$. So,

$$\forall h \in V, \forall C_i \in h, e^+[var(C_i)] \in rel(C_i)$$

Projecting onto the local version spaces of each local bias B_i, we obtain the following property:

Property 2 (Projection property of S_i's) *Each local specific boundary S_i must accept all the positives instances. $L(S_i)$ is thus the set of maximally specific relations (minimal w.r.t. $\leq_g$) of $L(B_i)$ that accept all E^+:*

$$L(S_i) = min_{\leq_g}\{r \in L^H(B_i)/\forall e^+ \in E^+, e^+[var(B_i)] \in r\}$$

Corollary 1 *The specific boundary S is the Cartesian product of the local specific boundaries S_i's, i.e., the set of hypotheses, where each constraint takes its relation from $L(Si)$:*

$$S = \underset{i \in 1..m}{\times} S_i$$

From Property 2, when a positive instance e^+ is presented, each local bias B_i can be processed individually (line 2 of Algorithm CONACQ). If the specific boundary of a constraint already accepts this positive instance, it is skipped (line 3), else the boundary goes up to the most specific relations of the local version space (i.e., the relations of $L^H(B_i)$ between $L(S_i)$ and $L(G_i)$) that accept e^+ (line 4). If no such relation exists, this means that no hypothesis can accept this positive instance. Then, the algorithm terminates since a collapsing state has been encountered (line 5).

6.2 Instances from E^-

A negative instance e^- must be a non solution for all the networks $(\mathcal{X}, \mathcal{D}, h)$ where $h \in V$. So,

$$\forall h \in V, \exists C_i \in h/e^-[var(C_i)] \notin rel(C_i)$$

Since at least one violated constraint is sufficient for an instance to be regarded as negative, instead of all satisfied constraints necessary in the case of a positive instance, G does not have the projection property exhibited by S:[2]

$$L(G_i) \neq max_{\leq_g}\{r \in L^H(B_i)/\forall e^- \in E^-, e^-[var(B_i)] \notin r\}$$

We can only say that $\forall e^- \in E^-, \exists i/\forall r \in L(G_i), e^-[var(B_i)] \notin r$. However, the cause of the rejection (which constraint(s) has been violated) may not be obvious. Furthermore, storing only the local general boundaries G_i's is not sufficient to express this uncertainty.

---

[2]If this was not the case the constraint defined on $rel(B_i)$ would be sufficient to reject all negative instance of E^-.

The traditional approach to version space learning involves storing the set of all possible global boundaries G. However, this can require exponential space and time [4]. In order to ensure our algorithm remains polynomial, we do not store this set, but encode each negative instance e^- as a clause, Cl. Each constraint that could possibly be involved in the rejection of a negative example e^- will be encoded as a meta-variable in the clause Cl. Semantically, the clause Cl represents the disjunction of the possible explanations for the rejection of this negative instance. In other words, it encodes a disjunction of the constraints that could have been responsible for the inconsistency in the instance.

When a negative instance e^- is presented, a new clause, initially empty, is built by processing each local bias B_i one-by-one (lines 12-14). Those biases whose specific boundary, $L(S_i)$, already accepts the negative instance, e^-, are skipped (line 15). The reason being that S_i is the maximally specific boundary of the local version space for B_i and, by definition, we know that at each step of the learning process the constraint defined on $rel(B_i)$ cannot be involved in the rejection of e^-, since this has already been deemed acceptable by at least one positive example.

For all the other constraints, a subset of which is responsible for the rejection e^-, we compute A_i, the subset of maximally specific relations (w.r.t. $\leq_g$) between $L(S_i)$ and $L(G_i)$ which accept $e^-[var(B_i)]$, i.e. the least upper bound that B_i must not take if it is proven to be a contributor to the rejection of e^- (line 16). Depending on this set of relations we have two alternative courses of action to consider. Firstly, if the set A_i is empty it means that all possible relations for the constraint defined on $rel(B_i)$ already reject e^-. Therefore, every hypothesis in the version space is consistent with e^- so there is nothing to do for e^-; we are then ready to process the next instance (line 17). Secondly, if A_i is not empty, we add the meta-variable $(L(G_i) <_g A_i)$ to the clause Cl (line 18). The semantic of this meta-variable is *"if B_i is involved in the rejection of e^-, then G_i must be made more specific than A_i"*.

To reject e^-, a sequence of constraints h must satisfy at least one meta-variable in the clause Cl encoding e^-. We will denote this as $h \models Cl$. The set of clauses, characterizing all the set E^-, is denoted as $\mathcal{K}$. Below we will summarise the maintenance of these clauses for clarity.

6.3 Maintenance of the set of clauses

i Maintenance of clauses when positive instances are added.

If a clause Cl contains the meta-variable $(L(G_i) <_g A_i)$ and if after the processing of positive instances, $L(S_i) \cap A_i$ becomes not empty, then the relations in $L(S_i) \cap A_i$ are no longer a possible explanation for the rejection of the negative instance denoted by Cl. Let A_i' be the set of relations of A_i that are not in $L(S_i)$. If A_i' is not empty, the new explanation becomes $(L(G_i) <_g A_i')$. Otherwise the meta-variable $(L(G_i) <_g A_i)$ is erased from Cl (lines 6-9).

ii Empty clause implies that the version space has collapsed.

When a clause Cl, encoding a negative instance e^-, is empty, either during its construction (line 19), or following the addition of some positive instances (line 10), it implies that there does not exist a possible explanation for rejecting the negative instance e^-, then the algorithm collapses.

Algorithm 1: The CONACQ Algorithm

$\mathcal{K} \leftarrow \emptyset$
foreach B_i **do** $L(S_i) \leftarrow \{\bot\}$; $L(G_i) \leftarrow \{\top\}$
foreach *training instance e* **do**

1   **if** $e \in E^+$ **then**
2   **foreach** B_i **do**
3   **if** $\exists r \in L(S_i)/e[var(B_i)] \notin r$ **then**
4      $L(S_i) \leftarrow min_{\leq_g}\{r/S_i \leq_g r \leq_g G_i \text{ and } e[var(B_i)] \in r\}$
5   **if** $L(S_i) = \emptyset$ **then** "collapsing"
6   **foreach** $Cl/(L(G_i) <_g A_i) \in Cl \text{ and } A_i \cap L(S_i) \neq \emptyset$ **do**
7       $Cl \leftarrow Cl \setminus (L(G_i) <_g A_i)$
8       $A'_i \leftarrow A_i \setminus L(S_i)$
9   **if** $A'_i \neq \emptyset$ **then** $Cl \leftarrow Cl \cup (L(G_i) <_g A'_i)$
10   **if** $Cl = \emptyset$ **then** "collapsing"
11   **if** $Cl = \{(L(G_i) <_g A_i)\}$ **then**
       $G_i \leftarrow max_{\leq_g}\{r/S_i \leq_g r \leq_g G_i \text{ and } r <_g A_i\}$; $\mathcal{K} \leftarrow \mathcal{K} \setminus Cl$

12   **if** $e \in E^-$ **then**
13    $Cl \leftarrow \emptyset$; $reject \leftarrow false$
14   **foreach** B_i ***while*** $\neg reject$ **do**
15   **if** $\exists r \in L(S_i)/e[var(B_i)] \notin r$ **then**
16      $A_i \leftarrow min_{\leq_g}\{r/S_i \leq_g r \leq_g G_i \text{ and } e[var(B_i)] \in r\}$
17   **if** $A_i = \emptyset$ **then** $reject \leftarrow true$
18   **else** $Cl \leftarrow Cl \cup (L(G_i) <_g A_i)$

   if $\neg reject$ **then**
19   **if** $Cl = \emptyset$ **then** "collapsing"
20   **if** $Cl = \{(L(G_i) <_g A_i)\}$ **then**
     $G_i \leftarrow max_{\leq_g}\{r/S_i \leq_g r \leq_g G_i \text{ and } r <_g A_i\}$; $\mathcal{K} \leftarrow \mathcal{K} \setminus Cl$
21   **else if** $\nexists Cl'/Cl' \subseteq Cl$ **then** $\mathcal{K} \leftarrow \mathcal{K} \cup Cl$
22   **foreach** $Cl''/Cl \subset Cl''$ **do** $\mathcal{K} \leftarrow \mathcal{K} \setminus Cl''$

---

iii The one-meta-variable clauses.

The one-meta-variable clauses represent the only possible explanation for the rejection of the coded negative instances. They must be reported on the local version space then removed from $\mathcal{K}$. Let $(L(G_i) <_g A_i)$ be a such clause: $L(G_i)$ must be made more specific than A_i.(lines 11 and 20).

iv Subsumption of negative instances.

A negative instance e_1^- (encoded by Cl_1) subsumes e_2^- (encoded by Cl_2) iff $Cl_1 \subseteq Cl_2$. Indeed, if Cl_1 is satisfied, then Cl_2 too. It is thus useless to store

Cl_2. Lines 21-22 of Algorithm CONACQ maintain this minimality of the base of clauses $\mathcal{K}$.

A proof of Correctness of Algorithm CONACQ can be found in [1]

Example 2 In Figure 2, we describe the learning process on a single constraint C_{12} and where B_{12} is the bias of Figure 1. Initially $L(S_{12}) = \{\bot\}$, and $L(G_{12}) = \{\top\}$. When the positive instance $e_1^+ = (1,1)$ is received, $L(S_{12})$ goes up in $L^H(B_{12})$ to the most specific relations accepting this tuple (a), namely $\{=\}$. We know now that the final relation of constraint C_{12} will be more general than or equal to "=". When the negative instance $e_2^- = (2,1)$ is received, it is necessary to restrict $L(G_{12})$ such that it will reject this tuple (b). At this step: $L(S_{12}) = \{=\}$, and $L(G_{12}) = \{\leq\}$. The negative instance $e_3^- = (0,3)$ forbids the relation "$\leq$" (c). Then $L(S_{12}) = L(G_{12}) = \{=\}$, that is a local convergence.

E	X_1	X_2
e_1^+	1	1
e_2^-	2	1
e_3^-	0	3

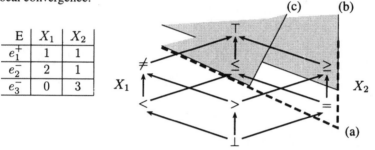

Figure 2: A local example

Example 3 In Figure 3, we present an example of our algorithm using a constraint network involving three variables X_1, X_2 and X_3. The biases used are $\{B_{12}, B_{23}\}$, where $var(B_{12}) = (X_1, X_2)$, $var(B_{23}) = (X_2, X_3)$ and $L^H(B_{12}) = L^H(B_{23})$, which for the purposes of this example we will assume to be the same as that presented as $L^H(B_i)$ in Figure 1. When processing the positive example $e_1^+ = (2,2,5)$, due to the projection property of S, S_{12} **and** S_{23} go up (i.e., $L(S_{12}) \leftarrow \{=\}$ and $L(S_{23}) \leftarrow \{<\}$) (a) and (b).

However, since G does not have this projection property: when $e_2^- = (1,3,2)$ is received, either C_{12} must reject the tuple $(1,3)$ **or** C_{23} must reject $(3,2)$. Therefore, we build the clause $Cl = (rel(C_{12}) <_g^L \{\leq\}) \vee (rel(C_{23}) <_g^L \{\neq,\})$ to store these alternatives (c) or (d). When the negative instance $e_3^- = (1,1,0)$ is received, we know that the constraint C_{12} is not involved in its rejection, because $e_3^-[var(C_{12})] = (1,1)$ is an allowed tuple of $L(S_{12}) = \{=\}$. The only explanation for the rejection of e_3^- is $Cl' = (rel(C_{23}) <_g^L \{\neq,\})$ (d). Note than Cl' subsumes Cl (i.e., $Cl' \subseteq Cl$). The explanation of the rejection of e_3^- (d) is also a valid one for e_2^-: Cl becomes subsumed by Cl', and thus is discarded (the explanation (c) is discarded too). After these three instances, the CONACQ result is $L(S_{12}) = \{=\}$, $L(G_{12}) = \{\top\}$, C_{23}: $L(S_{23}) = \{<\}$ and $L(G_{23}) = \{\leq\}$.

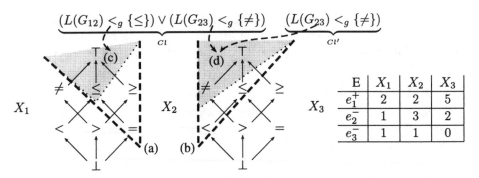

Figure 3: A global example

7 Experiments and Observations

We report here on some preliminary experiments to evaluate the learning capabilities of our approach. Rather than focusing on techniques for minimising the number of inter-actions, our focus here is on studying a number of properties of the CONACQ algorithm which provide motivation for our research agenda.

We performed experiments with a simulated teacher, which plays the role of the user, and a simulated learner that uses the algorithm presented earlier. The teacher has the knowledge of a randomly generated (target) network, represented by the triple $< 50, 8, C >$, defining a problem involving 50 variables with domains $\{1, ..8\}$, and a number C of constraints. Each constraint is randomly chosen from the bias $\{<, =, >, \leq, \neq, \geq\}$. The teacher provides the learner with solutions and non solutions. The learner acquires a version space for the problem using CONACQ algorithm.

7.1 Experiment 1: Effect of the order of the instances

In this following experiment, we assess aspects of the runtime characteristics of the CONACQ algorithm. In particular, we study computing time and the size of the version space, while varying the order in which examples are presented. Instances from a set E of size 100 are given by the teacher to the learner based on a $< 50, 8, 50 >$ network. The set E contains 10 positive and 90 negative instances.

Table 1 presents the time needed by the learner to acquire the version space, V, for the example set while varying the arrival time of the 10 positive instances. The positive instances were presented at the beginning (a), middle (b), and end (c) of the interaction between teacher and learner.

Table 1: Effect of the timing of the introduction of positive instances

Introduction time for positives	0 (a)	50 (b)	90 (c)
Computing time (in sec.)	3.3	5.1	8.6
$log(|V|)$	2,234	2,234	2,234

We observe that *"the sooner, the better"* seems to be the good strategy for the introduction of positive instances. Indeed, the specific bound S rises quickly in the space of hypotheses with positive instances, reducing the size of the version space.

Because of that, the CPU time needed is also reduced when positive instances arrive at the beginning. But we can see that the final size of the version space is not affected by the order of the instances. This is due to the commutativity property of version spaces, discussed in Section 5.

7.2 Experiment 2: Utility of partial instances

In some cases, the user can reject an instance while justifying it by a negative sub-instance. For example, in a real-estate setting the customer (teacher) might reject an apartment citing the reason that *"this living-room is too small for me"*. The estate agent (learner) knows that the violation is due to the variables defining the living room, which can being very helpful for handling negative examples. The utility of such justified rejections can be measured by providing our learner with partial instances. In the following experiment (Table 2), the teacher provides the learner with 90 partial negative instances (after 10 complete positive ones) in the training data. We consider partial instances involving 2, 5, 10 variables, and report the size of the version space and of the set of clauses after 100 instances have been given.

Table 2: Effect of the partial instances

Nb of variables involved in instances of E^-	50	10	5	2
$log(|V|)$	2,234	2,233	2,225	2,144
$|K|$ (10^4 meta-variables)	7.6	6.1	3.2	0

We observe that partial instances speed up the process of convergence of the version space. The smaller these partial instances are, the more helpful they are. This opens a promising way of helping the learning process: asking the user to justify why she rejects some instances can assist in reducing the length of the dialog with the teacher. This is a critical issue if we are learning in an interactive setting from a human user.

7.3 Experiment 3: Non-representable constraints and version space collapse

We have seen that our algorithm learns a network expressed using a given bias. An overly restrictive bias leads to version space collapse since it is unlikely to be capable of expressing the target network. This happens because some of the constraints of the target network are non-representable in the given bias. In the following experiment, (Table 3), we analyse the effect on the speed of version space collapse by varying the proportion of non-representable constraints in the target network. For each proportion of non-representable constraints we learned 100 different $< 50, 8, 50 >$ target networks. Non-representable constraints, generated randomly, were not members of our bias $\{<, =, >, \leq, \neq, \geq\}$. The table presents the number of times the version space collapsed after 1,000 instances where presented. Note that the focus of this experiment is related to automatic reformulation rather than interactive modelling.

We observe that the more non-representable constraints in the target network, the faster the version space collapses. This is to be expected since version spaces are sensitive to noise (errors) in the training data. However, an interesting observation was

Table 3: Effect of non-representable constraints

Ratio of non representable constraints	10%	25%	50%
% of collapsing	47	78	100

made during this analysis. On a number of constraint networks containing very few non-representable constraints we observed that the version space did not collapse, even after millions of instances were presented. This seems to violate Mitchell's theorem of representability [6]. However, what occured in these situations was that the non-representable constraints in the target *become* representable by propagation of other constraints. As an example, consider three variables X_1, X_2, and X_3 linked by the following constraints in the target network: $X_1 = X_2$, $X_2 = X_3$, and $(X_1 = X_3) \vee (X_1 = X_3 + 5)$. Obviously, the constraint between X_1 and X_3 is not representable in the bias $\{<, =, >, \leq, \neq, \geq\}$, and every network containing it is expected to cause the version space to collapse. However, this is not the case in this example, because we can restrict the constraint between X_1 and X_3 to $X_1 = X_3$ by transitivity. This transitive closure constraint is representable.

It is worth noting that if we had used a technique that learned each constraint in the network separately, the version space for our problem would have collapsed had we attempted to acquire the constraint between X_1 and X_3.

7.4 Observation: Implicit constraints

The general phenomenon of constraints that can be inferred by other constraints can have another effect, which is to prevent the version space from converging to the smallest possible on each constraint taken separately. Consider again an example with three variables X_1, X_2 and X_3, linked in the target network by the constraints $X_1 = X_2$, $X_2 = X_3$, and $X_1 = X_3$. Furthermore, consider what occurs at some point in the learning process when the version space local to the constraint defined on (X_1, X_3) contains both $X_1 = X_3$ and $X_1 \leq X_3$. If the training data contains only complete instances, it is impossible to converge to the constraint $X_1 = X_3$ because every negative instance that would permit us to discard $X_1 \leq X_3$ from the version space (e.g., $((X_1, 1), (X_2, 2), (X_3, 2)))$ will also be rejected by $X_1 = X_2$ or by $X_2 = X_3$. Thus, the boundary G will never determine that culpability lies with $X_1 \leq X_3$.

Applying some levels of local consistency seems to be a promising approach to improving the reduction of the version space, by adding implicit constraints to the learned network. In the previous example, path-consistency would be enough to deduce that the only candidate between X_1 and X_3 is the constraint $X_1 = X_3$. This phenomenon can cause the VS to keep a size bigger than it should have.

8 Conclusion

We have proposed an original method to learn constraint networks from instances that should or should not be solutions. The technique used is based on version spaces, a machine learning paradigm that has good properties (e.g., incrementality, commutativity, wrt the training data) that will be essential in a process interacting with a user.

Even if this paper is mainly a description of the general process of learning a constraint network from instances, we can easily foresee the many applications it could have, in assisting a novice in modelling her problem, or helping an expert to test whether a given library of constraints with good computational properties can encode her problem.

We have presented preliminary experiments that show that our approach raises several important issues, such as the speed of the learning process, or the question of the implicit constraints. Based on these experiments, and the framework in general, we have given an insight into some of the very interesting research issues which are raised by our work.

References

[1] R. Coletta, C. Bessiere, B. O'Sullivan, E.C. Freuder, S. O'Connell, and J. Quinqueton. Semi-automatic modeling by constraint acquisition. In *CP-03 Second Workshop on Reformulating Constraint Satisfaction Problems*, 2003.

[2] E.C. Freuder and B. O'Sullivan. Generating tradeoffs for interative constraint-based configuration. In Toby Walsh, editor, *Proceedings of the Seventh International Conference on Principles and Practice of Constraint Programming*, pages 590–594, November 2001.

[3] E.C. Freuder and R.J. Wallace. Suggestion strategies for constraint-based matchmaker agents. In *Principles and Practice of Constraint Programming - CP98*, pages 192–204, October 1998.

[4] Haym Hirsh. Polynomial-time learning with version spaces. In *National Conference on Artificial Intelligence*, pages 117–122, 1992.

[5] J. Little, C. Gebruers, D. Bridge, and E.C. Freuder. Capturing constraint programming experience: A case-based approach. In *CP-02 Workshop on Reformulating Constraint Satisfaction Problems*, 2002.

[6] T. Mitchell. Concept learning and the general-to-specific ordering. In *Machine Learning*, chapter 2, pages 20–51. McGraw Hill, 1997.

[7] U. Montanari. Networks of constraints: Fundamental properties and applications to picture processing. *Information Sciences*, 7(95-132), 1974.

[8] S. O'Connell, B. O'Sullivan, and E.C. Freuder. Query generation for interactive constraint acquisition. In *Proceedings of the 4th International Conference on Recent Advances in Soft Computing (RASC-2002)*, pages 295–300, December 2002.

[9] F. Rossi and A. Sperduti. Learning solution preferences in constraint problems. *Journal of experimental and theoretical computer science*, 10, 1998.

[10] M. Wallace. Practical applications of constraint programming. *Constraints*, 1(1–2):139–168, 1996.

SESSION 2A:

**KNOWLEDGE DISCOVERY IN DATA
(ASSOCIATION RULES, CLUSTERING AND
CLASSIFICATION)**

Strategies for Partitioning Data in Association Rule Mining

Shakil Ahmed, Frans Coenen, and Paul Leng

Department of Computer Science, University of Liverpool
Liverpool L69 7ZF, United Kingdom
{shakil, frans, phl}@csc.liv.ac.uk

Abstract. The problem of extracting association rules from databases is well known. The most demanding part of the problem is the determination of the *support* for all those sets of attributes which occur often enough to be of possible interest. We have previously described methods we have developed that approach the problem by first constructing a tree (the *P*-tree) that contains a record of all the relevant information in the database and a partial computation of the support totals. This approach offers significant performance advantages over comparable alternative methods, which we have demonstrated experimentally with store-resident datasets. In practice, however, the real focus of interest is on much larger databases. In this paper we discuss strategies for partitioning the data in these cases, and present results of the performance analysis.

Keywords: Association Rules, Partial Support, Data Structures, Partitioning.

1 Introduction

A well-known method for knowledge discovery in databases (KDD) involves the extraction of *association rules* [2] from a binary database. In a database of this kind, each attribute simply records the presence or absence of some property, or *item*, in the record. An association rule is a probabilistic relationship, of the form $A \Rightarrow B$, between disjoint sets of these items, obtained from examination of the data. The task is to discover, in applications such as supermarket shopping-basket analysis, important associations among items such that the presence of some items in a transaction will imply the likely presence of other items in the same transaction; that is, rules that associate one set of attributes of a relation to another.

A rule is usually only of potential interest if the set of attributes it associates occurs together relatively frequently in the data being examined. We define these *frequent* sets to be those which exceed some defined level of *support*. The support for the rule $A \Rightarrow B$ is the number (or proportion) of database records which contain $A \cup B$. The principal problem in association rule mining is the search for sets which exceed the support threshold. Once these frequent sets have been found, it is relatively straightforward to identify the rules that are likely to be of interest.

Finding all the frequent sets is a computationally demanding problem because of the exponential scale of the search space. The well-known *Apriori* algorithm [3] was one of the first to address this problem, and many subsequent algorithms have been described, many based on Apriori. We have previously introduced methods that begin by preprocessing the data in a single pass of the database which performs a partial summation of the support totals. These partial counts are stored in a set-enumeration tree structure which we call the *P*-tree. We then apply to this structure an algorithm, Apriori-TFP, which completes the summation of the final support counts, storing these in a second, differently-ordered, set-enumeration tree (the *T*-tree).

In experiments comparing the performance of this approach with other published methods, Apriori-TFP has compared favourably. To provide a fair basis for comparison, it is usual to examine data which can be wholly retained in main memory during all the computation. In reality, however, most of the most demanding applications of association-rule mining will involve data on a much larger scale. Not all methods translate easily to an implementation involving non-store-resident data, and performance in these cases may not scale linearly with the database size.

In this paper we examine possible methods for partitioning data in order to apply the Apriori-TFP algorithm in implementations which assume the data cannot be store-resident. We consider both "horizontal" partitioning, which divides the original data into smaller sets of records, and "vertical" partitioning, which divides the data by attribute. We present an experimental evaluation of the approaches.

2 Background

The biggest problem in deriving association rules is the exponential complexity of the task of computing support counts for all possible combinations of items. All practical algorithms, therefore, try to identify those sets of items which may possibly exceed the required threshold of support. Most methods are based to a greater or lesser extent on the "Apriori" algorithm [3]. Apriori performs repeated passes of the database, successively computing support-counts for sets of single attributes, pairs, triplets, and so on. At the end of each pass, sets which fail to reach the required support threshold are eliminated, and *candidates* for the next pass are constructed as supersets of the remaining (frequent) sets. Since no set can be frequent which has an infrequent subset, this procedure guarantees that all frequent sets will be found. The method may still be computationally expensive, however, especially for low support thresholds and when the database is very densely-populated, as in these cases the number of candidates to be considered may become very large, and many passes of the data may also be required.

Strategies to improve on the basic Apriori algorithm include algorithms which begin by partitioning [12] or sampling [10] the database to estimate the likely candidate set, or by checking subsets dynamically [11]. These methods reduce the number of database passes involved, but tend to generate more candidates to be counted. Other methods [4] [5] [13] reduce the search space by aiming to identify *maximal* frequent sets without first examining all their subsets. These algorithms may cope better with densely-populated databases than the other algorithms described, but at the cost of multiple database passes.

We have previously described [9] a class of methods we have introduced which begin by performing a single database pass to perform a restructuring of the relevant data and a partial computation of the support totals. We construct a tree, which we call the *P-tree*, which contains all the sets of items present as distinct records in the database (plus a few additional sets required to maintain the tree structure efficiently). These sets are stored in lexicographic order, in a form such that each subtree contains only lexicographically following supersets of its parent node. This order makes it easy and efficient, as the tree is constructed, to count for each node the number of occurrences of lexicographically-following supersets in the data. Figure 1 illustrates a P-tree for the attribute-set $\{A, B, C, D\}$. The illustration is of a complete tree, that would arise if every combination of attributes were present in the database; in practice, this will not occur in real large-scale data.

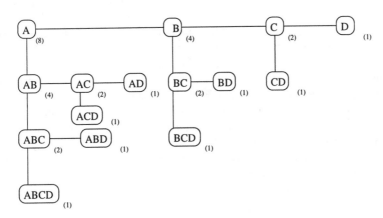

Fig. 1. Example of a P-tree

To complete the counting of support for a set S, then, we need only find S and its lexicographically-preceding immediate supersets in the P-tree. The algorithm we have used for this purpose, which we call Apriori-TFP, is described in [7]. Apriori-TFP (Total-from-Partial) uses the basic Apriori methodology, applied to the P-tree rather than to the original database. The candidate sets to be considered are stored in a second set-enumeration tree, the *T-tree*, ordered in the opposite way to the P-tree. On completion of the algorithm, the T-tree contains just the frequent sets, with their final support totals.

The performance of Apriori-TFP improves on the original Apriori for two reasons: firstly, the initial very efficient partial computation carried out when constructing the P-tree avoids some less efficient computation that Apriori must carry out repeatedly, on each pass; and secondly, the structure of the T-tree provides a very efficient way of locating the candidates for which support is to be counted in the passes of Apriori-TFP. Experimental results reported in [7] confirm this gain, and also demonstrate improved performance over the *FP-growth* [6] algorithm, which has some similar properties.

Like most experimental work on association-rule algorithms, our performance evaluation has been based on measurements using main-store-resident data, because this provides the firmest basis for performance measurement. It is clear, however, that for most applications only those methods that will cope effectively with much larger datasets will be suitable. Not all methods can be readily adapted to deal with non-store-resident data. For example, the otherwise very efficient *DepthProject* [1] algorithm is explicitly targeted at memory-resident data, while the multiply-linked structure of the *FP*-tree used in [6] also causes problems for non-store-resident implementations.

In this paper we examine strategies for implementing Apriori-TFP in cases when it will be impossible to contain all the data required in main memory. The memory requirement for Apriori-TFP, as for most other methods, is twofold. Firstly, the original data (in our case, transformed into a P-tree) must be contained in primary memory or else read repeatedly for each pass of the data. Secondly, we require to contain in primary memory the *candidate* sets of attributes whose support is being counted. The number of such candidates can become very large, especially if a low threshold of support is required. The overall memory requirement, therefore, includes both these factors. Two broad approaches for reducing this suggest themselves. First, "horizontal" partitioning: we can divide the database into a number of non-overlapping segments each of which is small enough to be handled in main memory. Alternatively or additionally, we can partition "vertically", dividing by attribute, and hence defining subsets of the candidates that can be counted separately. From these approaches, we have defined four methods for carrying out the counting of support totals needed, described in the following sections.

3 Method I: TFP with Horizontal Partitioning

Method 1 may be regarded as the 'natural' implementation of the Total- from Partial- support (TFP) method in this context. We begin by dividing the data into equal-sized segments, and create a separate P-tree for each segment. In this and the other methods described, the P-trees thus created enumerate all the sets present as distinct itemsets in the segment under consideration, recording for each an incomplete summation of their support-count. The stored P-trees are then treated as a composite structure from which we compute the final support totals for all the frequent sets, storing these in a T-tree. Detailed descriptions of the algorithms for building a P-tree in a single database pass and for counting support totals using a T-tree are given in [7] [9].

The first stage is to build a P-tree for each segment, storing this on backing store. For this purpose, the P-tree is converted to a table (array of arrays) form. The rows of the P-tree table consist of corresponding levels of the P-tree; so that all 1-itemsets of the P-tree are included in level 1 of the table, 2-itemsets in level 2, and so on. This is possible because the Apriori-TFP algorithm does not require the linkage between nodes in the tree to be maintained, and can traverse the P-tree in any order. Thus, it is possible to treat the stored P-trees as a single structure, divided into segments of manageable size.

To build a single T-tree from the P-trees stored on backing store, we use a form of the Apriori-TFP algorithm described in [7]. The algorithm is (for $K = 1, 2,\dots$):

1. Build level K in the T-tree.
2. Read all the stored P-trees in turn, adding interim supports associated with individual P-tree nodes to the level K nodes established in (1).
3. Remove any level K T-tree nodes that do not have an adequate level of support.
4. Repeat steps (1), (2), and (3); until a level K is reached where no nodes are adequately supported.

The method creates a final single T-tree in main memory, that contains all the frequent sets and their support-counts. Note that the main memory requirement is for storage to contain the P-tree for a single segment of the data, plus the whole of the T-tree.

4 Method II: TFP using Negative Border

The method described above is the most obvious and simplest way of transforming our Apriori-TFP algorithm into a form applicable when data is not resident in main memory. The drawback, of course, is that the basic Apriori methodology requires repeated passes to be made of the database to compute the support for single items, pairs etc., in turn. For Apriori-TFP, the P-tree is used instead of the database, but we will still require to read each P-tree segment repeatedly from backing store.

The concept of the *negative border* [10] tries to avoid this by obtaining an early estimate of the possible frequent sets, which can then be counted in one pass. To do this, we take a single segment of data, find all the sets that are frequent in this segment, then verify the results with the rest of the database. Because there may be sets that are frequent in the entire database but not in our chosen segment, however, we need to enlarge the set of candidates to be considered. First, the support threshold is lowered so much that it is very unlikely that any frequent sets are missed. Then, after finding all the *locally frequent* sets in the segment being examined, this collection is augmented by adding its 'negative border'. The *negative border* is the collection of all candidates that are not frequent in the segment but all its subsets are. The significance of the negative border is that it defines a boundary between the frequent and non-frequent sets. If no set on the negative border is finally found to be frequent, then no sets 'outside' the border can be frequent either.

The application of this method in our case can be divided into three stages:

1. First, build and store P-trees for each segment of data, as for Method 1.
2. Build a T-tree with its negative border for the first segment of data (for simplicity, we will assume that the data is randomly distributed, so that the first segment can be taken as an accurate sample of the whole).
3. Update the T-tree for the other segments of data.

An initial T-tree with negative border is built, using a lowered support threshold, from the first stored P-tree segment, using a slightly modified Apriori-TFP algorithm. Although this will again require repeated passes of the P-tree segment, if this can be contained in main memory then it will be read once only. The negative border is easily obtained. In Apriori-TFP, a candidate set is added to the tree when its subsets are all frequent. If after counting its support, the set is found to be infrequent, it is deleted from the tree. In this variant, we retain these sets on the tree, but do not use them to construct further (superset) candidates. Thus, these sets are not themselves frequent, but have only frequent subsets, and have no supersets in the final tree.

For each of the other segments of data, we read the P-tree into main memory, then perform a single traversal of this to count the support of all the sets in the T-tree, adding these to the totals already stored. The final T-tree contains the final support-counts for all the candidate sets identified in the first section, including those on their negative border. Sometimes, unfortunately, it may happen that we find out that all necessary sets have not been evaluated. There has been a *failure* in the building if all frequent sets are not found in one pass. If there are no misses, then the method is guaranteed to have found all frequent sets. Misses indicate a potential failure; if there is a miss of any set, then some superset of the missed set might be frequent but not evaluated. A miss is identified by checking the negative border. If any superset can be constructed, all of whose subsets are frequent, then it will be necessary to perform another pass to count its support.

5 Methods III and IV: TFP with Vertical Partitioning

Both methods described above require main memory sufficient to contain the P-tree for a single segment of data together with the whole of the T-tree. Because there is no partitioning of the T-tree, these may face problems in dealing with very large candidate sets. A possible alternative way of reducing the requirement to manageable proportions is to divide the set of attributes under consideration into subsets, corresponding to which there is a partitioning of both the P-tree and the T-tree into subtrees that can be processed separately. The problem with this "vertical" partitioning strategy is that, although subtrees of the T-tree properly represent subsets of the candidate set, the subtrees of the P-tree do not map directly on to this. This is because although *succeeding* supersets of a set S are located in the subtree rooted at S, *predecessor* supersets are scattered throughout the preceding part of the P-tree, which must therefore be traversed in order to compute the support for S.

The problem can be overcome by increasing the amount of counting done during the construction of the P-tree. We begin by dividing the ordered attribute-set into (say) 4 subsequences, labeled 1, 2, 3, 4. We then proceed to construct separate *Partition-P*-trees, which we will label PP1, PP2, PP3, PP4 respectively, for these attribute-sets. PP1 is a normal P-tree for the attributes in subset 1. PP2, however, counts all those sets which include at least one item from subset 2, in a tree which includes both set 2 and its predecessors. PP4, finally, will include all attributes, but will count only those sets which include at least one item from subset 4. Suppose, for example, the attribute-set of figure 1 was used to define 4 PP-trees for items A, B C and D respectively. Then, a record comprising the itemset ACD would be counted in PP1 (as A), PP3 (AC), and PP4 (ACD).

The effect of this is that the total support for any set S can now be obtained from the PP-tree within which S is located. The apparent drawback is that we now need to construct not one but several P-trees, of increasing size. In our example, the "tree" PP1 will comprise only the single node A, whereas at first sight it appears that PP4 will be as large as the original P-tree. In practice, however, this is not the case as only those records which contain a D will be represented in PP4. The size of the largest PP-tree can be further reduced if we order the attributes by descending expected frequency (a heuristic that also, as we have found in previous work [8], improves the performance of Apriori-TFP).

Method 3, therefore, may be summarized thus:

1. Choose an appropriate partitioning of the attribute-set into sequences 1, 2,...k.
2. Perform k passes of the database to build *Partition-P*-trees PP1, PP2...PPk.
3. Read PP1 into memory, and build a T-tree to count the total support for all frequent sets formed from members of set 1 only.
4. Read PP2 into memory, and build a T-tree counting the support for frequent sets formed from members of set 2 with its predecessors.
5. Repeat step 4 for PP3, PP4, etc.

The method reduces the maximum primary memory requirement, as we now need to contain in memory only a PP-tree together with the subtree of the T-tree corresponding to that partition. A further advantage of the method is that more of the counting is done by the relatively efficient procedures used when constructing the P-tree. The chief drawback, however, is that repeated passes of the database are now required to construct the PP-trees. To overcome this, we can combine the "vertical" partitioning of Method 3 with a "horizontal" segmentation of the database as in Methods 1 and 2. In this case, (Method 4) we will first build PP-trees, as described for Method 3, for each segment of the database (choosing a segment size which allows this to be done entirely in primary memory). Then, the stored PP-trees are processed in the order of the vertical partitioning, to construct the complete T-trees for partition 1, 2 ...in turn. In this case the maximum memory requirement is for the PP-trees for one partition, plus the corresponding T-tree partition, and the PP-trees stored for each segment need be read once only.

6 Results

In this section we describe our experiments and the performance results for the methods described above. All the programs were written in standard C++ and run under the Linux operating system. We performed our experiments on an AMD Athlon workstation with a clock rate of 1.3 GHz, 256 Kb of cache, and 512 Mb of RAM. The data was stored on an NFS server (1 Gb filestore).

We used synthetic data sets constructed using the QUEST generator described in [3]. This uses parameters T, which defines the average number of items found in a set; and I, the average size of the maximal supported set. Higher values of T and I in relation to the number of items (attributes) N correspond to a more densely-populated database. For all the experiments described here, we have used the parameters T =10, I =5, $N = 500$.

We first examined the two "horizontal" partitioning methods, 1 and 2. For these experiments, we generated a database of 500,000 records, and investigated partitions of this into 5, 10 and 20 equal segments, for each of which a separate P-tree was constructed and stored as described above. The time to create the P-trees was 30.25, 25.78 and 22.82 seconds for 5, 10 and 20 segments respectively. Interestingly, because the size of the trees reduces as the number of segments increases, the time to build the trees reduces for more segments. Table 1 then compares the performance of the methods (times in seconds) in using the stored P-trees to compute final support totals for all frequent sets, for varying support thresholds. For method 2, the actual support thresholds were reduced in each case to 2/3 of the chosen figure when constructing the initial T-tree, with the aim of avoiding failure to find all frequent sets in one pass.

Support threshold	1.0	0.5	0.1	0.05
Method 1 (5 segs)	18.54	19.69	89.10	210.01
Method 1 (10 segs)	18.67	19.99	89.59	213.46
Method 1 (20 segs)	19.77	20.96	93.91	221.78
Method 2 (5 segs)	6.45	7.62	80.47	199.51(Fail)
Method 2 (10 segs)	6.30	7.22	75.76(Fail)	216.59(Fail)
Method 2 (20 segs)	6.59	7.45	89.01(Fail)	241.16(Fail)

Table 1: Times to find frequent sets for T10I5N500D500000

As can be seen, the performance of Method 1 varies only slightly for the three different segmentations, especially if the time to build the P-tree is taken into account. This suggests that the method will scale well for larger datasets, requiring more partitions. Method 2 outperforms Method 1 for relatively high support thresholds, gaining because of the reduced number of passes of the stored P-trees that are required. At lower support thresholds, however, the advantage begins to be offset by the increased cost of managing a larger T-tree, and, worse, the heuristic used to estimate the candidate set proves to be inadequate in some cases, so that the algorithm fails to find all the frequent sets in one pass. In this event, another full pass of the disk-resident data would be required to complete the counting of supports (the time for this is not included here).

Table 2 shows the storage requirements for these experiments. The figures tabulated, in megabytes, are the sum of the store required to contain the largest P-tree segment, plus the whole of the T-tree. Thus, in each case, the table records the maximum main memory requirement for the Method. These results illustrate the problem with these methods; at low support thresholds (or with data of high density), the number of candidates to be included in the T-tree increases sharply. This is the cause of the sharp increase in execution times observed in Figure 1 as the support threshold is reduced. This adverse scaling is, of course, a characteristic of all methods of finding frequent sets. The further effect, however, is that the reduction in memory requirement brought about by partitioning the data is ineffective as the store required for the candidate set becomes dominant, and in the most extreme cases, this may make the methods infeasible. Method 2 scales less well than Method 1 in this respect. because of the larger candidate sets imposed by the reduced support threshold and negative border.

Support threshold	1.0	0.5	0.1	0.05
Method 1 (5 segs)	3.6	3.8	7.6	50.4
Method 1 (10 segs)	1.9	2.0	5.9	48.5
Method 1 (20 segs)	0.1	0.3	4.1	46.8
Method 2 (5 segs)	3.7	4.1	37.1	141.6
Method 2 (10 segs)	2.0	2.3	32.7	145.4
Method 2 (20 segs)	0.2	0.6	37.6	141.7

Table 2: Memory requirements for T10I5N500D500000

In examining Method 3, we first examined the effect of different degrees of partitioning. We investigated partitions comprising 50, 25, 10 and 1 items: that is, for $N =500$ attributes, dividing the set into 10, 20, 50 and 500 partitions. In each case the partitioning was naive; the attribute set was placed in descending order of frequency, and divided into equal-sized ranges. This is, of course, unlikely to be optimal because, as we have explained, the size of trees produced tends to increase towards the higher end of the attribute-sequence, although this effect is reduced by the ordering of attributes. In some preliminary experiments, we found the scaling of the methods was close to linear as the database size increased, so for experimental convenience the remaining experiments were carried out with a database size $D = 50,000$, while continuing to require that all trees are stored on disk and re-read whenever required.

Table 3 shows the times required to compute the frequent sets (from the stored PP-trees), and Table 4 the maximum memory requirements (largest PP-tree + largest T-tree partition) for these experiments. For lower support thresholds, a higher degree of partitioning appears to offer better results, both in time and memory requirements. This is offset, however, by the greater cost of constructing the PP-trees; because each tree requires a pass of the database, the time for this scales linearly with the number of partitions. Although in some applications it might be reasonable to write off the PP-tree construction as an initial preprocessing cost, in general this cost will be a significant weakness of Method 3.

Support threshold	1.0	0.5	0.1	0.05	0.01	0.005
50 items/partition	2.26	2.32	3.44	8.05	31.09	61.80
25 items/partition	2.80	2.97	3.79	7.56	28.73	53.36
10 items/partition	3.43	3.50	4.23	6.72	25.97	46.89
1 item/partition	4.41	4.53	4.66	5.71	15.56	33.58

Table 3: Method 3: Times to find Frequent sets for T10I5N500D50000

Support threshold	1.0	0.5	0.1	0.05	0.01	0.005
50 items/partition	1.2	1.2	1.5	3.9	24.7	48.2
25 items/partition	0.9	0.9	1.0	2.5	12.9	24.6
10 items/partition	0.5	0.5	0.6	1.4	6.5	10.9
1 item/partition	0.1	0.1	0.1	0.7	1.4	2.1

Table 4: Method 3: Memory requirements for T10I5N500D50000

This drawback is overcome in Method 4. Table 5 shows the results obtained for this, using "vertical" partitioning as for Method 3, together with a horizontal segmentation of the data into 5 segments. Thus, for each segment of 10,000 records, PP-trees were constructed in primary memory in a single pass.

Support threshold	1.0	0.5	0.1	0.05	0.01	0.005
50 items/partition	2.44	2.50	3.67	8.91	33.71	63.97
25 items/partition	3.13	3.19	4.10	8.26	30.64	55.96
10 items/partition	3.56	3.79	4.59	7.16	27.77	48.94
1 item/partition	4.85	5.20	5.55	6.48	16.11	32.96

Table 5: Method 4: Times to find Frequent sets for T10I5N500D50000

The times for Method 4 were very close to those for Method 3, and the memory requirements for the method, not tabulated here, were also similar. In these experiments we are dealing with a relatively small database, but for larger databases the segmentation used will ensure that the memory required while constructing the PP-trees will continue to be manageable.

The major advantage of Method 4 is the reduced time taken to build the PP-trees. Table 6 shows this; Method 4 is significantly less, especially when the partitioning is increased, requiring more data passes in Method 3. By comparison, the overall P-tree construction time for Methods 1 and 2, for this data, was 1.92 seconds.

Items/partition	50	25	10	1
Method 3	10.58	15.08	24.63	153.90
Method 4 (5 segs)	7.01	8.71	10.46	15.67

Table 6: Time to construct PP-trees for T10I5N500D50000

The final tabulation compares the results for all four methods on this dataset. Here we have shown the results for a vertical partitioning of 1 item/partition (Methods 3 and 4), and a horizontal partitioning into 5 segments (Methods 1, 2 and 4). As we can see, at the lower support thresholds Methods 3 and 4 strongly outperform Methods 1 and 2 in both execution time and primary memory requirement. Even when the time taken to construct the P-trees is taken into account, Method 4 is clearly the best for this data.

Support threshold	1.0	0.5	0.1	0.05	0.01	0.005
Method 1	1.95	2.02	8.74	18.27	61.45	185.80
Method 2	0.70	0.78(Fail)	10.66(Fail)	25.04(Fail)	-	-
Method 3	4.41	4.53	4.66	5.71	15.56	33.58
Method 4	4.85	5.20	5.55	6.48	16.11	32.96

Table 7: Times to find Frequent sets for T10I5N500D50000

Support threshold	1.0	0.5	0.1	0.05	0.01	0.005
Method 1	0.4	0.4	1.8	16.9	127.4	274.9
Method 2	0.4	0.6	19.5	62.5	overflow	-
Method 3	0.1	0.1	0.1	0.7	1.4	2.1
Method 4	0.1	0.1	0.2	0.7	1.4	2.1

Table 8: Maximal memory requirements for T10I5N500D50000

7 Conclusions

We have in this paper described the results of a number of experiments carried out to investigate the performance of methods for extracting association rules from databases in cases where the data is too large to be contained in main memory, demanding some strategy for partitioning the data. In all cases, we have been examining methods that use an initial preprocessing of the database into a reordered form that includes a partial computation of support totals: the P-tree structure. In previous work we have shown this to offer significant performance advantages to Apriori-based algorithms, and our aim here was to examine how best to apply the approach to non-store-resident data. Two of the methods examined are established methods, modified slightly to make use of our data structures, and two others are new methods, using the tree structures to produce a "vertical" partitioning of the data.

The first method examined is, essentially, a straightforward adaptation of Apriori in this context, involving a simple partitioning of the data into segments. We have shown that the method scales well for increasing number of partitions, but, like the original Apriori, its performance drawback is the repeated passes of disk-resident data that it involves, especially when low support thresholds and/or high-density data is involved. The sampling method of [10] was developed specifically to avoid the cost of multiple database passes when data is non-store-resident. Our results confirm its effectiveness for relatively high support thresholds, but, at very low support thresholds, as candidate sets become very large, the additional memory requirement of the method becomes an increasing overhead, and in the extreme the method requires an additional database pass to find all the frequent sets.

The new methods we have introduced aim to reduce the memory requirement by a partitioning of the attribute set, and a corresponding construction of trees that each contain some subset of the candidates to be counted. Our results show these methods to be extremely effective in limiting the maximum primary memory requirement, even at very low support thresholds, because they enable both the original data (as represented by PP-trees) and the candidate set to be partitioned for memory management. For the most computationally demanding cases, at low support thresholds, a high degree of partitioning appears to work best, and in these cases these methods are significantly faster than the others we have considered. With a very high degree of partitioning, the increased cost of preprocessing the data to produce PP-trees may become a problem. We have shown, however, that this problem can be overcome by applying a horizontal segmentation of the data together with the vertical partitioning. In our experiments, this substantially reduced the preprocessing time with little effect on performance in generating the frequent sets. At low support thresholds, this method significantly outperforms all others in both time and space requirements. Work remains to be done to establish the optimal degree of partitioning and segmentation in different cases.

References

1. Agarwal, R., Aggarwal, C. and Prasad, V. Depth First Generation of Long Patterns. In Proc. of the ACM KDD Conference on Management of Data, Boston, pages 108-118, 2000.
2. Agrawal, R., Imielinski, T. and Swami, A. Mining Association Rules between Sets of Items in Large Databases. In Proc. of the ACM SIGMOD Conference on Management of Data, Washington, D.C., pages 207-216, May 1993.
3. Agrawal, R. and Srikant, R. Fast Algorithm for Mining Association Rules. In Proc. of the 20th VLDB Conference, Santiago, Santiago, Chile, pages 487-499, September 1994.
4. Bayardo, R.J. Efficiently Mining Long Pattern from Databases. In Proc. of the ACM SIGMOD Conference on Management of Data, pages 85-93, 1998.
5. Bayardo, R.J., Agrawal, R. and Gunopulos, D. Constraint-Based Rule Mining in Large, Dense Databases. In Proc. of the 15th Int'l Conference on Data Engineering, 1999.

6. Han, J., Pei, J. and Yin, Y. Mining Frequent Patterns without Candidate Generation. In Proc. of the ACM SIGMOD Conference on Management of Data, Dallas, pages 1-12, 2000.

7. Coenen, F., Goulbourne, G., and Leng, P. Computing Association Rules using Partial Totals. PKDD 2001, pages 54-66, 2001.

8. Coenen, F. and Leng, P. Optimising Association Rule Algorithms Using Itemset Ordering. Research and Development in Intelligent Systems XVIII: Proc ES2001 Conference, eds M Bramer, F Coenen and A Preece, Springer, pp53-66.

9. Goulbourne, G., Coenen, F. and Leng, P. Algorithms for Computing Association Rules Using a Partial-Support Tree. J. Knowledge-Based System 13 (2000), pages 141-149. (also Proc ES'99.)

10. Toivonen, H. Sampling Large Databases for Association Rules. In Proc. of the 22th VLDB Conference, Mumbai, India, pages 1-12, 1996.

11. Brin, S., Motwani, R., Ullman, J. D. and Tsur, S. Dynamic Itemset Counting and Implication Rules for Market Basket Data. In Proc. of the ACM SIGMOD Conference on Management of Data, USA, pages 255-264, 1997.

12. Savasere, A., Omiecinski, E. and Navathe, S. An Efficient Algorithm for Mining Association Rules in Large Databases. In Proc. of the 21th VLDB Conference, Zurich, Swizerland, pages 432-444, 1995.

13. Zaki, M.J. Parthasarathy, S. Ogihara, M. and Li, W. New Algorithms for fast discovery of association rules. Technical report 651, University of Rochester, Computer Science Department, New York. July 1997.

A Self-Organising Hybrid Model for Dynamic Text Clustering

Chihli Hung and Stefan Wermter
Centre for Hybrid Intelligent Systems
The University of Sunderland
[chihli.hung; stefan.wermter]@sunderland.ac.uk
www.his.sunderland.ac.uk

Abstract

A text clustering neural model, traditionally, is assumed to cluster static text information and represent its inner structure on a flat map. However, the quantity of text information is continuously growing and the relationships between them are usually complicated. Therefore, the information is not static and a flat map may be not enough to describe the relationships of input data. In this paper, for a real-world text clustering task we propose a new competitive Self-Organising Map (SOM) model, namely the Dynamic Adaptive Self-Organising Hybrid model (DASH). The features of DASH are a dynamic structure, hierarchical clustering, non-stationary data learning and parameter self-adjustment. All features are data-oriented: DASH adjusts its behaviour not only by modifying its parameters but also by an adaptive structure. We test the performance of our model using the larger new Reuters news corpus based on the criteria of classification accuracy and mean quantization error.

1 Introduction

Clustering by document concepts is a helpful way for linking a query to relevant information. One well-known project is WebSOM [1]. WebSOM employs a Self-Organising Map (SOM) for clustering documents and presents them on a 2-dimensional map. The SOM, proposed by Kohonen in the 1980s, applies a pre-defined topological structure and a time-based decaying learning rate to function as a powerful tool for non-linear projection, vector quantization, and data clustering tasks [2]. In terms of a real-world text clustering task, however, the quantity of text information is continuously growing so the information is not static. This information usually has some relationship with time, for instance, news. Some specific events often occur during a specific period and the recent information is more important. Moreover, it is not easy to decide the number of clusters for a complicated text set, which should be further analysed based on a hierarchical architecture.

Therefore, a SOM clustering model with a very large map is not preferred. A model which contains a time-based decaying learning function and pre-defined topological structure is not suitable for such a real-world text clustering task. Several alternative models have been proposed to enhance the practicability of the SOM. However, none of the existing models meet all the needs of the features required for a real-world text clustering task. This leads to the development of a new algorithm, the Dynamic Adaptive Self-Organising Hybrid model (DASH).

The remainder of this paper is organised as follows. In Section 2, we give a brief survey of the related competitive neural learning models. In section 3, we introduce the features of the DASH and its algorithm. Section 4 includes the experiments and comparisons using three scenarios which test our model based on the static data set and non-stationary data set. A conclusion is given in section 5.

2 The Competitive Neural Learning Models

Due to the deficiencies of the SOM, several related unsupervised neural learning models have been proposed. They are based on the competitive learning technique whose learning adjustments are confined to a neuron that is most activated to the stimulus currently being presented [2, 3]. This pure competitive learning has a feature of "winner-take-all". Compared with a neural system, the neighbours of the winner neuron are also activated to a stimulus. The lateral relationships of neurons and the winner affect the extent of activation for the neighbours of the winner. Thus both the winner and its neighbours are activated to a stimulus, which form a "winner-take-most" model.

In a clustering task, we use a unit to represent the neuron, a connection to represent the relationship and an input data vector to represent the stimulus. All the relationships of the units form a topology of a competitive neural model. The winner is represented by the Best Matching Unit (BMU) which is defined as the unit of the model with the shortest Euclidean distance to its associated input vectors. A common goal of these algorithms is to map a data set from a high-dimensional space onto a low-dimensional space, and keep its inner structure as faithful as possible. We divide these models into four groups, which are static models, dynamic models, hierarchical models and non-stationary distribution learning models.

Static models, such as the Neural Gas (NG) [4], and dynamic models, such as the Growing Grid (GG) [5], Growing Cell Structure (GCS) [6], Growing Neural Gas (GNG) [7], Incremental Grid Growing (IGG) [8] and Growing SOM (GSOM) [9], try to define a new architecture with no need of prior knowledge for a topological structure or the number of output units. They develop the map periodically. Some models, e.g. the GCS, GNG and IGG also contain a unit-pruning or connection-trimming function which is based on a pre-defined constant threshold, to further tune the structures. Hierarchical models, such as the TreeGCS [10], Multilayered Self-Organising Feature Maps (M-SOM) [11] and Growing Hierarchical Self-Organizing

Map (GHSOM) [12], offer a detailed view for a complicated clustering task. Non-stationary distribution learning models, such as the Growing Neural Gas with Utility criterion (GNG-U) [13], Plastic Self Organising Map (PSOM) [14] and Grow When Required (GWR) [15] are focused on the ability of continuous learning under a dynamic environment.

We focus on the models with a continuous learning or hierarchical training function. For a model to offer automatic hierarchical clustering, it needs a function to further prune the map by removing unsuitable units to form several partitions on a map. Hodge and Austin [10] use this technique to form synonym clusters as an automatic thesaurus. However, the unit-pruning function seriously depends on a pre-defined constant threshold. Based on the unknown data distribution, this threshold is very difficult to determine. Second, the partition is formed because of the nature of the input data. We cannot foresee that a hierarchy must be built by a competitive model with the unit-pruning function. A proper policy may build such a hierarchy by further developing a whole map from a unit with many input data mapped to this unit or with higher error information, e.g. [11] and [12].

For the non-stationary data set, a trained unit or training unit should be replaced by a unit which is trained with new input samples. A model with the unit-pruning function or with the connection-trimming function which should be based on the global consideration can handle this task. That is, a model, e.g. the GNG and GWR, using the connection-trimming function based on a local aged consideration can be treated as an incomplete non-stationary model only. On the other hand, the stop criterion of models should not be a time-dependent threshold, such as iteration or epoch. However, this stop criterion is used for all models in our survey. Moreover, if a model does not use a time-dependent stop criterion, an unsuitable constant unit-pruning or a connection-trimming threshold may make the model train forever but learn nothing. This constant value can be very small or very large, which is totally dependent on trial-and-error. However, it is not a good idea to use such a constant threshold for a big data set. We argue that a unit-pruning or a connection-trimming threshold should be automatically adjusted to suit different data sets during training.

3 Dynamic Adaptive Self-organising Hybrid (DASH) Model

3.1 The Features of DASH

DASH is a growing self-organising model which contains a dynamic structure, hierarchical training, non-stationary data learning and parameter self-adaptation. All features are data-oriented. We need to define three main parameters, which have an impact on the style of the DASH architecture. The first one is τ, which influences how well DASH represents the current data set. The second one is S_{min}, a minimum number of input samples which a map represents. The third one is a connection-trimming threshold, β. These three parameters are percentage-like. S_{min} can also be a real number. For example, a child map is not built when a unit is associated with the input vectors whose number is less than S_{min}. β is a self-adjusting variable when the units do not grow continuously to meet the requirement of a map quality, the AQE, which is defined as the average distance between every input vector and its Best Matching Unit (BMU) [16].

DASH starts with two units and stops when all units represent their associated input vectors well, or the number of inputs is too few to build a sub-map. The recursive training continues for the individual unit whose AQE does not meet the requirement of DASH. We use the Competitive Hebbian Learning (CHL) principle to connect the BMU and the Second Matching Unit (SMU) for an input stimulus [17]. A connection is trimmed if it is relatively old compared to other connections and a unit without any connection is removed. However, if the model has met its quality requirement, the connection-trimming function is restrained. This is not a problem for training non-stationary data sets because the stop criterion is based on the map quality. Thus, τ affects the size of a single map, S_{min} influences the depth of a hierarchy, and β controls the separation criterion of the clusters. An example of the DASH structure is given in (Figure 1a).

DASH also offers a cue to decide the number of clusters, which is usually determined by subjective human judgement in other competitive learning models. Because of the features of structure separation and hierarchical training, DASH treats a single training map as a two-level hierarchy, i.e. one for a whole sub-map and the other for the partitions in a sub-map. For example, a map in layer 1 contains four partitions (Figure 1a). This map is treated as a local root that has four branches and each branch has a different number of stems. Finally, DASH offers the potential for shorter training. A hierarchical training function can be seen as a distributed model, which trains a whole input set by training several smaller input sub-sets separately.

3.2 The DASH Algorithm

DASH consists of two main iterations and seven processes (Figure 1b). The inner iteration is a learning procedure for each map in a hierarchy. The outer iteration offers a stop criterion for the whole model. In terms of the concept, DASH is a combination of GNG and GHSOM but with several unique features mentioned in the previous section. For convenience, we describe the main structure of the model as follows:

Let $A=\{L_1,L_2,...L_l\}$, where A is the set of sub-maps. Let $L=\{U_1,U_2,...U_u\}$, where U_i is the unit i in the map L. Each U_i has an error variable, err_i. Let C_{ij} be the binary connection between U_i and U_j. Each C_{ij} has a variable, age_{ij}, to store the connection age. Let the input distribution be $p(X)$ for the input set X. Let $X=\{x_1,x_2,...x_n\}$, where x_i is the input sample i in the input set X. We define the weight vectors for an input sample and for a unit as x_i and w_i respectively. Then the precise processes of the DASH algorithm are as below.

1) Global network initialisation

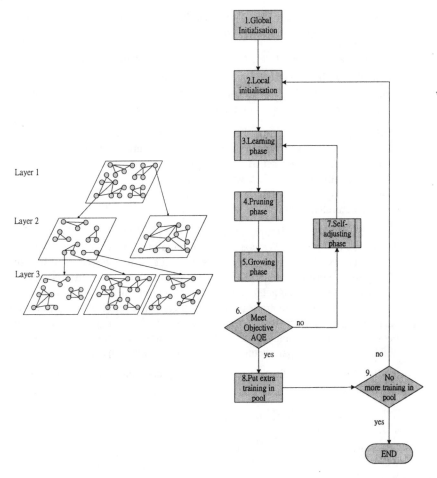

Figure 1. a) The hierarchical structure of   b) The flow chart of DASH algorithm
         DASH

1.1) Define a map quality index, τ , where $0 < \tau \le 1$. τ decides the objective AQE for a child map. It controls the extent of the size for a single map and is also the stop criterion for the child map training. A smaller τ builds a bigger map. We suppose that before training there is a virtual map L_0 above the first map L_1. L_0 contains only one unit whose weight vector, w_0, is the mean value of the untrained input data set, X, which contains N input samples.

$$w_0 = \frac{1}{N}\sum_{i=1}^{N} x_i \qquad \text{(Eq. 1)}$$

Thus, the AQE of L_0 is:

$$AQE_0 = \frac{1}{N}\sum_{i=1}^{N} \|x_i - w_0\| \qquad \text{(Eq. 2)}$$

1.2) Define learning rates α_b and α_s for the Best Matching Unit b, and its neighbours s, respectively, where $0 < \alpha_s < \alpha_b < 1$.

1.3) Define an age threshold, β, for a connection C_{ij}, where $0 < \beta \leq 1$. The β cooperates with the current highest age of connection to decide whether a connection is too old. A β adjusting parameter, J_β, is defined as well, which is used to modulate β based on the current data samples.

1.4) Define S_{min}, a minimum number of input samples which a map represents. The default value is two because the minimum number of units is two in a map. S_{min} can also be set as a proportion of the size of input data, where $0 < S_{min} < 1$. In this case, S_{min} will be found by $S_{min} \times N$. S_{min} influences the depth of a DASH hierarchy. A smaller S_{min} makes DASH expand deeper down a hierarchy.

1.5) Let O_l be a temporal maximum number of units in a map for the layer l. It is defined by Equation 3. We use 3 as the minimum of O_l because a sub-map of DASH starts with 2 units, which allows the model with one spare unit to grow. We apply a constant, 100, in (Eq. 3) for two reasons. The first is that the model is better if it can achieve the quality requirement using a smaller map. We force the model to train properly rather than adding units to pursue a smaller AQE. The second reason is that a very large map is not preferred because it is hard to analyse or visualise. Besides the parameter, O_l, we also define a γ adjusting parameter, J_r, to modify O_l, where $0 < J_\gamma \leq 1$. O_l will be modified in the self-adjusting phase, if a map contains O_l units but does not meet the map quality.

$$
\begin{cases}
O_l = \max(3, \min(100, \dfrac{S_{min}}{2})), \text{ where } l = 1 \\
O_l = \max(3, \min(O_{l-1} \times \dfrac{\tau}{2}, \dfrac{S_{min}}{2})), \text{ where } l > 1
\end{cases}
\tag{Eq. 3}
$$

2) Local network initialisation

2.1) Determine an objective AQE based on the AQE in the direct parent map.

$$objective\ AQE_l = AQE_{l-1} \times \tau \tag{Eq. 4}$$

2.2) Based on O_l, define how often the unit grows as follows:

$$IterGrow = \frac{N_l}{O_l - 1}, \text{ where } N_l \text{ is the number of current input data.} \tag{Eq. 5}$$

2.3) Create two units and initialise weights randomly from $p(X)$.

2.4) Re-order the current data set randomly.

3) Learning Phase

3.1) Generate a data sample x_i for the model.

3.2) Calculate the Euclidean distance of each unit to x_i and decide the Best Matching Unit, b, and the Second Best Matching Unit, s, by

$$b = \arg\min_{n \in L}\|x_i - w_n\| \text{ and} \qquad \text{(Eq. 6)}$$

$$s = \arg\min_{n \in L/\{b\}}\|x_i - w_n\| \qquad \text{(Eq. 7)}$$

and connect them as C_{bs}, if it does not exist.

3.3) Update the weights to the BMU b, and other units n, with a connection from b:

$$w_b(t+1) = w_b(t) + \alpha_b \cdot (x_i - w_n) \text{ and} \qquad \text{(Eq. 8)}$$

$$w_n(t+1) = w_n(t) + \alpha_s \cdot (x_i - w_n) \qquad \text{(Eq. 9)}$$

3.4) Add 1 to the age variables for all connection C, but zero to C_{bs}.

$$\begin{cases} age = age + 1 \\ age_{bs} = 0 \end{cases} \qquad \text{(Eq. 10)}$$

3.5) Increase the error to the BMU error variable, err_b:

$$err_b(t+1) = err_b(t) + \|x_i - w_b\| \qquad \text{(Eq. 11)}$$

4) Pruning Phaseat: each n *IterGrow* iteration, where n is ≥ 1.

   4.1) Find the maximum age of connections currently.

$$age_{max} = \arg\max(age) \qquad \text{(Eq. 12)}$$

   4.2) Remove any connection whose age is larger than a portion of the maximum age of connections currently. This will be carried out if the number of units is more than two.

$$\begin{cases} remove\ connection\ C_{ij}, \text{ if current number of units} > 2 \text{ and } \dfrac{age_{ij}}{age_{max}} > \beta \\ do\ nothing, \qquad\qquad otherwise \end{cases} \qquad \text{(Eq. 13)}$$

   4.3) Prune any unit without any connection but still keep the minimum number of units, 2.

5) Growing Phase: at each *IterGrow* iteration, insert a new unit as follows:

   5.1) Find the unit q with maximum accumulated error:

$$q = \arg\max_{u \in L}(err) \qquad \text{(Eq. 14)}$$

   5.2) Find the unit f, the unit with the highest accumulated error amongst the neighbours of q.

$$f = \arg\max_{u \in Neighbours_q}(err) \qquad \text{(Eq. 15)}$$

   5.3) Insert a new unit r to a map and initialise its weight by interpolating weight vectors q and f.

$$w_r = \frac{w_q + w_f}{2} \qquad \text{(Eq. 16)}$$

   5.4) Set up the err variables for units q, f and r.

$$err_q = \frac{err_q}{2} \qquad \text{(Eq. 17)}$$

$$err_f = \frac{err_f}{2} \qquad \text{(Eq. 18)}$$

$$err_r = \frac{err_q + err_f}{2} \qquad \text{(Eq. 19)}$$

5.5) Connect unit r to unit q and f. Set up the age variable for these two connections, i.e. C_{rq} and C_{rf}.

$$age_{rq} = age_{rf} = age_{qf} \qquad \text{(Eq. 20)}$$

5.6) Remove the connection between unit q and unit f.

6) Check the condition whether the map AQE meets the objective AQE at each *IterGrow* iteration.

6.1) Evaluate the AQE for a map l:

$$AQE_l = \frac{1}{N_l}\sum_{i=1}^{N_l}\left\|x_i - w_{b(i)}\right\|, \qquad \text{(Eq. 21)}$$

where $w_{b(i)}$ is the weight vector of BMU for input sample i.

6.2) If $AQE_l \leq objective\ AQE_l$, then stop training for this map, or go to the self-adjusting phase.

7) Self-adjusting Phase: at some *IterGrow* iteration, modify some parameters to suit the object AQE_l.

7.1) Increase the age threshold, β by the adjusting parameter, J_β, if units are not growing.

$$\beta(t+1) = \beta(t) \times (2 - J_\beta), \text{where } 0.5 < J_\beta \leq 1. \qquad \text{(Eq. 22)}$$

7.2) Decrease the age threshold, if the number of units reach O_l, which is the reference number of units in a map:

$$\beta(t+1) = \beta(t) \times J_\beta, \qquad \text{(Eq. 23)}$$

7.3) Increase the reference number of units in a map, if the number is reached.

$$O_l(t+1) = O_l(t) \times (2 - J_\gamma), \text{where } 0.5 < J_\gamma < 1. \qquad \text{(Eq. 24)}$$

8) Put all units whose AQEs are greater than the objective AQE in the same layer into the training pool if the number of their associated input vectors is greater than S_{min}.

9) Continue the hierarchical training until there are no training requirements in the training pool.

4 Experiments and Comparisons

4.1 The New Reuters Corpus

We work with the new version of the Reuters corpus, RCV1, since this news corpus is a representative test for text classification, a common benchmark and a fairly recent comprehensive data source [18]. In this paper, we initially concentrate on the

8 most dominant topics and the first 10,000 full-text articles associated with these topics for our data set. Because a news article can be pre-classified as more than one topic, we consider the multi-topic as a new combination of topics in our task. Thus the 8 chosen topics are expanded into 40 combined topics for the first 10,000 news articles. We use a traditional vector space model such as TFxIDF to represent a full-text document as a numeric vector [19]. Some feature selection techniques are necessary because of the huge dimensionality of vectors. We remove the stop words, confine words shown in WordNet [20], which only contains open-class words, i.e. nouns, verbs, adjectives and adverbs and lemmatise each word to its base form. After this pre-processing, we still have 16,122 different words in the master word list. We further pick up the 1,000 most frequent words from the master word list since this method is as good as some dimensionality reduction techniques [21]. We evaluate our model by the AQE and classification accuracy, which have also been used in the work of Kohonen et al. [22]. The AQE tests the distortion of the representation for the model. Classification accuracy is used since it tests the ability of the model to simulate human categorisation when tackling pre-labelled data sets.

4.2 Static Data Set

We use 10,000 full-text documents as our test-bed. We use a normalized TFxIDF as the vector representation approach [23]. In this experiment, three different τ, i.e. 95%, 90% and 85% of DASH are applied. For convenience, they are termed DASH95, DASH90 and DASH85 in this paper. Different τ means different objective AQEs for DASH, which affects the size of maps. We compare the results with five other models, i.e. SOM, NG, GG, GCS and GNG. We use 15x15 = 225 units for each model, but this number is only an estimate for dynamic models, i.e. the GG, GCS and GNG. All learning rates of models are initialised to 0.1. Such a learning rate is decayed in some models, such as SOM and NG. SOM fine-tuning training starts with a 0.001 learning rate. Other models, such as the GG, GCS, GNG and DASH, also use an extra learning rate which is 0.001 for training runner-up units of BMU. Except DASH, all models stop at 50,000 iterations. The DASH stop criterion is defined by objective AQE. According to the results in (Table 1), the classification accuracy of GG is the lowest. Other models have similar results.

Another evaluation criterion used in this paper is the AQE, which can be used to describe the degree of distortion for models. The smaller AQE, the more cohesive the cluster. We notice that the stricter structure of models, e.g. SOM and GG have higher AQEs. That is, the performance of vector quantization is a significant feature for clustering. The pre-defined structure for models, e.g. SOM and GG, is not the same as the real structure of the input data set.

Other parameters for three DASH models are the same. However, the β variable is self-adjusting based on the input data set. DASH85 contains only one map whose units have all reached the stop criterion. Compared with other DASH models, DASH85 applies a bigger map with 239 units. The β parameter is adapted from 95% to 17.6%. Thus, this is a flat DASH. The number of units in the first map for the DASH95 and DASH90 are 58 and 124, respectively. Several units in the first map of the DASH95 and DASH90 do not meet the stop criterion. Therefore, they develop the recursive training until the stop criterion is met. In our experiments,

DASH95 and DASH90 contain 30 and 14 sub-maps, respectively. The performance of the DASH is comparable to other models and offers an extra hierarchical structure based on the static data set.

	SOM	NG	GG	GCS	GNG	DASH95	DASH90	DASH85
AQE	0.930	0.837	0.881	0.820	0.823	0.818	0.790	0.802
Accuracy	69.16%	69.54%	69.82%	68.18%	68.60%	66.60%	70.42%	68.37%

Table 1. A comparison of several competitive methods based on the criteria of classification accuracy and AQE for 10,000 full-text news articles. Parameters for DASH are: S_{min}: 1% and β: 95%. Please note that β is an adjustable parameter during training.

4.3 Knowledge Acquisition

In this section, we keep the same pre-processing and vector representation approaches as that in the previous section but we want to test the ability of models to handle the non-stationary data set. We use three experiments in this section. We treat the new data set as new knowledge that complements the existing knowledge. The first 5,000 full-text documents are applied as an existing data set and the second 5,000 full-text documents as a new data set. The existing data set is used for all experiments in the beginning. The new data set is introduced in experiment 1 at iteration 10,000, experiment 2 at iteration 30,000 and experiment 3 at iteration 50,000. SOM rough-training is stopped at iteration 30,000 and its fine-tuning training is stopped at 50,000 iterations. The stop criterion of DASH is finding the objective AQE. According to our experiments, the SOM does not suffer from the new data set seriously, if the distribution of the new data set is similar to that of the existing data set or the new data set comes from the same collection of the existing data set (Table 2). In this case, the performance of the SOM is comparable to the non-stationary model, DASH.

		10,000 iterations	30,000 iterations	50,000 iterations
SOM	AQE	0.937	0.938	0.940
	Accuracy	69.06%	68.44%	69.08%
DASH90	AQE	0.771	0.780	0.802
	Accuracy	72.23%	71.42%	70.39%

Table 2. A comparison of SOM and DASH. A new data set is added to the existing data set at iteration 10,000 in experiment 1, iteration 30,000 in experiment 2 and iteration 50,000 in experiment 3. Parameters for DASH are: τ: 90%, S_{min}: 1% and β: 95%. Please note that β is an adjustable parameter during training.

4.4 Knowledge Update

In this section, we want to compare the performance of models under a non-stationary environment as well, but we treat the existing knowledge as out-of-date, which should be updated by the new knowledge, i.e. the new data set. We use the same pre-processing procedure mentioned above and use 10,000 full-text documents as our test-bed. To mimic the non-stationary data set, we use the normalized TFxIDF vector representation as our new data set but use the non-normalized TFxIDF as the existing data set. The averaged weights of the existing set are much higher than those of the new data set. Thus, the AQEs are also much higher when models deal with the existing data set. Like the strategy mentioned in the previous section, we introduce the new data set at iteration 10,000 for experiment 1, iteration 30,000 for experiment 2 and iteration 50,000 for experiment 3. According to our experiments, the SOM clearly suffers from the decayed learning rate (Table 3). The new data samples are not learnt completely, so the accuracy drops while the AQE increases. On the other hand, DASH removes all unsuitable trained units very fast and adjusts its new objective AQE automatically. Thus, there is no big difference between the performance at each point when a new data set is introduced during training for DASH.

		10,000 iterations	30,000 iterations	50,000 iterations
SOM	AQE	0.948	1.352	2.513
	Accuracy	64.37%	21.52%	25.75%
DASH90	AQE	0.784	0.776	0.793
	Accuracy	71.40%	72.25%	69.30%

Table 3. A comparison of SOM and DASH. A new data set substitutes for the existing data set at iteration 10,000 in experiment 1, iteration 30,000 in experiment 2 and iteration 50,000 in experiment 3. Parameters for DASH are: τ: 90%, S_{min}: 1% and β: 95%. Please note that β is an adjustable parameter during training.

4.5 An Analysis of the Non-Stationary and Hierarchical DASH

We use the second experiment in the previous section, which updates the existing data set at iteration 30,000 to further the analysis of our model. Please note that a 15×15 SOM is used in this experiment. The DASH starts with 2 units and adjusts its architecture and parameters based on the current data set. The DASH satisfies the objective AQE by developing 23 sub-maps. A part of the hierarchical structure is shown in (Figure 2). The concepts of units in a neighbourhood are similar. We use two terms whose weights are the most significant to represent the labels of the unit in the root map and use the second and third significant terms to represent its child map. Thus, a unit of the map in the lower layer of a hierarchy is associated with more terms, which represent news articles with more specific concepts.

In the beginning of the training stage, the SOM has a smaller AQE because the number of units is much larger than that of the DASH (Figure 3a). However, the AQE of the DASH is smaller than that of the SOM from iteration 8,000 (Figure 3). At this point, the DASH only contains 34 units while the SOM has 255 units (Figure 4a). When the existing data set is replaced by the new data set, the AQEs of both models are much smaller. Based on the criterion of the AQE, the DASH outperforms the SOM.

The non-stationary learning feature of the DASH can be illustrated by Figure 4. The DASH adjusts its architecture by the unit-growing and global connection-trimming functions. The number of units for the DASH is continuously growing in general. When the existing data set is replaced by the new data set at iteration 30,000, many unsuitable units are removed (Figure 4a). This is performed by the connection-trimming variable, β. We set an initial value of 95% for β. It is adjusted automatically based on the current data set. The final value of β is about 0.4 (Figure 4b). Some non-stationary competitive models such as GNG-U and GWR have been tried in these experiments. However, it is not possible to use their unit-pruning and connection-trimming constant thresholds for both data sets. When a proper threshold is set for the existing data set, this threshold is always too large for the new data set. Thus, models do not grow. Conversely, if a threshold is suitable for the new data set, this threshold is always too small for the existing data set. However, we should not set such a threshold by presuming the distribution of the new data set. Therefore, we only present our model and SOM in these experiments.

The Root Map of the DASH

yen mi	yen specify		yen billion	billion crown	crown billion	profit crown	profit earnings	profit earnings		net loss	net share
			franc billion							share dividend	share net
			franc swiss			yuan million	yuan million		rupee share		share rupee
beat game		sept latest	budget sept			yuan million	percent mark		markka singapore		share rupee
			officer chief		tax hotel	hotel percent	percent hotel	pct percent			peso rate
play match		drug company	softw are company			gold hotel		pct pc	pct pc		
		drug study	tobacco company	tobacco company			cattle source		pct bank		rate bank
england test			airline tobacco	tobacco pow er						bank rate	bank rate
iraq mother	nuclear treaty	china nuclear	airline european			import oil		coffee crude			bond bank
iraq king	china taiw an	china court		port cargo		oil tonne		cent coffee			bond coupon
		court minister				tonne gas		tonne wheat			bond coupon
police refugee	police rebel	minister russian	minister election	clinton minister		gas british	tonne rice	tonne wheat	wheat tonne		trader price

Oil and Tonne

tonne price	tonne crude	import tonne		chinese petroleum	chinese petroleum	company chinese
		win million				company percent
gas output	gas tonne	gas tonne	gas tonne	gas crude		company tender
		gas field		company field		
field crude			field petroleum		company iran	iran company
oil production	field production	field barrel	field barrel	barrel field	venture energy	energy venture

Figure 2. A part of the hierarchical structure of a DASH. The two most significant terms are the shown in the upper map and the second and third most significant terms are show in its child map.

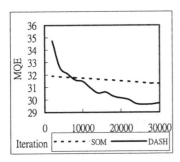
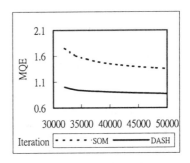

Figure 3. a) AQEs of SOM and DASH for the existing data set   b) AQEs of SOM and DASH for the new data set

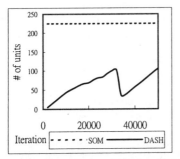
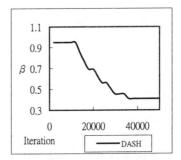

Figure 4. a) Units of SOM and DASH   b) The β parameter of DASH

5 Conclusion

In this paper, we have presented a new type of self-organising dynamic growing neural network which can deal with non-stationary data sets and represent the inner data structure by a hierarchical view. In terms of the concept, DASH is a hybrid model of GHSOM and GNG. It contains several unique features, such as parameter self-adjustment, hierarchical training and continuous learning. Based on these features, a real-world document clustering task has been demonstrated in this paper. We also analyse the deficiencies of current models. Those models which are designed for the non-stationary data sets may not be suitable for clustering a real-world task. The main reason is the difficulty of determining constant unit-pruning and connection-trimming parameters. Furthermore, those non-stationary models should not use a time-dependent stop criterion. For more complex data sets, such as a document collection, a hierarchical structure is preferable. This hierarchical training also benefits from a distributed model which trains several small maps separately instead of a huge map. That is, the DASH is a new hierarchical neural model which functions as a non-stationary distribution learning facility.

References

1. Honkela, T., Kaski, S., Lagus, K., and Kohonen, T. Newsgroup exploration with WEBSOM method and browsing interface. Report A32, Helsinki University of Technology, 1996
2. Kohonen, T. Self-organization and associative memory. Springer-Verlag, Berlin, 1984

3. Grossberg, S. Adaptive pattern classification and universal recoding: I. Parallel development and coding of neural feature detectors. Biological Cybernetics, 1976, 23:121-131

4. Martinetz, T. and Schulten, K. A 'Neural-Gas' network learns topologies. Artificial Neural Network, 1991, 1:397-402

5. Fritzke, B. Growing grid-a self-organizing network with constant neighborhood range and adaptation strength. Neural Processing Letters, 1995, 2(5):9-13

6. Fritzke, B. Growing cell structures – a self-organizing network for unsupervised and supervised learning. Neural Networks, 1994, 7(9):1441-1460

7. Fritzke, B. A growing neural gas network learns topologies. Advances in Neural Information Processing Systems 7, Tesauro, G., Touretzky, D.S. and Leen, T.K. (Eds) , MIT Press, Cambridge MA, 1995: 625-632

8. Blackmore, J. and Miikkulainen, R. Incremental grid growing: encoding high-dimensional structure into a two-dimensional feature map. Proceedings of the IEEE International Conference on Neural Networks (ICNN'93), 1993

9. Alahakoon, D., Halgamuge, S.K., and Srinivasan, B. Dynamic self-organizing maps with controlled growth for knowledge discovery. IEEE Tractions on Neural Networks, 2000, 11(3):601-614

10. Hodge, V. and Austin, J. Hierarchical growing cell structures: TreeGCS. Proceedings of the Fourth International Conference on Knowledge-Based Intelligent Engineering Systems, 2000

11. Chen, H., Schuffels, C. and Orwig, R. Internet categorization and search: a self-organizing approach. Journal of Visual Communication and Image Representation, 1996, 7(1):88-102

12. Rauber, A., Merkl, D. and Dittenbach, M. The growing hierarchical self-organizing maps: exploratory analysis of high-dimensional data. IEEE Transactions on Neural Networks, 2002, 13(6):1331-1341

13. Fritzke, B. A self-organizing network that can follow non-stationary distributions. Proceedings of ICANN-97, International Conference on Artificial Neural Networks, Springer, 1997:613-618

14. Lang, R. and Warwick, K. The plastic self organising map. IEEE World Congress on Computational Intelligence, 2002

15. Marsland, S., Shapiro, J. and Nehmzow, U. A self-organising network that grows when required. Neural Networks, 2002, 15:1041-1058

16. Kohonen, T. Self-organizing maps. Springer-Verlag, 2001

17. Martinetz, T.M. Competitive Hebbian learning rule forms perfectly topology preserving maps. International Conference on Artificial Neural Networks, ICANN'93, Amsterdam, 1993:427-434

18. Wermter, S. and Hung, C. Selforganizing Classification on the Reuters News Corpus. COLING2002, 19th International Conference on Computational Linguistics, Taipei, Taiwan, 2002:1086-1092

19. Salton, G. Automatic Text Processing: the Transformation, Analysis, and Retrieval of Information by Computer. Addison-Wesley, USA, 1989

20. Miller, G.A. WordNet: a dictionary browser. Proceedings of the First International Conference on Information in Data, 1985

21. Chakrabarti, S. Data mining for hypertext: a tutorial survey. ACM SIGKDD Explorations, 2000, 1(2):1-11

22. Kohonen, T., Kaski, S., Lagus, K., Salojärvi, J., Honkela, J., Paatero, V. and Saarela, A. Self organization of a massive document collection. IEEE Transactions on Neural Networks, 2000, 11(3):574-585

23. Salton, G. and Buckley, C. Term-weighting approaches in automatic text retrieval. Information Processing & Management, 1988, 24(5):513-523

POLYNOMIAL-FUZZY DECISION TREE STRUCTURES FOR CLASSIFYING MEDICAL DATA.

Ernest Muthomi Mugambi[1], Dr Andrew Hunter[2], Dr Giles Oatley[1], and Prof Lee Kennedy[1]

[1] Sunderland University (Computer Science Dept, Science Lab, South Rd Durham DH1 3LE)
[2] Durham University
ernest.mugambi@dur.ac.uk

Abstract. Decision tree induction has been studied extensively in machine learning as a solution for classification problems. The way the linear decision trees partition the search space is found to be comprehensible and hence appealing to data modelers. Comprehensibility is an important aspect of models used in medical data mining as it determines model credibility and even acceptability. In the practical sense though, inordinately long decision trees compounded by replication problems detracts from comprehensibility. This demerit can be partially attributed to their rigid structure that is unable to handle complex non-linear or/and continuous data. To address this issue we introduce a novel hybrid multivariate decision tree composed of polynomial, fuzzy and decision tree structures. The polynomial nature of these multivariate trees enable them to perform well in non-linear territory while the fuzzy members are used to squash continuous variables. By trading-off comprehensibility and performance using a multi-objective genetic programming optimization algorithm, we can induce polynomial-fuzzy decision trees (PFDT) that are smaller, more compact and of better performance than their linear decision tree (LDT) counterparts. In this paper we discuss the structural differences between PFDT and LDT (C4.5) and compare the size and performance of their models using medical data.

Keywords: Decision tree; Comprehensibility; Performance; Multiobjective genetic programming.

1   Introduction

Decision trees have been popularly univariate (also known as axis-parallel) in nature which implies that they use splits based on a single attribute at each internal node. Although several methods have been developed for constructing multivariate trees, this body of work is not well-known [1]. Most of the work on multivariate splits considers linear (oblique) trees [2][10]. The problem of finding an optimal linear split is known to be intractable [11] hence the need to find good, albeit suboptimal, linear splits. While there exist methods used for finding good linear splits ranging from linear discriminant analysis [12], hill-climbing search [13] to perceptron training [14], the use of evolutionary algorithms which are known to be powerful global search mechanisms, is little-known. In this paper, we use a genetic programming algorithm to optimize polynomial-fuzzy decision structures.

For many practical tasks, the trees produced by tree-generation algorithms are not comprehensible to users due to their size and complexity. It is desirable that the classifier "provide insight and understanding into the predictive structure of the data" [24] as well as explanations of its individual predictions [15]; in medical data mining such characteristics are a prerequisite for model acceptability and credibility. It can be argued that the incomprehensibility of some models is caused by the model induction process being primarily based on predictive accuracy or performance [6]. To address this concern, we use a multi-objective genetic programming algorithm to optimize decision trees for both classification performance and comprehensibility, without discriminating against either of them. There is a lack of a proper empirically tested theory on comprehensibility; the comprehensibility ideas used are based on some limited studies in the literature [17][18].

2 Decision trees

Decision trees are a way to represent underlying data hierarchically by recursively partitioning the data [24][25]. The decision tree formalism has been found to be intuitively appealing and comprehensible because the way they perform classification by a sequence of tests is easy for a domain expert to understand. For this reason among others, decision trees have found their way into many a data mining researcher's / practitioner's tool box. There are three main types of decision trees based on how they partition the feature space :

Univariate or axis-parallel decision tree - This type of decision trees carry out tests on a single variable at each non-leaf node. Their mode of splitting the data is equivalent to using axis-parallel hyperplanes in the feature space.

Multivariate linear or oblique - The tests are geometrically equivalent to hyperplanes at an oblique orientation to the axis of the feature space.

Non-linear multivariate decision trees - They perform non-linear partitioning of the feature space by constructive induction.

Linear decision trees(C4.5) belong to the axis-parallel class of decision trees while our polynomial-fuzzy decision tree (PFDT) models are more akin to the non-linear multivariate type of trees.

3 Structure of polynomial-fuzzy decision tree (PFDT)

The polynomial-fuzzy decision tree is a hybrid model comprising three different structures:

Polynomial structures - Polynomial function are of the form : $a_n x^n + a_{n-1} x^{n-1} + \ldots\ldots + a_2 x^2 + a_1 x + a_0$

Decision tree structures - This constitutes a novel *soft-if* operator envisaged and used by Hunter [8]. *soft-if* is a decision tree structure mathematically defined as: $\phi(x_i - c_i)x_{i+1} + (1 - \phi(x_i - c_i))x_{i+2}$ where $i > 0$, x_i represents attribute values, ϕ is a sigmoid operator $- \phi(x) = 1/(1 + \exp^{-x})$ and c_i are coefficients.

Fuzzy membership functions - These operators are used to squash continuous variables. Several membership functions such as sigmoid and bell-shaped functions are used.

4 Comparison between the polynomial-fuzzy decision trees(PFDT) and linear decision trees(LDT)

4.1 Comprehensibility

Linear or univariate trees are, in the raw form, clearly the simplest and most comprehensible of the decision trees structures. But due to their inability to handle non-linear feature spaces they compensate by using more splits – a feature that affects their comprehensibility. PFDT are more complex in structure. The polynomial nature of PFDT gives them the power and compactness to express very complex non-linear relationships using very few internal and leaf nodes.

One major setback, for linear decision trees comprehensibility, is a condition known as sub-tree replication. It is characterized by repeated occurrence of the same sub-tree in several disjuncts of the decision tree. Sub-tree replication increases the complexity of the tree structure. PFDT are devoid of this phenomenon.

4.2 Performance

Linear decision trees are known to perform well in small and linear feature spaces but very poorly in large and non-linear ones. PFDT should perform better in non-linear territory primarily because they have the mechanism to handle non-linearity. Another feature that acts as an impetus for PFDT is constructive feature induction [3]. This enables them to combine features that are better conjunctively than on their own. The discriminant capability provided by constructive induction creates new ground upon which the feature space can be partitioned and could therefore improve performance [6]. Fuzzy membership functions are used in PFDT on continuous variables and tend to create a level ground for all the variables. The lack of this capability in LDT creates an induction bias in favor of continuous attributes. Large continuous variables have to be split many times which translates to longer tree structures and increases probability of sub-tree replication.

4.3 Model simplification

Most induction models aspire to improve comprehensibility by model simplification either for its own sake or to improve performance, or both [20][21][22][23] ; it is generally accepted that simpler models usually have better generalization [26][27]. A review on decision tree literature [6] indicates that there are five main criteria for simplifying decision tree structure

1. controlling tree size by pre-pruning or post-pruning (editing).
2. modifying the space of states(trees) searched.
3. modifying the search algorithm used.
4. restricting the data either by removing cases or certain features from being considered by the search algorithm.
5. translating the tree structure into another data structure such as a set of rules.

Simplification of linear decision trees usually comes in the form of controlling tree-size either by pre-pruning or post-pruning or incrementally resizing the induced trees. Pre-pruning entails imposing a non-trivial stopping criterion on tree expansion while post-pruning involves editing the induced trees. One shortcoming of using this simplification method is that it might occur at the expense of performance. The PFDT exhibits the third tree simplification criterion which involves modifying the search algorithm such that it is carried out along two non-dominating fronts; size and performance. The tree size of the PFDT models can also be controlled by fixing the maximum size/depth of trees searched.

5 Structure and Comprehensibility

Despite model comprehensibility being at the center of model credibility and acceptability in medical data mining there is a clear lack of a scientific methodology of characterizing and measuring it. We shall restrict our definition of comprehensibility to the ability of users to understand the solutions accrued from decision tree models. It is generally accepted that model comprehensibility is affected by model complexity - determined by syntactic and semantic simplicity/complexity [17] - and the ability of the model to offer explanation [18]. We shall only concentrate on the aspects of model complexity that affect comprehensibility:

Syntactic simplicity - This refers to the size of a pattern or number of interacting terms in a model; also known as complexity. Most models, including linear decision trees, attempt to augment comprehensibility by inducing smaller models (pre-pruning) or trimming the induced models (post-pruning). There are two ways of controlling syntactic simplicity in PFDT : by trading-off size and performance (see section 8), smaller sized models that are of good performance are encouraged and controlling the size (depth) of the individuals in the initial generation of the genetic programming optimization.

Semantic simplicity - This is a lesser used aspect of model complexity borrowed from fuzzy inference [17]; the type and order of operators / structures used in the model. While this notion does not affect linear decision trees by virtue of having a homogenous structure, it is highly pertinent to our hybrid PFDT models. In order to improve this aspect, the model is structured in such a way that the decision tree structures (soft-if) are at the top followed by polynomial structures (* and + operators) and lastly the fuzzy membership functions are relegated to the leaf nodes at the bottom of the tree. Fig 10 illustrates a structured(a) and unstructured(b) PFDT model.

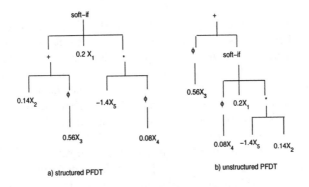

a) structured PFDT

b) unstructured PFDT

NB. ϕ represents a logistic fuzzy membership function

Fig. 1. Structured and unstructured PFDT models.

6   Genetic Programming(GP)

PFDT is optimized using a genetic programming algorithm [28]. Genetic programming is a global, random search method for solving genetic tree-like programs. It is suitable for solving NP-hard computational problems such as those that arise in non-linear decision tree modelling [30]. GP has been successful in such areas as symbolic regression[28], pattern recognition [29] and concept learning [32] among others. GP offers a very natural and versatile way to represent the hybrid structures the likes used in the PFDT models [31]. GP uses several operators such as *crossover* and *mutation* to optimize the expression tree.

7   Coefficient Optimization

While GP is good at optimizing the structure of the tree, it is known to be deficient in the capability to optimize the coefficients in the expression tree

[8]. We have incorporated a Quasi-Newton optimization [33] technique to augment the power of the GP coefficient optimization. This technique uses an error propagation algorithm that efficiently calculates the gradient of the error function with respect to the coefficients embedded in the GP expression tree. In order to calculate these gradients, the structures that contain the coefficients have to be differentiable. For this reason among others, linear decision tree structures cannot be incorporated into our PFDT system and hence the need to improvise using *soft-if* structures that closely emulate LDT features and are differentiable.

8 Multi-objective Optimization(MOO)

At the heart of the genetic programming algorithm is the multi-objective optimization which ensures that the search is carried out along two "conflicting" fronts. Multi-objective optimization is defined as "a vector of decision variables which satisfies constraints and optimizes a vector function whose elements represent the objective functions". Most linear decision trees use either classification performance or model size as the sole objective of the induction process. While performance is an important objective, other characteristics such as tree size and comprehensibility might not be any less important. MOO therefore offers a suitable way to optimize PFDT without discriminating against any of the objectives by using *Pareto optimality* concept. According to this concept a feature solution A is better than B if A is better than B in at least one objective and not worse-off in any of the remaining objectives. A set of solutions, where none is better than any other, is known as a *non-dominated set* and if such a set dominates all other solutions, it is referred to as the *Pareto front*. MOO algorithms [7][19] attempt to find this *Pareto front*.

There are two main objectives we are interested in: tree size and classification performance. Tree size is a straightforward measure of the size of the decision tree, which we aim to minimize. It is accepted that smaller decision tree are more comprehensible and have better generalization capabilities. The second objective we mean to maximize is classification performance, which is measured using the Receiver Operating Characteristic curve [9], *sensitivity* [3] and *specificity* [4] measures. ROC is a standard technique, widely used in medical applications, which characterizes the performance of a classifier as the decision threshold is altered, by trading-off the *sensitivity* versus *1-specificity*.

9 PFDT Optimization Algorithm

PFDT is optimized using a multi-objective genetic programming algorithm(MOGP). MOGP algorithm commences with the initialization of the PFDT structures

---

[3] percentage of positively classified instances that the classifier gets right.
[4] percentage of negatively classified instances that the classifier gets right.

in the form of genetic programming expression trees. The trees are *strongly-typed* to ensure that only specific orders of operators are allowed (see section 5). This is in line with the need to develop perspicuous tree structures. Although the generation of terminals and non-terminals is purely random, there are strict controls to ensure that the expression trees are valid. During initialization the training set is also set to half the data set, the cross validated test set is set to the remaining data set and the terminals set to the attributes contained in the data set. After initialization the initial population is evaluated and the *elite set* which is made up of the "best" individuals of that population is constituted. MOGP is an elitist evolutionary algorithm but great caution is taken to ensure that the elite set does not have undue influence on the ability of the algorithm to explore diverse feature spaces. The selection of the elite is based on two objectives: the performance on the Receiver Operating Characteristic curve and the size of the decision tree. The *Pareto optimality* concept is used for the multi-objective evaluation after the coefficient optimization of the expression tree. The *mating pool* is made up of individuals from population and the elite set chosen by binary tournament selection where the winner is determined by *fitness sharing*. Reproduction is carried out by the mating pool using *crossover* and *mutation*. Crossover and mutation operations are strictly controlled to ensure that they give valid offsprings.

10 Experiments and Results

After conducting many experiments using the algorithm, the following control parameters for the algorithm were arrived at (see Table 1). Experiments were conducted on two different medical data sets; Diabetes and Trauma. The two data sets are different fundamentally since they address different medical conditions and structurally in terms of number of instances and attributes (continuous and discrete).

The Diabetes data set constitutes 2304 records of patients that attend a diabetic clinic. Each patient corresponds to a record in the data set. Each record contains readings taken from the patients and their medical history. The 29 patient attributes constitute factors that are associated with Diabetes and the type of complications the patients may have suffered in the period they have had diabetes. The aim of this classification exercise is to build decision tree models that can predict patients whose diabetic status is likely to deteriorate leading to complications that are normally associated with the disease. The training set is made up of 1300 cases while the test set constitutes the remaining 1004 cases.

The graph 2 shows the performance of PFDT algorithm along the generations peaking at the 90th generation.

At the end of a run, MOGP gives a range of non-dominating solutions that comprise the elite set. Moreover, since all the individuals in the population are stored, it is possible to process all the individuals in the population

Table 1. MOGP Settings

Population	100
Non-dominated set size	25
Tournament size	2
Dominance group size	10
Generations	200
Crossover rate	0.3
Mutation rate	0.3

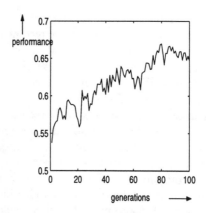

Fig. 2. Generational Performance of MOGP.

finding the best models in any given complexity (model size) level. Fig 3 shows ROC (Receiver operating characteristic) curves for the best models at various complexities.

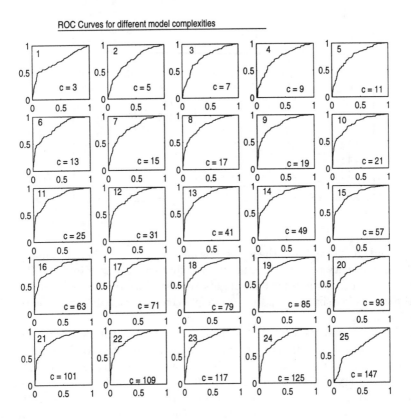

Fig. 3. ROC Performance of PFDT models at different complexity levels. $C = $ *complexity*.

We now compare the performance of PFDT and LDT(C4.5). The comparison is based on the model size and performance; measured by *sensitivity* and *specificity* respectively. Where there are no performance values (indicated by '-') there is no model of the corresponding size. Table 2 shows some, but not all, sensitivity and specificity values for PFDT and C4.5 models.

To compare the capability of PFDT and C4.5 to trade-off size and performance, refer to Fig 4. From the graph it is evident that PFDT is capable of inducing better models in terms of size and performance. All the PFDT models fall in the model size range of 3-149 compared to the C4.5's 55-313. PFDT models as small as 30 and 39 outperform the best C4.5 models which

Table 2. Comparing PFDT and C4.5 Models

Model No	Model Size	C4.5	Model Size	PFDT
1	-	-	3	0.337,0.877
2	-	-	11	0.748,0.603
3	-	-	21	0.599,0.816
4	-	-	31	0.653,0.801
5	-	-	39	0.708,0.743
6	55	0.790,0.640	55	0.663,0.745
7	65	0.780,0.650	65	0.743,0.668
8	93	0.698,0.641	93	0.719,0.673
9	119	0.780,0.620	117	0.798,0.615
10	-	-	125	0.724,0.727
11	173	0.740,0.610	-	-
12	203	0.739,0.607	-	-
13	229	0.736,0.587	-	-
14	259	0.726,0.568	-	-
15	313	0.718,0.554	-	-

are 55 and 65 in size. From the graph it is also evident that there is a marginal possibility of very poor performing models finding their way into the PFDT elite set, a phenomenon that highlights the difficulty of the multi-objective optimization consistently inducing models that are globally superior in all the feature spaces.

We also compared the two models using Trauma Survival data. The aim of the excercise is to predict the survival of patients admitted to Trauma units. Although the Trauma data set consists of over 15,000 cases we could only manage to carry out experiments with 3,000 cases (2,000 for training and the rest for testing the models) due to time constraints. With only 8 attributes, the Trauma data set is much smaller than Diabetes data set. A smaller data set favours C4.5; fewer partitions/splits hence a smaller tree, more than the PFDT which is a feature selection algorithm. Fig 5 compares the capability of the two models to trade-off performance and complexity. As suspected, a C4.5 model (size 13 and performance 0.9) outperforms all the PFDT models. PFDT though, produces more models (with more diversity) that perform very well and with smaller complexity levels than C4.5. The importance of having diverse solutions in terms of complexity and composition cannot be overemphasized because medical data collection is costly, time-consuming and at times invasive.

11   Conclusion

We have introduced a structured non-linear fuzzy multi-objective decision tree model (PFDT) that is optimized using genetic programming. We have also compared the structure and performance between it and linear decision

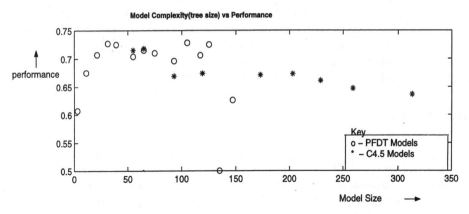

Fig. 4. Complexity vs Performance trade-off of PFDT and C4.5 models using *Diabetes data*.

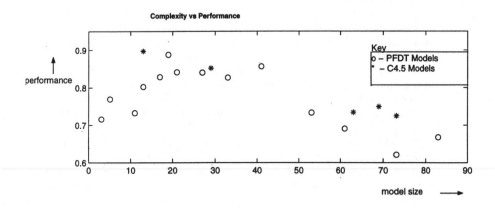

Fig. 5. Complexity vs Performance trade-off of PFDT and C4.5 models using *Trauma data*.

tree (C4.5). As expected PFDT trades-off performance and complexity better than C4.5 when used on the larger data set (Diabetes) and relatively well on Trauma data. Due to the lack of a proper scientific theory on comprehensibility we had to contend with carrying out our comparative analysis based on model complexity (size) and performance. In future we intend to research more on methods that can be used to measure model comprehensibility in a bid to make such comparative work more beneficial.

References

[1]   S. K Murthy. Automatic construction of decision trees from data: a multidisciplinary survey. *Kluwer academic publishers, Boston.1-49, 1998.*

[2]   A. Ittner and M. Schlosser. Discovery of relevant new features by generating non-linear decision trees. *Proc. of 2nd International Conference on Knowledge Discovery and Data Mining, 108-113.AAAI Press, Menlo Park, CA, Portland, Oregon, USA,1996.*

[3]   A. Ittner. Non-linear decision trees NDT. *International conference on machine learning, 1996.*

[4]   N. Nikolaev and V. Slavov. Concepts of inductive genetic programming. *EuroGP:First European workshop on genetic programming, lecture notes in computer science. LNCS 1391, Springer, Berlin,1998, pp.49-59.*

[5]   M.C.J Bot and W.B. Langdon. Application of genetic programming to induction of linear classification trees. *EuroGP 2000:European conference, Edindburgh, Scotland, UK, April 2000.*

[6]   L.A Breslow and D.W. Aha. Simplifying decision trees: a survey. *Navy Center for Applied Research in Knowledge Engineering Review Technical Report, 1998.*

[7]   C. Emmanouillidis. Evolutionary multi-objective feature selection and ROC analysis with applocation to industrial machinery fault diagnosis. *Evolutionary methods for design, optimization and control, Barcelona 2002.*

[8]   A. Hunter. Expression Inference - genetic symbolic classification integrated with non-linear coefficient optimization. *AISC 2002:117-127.*

[9]   J. Hanley and B. McNeill. The meaning and use of the area under a receiver operator characteristic curve. *Diagn.Radiology, 143;29-36, (1982).*

[10] A. Ittner, J. Zeidler, R. Rossius, W. Dilger and M. Schlosser. Feature space partitioning by non-Linear and fuzzy decision trees. *Chemnitz University of Technology, Department of Computer Science, Chemnitz, 1997.*

[11] L. Hyafil and R.L. Rivest. Constructing optimal binary decision trees is NP-complete. *Information Processing Letters, 5(1):15-17, 1976.*

[12] W. Loh and N. Vanichsetakul. Tree structured classification via generalized discriminant analysis. *J.of the American Statistical Association,83(403):715-728,1988.*

[13] S. Murthy, S. Kasif, S. Salzberg and R. Beigel. A system for induction of oblique decision trees. *J. of Artificial Intelligence Research, 2:1-33, August 1994.*

[14] S.E Hampson and D.J. Volper. Linear function neurons:Structure and training. *Biological Cybernetics, 53(4):203-217, 1986.*

[15] D. Michie. Inducing knowledge from data; First Principles. *Unpublished manuscript for a talk given at the Seventh International Conference on Machine Learning.Austin, Texas.*

[16] L. Breiman, J.H. Friedman, R.A. Olshen, and C.J. Stone. Classification and regression trees. *Belmont, CA:Wadsworth International Group.*

[17] C. Pena-Reyes, and M. Sipper. Fuzzy CoCo:Balancing accuracy and interpretability of fuzzy models by means of coevolution. *Logic Systems Laboratory, Swiss Federal Institute of Technology in Lausanne, CH-1015 Lausanne, Switzerland.*

[18] N. Lavrac. Selected techniques for data mining in medicine. *Artificial Intelligence in Medicine 16(1999) 3-23.*

[19] A. Hunter. Using multiobjective genetic programming to infer logistic polynomial regression models. *15th European Conference on Artificial Intelligence, Lyon, France, 2002.*

[20] M. Bohanec, and I. Bratko. Trading accuracy for simplicity in decision tree. *Machine Learning, 15:223-250, 1994.*

[21] J.J. Oliver, and D.J. Hand. On pruning and averaging decision trees. *Proceedings of the 12th International Machine Learning Conference(pp.430-437).Tahoe City, CA:Morgan Kaufmann, 1995.*

[22] L.B. Holder. Intermediate decision trees. *Proceedings of Fourteenth International Joint Conference on Artificial Intelligence(pp.1056-1063). Montreal:Morgan Kaufmann, 1995.*

[23] G.I. Webb. Further experimental evidence against the utility of Occam's razor. *JAIR, 4, pp.397-417, 1996.*

[24] L. Breiman, J.H. Friedman, R.A. Olsen, and C.J. Stone. Classification and regression trees. *Belmont,CA:Wadsworth International Group,1984.*

[25] J.R. Quinlan. Induction of decision trees. *Machine Learning, 1:81-106, 1986.*

[26] A. Blumer, A. Ehrnfecht, A. Hausler and M.K. Warmuth. Occam's razor. *Information processing letters, 24:377-380, 1987.*

[27] J. Risannen. Stochastic complexity modelling. *Ann.Statist, 14:1080-1100, 1986.*

[28] J.R. Koza. Genetic Programming: On the Programming of Computers by Means of Natural Selection. *MIT Press, Cambridge, MA, USA, 1992.*

[29] K. Krawiec. Genetic programming using partial order of solutions for pattern recognition. *Proceedings of II National Conference 'Computer Recognition Systems' KOSYR2001, pp. 427-433.*

[30] N.I. Nikolaev and V. Slavov. Inductive genetic programming with decision trees. *Intelligent Data Analysis 2(1998) 31-44.*

[31] R.V. Katya and P.J. Fleming. Multiobjective genetic programming: A nonlinear system identification application. *Electronics Letters, 34(9), pp. 930-931.*

[32] K.C. Tan, Q. Yu, C.M Cheng and T.H. Lee. Evolutionary computing for knowledge discovery in medical diagnosis. *Artificial Intelligence in medicine 27(2003) 129-154.*

[33] C.M. Bishop. Neural Networks for PatternRecognition. *Oxford University Press, 1995.*

A Comparison of Generic Machine Learning Algorithms for Image Classification

Raphaël Marée, Pierre Geurts, Giorgio Visimberga [†],
Justus Piater, Louis Wehenkel
Montefiore Institute, University of Liège
Liège, Belgium
http://www.montefiore.ulg.ac.be/~maree/

[†] On leave from Politecnico Di Bari
Bari, Italy

Abstract

In this paper, we evaluate 7 machine learning algorithms for image classification including our recent approach that combines building of ensembles of extremely randomized trees and extraction of sub-windows from the original images. For the approach to be generic, all these methods are applied directly on pixel values without any feature extraction. We compared them on four publicly available datasets corresponding to representative applications of image classification problems: handwritten digits (MNIST), faces (ORL), 3D objects (COIL-100), and textures (OUTEX). A comparison with studies from the computer vision literature shows that generic methods can come remarkably close to specialized methods. In particular, our sub-window algorithm is competitive with the state of the art, a remarkable result considering its generality and conceptual simplicity.

1 Introduction

Image classification is an important problem which appears in many application domains like quality control, biometry (face recognition), medicine, office automation (character recognition), geology (soil type recognition)...

This problem is particularly difficult for traditional machine learning algorithms mainly because of the high number of input variables that may describe images (i.e. pixels). Indeed, with a high number of variables, learning methods often suffer from a high variance (models are very unstable) which deteriorates their accuracy. Futhermore, computing times can also be detrimental in such extreme conditions. To handle this high dimensionality, image classication systems usually rely on a pre-processing step, specific to the particular problem and application domain, which aims at extracting a reduced set of interesting features from the initial huge number of pixels. The limitation of this approach is clear: When considering a new problem or application domain, it is necessary

At the same time, recent advances in automatic learning have produced new methods which are able to handle more and more complex problems without requiring any a priori information about the application. These methods are increasingly competitive with methods specifically tailored for these domains. In this context, our aim in this paper is to compare several of these recent algorithms for the specific problem of image classification. Our hypothesis is that it will be possible to obtain with some of these approaches competitive results with specialized algorithms without requiring any laborious, manual pre-processing step.

In this goal, our approach was to choose several problems which we think are representative of the image classification domain and then to apply several learning algorithms on each of these problems, without any specific pre-processing, i.e. by directly using the pixel values. Among recent learning algorithms potentially able to handle this complex problem, we have chosen a panel of 7 algorithms, including one generic approach that we have recently proposed for image classification [17]. These algorithms will be compared essentially on two criteria: accuracy of the models and computational efficiency (of the learning and test phases). Although several of these algorithms have been already applied to image classification, usually these studies either do not compare several algorithms or are focused on only one particular application problem.

The paper is structured as follows. In Section 2, we briefly describe the machine learning algorithms chosen for our comparison. Of course, we spend more time on the description of our own proposal. The essential characteristics of the four datasets used for the comparison are summarized in Section 3. The experimentation protocols and the results of the experiments are discussed in Section 4. We end the paper with our conclusions and discusssions about future work directions.

2 Algorithms for generic image classification

The input of a generic learning algorithm for image classification is a training set of pre-classified images,

$$LS = \{(A^i, c^i), i = 1, \ldots, N\}$$

where A^i is a $W_x \times W_y$ matrix describing the image and $c^i \in \{1, \ldots, M\}$ is its classification (among M classes). The elements $a_{k,l}^i$ of A^i ($k = 1, \ldots, W_x$, $l = 1, \ldots, W_y$) describe image pixels at location (k, l) by means of an integer value in the case of grey level images or by means of 3 integer RGB values in the case of color images.

Then, to handle information from pixels without any pre-processing, the learning algorithm should be able to deal efficiently with a large amount of data, first in terms of the number of images and classes of images in the learning set, but more importantly in terms of the number of values describing these images (i.e. the attributes). Assuming for example that $W_x = W_y = 128$, there are already $128 * 128 = 16384$ integer values describing images and this number is further multiplied by 3 if colors are taken into account.

We describe below seven classification algorithms that we think could work in such difficult conditions and that we have compared in our experiments. The common characteristics of these methods is that they are essentially non parametric and that they can efficiently handle very large input spaces.

2.1 Decision trees

Decision tree induction [3] is one of the most popular learning algorithms with nice characteristics of interpretability, efficiency, and flexibility. However, the accuracy of this algorithm is often not competitive with other learning methods due to its high variance [9]. In this study, we therefore do not expect decision trees to be satisfactory but we still evaluate it as it is the basis of other promising and recent algorithms.

2.2 Ensemble of decision trees

Ensemble methods are very popular in machine learning. These methods improve an existing learning algorithm by combining the predictions of several models obtained by perturbing either the learning set or the learning algorithm parameters. They are very effective in combination with decision trees that otherwise are often not competitive with other learning algorithms in terms of accuracy. Several ensemble methods have been applied to image classification problems, either in combination with traditional algorithms or with ad hoc computer vision system (e.g. in [7] and [12]). In this paper, we propose to compare four different ensemble methods based on decision trees. Two of these methods are the now famous bagging and boosting techniques. The two other methods, random forests and extra-trees, are two recent methods that essentially improve bagging in terms of accuracy but also in terms of computational efficiency. As the extra-trees method is our own proposal, we give below a more detailed description of it.

2.2.1 Bagging

Bagging [1] (for "boostrap aggregating") consists in drawing T boostrap learning samples from the original learning set (by random re-sampling without replacement) and then in producing from each of them a model using the classical decision tree algorithm. Then, a prediction is computed for a test instance by taking the majority class among the predictions given by the T trees for this instance.

2.2.2 Random forests

With Random Forests [2], each of the T trees is grown on a bootstrap sample of the original learning set like in bagging. But here, during tree construction, at each node of the tree, only a small number (k) of attributes randomly selected

Build_extra_tree(input: a learning sample, LS):

- If LS contains images all of the same class, return a leaf with this class associated to it;

- Otherwise:

    1. Set $[a_{k,l} < a_{th}]$=Choose_a_random_split(LS);
    2. Split LS into LS_{left} and LS_{right} according to the test $[a_{k,l} < a_{th}]$ and build the subtrees T_{left} = build_extra_tree(LS_{left}) and T_{right} = build_extra_tree(LS_{left}) from these subsets;
    3. Create a node with the test $[a_{k,l} < a_{th}]$, attach T_{left} and T_{right} as successors of this node and return the resulting tree.

Choose_a_random_split(LS):

1. Select a pixel location (k, l) at random;

2. Select a threshold a_{th} at random according to a distribution $N(\mu_{k,l}, \sigma_{k,l})$, where $\mu_{k,l}$ and $\sigma_{k,l}$ are resp. the mean and standard deviation of the pixel values $a_{k,l}$ in LS;

Table 1: Extra-tree induction algorithm for image classification

among the whole set of attributes is searched for the best test. In [2], it has been shown that random forests give better results than bagging and often yield results competitive with boosting (see below). It is also faster than these two algorithms since it requires to consider only a small subset of all attributes when developping one node of the tree.

2.2.3 Extremely randomized trees

Extremely randomized trees [9], [10] (extra-trees in short) are another ensemble method for decision trees that is extreme in terms of the randomization introduced when growing the trees of the ensemble. Indeed, an extremely randomized tree is grown by selecting at each node of the tree the parameters of the test fully at random. In the context of image classification, this yields the very simple recursive function shown in Table 1 to build an extra-tree. Several extra-trees are then built according to this algorithm and their predictions are aggregated just like in other ensemble methods. Experiments in [9] have shown that this method gives better results than bagging and is also competitive with boosting. Its main advantage with respect to other ensemble methods for decision trees is that it is also extremely fast. The complexity of the algorithm of Table 1 is independent of the number of attributes and, like other decision tree based algorithms, it is (empirically) linear with respect to the learning sample size.

2.2.4 Boosting

Boosting also builds an ensemble of decision trees but, contrary to previous ensemble methods, it produces the models sequentially and is a deterministic algorithm. It sequentially applies the learning algorithm to the original learning sample by increasing weights of misclassified instances. So, as the iteration proceeds, the models are forced to focus on the "difficult" instances. Several variants of this algorithm have been proposed in the literature. In our experiment, we will use the original algorithm, called AdaBoost.M1, described in [8] and we will apply it to decision trees.

2.3 Support Vector Machines

Support Vector Machine (SVM) is a machine learning algorithm originally motivated by advances in statistical learning theory [24]. It first applies a transformation of the initial input space into a new potentially very high dimensional transformed input space where classes are very likely to be linearly separable and then deriving a hyperplane to separate each pair of classes in this transformed input space. There exist several efficient implementations of this algorithm. In our experiment, we use the algorithm proposed in [5] with Gaussian and polynomial kernels. SVMs already gave very impressive results in terms of accuracy and computational efficiency in many complex domains including image classification problems (e.g. in [4], [11] or [23]).

2.4 Extra-trees with sub-window extraction

Even though ensemble methods with decision trees can handle a very large number of input variables efficiently (especially our extra-trees), the tree complexity (and, hence, the number of pixels that are combined along a path from the root node to a leaf in the tree) is limited by the size of the learning set. When the number of images is small compared to the total number of pixels, a tree cannot combine enough pixels to provide acceptable models. To solve this problem, we have adopted another generic approach that is popular in image classification (e.g. [13] and [6]). It artificially augments the number of images in the learning set by building models from sub-windows extracted from original images of the learning set.

Although it can be combined with any learning algorithm, we have combined this idea with extra-trees, essentially for computational efficiency reasons. In this variant, the construction of one extra-tree from the ensemble is carried out in two steps, given a window size $w_1 \times w_2$ and a number N_w:

- Extract N_w sub-windows at random from training set images (by first selecting an image at random from LS and then selecting a sub-window at a random location in this image) and assign to each sub-window the classification of its parent image;

- Grow an extra-tree to classify these N_w sub-windows by using the $w_1.w_2$ pixel values that characterize them.

Table 2: Database summary

DBs	# images	# attributes	# classes
MNIST	70000	784 $(28 * 28 * 1)$	10
ORL	400	10304 $(92 * 112 * 1)$	40
COIL-100	7200	3072 $(32 * 32 * 3)$	100
OUTEX	864	49152 $(128 * 128 * 3)$	54

To make a prediction for an image with an ensemble of extra-trees grown from sub-windows, the following procedure is used:

- Extract all possible sub-windows of size $w_1 \times w_2$ from this image;

- Assign to the image the majority class among the classes assigned to the sub-windows by the ensemble of extra-trees.

3 Four image classification problems

To evaluate the machine learning algorithms for generic image classification and to allow replication of our experiments, we selected four publicly available datasets corresponding to common image classification problems: recognition of handwritten characters (here, digits), faces, objects, and textures. The main characteristics of the datasets are summarized in Table 2 and an overview of their images is given in Figure 1. We briefly describe each problem below.

3.1 MNIST, database of handwritten digits

The MNIST database[1] [16] consists of 70000 handwritten digits that have been size-normalized and centered in images of 28 × 28 pixels with 256 grey levels per pixel. The goal is to build a model that classifies digits. Different writing styles are characterized by thin or thick strokes, slanted characters, etc.

3.2 ORL, face database

The ORL database[2] from AT&T contains faces of 40 distinct persons with 10 images per person that differ in lighting, facial expressions (open/closed eyes, smiling/not smiling), facial details (glasses/no glasses) and contain minor variations in pose. The size of each image is 92 × 112 pixels, with 256 grey levels per pixel. The goal is to identify faces.

---

[1] http://yann.lecun.com/exdb/mnist/
[2] http://www.uk.research.att.com/facedatabase.html

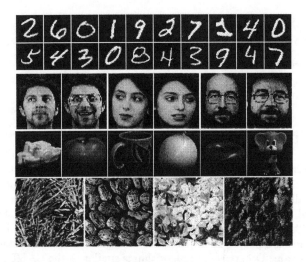

Figure 1: Overview of the four databases: MNIST, ORL, COIL-100, OUTEX

3.3 COIL-100, 3D object database

The Columbia University Object Image Library[3] COIL-100 is a dataset with colored images of 100 different objects (boxes, bottles, cups, miniature cars, etc.). Each object was placed on a motorized turntable and images were captured by a fixed camera at pose intervals of 5 degrees. This corresponds to 72 images per object. In COIL-100, each image has been normalized to 128×128 pixels and are in true color. For our experiments, we have resized the original images down to 32×32 pixels.

3.4 OUTEX, texture database

Outex[4] [21] provides a framework for the empirical evaluation of texture analysis algorithms. The Contrib_TC_0006 dataset we took from Outex has been derived from the VisTeX dataset. It contains 54 colored textures and 16 images of 128×128 pixels in true colors for each VisTex texture.

4 Experiments

In this section, the seven classification algorithms are compared on the four problems. Before describing the experimentation protocol and discussing the results, the next subsection discusses some implementation details and the way we have tuned the different parameters of the methods.

---

[3]http://www.cs.columbia.edu/CAVE/
[4]http://www.outex.oulu.fi/

4.1 Implementation and determination of the parameters

For all algorithms except for SVM, we have used our own software which is implemented in C. For SVM, we have used the LibSVM [5] package which is a C++ implementation of the algorithm presented in [5].

For each machine learning method, the values of several parameters need to be fixed. We discuss this tuning stage for each method below. For some algorithms, the values of the parameters are fixed on the basis of the resulting error on the test sample. We are aware that this would lead to slightly underestimated error rates, however, we believe that this will not be detrimental for comparison purposes, especially since the number of parameters in each method is quite small.

Classical decision trees are fully developed, i.e. without using any pruning method. The score measure used to evaluate tests during the induction is the score measure proposed in [25] which is a particuler normalization of the information gain. Otherwise our algorithm is similar to the CART method [3].

Ensemble methods all are influenced by the number of trees T which are aggregated. Usually, the more trees are aggregated, the better the accuracy. So, in our study, we have used for each problem and for each algorithm, a number of trees that appeared to be large enough to give stable error rates on the test samples. Usually, extra-trees that are more randomized requires more trees than the other variants (from 50 on MNIST to 500 on ORL and COIL-100). Extra-trees with sub-windows however are stabilized much sooner (10 trees are sufficient in all problems).

Random forests depends on an additional parameter k which is the number of attributes randomly selected at each test node. In our experiments, its value was fixed to the default value suggested by the author of the algorithm which is the square root of the total number of attributes. According to [2] this value usually gives error rates very close to the optimum.

Boosting does not depend on another parameter but it nevertheless requires that the learning algorithm does not give perfect models on the learning sample (so as to provide some misclassified instances). Hence, with this method, we used with decision trees the stop-splitting criterion described in [25]. It uses an hypothesis testing based on the G^2 statistic [14] to determine the significance of a test. In our experiments, we fixed the nondetection risk α to 0,005.

For SVM, we used LibSVM with default parameters. We tried their implementation of linear, polynomial (with degree 2 and 3) and radial basis kernel functions. Again, the best kernel was choosen on the test sample.

For extra-trees on sub-windows, additional parameters are the size of sub-windows $w1 \times w2$ and the number N_w of them extracted during the learning phase. Like for the number of trees in the ensemble, accuracy appears to be a monotonically increasing function of N_w. On the last three problems, N_w was fixed to 120000. On MNIST, as the initial learning sample size is already quite large, we further increase this number to 360000. Accuracy is on the

---

[5]http://www.csie.ntu.edu.tw/~cjlin/libsvm/

Table 3: Results on all problems

MNIST

Algorithm	Error rate
Classical Decision Tree	11.5%
Bagging ($T = 50$)	4.42%
Extra-Trees ($T = 100$)	3.17%
Random Forests ($T = 100$)	3.0%
Extra-Trees + Sub-Window	2.54%
Boosting ($T = 50$)	2.29%
SVMs (poly2)	1.95%
LeNet-4[16]	0.7%

ORL

Algorithm	Error rate
Classical Decision Tree	29.25% ± 6.89
Bagging ($T = 50$)	9.5% ± 5.7
Boosting ($T = 50$)	3.75% ± 2.79
Random Forests ($T = 200$)	1.25% ± 1.68
Extra-Trees ($T = 500$)	1.25% ± 1.68
SVMs (linear)	1.25% ± 1.25
Extra-Trees + Sub-Window	0.5% ± 1.0
-	-

COIL-100

Algorithm	Error rate
Classical Decision Tree	20.80%
Bagging ($T = 50$)	2.24%
Extra-Trees ($T = 500$)	1.96%
Random Forests ($T = 500$)	1.17%
Boosting ($T = 100$)	0.54%
SVMs (linear)	0.44%
Extra-Trees + Sub-Window	0.35%
Local Affine Frames [20]	0.1%

OUTEX

Algorithm	Error rate
Classical Decision Tree	89.35%
Bagging ($T = 50$)	73.15%
SVMs (linear)	71.99%
Boosting ($T = 50$)	69.44%
Random Forests ($T = 1000$)	66.90%
Extra-Trees ($T = 1000$)	65.05%
Extra-Trees + Sub-Window	2.78%
RGB Histograms [18]	0.2%

other hand very much influenced by the size of sub-windows. The optimal size is problem-dependent and has been tuned manually on each problem.

4.2 Protocols and results

The test protocols are discussed in this section on each problem. Results are summarized in Table 3. For each problem, the methods are sorted by decreasing error rates.

4.2.1 MNIST

In the literature, the first 60000 images are often used for learning and the remaining 10000 examples are used for validation. In [16], the results of many learning methods are reported, they range from 12% with a one-layer neural network to 0.7% with the authors' method "Boosted LeNet-4". Our results are obtained by strictly following this protocol. Error rates with generic methods vary from 11.5% with a classical decision tree to 1.95% with support vector machines. Using sub-windows, the error rate is 2.54% (with $T = 10$, $N_w = 360000$ and $w_1 = w_2 = 24$) which is less accurate than Boosting and SVM. In [4], an error rate of 1.1% was obtained with another implementation of SVM.

4.2.2 ORL

In the literature, various algorithms with pre-processing steps have been tested on this dataset, including hidden Markov models [19], convolutional neural networks [15], SVMs [11], and variants of nearest neighbors [22]. But the protocol for testing is different from one paper to another. Given the fact that this database is quite small and as there is no well-defined test protocol, our experiments use 10-fold cross-validation to provide a fair assessment of the generic methods. It means that the learning set was randomly partitioned into 10 learning samples with 360 images (9 views per subject) while the remaining images (1 view per subject) used for tests samples. Following this procedure, we get an average error rate (10 runs) of 29.25%, with a classical decision tree, down to 0.5% with our sub-windows (with $T = 10$ and $w_1 = w_2 = 32$). Random Forests, Extra-Trees, and SVM give a slightly inferior result with an average error rate of 1.25%.

4.2.3 COIL-100

This problem was approached in the literature with different methods, some of them specific to 3D object recognition, that use different matching techniques of local or global features (color histograms, eigenwindows, locale affine frames [20], etc.). For the learning sample, we took 18 views for each of the 100 objects, starting with the pose at 0 and then going on with intervals of 20. The remaining views were devoted to the test sample. Methods in the computer vision literature provide error rates from 12.5% to 0.1%. Using this protocol, classical decision tree yields an error rate of 20.80% that drops down to 0.35% with the combination of extra-trees and sub-windows (with $T = 10$ and $w1 = w2 = 16$). Boosting and SVMs are close to our approach with respectively an 0.54% and 0.44% error rate.

4.2.4 OUTEX

This dataset has a small number of objects but a very large number of attributes. The OUTEX framework precisely defines the images to use in the learning and test sample (8 images for each texture in both ensembles). The paper [18] evaluates several feature extraction techniques and image transformation methods in combination with a traditional nearest neighbors algorithm. Their resulting error rates on this dataset vary from 9.5% to 0.2%. Using the same protocol, most of the popular learning methods are especially bad with an error rate varying from 89.35% (classical decision tree) to 66.90% (random forests). Extra-trees are also not satisfactory with an error rate of 65.05% (even with $T = 1000$). On the other hand, sub-windows reduce error rates down to 2.78% (with $T = 10$ and $w1 = w2 = 4$). These results can be explained by the nature of the problem. As textures are generally based on the repetition of small patterns, one can extract small sub-windows from the original images that are quite well classified by models since they contain sufficient information to classify the whole image. This statement is further confirmed by the fact that small sub-windows of size 4×4 give the best results on this problem. On the other hand, extra-trees alone and other learning algorithms are not able to find relevant information among the high number of pixels describing the textures because the characteristics patterns are not associated with specific image locations.

4.3 Discussion

As expected, for each problem, classical decision trees are not satisfactory. This is explained by the high variance of this method. However, ensemble methods are well-known in the literature for improving accuracy and this is confirmed by our experiments. Indeed, Bagging and in a more impressive way Boosting give much more accurate results for each problem. Random forests and Extra-Trees are competitive with Boosting. SVM is very close to boosting but maybe slightly better in average. Extra-trees with sub-windows is the best generic method in terms of accuracy on three of the four problems (ORL, COIL-100, OUTEX) but it is nevertheless beaten by boosting and SVM on MNIST. On all problems, the best results, always obtained either by SVM or extra-trees with sub-windows, are competitive with state-of-the-art techniques in computer vision. This is remarkable considering that these algorithms are very easy to use.

Another criterion for comparing algorithms for computer vision is their computational efficiency. To give an idea of the difference between the algorithms, Table 4 reports the computing times [6] for learning each model on the COIL-100 and MNIST problems. Extra-trees is undoubtedly the fastest method. On COIL-100, growing 500 extra-trees is even faster than growing one single decision tree. Not surprisingly, bagging and boosting that build T trees with the classical decision tree induction algorithm are the slowest methods. Random forests are much faster but still slower than the extra-trees (especially on COIL-100). SVMs are very fast on COIL-100 but slower on MNIST which consists of much more images. Our sub-windows method increases significantly the computing times of extra-trees but the resulting algorithm is still much faster than bagging and boosting on COIL-100. On MNIST, high computing times are attributed to the augmented learning sample ($N_w = 360000$).

The prediction times for all tree-based algorithms are negligible. With sub-windows however, the test of a new image requires the propagation of all sub-windows in the trees of the ensemble and it depends mostly on the size of the sub-windows. For example, it takes about 54s to predict the classes of the 5400 test objects on COIL-100 and about 12s to test the 10000 images on MNIST. Although our implementation is not optimal, we believe that these times are nevertheless reasonable. With SVM, prediction times depends on the number of support vectors. On both problems, it was the slowest method for testing with a prediction time of 3m19s for COIL-100 and 8m09s on MNIST.

5 Conclusions

We compared seven generic algorithms for image classification including our recent approach that combines building of ensembles of extremely randomized trees and extraction of sub-windows from the original images. Classical decision tree, Bagging, Boosting, Random Forests and SVM are the other meth-

---

[6]On a Pentium IV 2.53Ghz.

Table 4: Learning time on MNIST and COIL-100

MNIST		COIL-100	
Algorithm	**Time**	**Algorithm**	**Time**
Boosting ($T = 50$)	6h22m29s	Boosting ($T = 100$)	5h25m01s
Extra-Trees + Sub-Window	5h06m24s	Bagging ($T = 50$)	1h53m25s
Bagging ($T = 50$)	5h01m11s	Random Forests ($T = 500$)	51m34s
SVMs (poly2)	28m28s	*Extra-Trees + Sub-Window*	45m45s
Random Forests ($T = 100$)	20m16s	Classical Decision Tree	3m08s
Extra-Trees ($T = 100$)	11m39s	SVMs (linear)	1m02s
Classical Decision Tree	7m17s	*Extra-Trees ($T = 500$)*	9s

ods we evaluated on four different image classification problems for which test protocols were rigorously specified. The accuracy of our generic sub-window technique is the best on three of the four problems and is comparable to state-of-the-art techniques but slightly inferior to the best known results. In fact, our experiments demonstrate that generic methods, in particular our sub-window algorithm, can come remarkably close to specialized methods. In many practical application contexts, a slight performance drop in exchange for reduced task-specific pre-processing and manual intervention may constitute a very desirable trade-off.

The future directions are two-fold. First, as our wrapping method of extraction and classification of sub-windows from images is generic, it is attractive to combine it with other learning algorithms (in particular Boosting and SVMs). Second, experiments should be carried out to compare the robustness of these generic approaches to rotation, scaling, occlusion, and noise. Although some algorithms are close in terms of accuracy, it is not sure that they would be all affected in the same way by these perturbations. In [17], we provided a preliminary study of the behavior of our sub-window approach in the presence of rotation, scaling, and occlusion on the COIL-100 problem. We observed good robustness to small transformations introduced in test images and also suggested some improvements that preserve the generic nature of the algorithm.

6   Acknowledgments

Raphaël Marée is supported by the "Région Wallonne" (Belgium). Pierre Geurts is a research associate of the F.N.R.S., Belgium.

References

[1] L. Breiman. Bagging predictors. *Machine Learning*, 24(2):123–140, 1996.

[2] L. Breiman. Random forests. *Machine learning*, 45:5–32, 2001.

[3] L. Breiman, J.H. Friedman, R.A. Olsen, and C.J. Stone. *Classification and Regression Trees*. Wadsworth International (California), 1984.

[4] C. J. C. Burges and B. Schölkopf. Improving the accuracy and speed of support vector machines. In M. C. Mozer, M. I. Jordan, and Thomas Petsche, editors, *Advances in Neural Information Processing Systems*, volume 9, page 375. The MIT Press, 1997.

[5] Chih-Chung Chang and Chih-Jen Lin. Libsvm : a library for support vector machines. Technical report, Computer Science and Information Engineering, National Taiwan University, 2003.

[6] J. Dahmen, D. Keysers, and H. Ney. Combined classification of handwritten digits using the 'virtual test sample method'. In *Proc. Second International Workshop, MCS 2001 Cambridge, UK*, pages 99–108, July 2001.

[7] H. Drucker. Fast decision tree ensembles for optical character recognition. In *Proc. Fifth Annual Symposium on Document Analysis and Information Retrieval*, pages 137–147, 1996.

[8] Y. Freund and R. E. Schapire. Experiments with a new boosting algorithm. In *Proc. Thirteenth International Conference on Machine Learning*, pages 148–156, 1996.

[9] P. Geurts. *Contributions to decision tree induction: bias/variance tradeoff and time series classification*. Phd. thesis, Department of Electrical Engineering and Computer Science, University of Liège, May 2002.

[10] P. Geurts. Extremely randomized trees. Technical report, Department of Electrical Engineering and Computer Science, University of Liège, 2003.

[11] G.-D. Guo, S. Li, and K. Chan. Face recognition by support vector machines. In *Proc. International Conference on Automatic Face and Gesture Recognition, 196-201.*, 2000.

[12] G.-D. Guo and H.-J. Zhang. Boosting for fast face recognition. In *Proc. IEEE ICCV Workshop on Recognition, Analysis, and Tracking of Faces and Gestures in Real-Time Systems*, pages 96–100, 2001.

[13] M.S. Hoque and M. C. Fairhurst. A moving window classifier for offline character recognition. In *Proc. of the Seventh International Workshop on Frontiers in Handwriting Recognition, Amsterdam*, pages 595–600, September 2000.

[14] T.O. Kvålseth. Entropy and correlation : Some comments. *IEEE Trans. on Systems, Man and Cybernetics*, SMC-17(3):517–519, 1987.

[15] S. Lawrence, C. Lee Giles, A. C. Tsoi, and A. D. Back. Face recognition: A convolutional neural network approach. *IEEE Transactions on Neural Networks*, 8(1):98–113, 1997.

[16] Y. LeCun, L. Bottou, Y. Bengio, and P. Haffner. Gradient-based learning applied to document recognition. *Proc. of the IEEE*, 86(11):2278–2324, 1998.

[17] R. Marée, Geurts P., Piater J., and Wehenkel L. A generic approach for image classification based on decision tree ensembles. Submitted.

[18] T. Menp, M. Pietikinen, and J. Viertola. Separating color and pattern information for color texture discrimination. In *Proc. 16th International Conference on Pattern Recognition*, 2002.

[19] A. Nefian and M. Hayes. Face recognition using an embedded HMM. In *Proc. IEEE Conference on Audio and Video-based Biometric Person Authentication*, pages 19–24, March 1999.

[20] S. Obrzalek and J. Matas. Object recognition using local affine frames on distinguished regions. In *Electronic Proceedings of the 13th British Machine Vision Conference, University of Cardiff*, 2002.

[21] T. Ojala, T. Menp, M. Pietikinen, J. Viertola, J. Kyllnen, and S. Huovinen. Outex - new framework for empirical evaluation of texture analysis algorithms. *Proc. 16th International Conference on Pattern Recognition, Quebec, Canada, 1:701-706*, 2002.

[22] R. Paredes and A. Perez-Cortes. Local representations and a direct voting scheme for face recognition. In *Pattern Recognition in Information Systems, Proc. 1st International Workshop on Pattern Recognition in Information Systems*, pages 71–79, July 2001.

[23] M. Pontil and A. Verri. Support vector machines for 3d object recognition. *IEEE Transactions on Pattern Analysis and Machine Intelligence*, 20(6):637–646, 1998.

[24] V.N. Vapnik. *The nature of statistical learning theory*. Springer Verlag, 1995.

[25] L. Wehenkel. *Automatic learning techniques in power systems*. Kluwer Academic, Boston, 1998.

SESSION 2B:

CONSTRAINT PROGRAMMING 2

Turtle: A Constraint Imperative Programming Language

Martin Grabmüller

Petra Hofstedt

Fakultät IV Elektrotechnik und Informatik, Technische Universität Berlin

Berlin, Germany

Abstract

Ideally, in constraint programs, the solutions of problems are obtained by specifying their desired properties, whereas in imperative programs, the steps which lead to a solution must be defined explicitly, rather than being derived automatically. This paper describes the design and implementation of the programming language TURTLE, which integrates declarative constraints and imperative language elements in order to combine their advantages and to form a more flexible programming paradigm suitable for solving a wide range of problems.

1   Introduction

Programming languages can be divided into two main categories: imperative and declarative languages. Imperative programming languages are statement-oriented and it is the task of the programmer to specify explicitly which steps a computer program has to perform in order to find the solution to a given problem. In declarative languages, the properties of the desired solutions are specified and it is mainly up to the programming system (compiler and run-time system) to find a way for obtaining the solutions.

Even though the advantages of declarative programming—e.g., more effective development and increased program correctness—are widely recognized, imperative programming languages are still used in industry as well as in academia. This is partly due to the fact that imperative programming languages are still more efficient than declarative ones for many applications, and because traditionally, software projects were started with imperative languages and there is the need to maintain them. One way to make use of the advantages of both programming paradigms is to integrate them into one language, so that whatever paradigm is better suited can be used to perform a given task.

The combination of constraint-based and imperative programming has been called *constraint imperative programming* (CIP) in literature [6]. The object-oriented programming language Kaleidoscope [10] is one of the first examples of a language in that paradigm, but other languages or systems also share properties of CIP [3, 1].

This paper describes the design and implementation of the higher-order constraint imperative programming language TURTLE[1]. Even though CIP as originally introduced [6] refers to imperative object-oriented programming languages, we will use a broader definition of CIP. In the following text, all languages which have both constraint and imperative features (including object-oriented ones) will be called constraint imperative programming languages.

The rest of this paper is organized as follows: We present the higher-order constraint imperative programming language TURTLE in Sect. 2. This is done by first defining the imperative part of the language and then enhancing it with four language extensions. Section 3 touches the semantics of TURTLE by a brief introduction of the TURTLE Abstract Machine (TAM) and sketches the implementation of our CIP language carried out based on this machine description. Finally, in Sect. 4, we discuss TURTLE with respect to related work and draw a conclusion.

2 The Design of Turtle

TURTLE was developed by starting with a base language which was then enriched with four concepts necessary for extending it to a constraint imperative language. This section describes both the base language and the constraint extensions and presents an example for constraint imperative programming with TURTLE.

2.1 The Base Language

The imperative subset of the TURTLE language consists of all programming constructs necessary for imperative, structured programming. These constructs include imperative control structures, variables, functions, a rich type system allowing the definition of new data types, a module system for structuring programs with polymorphic modules and higher-order functions.

Fig. 1 summarizes the syntax of the imperative part of the language. t stands for type expressions, which are used to denote data types. Statements s do not produce values, but are instead executed for their side effects. Statements are declarations, assignments, function calls and control structures. Expressions, denoted by e, are evaluated in order to produce values, and always appear as parts of statements. Note that functions can be both declared by statements as well as created by expressions which result in function values. Constants are named c in Fig. 1 and can be integer, boolean, real, character or string constants. Variables v represent storage locations into which values can be stored by assignment statements, and from which values can be fetched. The notation $e_1[e_2]$ stands for array accesses. Functions f receive input values as parameters and return values as their results. The calling convention in TURTLE is call-by-value.

The type system has primitive data types like integer or real numbers, boolean values, characters and strings. TURTLE supports tuples, arrays and lists of arbitrary base types. User-defined algebraic, recursive data types are

---

[1]Note that turtles normally live longer than most other animals.

$$
\begin{array}{lll}
t & ::= & t_{simple} \mid t_{cmplx} \\
t_{simple} & ::= & int \mid bool \mid real \mid char \\
t_{cmplx} & ::= & n < t_1, \ldots, t_n > \mid \textbf{string} \mid \textbf{array of } t \mid \textbf{list of } t \mid (t_1, \ldots, t_n) \\
s & ::= & \textbf{var } v : t; \mid f(e_1, \ldots, e_n); \mid e_1 := e_2; \\
& \mid & \textbf{datatype } n < n_1, \ldots, n_l >= v_1(l_{11} : t_{11}, \ldots, l_{1k} : t_{1k}) \textbf{ or } \ldots \\
& & \textbf{or } v_m(l_{m1} : t_{m1}, \ldots, l_{ml} : t_{ml}); \\
& \mid & \textbf{fun } f(v_1 : t_1, \ldots, v_n : t_n) : t \quad s; \ldots \textbf{ end}; \\
& \mid & \textbf{while } c \textbf{ do } s; \ldots \textbf{ end}; \mid \textbf{return } e; \\
& \mid & \textbf{if } c \textbf{ then } s_1; \ldots \textbf{ else } s_2; \ldots \textbf{ end}; \\
e & ::= & c \mid v \mid f(e_1, \ldots, e_n) \mid e_1[e_2] \\
& \mid & \textbf{fun } (v_1 : T_1, \ldots, v_n : T_n) : t \quad s; \ldots \textbf{ end}
\end{array}
$$

Figure 1: Base Language Syntax

introduced by **datatype** declarations, which declare data types n, possibly parameterized by other types, with several variants v_i, where each variant has a number of fields l_{ij}. The compiler automatically generates functions for creating values of user-defined types (constructor functions) and for selecting and modifying the fields stored in the values (selector and mutator functions). Since a data type can have one or more variants, functions for examining the variant a given value has (discriminator functions) are also generated.

In TURTLE, programs are composed of modules which define data types, functions and variables. Some or all of the definitions in a module can be exported, so that other modules of the same program can import and use them. By these means, various principles of software engineering, such as encapsulation, information hiding and the definition of interfaces between modules can be expressed in TURTLE.[2]

In addition to the imperative language discussed above, some functional programming concepts have also been integrated: functions in TURTLE are higher-order, so that functions can be arguments to and results from function calls and can be stored into arbitrary data structures. This feature was added because it proved very useful for code reusability and abstraction in other programming languages besides purely functional languages, for example in Scheme [9]. Another important feature—not specific to functional programming, but most common in these languages—is the possibility to make modules polymorphic. This means that modules can be parametrized by data types and that the types and functions defined in these modules can operate on any data type which is specified when importing them.

2.2 Constraint Programming Extensions

The extension of an imperative language to a constraint imperative one by adding declarative constraints allows for cleaner and more flexible programs,

---

[2]The syntax for defining modules has been omitted from Fig. 1 because of space limitations.

$$t \quad ::= \quad !\ t_{simple}$$

$$s \quad ::= \quad \textbf{constraint } f(v_1 : T_1, \ldots, v_n : T_n) \quad s; \ldots \textbf{ end};$$

$$\mid \quad \textbf{require } c_1 : p_1 \wedge \ldots \wedge c_n : p_n \textbf{ in } s; \ldots \textbf{ end};$$

$$\mid \quad \textbf{require } c_1 : p_1 \wedge \ldots \wedge c_n : p_n;$$

$$e \quad ::= \quad \textbf{var } e \mid !\ e \mid \textbf{constraint } (v_1 : T_1, \ldots, v_n : T_n) \quad s; \ldots \textbf{ end}$$

Figure 2: Constraint Extension Syntax

as will be shown in Sect. 2.3.

Four concepts have been found to be necessary for extending an imperative language to a constraint imperative one: constrainable variables, constraint statements, user-defined constraints and constraint solvers. These extensions are required because it must be possible to place constraints on variables, to abstract over constraints and finally, to solve the constraints. The syntactic extensions to the base language are shown in Fig. 2.

Constrainable variables are variables whose values can be determined by placing constraints on them. In TURTLE, constrainable variables are declared by giving them constraint types. This is done by annotating the type of the variable with an exclamation mark in the variable definition. Constrainable variables are distinguished from normal, imperative variables, because they behave differently. Normal variables are set to values by assignment statements, whereas constrainable variables are determined by constraints. So the former are imperative, whereas the latter are declarative. The separation into two classes of variables makes the semantics cleaner and it is easier to program with them, because the use and behavior of each variable can be deduced from the type of the variable. Normal variables cannot be determined by constraints, and if such a variable appears in a constraint, its value is taken as a constant when the constraint is solved. To make use of abstraction mechanisms like functions and abstract data types, it must be possible to pass constrainable variables to functions or user-defined constraints or to store them into data structures. Each constrainable variable is associated with a *variable object* which is explicitly created by a **var** expression and holds the value of the variable. By using variable objects, it is possible to share these objects between several constrainable variables and to place the variable object in different data structures, for example, for constraining several data structures at once. When the value of a constrainable variable is needed, it has to be extracted by the dereferencing operator !. This is shown in Fig. 2 as the expression extension $!\ e$.[3]

Constraint statements allow the programmer to place constraints on constrainable variables. In TURTLE, the **require** statement normally consists of a constraint conjunction $c_1 : p_1 \wedge \ldots \wedge c_n : p_n$ and a body $s; \ldots$ The body is a sequence of statements and the constraints in the conjunction are enforced as long as the body executes. Enforcing means that the built-in constraint solver

---

[3]The type system forbids expressions like !!! 7, which are meaningless.

tries to satisfy the constraint conjunction by adding it to the constraint store. All constraints of enclosing constraint statements are contained in the store. When the solver is able to solve the conjunction of the store together with the newly added constraints, each constrainable variable gets assigned a value such that the values of all constrainable variables form a solution of the constraint store. When the body of the constraint statement is left, all constraints added for that statement are removed from the store. Because sometimes constraints must stay in effect when the scope of a constraint statement is left (e.g. when constraints are to be placed on global variables), a variant of the **require** statement without a body is provided. The constraints defined with such a statement stay in effect as long as the variables they constrain exist.

User-defined constraints. In the same way as functions abstract over statements, user-defined constraints abstract over constraints. A user-defined constraint is similar to a function, but its purpose is not to collect a sequence of statements which might be executed in more than one place, but to collect constraints which might be needed in several constraint statements. In TURTLE, user-defined constraints are defined similarly to functions, but declared with the keyword **constraint** instead of **fun**. User-defined constraints cannot be called like normal functions, they may only be invoked from constraint statements. Functions, on the other hand, may be called from constraint statements. The returned value is then used in the constraint as a constant value, just as normal variables are treated in constraints. Calling user-defined constraints results in additional (primitive) constraints being placed onto their parameters, they do not produce values.

Constraint solvers. The last component necessary for CIP is a constraint solver, which is responsible for checking whether a constraint conjunction specified in a constraint statement can be satisfied together with the current constraint store, for adding the constraints to it and for determining values for the variables on success. It must also remove constraints from the store whenever the scope of a constraint statement is left.

One feature which is not strictly necessary for CIP, but very useful when modeling real-life problems is the possibility to define constraint hierarchies [5]. With a constraint solver supporting constraint hierarchies, it is possible to assign strengths to individual constraints which represent their importance. The solver respects these strengths when solving the constraint store and tries to satisfy the most important constraints, even if that means that less important ones (preferential constraints) are left unsatisfied. Especially for over-constrained problems, such as those appearing in graphical applications, this is very useful. In TURTLE, constraint hierarchies can be specified by assigning strengths to the individual constraints appearing in constraint statements. Syntactically, this is done by annotating the constraints with symbolic strengths (preferences) (p_i in Fig. 2). When no such annotation is given, the strength defaults to the strongest strength, called *mandatory*. Constraints with this strength always get satisfied by the solvers and if that is not possible, an exception is raised.

```
module layout;
import io;
fun main (args: list of string): int
    var lm: !real := var 0.0;
    var rm: !real := var 0.0;
    var gap: !real := var 0.0;
    var pw: !real := var 0.0;
    var col: !real := var 0.0;
    require lm = 2.0 and rm = 2.0 and pw = 21.0 and
      gap >= 0.5 and gap <= 2.0 and gap = 0.5 : medium and
      col <= 7.0 : strong and
      gap + lm + 2.0 * col + rm = pw in
        io.put ("lm="); io.put (!lm); io.nl ();
        io.put ("rm="); io.put (!rm); io.nl ();
        io.put ("gap="); io.put (!gap); io.nl ();
        io.put ("pw="); io.put (!pw); io.nl ();
        io.put ("col="); io.put (!col); io.nl ();
    end;
    return 0;
end;
```

Figure 3: Layout Example Program

The constraint programming model currently implemented in TURTLE only allows a single solution for the constraints, so that the solvers only determine the first (not necessarily best) solution. Note that since the constraint solver is only invoked at the beginning of a constraint statement, the values of all constrainable variables remain fixed as long as the body of the statement is executed. The restriction that at most one solution is found could be removed by adding backtracking to the TURTLE semantics, as with Alma-0 [2]. This is a topic of future consideration.

2.3 Programming In Turtle – An Example

This section presents an example of CIP in TURTLE. It will demonstrate the use of the constraint features of the language. More detailed examples may be found in [8]. Consider the example program in Fig. 3. The program is intended to calculate the margins, column width and inter-column gap for a simple layout problem. A program like this could be part of a typesetting system. The variables lm and rm represent the left and right margin of the paper, gap stands for the gap between the two columns and pw is the page width. col represents the width of both the left and the right column.

The program starts by declaring the variables as constrainable variables of type $real$ and initializes the variables. In this example, all variables are initialized to the value zero, because the actual values will later be determined by constraints. After the variable declarations, a constraint statement is used to specify the constraints on the variables. The constraints which are not annotated with a constraint strength are assigned the strongest strength, *mandatory*. *lm*, *rm* and *pw* are specified to take fixed values, because these values are normally fixed for a specific printer or paper size. The gap between the columns is constrained to lie in the interval [0.5, 2.0], with a *medium* preference at 0.5. This preference ensures that the gap will be as narrow as possible.

Another preferential constraint, but with more important strength *strong*, is placed on the variable *col*. This constraint tries to hold the value for *col* below or equal to 7.0. Together with the preferential constraint on *gap*, this will result in a gap as narrow as possible, unless *col* is smaller than 7.0. The gap will only get wider when the column width exceeds 7.0. When that happens, the constraint with strength *strong* will override the constraint labelled with *medium*. The constraint *col* <= 7.0 will be violated as soon as *gap* reaches its upper bound 2.0 in order to satisfy the overall constraint conjunction.

The results calculated for this example are as follows. *gap* will get its maximum value 2.0, and the *medium* constraint on *gap* will be violated as well as the *strong* constraint on *col*, so that the latter variable will get the value 7.5. *lm*, *rm* and *pw* will receive the values 2.0, 2.0 and 21.0, respectively, so that the main constraint *gap* + *lm* + 2.0*col* + *rm* = *pw* is satisfied by $2.0 + 2.0 + 2.0 * 7.5 + 2.0 = 21.0$.

Finally, in the body of the constraint statement, the values of all variables are printed out. The variables need to be dereferenced using the ! operator, because the values of the variable objects stored in the constrainable variables shall be printed, not the variable objects themselves.

The advantage of using a constraint imperative language instead of a traditional imperative one is that the problem specification (the constrainable variables and the constraints) is expressed declaratively, and it can easily be modified to solve a variety of problems: as given, it can be used to calculate the column width for a specific paper size, and by making the constraint on *pw* preferential, it can calculate the optimal paper size for a given column width.

Another important advantage of constraint imperative programming is that a constraint imperative programmer can re-use the algorithms present in the constraint solvers at a very high level. The resulting programs are easier to maintain and extend, thus increasing correctness and reliability.

3 Semantics and Implementation

In this section we describe the TURTLE Abstract Machine (TAM), which provides a formal semantics of TURTLE. Furthermore, we briefly sketch on the implementation of our constraint imperative language, which has been carried out based on this machine description.

3.1 The Turtle Abstract Machine

The TURTLE Abstract Machine provides an operational semantics for a subset of TURTLE called μTURTLE. Every TURTLE program can be converted
into an equivalent μTURTLE program by a straightforward syntactical transformation, where various syntactic entities are converted into simpler equivalent constructs. For a detailed description see [8]. The TAM is basically a
standard stack machine for imperative languages equipped with registers for
maintaining the computation environment, and extended with instructions
for managing the constraint store. There are four memory areas and a set of
registers in the TAM. The *memory* is divided into

- the *Code* area containing the machine instructions,

- the *Stack* for storing intermediate values,

- the *Store*, which holds all dynamic data structures created during execution (environments for storing local variables, closures for handling
  higher-order functions, continuation records for storing the machine
  state at function calls, and a chain of exception handlers, i.e. code
  addresses for resuming execution when an exception occurs plus corresponding continuations), and

- the constraint store *CStore*. The TAM itself accesses this store only
  by abstract machine instructions, whereas the integrated solvers are
  responsible for maintaining some representation of the constraints in
  the *CStore*.

The *register set* contains an accumulator *acc* for storing intermediate values
during program execution, the stack pointer *sp* which points to the top of the
Stack, and the program counter *pc* which always points to the next TAM instruction to be executed. The registers *cont*, *env*, and *ex* are used for access to
the chain of continuation records, to the environment holding the free variables
of the currently executing function, and to a list of exception handlers, resp.

The TAM instruction set can be divided into several classes: load and store
instructions fetch values from memory locations or constants to the accumulator or store the accumulator contents to memory. There are instructions
for closure and environment creation, instructions for function call and return, branching instructions to control the program flow, and an instruction
to halt the machine. The machine has several instructions for constraint and
constraint store management, i.e. for creation of constraint run-time representations from the constraint specifications and for the addition and removal
of constraints from and to the constraint store. Finally, instructions for exception handling allow to add and delete entries to and from the exception
handler chain and to raise an exception. These instructions are, among other
things, necessary to handle the violation of constraint stores (cf. Example 1).

The translation of a μTURTLE program into TAM code is performed according to a translation scheme given in [8]. We go not into detail wrt. this

```
1    var x: !int := var 0;
2    var y: int := 2;
3    require x < y and
4            x = 2 : strong in
6       f(!x,y);
7    end;
```

Figure 4: Cut-out of a TURTLE program example

```
1              load-constant 0          12          store-variable L[[t₂]]
2              push                     13          add-constraints L[[t₁]], L[[t₂]]
3              save-continuation l₀     14          handle l₁
4              load-variable rt_make_var 15         T[[f(!x,y)]]
5              call                     16          remove-constraints L[[t₁]], L[[t₂]]
6     l₀:      store-variable L[[x]]    17          unhandle
7              load-constant 2          18          jump l₂
8              store-variable L[[y]]    19   l₁:    remove-constraints L[[t₁]], L[[t₂]]
9              make-constraint (x < y), 0 20         raise
10             store-variable L[[t₁]]   21   l₂:    ...
11             make-constraint (x = 2), 2
```

Figure 5: TAM Code for the TURTLE Code of Fig. 4

scheme but discuss an example in the following. The execution of a μTURTLE program requires the preparation of the machine followed by the interpretation of the program's TAM instructions until a halt instruction is executed.

Example 1: Let us demonstrate the translation of a cut-out of a μTURTLE program into TAM instructions and their abstract machine interpretation.

In Fig. 4, a constrainable variable x and a normal variable y are declared. The variable x is initialized with 0, the value 2 is assigned to y. The constraints $x < y$ and $x = 2$ are required to hold during the function call f(!x,y).

Note, that since x is a constrainable variable, the behavior of the expression $x < y$ is different from one, where x and y are both simple variables. In the latter case at run-time it would be simply tested whether the current values of the variables fulfill the test, while in the case of a constraint the constrainable variable can be (re)set such that the corresponding constraint (and possibly further ones) is (are) satisfied. The first constraint has the strongest strength, i.e. it is *mandatory*. Its satisfaction by the solver is, thus, stronger desired than that of the second constraint with strength *strong*.[4]

Using the translation scheme the abstract machine code of Fig. 5 is produced. Lines 1–6 and 7–8 correspond to the initialization of the constrainable variable x to 0 and of the variable y to 2. For the constrainable variable x a function call is generated which creates a variable object (with initial value

---

[4]Since the constraint solver cannot satisfy both constraints at once, it will ignore the second constraint such that x will remain 0 finally.

0) at run-time (lines 1–6). For the variable y the constant 2 is loaded to the accumulator and afterwards stored into the *Store* at a corresponding location. At this, $\mathcal{L}$ is a function transforming variables to location descriptors at compile-time.

The remaining lines correspond to the **require** statement which involves management of the constraint store. Lines 9, 10 and 11, 12 create symbolic representations of the two constraints (including their strengths) and convey references to them from the accumulator into corresponding *Store* locations of newly created variables t_1 and t_2. Note that the constraint strengths are translated to non-negative integer constants. The strongest strength *mandatory* is 0 while numerically greater values represent weaker strengths. Line 13 adds the constraints to the constraint store and raises an exception if the newly built store cannot be satisfied. The expression $\mathcal{T}[\![f(!x,y)]\!]$ at line 15 represents the body of the **require** statement whose translation is left out in this example.[5] Line 16 removes the constraints from the store again and resolves it. Constraints must be removed from the store not only when the body finished normally as discussed above but also when an exception is raised during the execution of the body. Thus, in line 14 an exception handler is set up which removes the constraints before re-raising the exception (lines 19 and 20). Line 17 removes the exception handler when execution finishes without causing an exception.

As shown in the example, adding the constraint to the store automatically causes the constraint solver to resolve the store, i.e. to check whether the constraint store together with the newly added constraints is satisfiable. In that case, the store is modified accordingly. If any required constraint in the store is violated, the newly added constraint is removed from the store and an exception is raised. If any preferential constraint is not satisfied, the solver tries to satisfy as many preferential constraints as possible, but no exception is raised. When constraints are removed, the solver resolves its store, too.

3.2 The Turtle Compiler and the Run-Time System

In this section, we shortly sketch on the TURTLE compiler and the run-time system of TURTLE. To do this, we will consider the internal representation of constraints in more detail. The TURTLE compiler is fairly standard: the source program is parsed and first translated into a high-level intermediate form (called HIL), on which type checking and overload resolution are performed. The HIL code is then translated into a low-level intermediate language (LIL), from which finally the target code is generated (ANSI C in our implementation). LIL is the machine language of the TURTLE Abstract Machine (TAM), which defines the semantics of TURTLE.

Example 2: Figure 6 shows a part of the LIL code representation of Example 1 concerning the initialization of the variables and the creation of a constraint representation. Lines 1–5 and 6, 7 realize the variable declara-

---

[5]$\mathcal{T}$ stands for the translation function.

1	load-int #0	% **var** x: !int := **var** 0;
2	push	
3	make-int-variable	
4	variable-set	
5	store env(0, 1)	
6	load-int #2	% **var** y: int := 2;
7	store env(0, 2)	
8	load-int #0	% $x < y$: 0
9	push	
10	load env(0, 2)	
11	push	
12	load env(0, 1)	
13	push	
14	load-int #1	
15	push	
16	add-int-constraint #4, #1	
	. . .	
25	resolve-int-constraint	

Figure 6: LIL code representation of the TURTLE code of Fig. 4

tions and correspond to the lines 1–6 and 7, 8 in Fig. 5. The variable y is a normal variable which is initialized to the value 2 (lines 6, 7), whereas x is initialized with a constrainable variable object. This object contains a value slot which is initialized by the operand of the **var** expression, i.e. 0, and a pointer to a solver-specific data structure holding the information necessary for constraint solving. While the creation of constraint representations can be kept very abstract in the TAM code (lines 9, 10 and 11, 12 in Fig. 5), for the actual compiler implementation this needs a more detailed treatment, e.g. lines 8–16 realize the creation of the representation of the constraint $x < y$. The add-constraints instruction in the TAM code at line 13 is realized by a corresponding instruction for every constraint (e.g. in line 16) and one final resolve-int-constraint instruction per **require** statement.

The above example already gives a first impression about how the internal representation of constraints is realized. Let us consider this in more detail. Trivial constraints which do not contain any references to constrainable variables are translated like normal boolean expressions followed by a test whether the result was true or false. In the latter case and if the constraint was required, an exception is raised. More interesting is the compilation of non-trivial constraints. Since in TURTLE it must be possible to transfer constraints between the user program and the constraint solvers, the compiler must build a representation of the constraint. This representation must contain the strength of the constraint and references to the constrainable variables so that the solver can fetch their values and store new values into them.

The translation of non-trivial constraints partitions them into constants (including non-constrainable variables and function calls) which are evaluated before the constraint is created and into constrainable variables together with their coefficients. When translating a constraint[6] of a **require** statement first its strength is pushed onto the evaluation stack followed by the constant term and the constrainable variables with their correspondent coefficients. Finally, an indicator for the kind of constraint is pushed onto the stack as well as the number of constrainable variables.

Example 3: Consider again the creation of the constraint representation for $x < y$ in Fig. 6, lines 8–16. The instructions 'load-int #0' and 'push' load strength '0' of this *mandatory* constraint onto the stack. This is followed by pushing the constant term 'env(0,2)' (representing y), the constrainable variable stored in 'env(0,1)' (representing x) and its coefficient '#1' (lines 10-15). Note the difference between y and x. The value of y is used for calculating the constant term of the constraint (i.e. y itself), whereas the value of x (which is a variable object) is pushed onto the stack so that the constraint solver responsible for the constraint can access the variable. Finally, a '>'-constraint (coded by '#4') with one ('#1') constrainable variable is added to the constraint store by 'add-int-constraint #4, #1'.

Currently two experimental solvers for treating constraints for which the compiler cannot generate efficient straight-line code are integrated: a solver for acyclic linear real arithmetic constraints based on the Indigo algorithm [4] which is able to handle constraint hierarchies and a finite-domain solver over integers. The incorporated solvers are quite weak and the integration of more powerful and efficient solvers is a task of future work. The architecture of our system however is open for the inclusion of new solvers and the interface between the (imperative) run-time system and the constraint solvers is cleanly designed and flexible.

The constraint hierarchy support in TURTLE is restricted to the syntax necessary for specifying them and the interface between the run-time system and the constraint solvers which attaches strengths to the symbolic constraint representation. It is the task of the constraint solvers to make use of the strength information (as the Indigo solver does) or to ignore it (as in the currently implemented finite domain solver).

Even if the current TURTLE compiler implementation is an experimental one, it is quite usable as demonstrated by many TURTLE example programs including a web server and a TURTLE compiler front end (scanner, parser and abstract syntax tree implementation). The programs run with reasonable memory consumption and speed, i.e. purely imperative benchmark examples run slower for a factor of about 10 wrt. equivalent C programs, and provide enough debugging information to program comfortably.

---

[6]The described translation based on a partitioning into constants and constrainable variables used for the constraints of the currently integrated solvers will differ in general if other solvers are integrated.

4 Related Work and Conclusion

In this paper, we presented the design and implementation of the constraint imperative programming language TURTLE.

The name *constraint imperative programming* was introduced by Borning and Freeman-Benson [6, 7] and originally only referred to object-oriented languages with constraint programming extensions. We have extended this notion to include all languages with both imperative and constraint concepts. A further example of this paradigm is the language Alma-0 [2], which currently amalgamates concepts of pure logic and imperative languages but which is intended to be extended to a CIP language [3].

TURTLE's concept of constrainable variables and the idea to separate them from normal variables is similar to the "variables" and "unknowns" proposed for extensions of Alma-0 [3]. Our user-defined constraints perform a similar task as *constraint constructors* in the language Kaleidoscope [10]. Constraint statements similar to ours can also be found in that language. However, in contrast to Kaleidoscope, the separation of constrainable variables gives more control over the handling of constraints. Differing both from Alma-0 and Kaleidoscope, the variable objects in TURTLE are values which can be shared between data structures in order to build complex constraints. Additionally, TURTLE extends the CIP paradigm by integrating higher-order functions into the constraint imperative framework, thus making the language much more flexible and powerful. The algebraic data types of TURTLE come from the purely functional language Opal [11]. Besides the approach to create new programming languages which integrate both imperative and constraint programming, constraint libraries, like the constraint library ILOG [12] for C++ or JACK [1], a library for programming in Java, have been developed. Constraint libraries have the advantage of easier integration into existing programs, whereas in CIP, constraints and imperative constructs are more tightly combined, which makes the semantics cleaner and helps with optimization.

TURTLE is especially well suited for applications which consist of tasks with different requirements. The better integration of constraints can be exploited by optimizing compilers, because the optimizer knows about the semantics of constrainable variables and constraint statements. Another advantage of TURTLE when compared to constraint libraries for object-oriented languages is the availability of higher-order functions and polymorphic algebraic data types. To our knowledge, TURTLE is the first constraint imperative language including these features. The language TURTLE and its implementation are practical and the language has been used for implementing both imperative and constraint programs of different sizes. The major drawback of the current implementation is the lack of powerful and efficient constraint solvers, which is a topic of future work. The language design itself is flexible and expressive enough, such that TURTLE can be used for solving problems for which good imperative solution techniques are known as well as those for which declarative solutions are preferable. The implementation of TURTLE and the diploma thesis [8] describing the design and implementation in detail are available online: `http://uebb.cs.tu-berlin.de/~magr/turtle/home.html`

References

[1] S. Abdennadher, E. Krämer, M. Saft, and M. Schmauss. JACK: A Java constraint kit. In *WFLP 2001*. University of Kiel; Technical Report No. 2017, September 13–15 2001.

[2] K. R. Apt, J. Brunekreef, V. Partington, and A. Schaerf. Alma-0: An imperative language that supports declarative programming. *ACM Toplas*, 20(5):1014–1066, 1998.

[3] K. R. Apt and A. Schaerf. The Alma project, or how first order logic can help us in imperative programming. In *Correct System Design*, number 1710 in LNCS, pages 89–113. Springer, 1999.

[4] A. Borning, R. Anderson, and B. Freeman-Benson. The Indigo algorithm. Technical Report 96-05-01, Dept. of Computer Science and Engineering, University of Washington, July 1996.

[5] A. Borning, B. Freeman-Benson, and M. Wilson. Constraint hierarchies. *Lisp and Symbolic Computation*, 5:223–270, 1992.

[6] B. N. Freeman-Benson. *Constraint Imperative Programming*. PhD thesis, University of Washington, Dept. of Computer Science and Engineering, July 1991.

[7] B. N. Freeman-Benson and A. Borning. The design and implementation of Kaleidoscope'90, a constraint imperative programming language. In *Proc. of the IEEE Computer Society 1992 Int'l Conference on Computer Languages*, pages 174–180, April 1992.

[8] M. Grabmüller. Constraint Imperative Programming. Diploma Thesis, Technische Universität Berlin, February 2003.

[9] R. Kelsey, W. Clinger, J. Rees, et al. Revised[5] report on the algorithmic language Scheme. *ACM SIGPLAN Notices*, 33(6):26–76, September 1998.

[10] G. Lopez, B. Freeman-Benson, and A. Borning. Kaleidoscope: A constraint imperative programming language. In B. Mayoh, E. Tyugu, and J. Penjaam, editors, *Constraint Programming: Proc. 1993 NATO ASI Parnu, Estonia*, pages 305–321. Springer, 1994.

[11] P. Pepper. *Funktionale Programmierung in OPAL, ML, HASKELL und GOFER*. Springer, 2nd edition, 2003.

[12] J.-F. Puget. A C++ Implementation of CLP. In *Proceedings of the Second Singapore International Conference on Intelligent Systems*, Singapore, 1994.

Symmetry Breaking in Soft CSPs

Stefano Bistarelli

Istituto di Informatica e Telematica, CNR, Pisa, Italy

Dipartimento di Scienze

Universitá degli Studi "G. D'annunzio", Pescara, Italy

Jerome Kelleher and Barry O'Sullivan

Cork Constraint Computation Centre

Department of Computer Science

University College Cork, Ireland

Abstract

Exploiting symmetry in constraint satisfaction problems has become a very popular topic of research in recent times. The existence of symmetry in a problem has the effect of artificially increasing the size of the search space that is explored by search algorithms. Another significant topic of research has been approaches to reasoning about preferences. As constraint processing applications are becoming more widespread in areas such as electronic commerce, configuration, etc., it is becoming increasingly important that we can reason about preferences as efficiently as possible. We present an approach to dealing with symmetry in the semiring framework for soft constraints. We demonstrate that breaking symmetries in soft constraint satisfaction problems improves the efficiency of search. The paper contributes to the state-of-the-art in symmetry breaking, as well as in reasoning about preferences.

1   Introduction

Exploiting symmetry in constraint satisfaction problems has become a very popular topic of research in recent times [1, 2, 13, 17, 19, 22]. The existence of symmetry in a problem has the effect of artificially increasing the size of the search space that is explored by search algorithms. Therefore, a typical approach is to break the symmetries in the problem so that only unique solutions are returned (i.e. that only one exemplar of each symmetric equivalence class of solutions is returned). The complete set of solutions can be trivially computed using the symmetry in the problem. The significant advantage is that not only do we return fewer solutions, but we also reduce the search effort required to find these solutions by eliminating symmetric branches of the search tree.

Another significant topic of research in the constraint processing community is the ability to reason about preferences [3, 18]. It has been shown how preferences can be modeled as constraints [4, 11]. As constraint processing applications are becoming more widespread in areas such as electronic commerce, configuration, etc., it is becoming increasingly important that we can reason about preferences in as efficient a manner as possible. For example, a typical problem in e-commerce systems requires that we satisfy a set of user-specified preference constraints to a maximal degree. The user would typically wish to see a set of alternative solutions to their preferences, but would like to have diversity amongst the set presented to him. This is a well studied issue in the case-based reasoning community [23], but is less well studied in the constraint processing community. One obvious avenue to be explored here are notions of symmetry in preferences. Diversity in this case might be interpreted as the presentation of a set of solutions which are members of different symmetric equivalence classes. This is a potential application of the work presented in this paper.

The work reported is focused on symmetry breaking in soft constraint satisfaction problems. We present an approach to dealing with symmetry in the semiring framework for soft constraints [4, 6]. We first give definitions of symmetry, extending the work of Benhamou [2], and then relax them using the notion of degradation. The theoretical results are enforced by some empirical tests, showing that breaking symmetries in soft constraint satisfaction problems improves the efficiency of search.

The remainder of the paper is structured as follows. Section 2 presents a review of soft constraints and and overview of the state-of-the-art in the area of symmetry-breaking. We present the theoretical aspects of our approach to symmetry breaking in soft CSPs in Section 3 and give some examples in Section 4. Some empirical results are presented in Section 5. Some concluding remarks are made in Section 6.

2 Background

Before presenting an approach to dealing with symmetry in soft CSPs, we will first present a review of the background to this work. In Section 2.1 a brief state-of-the-art review of symmetry breaking in CSPs will be presented. In Section 2.2 the semiring-based approach to soft CSPs will be recapitulated for the convenience of the reader.

2.1 Symmetry Breaking

There is significant interest within the constraint programming community in exploiting symmetry when solving constraint satisfaction problems. As a consequence, a growing number of techniques are being reported in the literature. Benhamou [2] presented an early analysis of symmetry-breaking and placed it in the context of Freuder's work on interchangeability, a special case of symmetry [15].

A common approach to symmetry breaking involves carefully modeling the problem so that symmetries have been removed. For example, Crawford *et al.* [10] have demonstrated how constraints can be added to the model in order to break symmetries. Puget [21] has presented a formal approach to symmetry breaking that involves the addition of ordering constraints to break symmetries. Flener *et al.* [13] adopt a similar approach by adding ordering constraints to break symmetries in matrix models. Flener *et al.* [13] also remind us that symmetry detection is graph-isomorphism complete in the general case, pointing to the work of Crawford [9].

Brown *et al.* [8] have presented a modified backtracking algorithm that breaks symmetry by pruning branches of the search tree dynamically. This is done by ensuring that only one solution from each symmetric equivalence class is computed. Similarly, a general method for eliminating symmetries, known as symmetry breaking during search (SBDS), has been proposed by Gent and Smith [17]. The SBDS approach is based on earlier work by Backofen and Will [1]. Both of these methods can be regarded as examples of a class of approaches to handling symmetries that involve the addition of constraints during search to avoid symmetrical states in the search space. An implementation of SDBS based on the GAP computational abstract algebra system has been presented by Gent *et al.* [16].

Meseguer and Torras [20] have reported the use of search ordering heuristics to avoid symmetries during search. However, the method is less general than SBDS [17].

The notion of partial symmetry breaking has been explored by McDonald and Smith [19]. They show that there is a break-even point to be considered when breaking symmetries during search; there is a point where the benefit in reducing search from removing more symmetries is outweighed by the extra overhead incurred. By breaking a subset of the possible symmetries in a problem, rather than breaking all of them, significant savings in runtime can be accomplished.

Finally, symmetry breaking based on no-good recording methods have been presented by Fahle *et al.* [12] and Focacci and Milano [14]. The approach presented by the former is known as symmetry-breaking via dominance detection (SBDD) and it has been shown to compare well with SBDS; the latter approach is known as the global cut framework. Puget has presented an improvement on these approaches by using an auxiliary CSP for performing dominance checks based on no-good recording [22].

It should be noted that all of the approaches to dealing with symmetry presented above are defined for crisp constraints. In this paper we present, for the first time, a theoretical framework for exploiting symmetries in soft CSPs, and demonstrate the utility of the approach empirically using an SBDS-like approach. SBDS is chosen since it is a very flexible approach to breaking symmetries and is readily applicable to symmetry breaking in soft CSPs.

2.2 Soft CSPs

Soft constraints associate a qualitative or quantitative value either to the entire constraint or to each assignment of its variables. More precisely, they are based on a semiring structure $S = \langle A, +, \times, \mathbf{0}, \mathbf{1} \rangle$ and a set of variables V with domain D. In particular the semiring operation $\times$ is used to combine constraints together, and the + operator for projection.

Technically, a *constraint* is a function which, given an assignment $\eta : V \to D$ of the variables, returns a value of the semiring. So $\mathcal{C} = \eta \to A$ is the set of all possible constraints that can be built starting from S, D and V (values in A are interpreted as level of preference, importance or cost). Using the levels of preference, we can order constraints: to say that c_1 is better then c_2 we will write $c_1 \sqsupseteq c_2$.

When using soft constraints it is necessary to specify, via suitable combination operators, how the level of preference of a global solution is obtained from the preferences in the constraints. The combined weight of a set of constraints is computed using the operator $\otimes : \mathcal{C} \times \mathcal{C} \to \mathcal{C}$ defined as $(c_1 \otimes c_2)\eta = c_1\eta \times_S c_2\eta$. Moreover, given a constraint $c \in \mathcal{C}$ and a variable $v \in V$, the *projection* of c over $V - \{v\}$, written $c \Downarrow_{(V-\{v\})}$, is the constraint c' s.t. $c'\eta = \sum_{d \in D} c\eta[v := d]$.

3 Symmetry in Soft CSPs

Using an approach similar to [2], we can define two notions of *Semantic symmetry*.

Definition 1 (Symmetry for satisfiability) *Consider two domain values b and a for a variable v and the set of constraints C; we say that b and a are symmetrical for satisfiability ($a \approx b$) if and only if*

$$\forall \alpha, \exists \eta, \eta' : \bigotimes C\eta[v := a] = \alpha \iff \bigotimes C\eta'[v := b] = \alpha$$

Informally, two domain values a and b are *symmetrical for satisfiability* if whenever the assignment $v := a$ ($v := b$) leads to a solution with semiring value α, then, we can also obtain a solution with the same value α using the assignment $v := b$ ($v := a$).

Definition 2 (Symmetry for all solutions) *Consider two domain values b and a for a variable v and the set of constraints C; we say that b and a are symmetrical (w.r.t. the constraints C) ($a \simeq b$) if and only if*

$$\exists \phi, \eta', \eta'' : \forall \eta : \phi(\eta[v := a]) = \eta'[v := b], \text{ and } \phi(\eta[v := b]) = \eta''[v := a], \wedge$$

$$\bigotimes C\eta[v := a] = \bigotimes C\phi(\eta[v := a]) \wedge \bigotimes C\eta[v := b] = \bigotimes C\phi(\eta[v := b]).$$

Informally, two domain values a and b are *symmetrical (w.r.t. the constraints C)* if whenever we have the assignment $\eta[v := a]$ with semiring value α, there is also an assignment $\eta'[v := b]$ with the same semiring value, where $\eta'[v := b] = \phi(\eta[v := a])$ (for some bijective mapping ϕ), and vice versa.

Clearly symmetry for all solutions implies symmetry for satisfiability.

Theorem 1 *Symmetry for all solutions implies symmetry for satisfiability.*

Since finding the mapping ϕ is one of the most important steps when looking for symmetry, it could be useful to reformulate the definition of symmetry for all solutions using equivalent propositions.

Proposition 1 *The following propositions describing the notion of symmetry for all solutions ($a \simeq b$) are equivalent:*

$$\exists \phi, \eta', \eta'' : \forall \eta : \phi(\eta[v := a]) = \eta'[v := b], \text{ and } \phi(\eta[v := b]) = \eta''[v := a], \wedge$$

$$\tag{1}$$

$$\bigotimes C\eta[v := a] = \bigotimes C\phi(\eta[v := a]) \wedge \bigotimes C\eta[v := b] = \bigotimes C\phi(\eta[v := b]);$$

$$\exists \phi, \forall \eta : \bigotimes C\eta[v := a] = \bigotimes C\phi(\eta[v := a])[v := b] \wedge \tag{2}$$

$$\bigotimes C\eta[v := b] = \bigotimes C\phi(\eta[v := b])[v := a];$$

$$\exists \phi, \forall \eta : \bigotimes C\eta[v := a] = \bigotimes C\phi(\eta)[v := b] \wedge \tag{3}$$

$$\bigotimes C\eta[v := b] = \bigotimes C\phi(\eta)[v := a];$$

It also important to notice that, similar to the crisp case, the notion of Interchangeability for Soft CSPs [7] is a specific type of symmetry for all solutions obtained using as ϕ the identity function.

Theorem 2 *Consider two domain values b and a, for a variable v and the set of constraints C. If b is fully interchangeable with a on v ($FI_v(a/b)$) (that is, for all assignments η, we have $\bigotimes C\eta[v := a] = \bigotimes C\eta[v := b]$ [7]) then a and b are symmetrical (w.r.t. the constraints C) ($a \simeq b$). In particular, the symmetry hold using as ϕ the identity function.*

Symmetries in SCSPs are rarer than in classical CSPs. For this reason using a notion of threshold (similar to that defined by Bistarelli *et al.* [7]) is useful.

Definition 3 (Threshold symmetry for satisfiability) *Consider two domain values b and a for a variable v, the set of constraints C and a threshold $\bar{\alpha}$; we say that b and a are $_{\bar{\alpha}}$symmetrical for satisfiability ($a \approx_{\bar{\alpha}} b$) if and only if*

$$\forall \alpha \geq \bar{\alpha}, \exists \eta, \eta' : \bigotimes C\eta[v := a] = \alpha \iff \bigotimes C\eta'[v := b] = \alpha$$

Informally, two domain values a and b are $_{\alpha}$symmetrical for satisfiability if whenever the assignment $v := a$ ($v := b$) leads to a solution with value $\alpha \geq \bar{\alpha}$, then, there is also a way to obtain a solution with the same value α using the assignment $v := b$ ($v := a$).

Definition 4 (Threshold symmetry for all solutions) *Consider two domain values b and a for a variable v, the set of constraints C and a threshold $\bar{\alpha}$; we say that b and a are $_{\bar{\alpha}}$symmetrical for all solutions ($a \simeq_{\bar{\alpha}} b$) if and only if*

$$\exists \phi, \eta', \eta'', \alpha, \alpha' \geq \bar{\alpha} : \forall \eta : \phi(\eta[v := a]) = \eta'[v := b], \text{ and } \phi(\eta[v := b]) = \eta''[v := a],$$

$$\wedge \bigotimes C\eta[v := a] = \alpha \wedge \bigotimes C\phi(\eta[v := a]) = \alpha$$

$$\wedge \bigotimes C\eta[v := b] = \alpha' \wedge \bigotimes C\phi(\eta[v := b]) = \alpha'.$$

Informally, two domain values a and b are $_{\bar{\alpha}}$*symmetrical for all solutions* if whenever the assignment $\eta[v := a]$ leads to a solution whose semiring value is $\alpha \geq \bar{\alpha}$, then there is also a solution $\eta'[v := b]$ with the same semiring value, where $\eta'[v := b] = \phi(\eta[v := a])$ (for some bijective mapping ϕ), and vice versa.

We can prove that the number of symmetries increases when we increase the threshold level.

Theorem 3 *Given two domain elements a and b and two thresholds $\alpha_1 \leq \alpha_2$. Then,*

- *if $a \approx_{\alpha_1} b$, then $a \approx_{\alpha_2} b$;*
- *if $a \simeq_{\alpha_1} b$, then $a \simeq_{\alpha_2} b$.*

4 Examples

The example problem that will be studied here is based on the soft n-queens problem [5]. The example is a generalization of the usual n-queens problem, which can be found in [24]. The classical formulation requires that n queens are placed on a $n \times n$ chess-board in such a way that they do not attack each other. In this formulation, we may allow attacking queens, but we give a higher preference to solutions where queens attacking each other are farther apart. In order to formulate this problem as a constraint satisfaction problem, the location of the queens can be given by variables, and the *"do not attack each other"* requirement can be expressed in terms of a number of constraints. A simple way to do this is to assign a variable to each queen[1].

As the n queens must be placed in n different columns, we can identify each queen by its column, and represent its position by a variable which indicates the row of the queen in question. Let v_i stand for the row of the queen in the i-th column. The domain of each of the variables $v_1, \ldots, v_n$ is $\{1, 2, \ldots, n\}$. For any two different variables, v_i and v_j, the following two constraints must hold, expressing that the queens should be in different rows and on different diagonals:

$$v_i \neq v_j \text{ and } |v_i - v_j| \neq |i - j|$$

If we want to use soft constraints, the previous crisp constraints have to be assigned an element of the semiring. So, whenever $v_i = v_j$, instead of giving the boolean value *false* we assign the fuzzy value $|i - j|/n$. This means that the farther apart the two queens are, the higher this value will be. The same reasoning also holds for the two diagonals; in this case, when $|v_i - v_j| = |i - j|$ we assign the value $|i - j|/n$.

Notice that each solution of this generalized n-queens problem has a semiring value which is obtained by minimizing the semiring values of all its constraints. This comes from the choice of the fuzzy semiring, where the multiplicative operation is the *min*. Therefore, if a solution contains three pairs of attacking queens, each of the pairs will have a semiring value given by one of the constraints, and the value of this solution will be the minimum of these

---

[1]Note that this choice already eliminates some possible symmetries.

three values. Different solutions are then ordered using the other semiring operation, which in this case is the *max*. Note that the same problem can be solved also with a different semiring, obtaining a different way to compute a solution and a different ordering. For example, we could have chosen the semiring $\{\mathcal{R} \cup +\infty, min, +, +\infty, 0\}$, where the value of each solution would have been obtained by summing the values of each attacking pair, and solutions would have been compared using the min operator.

Let's now fix $n = 4$ and illustrate the definitions of the previous section using this example. Clearly we can see that, as in the crisp case, for any v_i with $i = 1, \ldots, 4$, we have $1 \simeq 4$ and $2 \simeq 3$. We have, in fact, for any configuration η,

$$\bigotimes C\eta[v_1 := 1] = \bigotimes C\phi^v(\eta)[v_1 := 4] \wedge$$
$$\bigotimes C\eta[v_1 := 4] = \bigotimes C\phi^v(\eta)[v_1 := 1];$$

where $\phi^v(\{v_1 := a_1, v_2 := a_2, v_3 := a_3, v_4 := a_4\}) = \{v_1 := 4 - a_1 + 1, v_2 := 4 - a_2 + 1, v_3 := 4 - a_3 + 1, v_4 := 4 - a_4 + 1\}$. The same happens for the variables $v_2, \ldots, v_4$ and for the pair $2 \simeq 3$. In Figure 1 some mappings are presented.

(a) A solution η with level $\frac{1}{4}$ and its symmetric equivalent ($1 \simeq 4$ for v_1).

(b) A solution η with level $\frac{1}{2}$ and its symmetric equivalent ($1 \simeq 4$ for v_1). (c) A solution η with level 1 and its symmetric equivalent ($2 \simeq 3$ for v_1).

Figure 1: Some mappings showing $1 \simeq 4$ and $2 \simeq 3$ for v_1.

Let's now consider the notion of $_\alpha$symmetry. For $n = 4$ we have many configurations with semiring value $\frac{1}{4}$. We only present in Figure 3 the configurations whose semiring value is greater or equal than $\frac{1}{2}$. All the configurations with levels $\frac{1}{2}$ and 1 can be obtained by applying the two geometric symmetries: 1. vertical symmetry $\phi^v(\{v_1 := a_1, \ldots, v_i := a_i, \ldots, v_n := a_n\}) = \{v_1 := n - a_1 + 1, \ldots, v_i := n - a_i + 1, \ldots, v_n := n - a_n + 1\}$ 2. horizontal symmetry $\phi^h(\{v_1 := a_1, \ldots, v_i := a_i, \ldots, v_n := a_n\}) = \{v_1 := a_n, \ldots, v_i := a_{n-i+1}, \ldots, v_n := a_1\}$. Notice also that in the soft 4-queen problem there are solutions with semiring value $\frac{3}{4}$ (see Figure 2) but these are excluded from our model, since we represent one queen in each column.

We want to show that when using a threshold $\bar{\alpha}$, more symmetries can be found. Suppose we fix $\bar{\alpha} = \frac{1}{2}$. By using Definition 4, looking for $_{\bar{\alpha}}$symmetry

Figure 2: A solution with level $\frac{3}{4}$ not permitted in our model.

(a) Solutions with level $\frac{1}{2}$.

(b) Solution with level 1.

Figure 3: Solutions for $n = 4$.

means that we need to check if there exists a mapping ϕ s.t. $a \simeq b$, but only when a and b are involved in a solution greater than the threshold $\bar{\alpha}$. Since in our example we want look for $\frac{1}{2}$ symmetries, it is sufficient to focus attention upon the configurations depicted in Figure 3.

We claim that $1 \simeq_{\frac{1}{2}} 3$ and $2 \simeq_{\frac{1}{2}} 4$ for variable v_2. To prove this, we need to give a mapping ϕ s.t. for any configuration η s.t. $\bigotimes C\eta[v_2 := 1] \geq \frac{1}{2}$ we have $\bigotimes C\eta[v_2 := 1] = \bigotimes C\phi(\eta)[v_2 := 3]$ and the opposite case (the same happens for $2 \simeq_{\frac{1}{2}} 4$). Let's consider the mapping ϕ similar to ϕ^v, s.t.

- $\phi(2, 4, 1, 3) = (3, 1, 2, 4)$, and $\phi(3, 1, 4, 2) = (2, 4, 1, 3)$,
- when restricted to variable v_1, v_3, and v_4 ($\phi_{\downarrow\{v_1, v_3, v_4\}} = \phi^v_{\downarrow\{v_1, v_3, v_4\}}$), and
- when restricted to v_2 ($\phi_{\downarrow\{v_2\}}(1) = 3, \phi_{\downarrow\{v_2\}}(2) = 4, \phi_{\downarrow\{v_2\}}(3) = 1, \phi_{\downarrow\{v_2\}}(4) = 2$.

The mapping just defined satisfies the condition of symmetry for all solutions greater than $\frac{1}{2}$. Figure 4 illustrates the mappings. Obviously the semiring value associated with a solution and its transformed equivalent is the same.

Obviously, we can check that the mapping maintains the same solution level, so $1 \simeq_{\frac{1}{2}} 3$ and $2 \simeq_{\frac{1}{2}} 4$. Similarly, we also have $1 \simeq_1 3$ and $2 \simeq_1 4$ (see Theorem 3).

5 Experiments

In this section we present some empirical results supporting the theoretical framework presented in Section 3. In particular, Section 5.1 demonstrates that

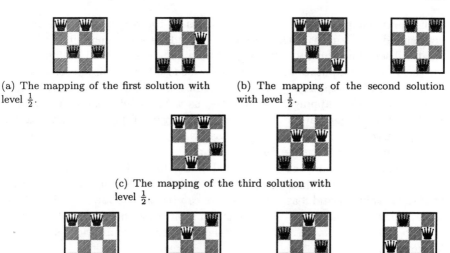

(a) The mapping of the first solution with level $\frac{1}{2}$.

(b) The mapping of the second solution with level $\frac{1}{2}$.

(c) The mapping of the third solution with level $\frac{1}{2}$.

(d) The mapping of the fourth solution with level $\frac{1}{2}$.

(e) The mapping of the solution with level 1.

Figure 4: The mappings of the solutions with level $\geq \frac{1}{2}$.

if values a and b for variable v are α_1 threshold symmetric, they are also α_2 threshold symmetric, where $\alpha_1 \leq \alpha_2$ (see Theorem 3), and that the number of mappings ϕ satisfying the definition for threshold symmetry for all solutions (Definition 4), increases with larger threshold value $\bar{\alpha}$.

In Section 5.2 we present results from an implementation of a Symmetry Breaking During Search algorithm that utilizes soft symmetries to reduce search effort and the number of solutions produced. Experimental results confirm the improvement in the search performance, and show a significant reduction in the number of distinct solutions found.

5.1 Counting Soft Symmetries

In crisp CSPs, the only mappings which can be used to find symmetrical values in the n-queens problem are the geometric mappings, for example, ϕ^v and ϕ^h, the vertical and horizontal axial symmetries, respectively. In the soft CSP framework, we can utilize the notion of threshold symmetry to find many more mappings, and hence more symmetrical values, which allow symmetry breaking methods to break more symmetries at each step.

In our experimental evaluations, we use a small subset of all possible mappings ϕ to test for threshold symmetry between two values a and b for a variable v. In particular, we chose to systematically generate the subset of all possible mappings for the soft queens problem in which domain values are mapped directly to other domain values *irrespective* of what variable they are assigned to. We computed this subset by generating $n!$ permutations of the domain values and mapping directly between values in the original domain and the corresponding position in the permuted one. This set of mappings is a very small subset of all the possible mappings ϕ among chess-board configurations; for the sake of computational tractability we chose to use this subset to enable us to find useful mappings. This subset allowed us to find a significant number of non-geometric mappings, and provides us with useful results. Many other methods for the generation of a manageable subset of mappings are possible. Using a larger set of mappings would potentially give rise to more symmetries, which is one possible avenue for future work.

In Table 1 we show the symmetrical values found for v_1 using this set of mappings for various values of threshold $\bar{\alpha}$ in the 5-Queens problem; we present results for values 1 and 3 as examples. We can see that at lower levels of $\bar{\alpha}$, we identify, for example, values 1 and 5 as symmetrical with 1 for v_1. At all levels of $\bar{\alpha}$ greater than this, we also identify these values as symmetrical, supporting Theorem 3.

Table 1: Table of symmetrical values for $a = 1$ and $a = 3$ for v_1 in 5-Queens problem at various values of threshold $\bar{\alpha}$.

$\bar{\alpha}$	$(v_1 := a)$	symmetric values
0.2–0.4	1	$\{1, 5\}$
	3	$\{3\}$
0.6–1.0	1	$\{1, 2, 3, 4, 5\}$
	3	$\{1, 2, 3, 4, 5\}$

Table 2 presents results attained by systematically evaluating the threshold symmetry for all solutions (Definition 4) for all (v, a, b, ϕ) combinations, using the set of mappings we generated as discussed above. Results shown in the table indicate the number of mappings that satisfy the definition for the specified value of $\bar{\alpha}$. The results clearly show that the number of mappings which give rise to symmetries is much larger at higher thresholds, a useful property when using symmetrical values to guide search in soft CSPs.

5.2 Exploiting Soft Symmetries during Search

To demonstrate the utility of the ideas developed in this paper we implemented an algorithm to break $_\alpha$symmetries in soft CSPs. In this algorithm we attempt to break symmetry in the search space to avoid searching for solutions which are symmetrical to solutions of the same (or higher) consistency which we have already found. Our implementation is based on the Symmetry Breaking During Search (SBDS) approach [17].

We implemented this search algorithm by augmenting a simple backtracker to break symmetry during search by avoiding sections of the search space which are symmetrical to those we have already successfully explored. In this way

Table 2: Number of times threshold symmetry for all solutions definition is satisfied with threshold $\bar{\alpha} = \frac{1}{n}$ and $\bar{\alpha} = 1$ when iterating through all (v, a, b, ϕ) combinations for soft queens problems of various sizes.

n	$\bar{\alpha} = \frac{1}{n}$	$\bar{\alpha} = 1$
2	6	6
3	15	27
4	24	68
5	40	100
6	54	1620

we can significantly reduce the search effort required to find a set of solutions and reduce the number of distinct solutions produced by providing a set of representative solutions instead of an exhaustive list of all possible solutions of the required consistency.

To enable us to prune symmetric states, we maintain a value exclusion set for each level of the search tree. Each time that we find a solution of the required consistency α, we update these exclusion sets with values $_\alpha$symmetric to the relevant value from that solution. To ensure that symmetries act locally, we empty value exclusion sets for subsequent levels of the search tree each time we backtrack to a choice point.

This approach does not improve on the effort required to find one solution to a soft CSP. However, in soft CSPs our goal is usually to find the best solution(s). Therefore, if we find a solution with a high level of consistency, we do not need to search for states which are symmetrical to this solution, significantly reducing search effort. Furthermore, we also reduce the effort involved in finding *all* solutions to a soft CSP.

The set of symmetrical values used for this algorithm is pre-computed by following an approach similar to that outlined above for computing the results in Table 2. In this case, we evaluate the threshold symmetry for all solutions definition for all $(v, a, b, \phi, \bar{\alpha})$ combinations possible in the relevant instance of the soft queens problem. We then store each (v, a, b) triple which is found to be $_\alpha$symmetric, thus avoiding the significant overhead of searching through a large set of mappings each time we wish to add to our value exclusion sets. Since we lack an efficient way to identify useful non-geometric mappings, we see this approach as a reasonable compromise between the added search efficiency gained by utilizing $_\alpha$symmetries and the off-line overhead of computing them.

The set of solutions produced by this algorithm can be seen as a representative subset of all possible solutions of the required consistency, which is a useful method of producing diverse solutions to a loosely constrained problem.

Results achieved using this approach are encouraging: we significantly reduce the number of distinct solutions found and the number of backtracks required to find those solutions. In Table 3 we present results demonstrating

Table 3: Results for our Soft SBDS Backtracker

		Soft SBDS		Backtracker	
n	α	#bts	#sols	#bts	#sols
2	1	2	0	2	0
2	0.5	2	1	4	4
3	1	4	0	4	0
3	0.667	3	1	5	2
3	0.333	14	8	27	27
4	1	10	1	13	2
4	0.75	10	1	13	2
4	0.5	11	6	26	16
4	0.25	30	16	256	256
5	1	4	1	43	10
5	0.8	4	1	43	10
5	0.6	4	1	43	10
5	0.4	103	66	233	184
5	0.2	363	243	3125	3125
6	1	87	2	131	4
6	0.833	50	6	155	32
6	0.667	67	20	197	70
6	0.5	124	61	358	198
6	0.333	485	304	3019	2642
6	0.167	1092	729	46656	46656

the utility of our approach to breaking soft symmetries, particularly in loosely constrained problems. For example, if we examine the results for $n = 6$ and $\alpha = \frac{1}{6}$ we can see that a very large reduction in the number of backtracks is attained to find a small representative subset of a large number of possible solutions.

6 Conclusions

Exploiting symmetry in constraint satisfaction problems has become a very popular topic of research in recent times. The existence of symmetry in a problem has the effect of artificially increasing the size of the search space that is explored by search algorithms. Another significant topic of research has been approaches to reasoning about preferences. As constraint processing applications are becoming more widespread in areas such as electronic commerce, configuration, etc., it is becoming increasingly important that we can reason about preferences as efficiently as possible.

We have presented an approach to dealing with symmetry in the semiring framework for soft constraints. We demonstrate that breaking symmetries in soft constraint satisfaction problems improves the efficiency of search. The paper contributes to the state-of-the-art in symmetry breaking, as well as in reasoning about preferences.

Acknowledgment

This work has received support from Enterprise Ireland under their Basic Research Grant Scheme (Grant Number SC/02/289) and their International Collaboration Programme (Grant Number IC/2003/88).

References

[1] R. Backofen and S. Will. Excluding symmetries in concurrent constraint programming. In *Proceedings of CP-99*, LNCS 1520, pages 72–86, 1999.

[2] Belaid Benhamou. Study of symmetry in constraint satisfaction problems. In *Proceedings of CP-94*, 1994.

[3] S. Bistarelli, H. Fargier, U. Montanari, F. Rossi, T. Schiex, and G. Verfaillie. Semiring-based CSPs and Valued CSPs: Frameworks, properties, and comparison. *Constraints*, 4(3), 1999.

[4] S. Bistarelli, U. Montanari, and F. Rossi. Semiring-based Constraint Solving and Optimization. *Journal of the ACM*, 44(2):201–236, Mar 1997.

[5] S. Bistarelli, U. Montanari, and F. Rossi. Semiring-based Constraint Logic Programming: Syntax and Semantics. *ACM Transactions on Programming Languages and System (TOPLAS)*, 23:1–29, 2001.

[6] S. Bistarelli, U. Montanari, and F. Rossi. Soft concurrent constraint programming. In *Proc. ESOP, April 6 - 14, 2002, Grenoble, France*, LNCS, pages 53–67, Heidelberg, Germany, 2002. Springer-Verlag.

[7] Stefano Bistarelli, Boi Faltings, and Nicoleta Neagu. A definition of interchangeability for soft csps. In *Recent Advances in Constraints*, LNAI 2627. Springer, 2003.

[8] C.A. Brown, L. Finkelstein, and P.W. Purdon Jr. Backtrack searching in the presence of symmetry. In T. Mora, editor, *Applied Algebra, Algebraic Algorithms and Error-Correcting Codes*, volume 357 of *LNCS*, pages 99–110. Springer-Verlag, 1988.

[9] J. Crawford. A theoretical analysis of reasoning by symmetry in first-order logic. In *Proc. of the AAAI-92 Workshop on Tractable Reasoning*, 1992.

[10] J. Crawford, G. Luks, M. Ginsberg, and A. Roy. Symmetry breaking predicates for search problems. In *Proceedings of KR-96*, pages 148–159, 1996.

[11] C. Domshlak, F. Rossi, B. Venable, and T. Walsh. Reasoning about soft constraints and conditional preferences: complexity results and approximation techniques. In *Proceedings of IJCAI-2003*, August 2003.

[12] T. Fahle, S. Schamberger, and M. Sellmann. Symmetry breaking. In *Proceedings of CP-01*, LNCS 2239, pages 93–107, 2001.

[13] P. Flener, A. Frisch, B. Hnich, Z. Kiziltan, I. Miguel, J. Pearson, and T. Walsh. Breaking row and column symmetries in matrix models. In *Proceedings of CP-02*, LNCS 2470, pages 462–476, 2002.

[14] F. Focacci and M. Milano. Global cut framework for removing symmetries. In *Proceedings of CP-01*, LNCS 2239, pages 75–92, 2001.

[15] E.C. Freuder. Eliminating interchangeable values in constraint satisfaction problems. In *Proceedings of the AAAI*, pages 227–233, 1991.

[16] I.P. Gent, W. Harvey, and T. Kelsey. Groups and constraints: Symmetry breaking during search. In *Proceedings of CP-02*, LNCS 2470, pages 415–430, 2002.

[17] I.P. Gent and B.M. Smith. Symmetry breaking in constraint programming. In W. Horn, editor, *Proceedings of ECAI-2000*, pages 599–603. IOS Press, 2000.

[18] U. Junker. Preference programming for configuration. In *Proceedings of the 4th International Workshop on Configuration (IJCAI-01)*, pages 50–56, August 2001.

[19] I. McDonald and B. Smith. Partial symmetry breaking. In *Proceedings of CP-02*, LNCS 2470, pages 431–445, 2002.

[20] Pedro Meseguer and Carme Torras. Exploiting symmetries within constraint satisfaction search. *Artificial Intelligence*, 129(1–2):133–163, 2001.

[21] J.-F. Puget. On the satisfiability of symmetrical constrained satisfaction problems. In *Proceedings of ISMIS-93*, LNAI 689, pages 350–361, 1993.

[22] J.-F. Puget. Symmetry breaking revisited. In *Proceedings of CP-02*, LNCS 2470, pages 446–461, 2002.

[23] B. Smyth and P. McClave. Similarity vs. diversity. In *Proceedings ICCBR-2001*, LNCS 2080, pages 347–361, 2001.

[24] P. van Hentenryck. *Constraint Satisfaction in Logic Programming*. MIT Press, Cambridge, MA, USA, 1989.

How to Classify Hard and Soft Constraints in Non-binary Constraint Satisfaction Problems

Miguel A. Salido

Dpto. Ciencias de la Computación e Inteligencia Artificial
Universidad de Alicante
03080 Alicante, Spain
msalido@dsic.upv.es[*]

Federico Barber

Dpto. de Sistemas Informáticos y Computación
Universidad Politécnica de Valencia,
46020 Valencia, Spain
fbarber@dsic.upv.es

Abstract

Nowadays many real problems can be modelled as Constraint Satisfaction Problems (CSPs) and solved using constraint programming techniques. In many situations, it is desirable to be able to state both *hard* constraints and *soft* constraints. Hard constraints must hold while soft constraints may be violated but as many as possible should be satisfied. Although the problem constraints can be divided into two groups, the order in which these constraints are studied can improve efficiency, particularly in problems with non-binary constraints. In this paper, we present a heuristic technique called *Hard and Soft Constraint Ordering Heuristic* (HASCOH) that carries out a classification of hard and soft constraints in order to study the tightest hard constraints first and to obtain ever better solutions. In this way, inconsistencies can be found earlier and the number of constraint checks can be significantly reduced.

1 Introduction

Many problems arising in a variety of domains such as planning, scheduling, diagnosis, decision support, scheduling and design can be efficiently modelled as Constraint Satisfaction Problems (CSPs) and solved using constraint programming techniques. Some of these problems can be modelled naturally using non-binary (or n-ary) constraints. Although, researchers have traditionally focused on binary constraints [14], the need to address issues regarding non-binary constraints has recently started to be widely recognized in the constraint satisfaction literature.

---

[*]This work has been partially supported by the grant (PPI-02-03) of visitor professor from the Polytechnic University of Valencia, and the project DPI2001-2094-C03-03 from the Spanish Government.

One approach to solving CSPs is to use a depth-first backtrack search algorithm [3]. General methods for solving CSPs include *Generate and test* [11] and *Backtracking* [10] algorithms. Many works have been carried out to improve the *Backtracking* method. One way of increasing the efficiency of *Backtracking* includes the use of *search order* for variables and values. Some heuristics based on *variable ordering* and *value ordering* [9] have been developed, because of the additivity of the variables and values. Constraints are also considered to be *additive*, that is, the order of imposition of constraints does not matter; all that matters is that the conjunction of constraints be satisfied [1].

Thus, a real life problem can be modelled as a CSP, and using some of the current ordering heuristics, it can be solved in a more efficiently way by some of the backtracking-based search algorithms (Figure 1).

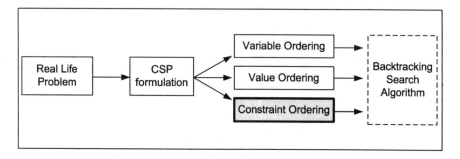

Figure 1: Constraint Ordering

In spite of the additivity of constraints, only a few works have be done on binary constraint ordering mainly for arc-consistency algorithms [15], [8]. However little work has be done on non-binary constraint ordering (disjunctive constraints [13]), and only some heuristic techniques classify the non-binary constraints by means of the arity. However, a low arity does not imply a tighter constraint. For instance, three integer variables ranged on the interval $[0, 10]$, (i.e. $x_1, x_2, x_3 : [0, 10]$), constraint $x_1 \leq 1$ is tighter than constraint $x_1 + x_2 + x_3 \leq 35$ that is redundant and it does not prune the search space. Otherwise, constraint $x_1 + x_2 + x_3 \leq 1$ is tighter than constraint $x_1 \leq 10$ that is redundant and it does not prune the search space. Thus, constraint ordering based on the arity of constraints is not useful in some techniques. Moreover, when all non-binary constraints have the same arity or these constraints are classified as hard and soft constraints, both *Backtracking* and *Generate and test* techniques are not useful.

In this paper, we propose a heuristic technique called *Hard and Soft Constraint Ordering Heuristic* (HASCOH) that classifies the non-binary constraints, independently of the arity so that hard constraints are studied before soft constraints and then the tightest constraints are studied before the loosest constraints. This is based on the *first-fail* principle, which can be explained as

"To succeed, try first where you are more likely to fail"

HASCOH carries out this constraint ordering to identify as soon as possible inconsistent tuples in order to significantly reduce the number of constraint checks. Without loss of generality, we do not consider preferences in soft constraints, that is, all soft constraints are equally important. Thus, soft constraints are studied after the hard constraints in order to satisfy as many soft constraints as possible.

In section 1, we formally define constraint satisfaction problems and describe two well-known ordering algorithms. Section 3 describes the constraint ordering in hard and soft non-binary constraints. Section 4 presents the computational complexity of HASCOH. The results of the evaluation are presented in section 5. Finally, in section 6, we present our conclusions and future work.

2 Definition and Algorithms

Briefly, a constraint satisfaction problem (CSP) consists of:

- a set of variables $X = \{x_1, x_2, ..., x_n\}$

- a set of domains $D = \{D_1, D_2, ..., D_n\}$, where each variable $x_i \in X$ has a set D_i of possible values

- a finite collection of constraints $C = \{c_1, ..., c_k, s_1, .., s_p\}$ restricting the values that the variables can simultaneously take.

A solution to a CSP is an assignment of values to all the variables (state) so that at least all the hard constraints are satisfied. The objective in a CSP may be to determine:

- whether a solution exists, that is, if the CSP is consistent.

- all solutions, many solutions, or only one solution, with no preference as to which one.

- an optimal, or a good solution by means of an objective function defined in terms of certain variables.

In some problems it is desirable to find all solutions, so that some techniques such as value ordering are not valid, so it is necessary to be able to efficiently find the *dead-ends* earlier in order to reduce the search tree.

Two ordering algorithms are analyzed in [12],[1]: variable ordering and value ordering. Let's briefly look at these two algorithms.

2.1 Variable Ordering

The experiments and analyzes by several researchers have shown that the ordering in which variables are assigned during the search may have substantial impact on the complexity of the search space explored. The ordering may be either a static ordering, or dynamic ordering. Examples of static ordering heuristics are *minimum width* [5] and *maximum degree* [4], in which the order of the variables is specified before the search begins, and it is not changed thereafter. An example of dynamic ordering heuristic is *minimum remaining values* [9], in which the choice of next variable to be considered at any point depends on the current state of the search.

Dynamic ordering is not feasible for all search algorithms, e.g., with simple backtracking, during the search, there is no extra information available that could be used to make a different choice of ordering from the initial ordering. However, with forward checking, the current state includes the domains of the variables as they have been pruned by the current set of instantiations. Therefore, it is possible to base the choice of the next variable on this information.

2.2 Value Ordering

Comparatively little work has been done on algorithms for value ordering even for binary CSPs [7],[6]. The basic idea behind value ordering algorithms is to select the value for the current variable which is most likely to lead to a solution. Again, the order in which these values are considered can have substantial impact on the time necessary to find the first solution. However, if all solutions are required or the problem is not consistent, then the value ordering does nor make any difference. A different value ordering will rearrange the branches emanating from each node of the search tree. This is an advantage if it ensures that a branch which leads to a solution is searched earlier than a branch which leads to a dead-end. For example, if the CSP has a solution, and if a correct value is chosen for each variable, then a solution can be found without any backtracking.

Suppose we have selected a variable to instantiate: how should we choose which value to try first? It may be that none of the values will succeed. In that case, every value for the current variable will eventually have to be considered and the order does not matter. On the other hand, if we can find a complete solution based on the past instantiations, we want to choose a value which is likely to succeed and unlikely to lead to a conflict.

3 Hard and Soft Non-binary Constraint Ordering

Our main objective is to classify the problem constraints in an appropriate order depending on the desired goals. One way to manage the problem constraints is by means of the natural order in which they are inserted into the problem. However, when managing hard and soft constraints there is a natural and reasonable order where the hard constraints are managed first and the soft constraints are managed later. This natural constraint ordering is presented in Figure 2. Each hard and soft constraint satisfies a portion of the search space, but no ordering is carried out to avoid constraint checking.

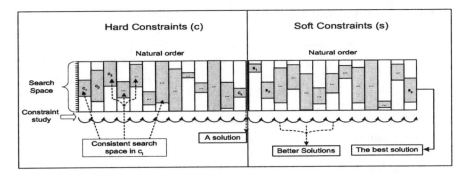

Figure 2: Natural ordering of hard and soft constraints

In many real problems, the main objective is to obtain a solution that satisfies hard constraints and as many soft constraints as possible. In this case, an any-time proposal may be appropriate. A feasible solution may be improved at any time by another solution that satisfies more soft constraints. Thus, both hard and soft constraints are classified from the tightest ones to the loosest ones. This constraint ordering is showed in Figure 3.

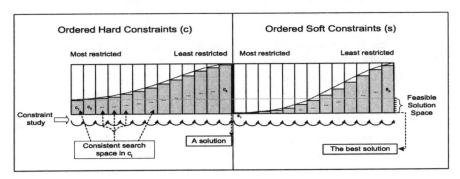

Figure 3: Constraint ordering in the any-time proposal

The search space of the correctly ordered hard and soft constraints has a behaviour which is similar to the behaviour of the left tails of normal curves, in which the height of each curve is bounded by the entire search space. The height of the tail of the hard constraints represents the valid search space for the problem. This restricted search space is the only valid search space for finding problem solutions and the rest of the search space can be removed.

Furthermore, the height of the tail of the soft constraints may be zero, because soft constraints are generally over-constrained. However, these constraints are dispensable and the objective is to satisfy as many soft constraints as possible. These soft constraints are classified from the tightest one to the loosest one. Thus, the first solution generated by the study of hard constraints is checked with all soft constraints and this solution is labelled with the number of satisfied soft constraints. Due to the any-time behaviour, the following solution satisfying all hard constraints is checked with the soft constraints from the tightest one to the loosest one, and this constraint checking is aborted when its label can not be greater than the label of the first solution. Thus, at any time, the best solution is maintained with its label, and a future solution is checked with soft constraints while its label may reach the label of the current best solution.

Here, we will focus on this any-time behaviour in which, depending on the user requirements, the solutions can be improved in order to satisfy more soft constraints. Thus, our main objective is to classify both hard and soft non-binary constraints in the appropriate order to be solved by some of the current techniques that manage non-binary constraints in a natural way [2].

3.1   Specification of HASCOH

HASCOH is a heuristic technique that carries out an appropriate classification of hard and soft constraints in order to obtain ever better solutions and reducing the number of constraint checks.

To this end, a preprocessing step carries out a classification based on a sample in finite population, in order to classify both hard and soft constraints so that hard constraints are studied before soft constraints and then the tightest constraints are studied before the loosest constraints. Figure 4 shows this preprocessing step in which a significant sample is chosen to statistically obtain an appropriate order of constraints.

Then, a *Generate and test* [11] or *Backtracking-based* [10] algorithm can be used to solve this ordered problem. The search algorithm tries to find a solution that satisfies hard constraints first. Once a solution is found, it is checked with the soft constraints and this solution is labelled with the number of satisfied soft constraints. Thus, the search algorithm can continue looking for a new solution that satisfies more soft constraints. Therefore, as an any-time proposal, and depending on the time available, these solutions may be improved in order to find a solution that satisfies as many constraints as possible.

Figure 4 shows that a (partial) state 1 is checked by the search algorithm with hard constraints in the appropriate order, generated by the preprocessing step, but the hard constraint 4 (the rectangle X) is returned as *unfeasible constraint* and the constraints checking (with the state 1) is aborted and a backtracking is carried out.

Once i backtracks have been performed, the state i is checked by the search algorithm with the ordered hard constraints and all hard constraints satisfy this state. Then, this state is a problem solution and a constraint checking is carried out with the soft constraints to know how good this solution is, that is, how many soft constraints satisfy this solution. Thus, a further solution can be compared with the last one to finally return the best solution. That is, state $i + j + k$ returns a better solution that state i. This is due to this new state satisfies more soft constraints than state i.

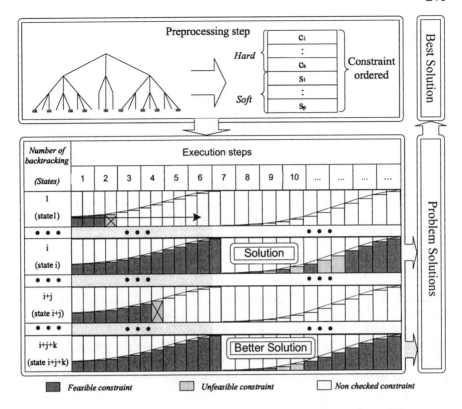

Figure 4: General scheme of HASCOH

Let's analyze the preprocessing step, the hard constraint management and the soft constraint management.

3.2 The Preprocessing Step

HASCOH is internally composed by an easy preprocessing step based on the sampling from a finite population in statistics, where there is a population, and a sample is chosen to represent this population. In our context, the population is composed by the states generated by means of the Cartesian Product of variable domain and the sample is composed by $s(n)$ random and well distributed states (s is a polynomial function) in order to represent the entire population. As in statistic, the user selects the size of the sample ($s(n)$). Figure 5 represents the distribution of the sample. This sample will be used to classify both hard and soft constraints.

With the selected sample of vertices $s(n)$, HASCOH checks how many states $sc_i : sc_i \leq s(n)$ satisfy each hard constraint. Thus, each hard constraint c_i is labelled with prc_i: $c_i(prc_i)$, where $prc_i = sc_i/s(n)$ represents the probability that c_i satisfies the whole problem. Thus, HASCOH classifies the hard con-

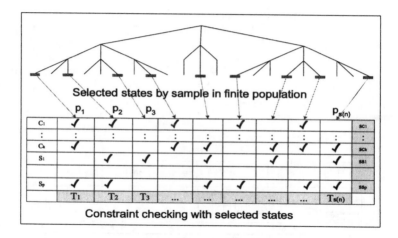

Figure 5: Sample in finite population

straints in ascending order of the labels prc_i. Idem for soft constraints s_i, which will be labeled with prs_i: $s_i(prs_i)$, where $prs_i = ss_i/s(n)$.

Therefore, HASCOH translates the initial non-binary CSP into an ordered non-binary CSP so that it can be studied by a CSP solver. In Figure 5, it can be observed that each hard and soft constraint is checked with each selected state. Furthermore, each state of the sample might store the evaluation value T_i to be used by a stochastic local search algorithm to restart the search.

The pseudo-code of HASCOH is presented in Figure 6.

3.3 Hard Constraint Management

As we pointed out in previous sections, hard constraints must hold. However, a solution (consistent state) that satisfies all hard constraints may be a partial state, that is, it is possible that all variables are not involved in the hard constraints. In this case, we can distinguish between *hard variables* and *soft variables*. A hard variable is a variable involved in at least a hard constraint while a soft variable is a variable only involved in soft constraints but not in hard constraints.

Once hard constraints have classified in the appropriate order by the pre-processing step, a *Generate and test* or *Backtracking-based* algorithm can be used to solve this ordered subproblem. The search algorithm tries to assign values to hard variables such that all hard constraints are satisfied. It must be taken into account that initial (partial) states to be checked with the tightest constraints must be located inside the search space of these tightest constraints. Thus, the search does not start at any point of the search space but rather in a 'reduced' portion of the search space (depending of the constrainedness of the tightest constraints). This valid and reduced search space can be seen below of the horizontal line in Figure 3. The search space can be significantly reduced

---

Hard and Soft Constraint Ordering Heuristic

Inputs: A set of n variables, $X_1,...,X_n$, their domains, $D_1...,D_n$, and a set of hard constraints, $c_1,...,c_k$ and a set of soft constraints $s_1,...,s_p$

Outputs: A set of ordered hard constraints, $c_{ord1}...,c_{ordk}$ and soft constraints $s_{ord1}...,s_{ordp}$

1.- Select $s(n)$ points from $D_1 \times ... \times D_n$: $s(n)$ a polynomial and well distributed sample.

2.- For each hard constraint c_i (soft constraint s_i) do
$\quad$ {
$\quad\quad sc_i = 0; \quad (ss_i = 0)$
$\quad\quad$ For each selected point p_j
$\quad\quad\quad$ {
$\quad\quad\quad\quad$ If satisfy(p_j, c_i) $\quad$ (satisfy(p_j, s_i))
$\quad\quad\quad\quad\quad sc_i = sc_i +1; \quad (ss_i = ss_i+1)$
$\quad\quad\quad$ }
$\quad$ }
$\quad prc_i = sc_i /s(n); \quad (prs_i = ss_i/s(n))$

3.- Classifies in ascending order of the labels constraints $\{c_i(prc_i),...,c_k(prc_k)\} \{s_j(prs_j),...,s_i(prs_i)\}$

Figure 6: Pseudo-code of Hard and Soft Constraint Ordering Heuristic

a priori and also inconsistencies can be found earlier with the corresponding savings in constraint checking.

3.4 Soft Constraint Management

The soft constraint management depends on the existence of the soft variables.

If the soft variables are not involved into the problem then a solution satisfying the hard constraints is a consistent state. This solution will only be checked with the ordered soft constraints and labelled with the number of satisfied soft constraints. Figure 7 shows an example in which the first solution satisfying all hard constraints is (1,4,3,3). This solution is checked with the soft constraints (13 soft constraints) and its label is 7, that is, this solution satisfies 7 soft constraints. The search algorithm looks for a new solution (1,4,3,4) and this solution is checked with the soft constraints. Due to the first solution did not satisfy 13-7=6 soft constraints, the soft constraint checking with the new solution (1,4,3,4) will be carried out while the number of unfeasible constraints is less that 6. In this case, the solution (1,4,3,4) does not satisfy the first four soft constraints, so the soft constraint checking continues and this solution satisfies 9 soft constraints and it is considered at this time as the best solution. Finally, the last solution (4,5,8,2) generated by the search algorithm is checked with the soft constraints. However, this solution (4,5,8,2) does not satisfy the first four soft constraints, so the following soft constraints will not be checked with the corresponding savings in constraint checking.

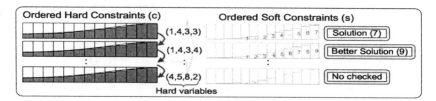

Figure 7: Example of soft constraint management without soft variables

If the soft variables are involved into the problem then a solution satisfying the hard constraints is a consistent partial state. Without loss of generality, a consistent state can be returned, using only hard constraints, by giving an assignment of values from their domains to the soft variables. However a backtracking search can be performed to the soft constraints in order to improve the current solution. Figure 8 shows an example in which an assignment of values to hard variables $(1,4,3,5,-,-)$ satisfies all hard constraints and a solution is found. However, soft variables can be a priori assigned to any value from their domains, but a backtracking search must be performed to find a solution that satisfies as many soft constraints as possible (solution $(1,4,3,5,3,2)$).

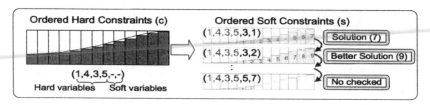

Figure 8: Example of soft constraint management with soft variables

Therefore, as an any-time proposal, and depending on the time available, these solutions may be improved in order to obtain ever better solutions.

Example: The 4-queens problem is a classical search problem in the artificial intelligence area. We have extended this problem to include soft constraints. The problem is to place four queens z_1, z_2, z_3, z_4 on a 4×4 chessboard so that no two queens can capture each other. Thus, hard constraints impose the condition that no two queens are allowed to be placed on the same row, the same column, or the same diagonal. We also add two soft constraints: queen 1 value must be less or equal than queen 2 value: $z_1 \leq z_3$ and the sum of queen 1 and queen 2 values must be less or equal than queen 3 value: $z_1 + z_2 \leq z_3$. This modified 4-queens problem is shown in Figure 9.

The preprocessing step checks how many partial states (from a given sample: 16 tuples $\{(1,1),(1,2),\cdots,(4,3),(4,4)\}$) satisfy each constraint and classifies them afterwards. It can be observed that some hard constraints are tightest than others. Constraints c_1, c_4, c_6 only satisfy 6 partial states, while constraints c_2 and c_5 satisfy 8 partial states and constraint c_3 satisfies 10 partial states.

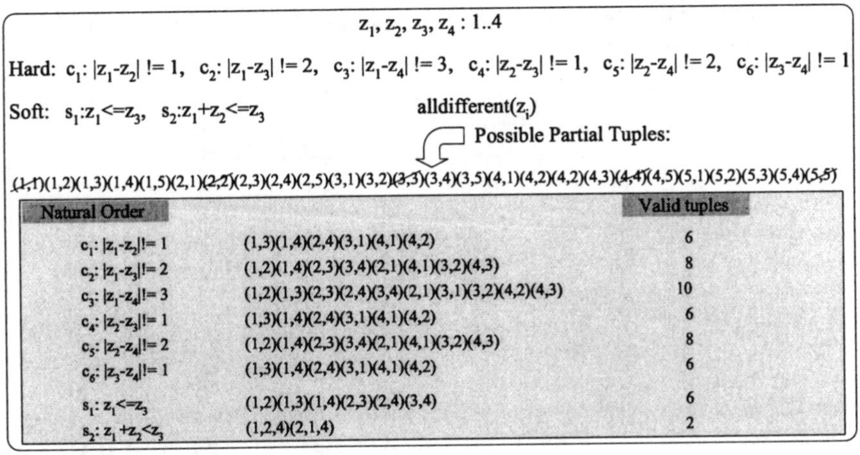

$$z_1, z_2, z_3, z_4 : 1..4$$

Hard: $c_1: |z_1\text{-}z_2| \mathrel{!=} 1$, $c_2: |z_1\text{-}z_3| \mathrel{!=} 2$, $c_3: |z_1\text{-}z_4| \mathrel{!=} 3$, $c_4: |z_2\text{-}z_3| \mathrel{!=} 1$, $c_5: |z_2\text{-}z_4| \mathrel{!=} 2$, $c_6: |z_3\text{-}z_4| \mathrel{!=} 1$

Soft: $s_1: z_1 <= z_3$, $s_2: z_1+z_2 <= z_3$ alldifferent(z_i)

Possible Partial Tuples:

(1,1)(1,2)(1,3)(1,4)(1,5)(2,1)(2,2)(2,3)(2,4)(2,5)(3,1)(3,2)(3,3)(3,4)(3,5)(4,1)(4,2)(4,3)(4,4)(4,5)(5,1)(5,2)(5,3)(5,4)(5,5)

Natural Order		Valid tuples
$c_1: |z_1\text{-}z_2| \mathrel{!=} 1$	(1,3)(1,4)(2,4)(3,1)(4,1)(4,2)	6
$c_2: |z_1\text{-}z_3| \mathrel{!=} 2$	(1,2)(1,4)(2,3)(3,4)(2,1)(4,1)(3,2)(4,3)	8
$c_3: |z_1\text{-}z_4| \mathrel{!=} 3$	(1,2)(1,3)(2,3)(2,4)(3,4)(2,1)(3,1)(3,2)(4,2)(4,3)	10
$c_4: |z_2\text{-}z_3| \mathrel{!=} 1$	(1,3)(1,4)(2,4)(3,1)(4,1)(4,2)	6
$c_5: |z_2\text{-}z_4| \mathrel{!=} 2$	(1,2)(1,4)(2,3)(3,4)(2,1)(4,1)(3,2)(4,3)	8
$c_6: |z_3\text{-}z_4| \mathrel{!=} 1$	(1,3)(1,4)(2,4)(3,1)(4,1)(4,2)	6
$s_1: z_1 <= z_3$	(1,2)(1,3)(1,4)(2,3)(2,4)(3,4)	6
$s_2: z_1 + z_2 < z_3$	(1,2,4)(2,1,4)	2

Figure 9: The 4-queens problem

Furthermore, soft constraint 2 is tightest than soft constraint 1. Thus, four groups of hard constraints and only one group of soft constraints are generated. The first group is composed by the *alldifferent* constraint. The second group is composed by constraints c_1, c_4, c_6, and the third and fourth group are composed by constraints c_2, c_5 and c_3, respectively. Finally, soft constraints are classified so that constraint s_2 is studied before constraint s_1.

4 Analysis of HASCOH

HASCOH selects a sample composed of $s(n)$ points, so the spatial cost is $O(s(n))$. HASCOH checks the consistency of the sample with each non-binary hard and soft constraint, so its temporal cost is $O((k+p)s(n))$. Then, HASCOH classifies each set of hard and soft constraints in ascending order. Its temporal complexity is $O(k\log k + p\log p)$. Thus, the temporal complexity of HASCOH is: $O(max\{(k+p)s(n), k\log k + p\log p\})$.

5 Evaluation of HASCOH

In this section, we compare the performance of HASCOH with two well-known and complete CSP solvers: *Generate and Test* (GT) and *Backtracking* (BT), because they are the most appropriate techniques for observing the number of constraint checks. This empirical evaluation was carried out with two different types of problems: benchmark problems and random problems.

Benchmark Problems: The n-queens problem is a classical search problem in the artificial intelligence area. The 4-queens problem was studied in the previous section.

Table 1: Number of constraint check saving using HASCOH with GT and BT in the n-queens problem.

queens	HASCOH+GT Constraint Check Saving	HASCOH+BT Constraint Check Saving
5	2.1×10^4	2.4×10^2
10	4.1×10^{11}	3.9×10^7
20	1.9×10^{26}	3.6×10^{18}
50	2.4×10^{70}	3.6×10^{52}
100	2.1×10^{143}	2.1×10^{106}
150	5.2×10^{219}	3.7×10^{161}
200	9.4×10^{295}	8.7×10^{219}

In Table 1, we present the amount of constraint check saving in the n-queens problem using GT with HASCOH (HASCOH+GT) and BT with HASCOH (HASCOH+BT). Here, our objective is to find all solutions. The results show that the amount of constraint check saving was significant in HASCOH+GT and HASCOH+BT due to the fact that HASCOH classifies the constraints in the appropriate order, so that the tightest constraints were checked first, and inconsistent tuples were discarded earlier.

Random Problems: Benchmark sets are used to test algorithms for specific problems. However, in recent years, there has been a growing interest in the study of the relation among the parameters that define an instance of CSP in general (i.e., the number of variables, number of constraints, domain size, arity of constraints, etc). Therefore, the notion of randomly generated CSPs has been introduced to describe the classes of CSPs. These classes are then studied using empirical methods.

In our empirical evaluation, each set of random constraint satisfaction problems was defined by the 4-tuple $< n, c, s, d >$, where n was the number of variables, c the number of hard constraints, s the number of soft constraints and d the domain size. The problems were randomly generated by modifying these parameters. We considered all hard constraints as global constraints, that is, all hard constraints had maximum arity so that there were not soft variables. Thus, Table 2 sets three of the parameters and varies the other one in order to evaluate the algorithm performance when this parameter increases. We evaluated 100 test cases for each type of problem and each value of the variable parameter.

The number of constraint checks using BT filtered by *arc-consistency* (as a preprocessing) (BT-AC) and BT-AC using HASCOH (HASCOH+BT-AC) is presented in Table 2, where the number of hard constraints was increased from 5 to 100 and the number of variables, soft constraints and the domain size were set at 5,5 and 10, respectively: $< 5, c, 5, 10 >$. The results show that the number of constraint checks was reduced in all cases.

Table 3 presents the number of constraint checks in problems where the domain size was increased from 10 to 110 and the number of variables, the

Table 2: Number of constraint checks using Backtracking filtered with Arc-Consistency in problems $< 5, c, s, d >$.

problems	BT-AC constraint checks	HASCOH+BT-AC constraint checks
$< 5, 5, 5, 10 >$	14226.5	2975.5
$< 5, 10, 5, 10 >$	60250.3	5714.2
$< 5, 20, 5, 10 >$	203542.2	12548.5
$< 5, 30, 5, 10 >$	325487.4	17845.7
$< 5, 50, 5, 10 >$	513256.7	24875.5
$< 5, 75, 5, 10 >$	704335.1	34135.3
$< 5, 100, 5, 10 >$	895415.3	43396.6

Table 3: Number of constraint checks using Backtracking filtered with Arc-Consistency in problems $< 3, 5, 5, d >$.

problems	BT-AC constraint checks	HASCOH+BT-AC constraint checks
$< 3, 5, 5, 10 >$	150.3	33.06
$< 3, 5, 5, 20 >$	260.4	55.2
$< 3, 5, 5, 30 >$	424.3	85.26
$< 3, 5, 5, 50 >$	970.5	180.1
$< 3, 5, 5, 70 >$	2104.8	380.9
$< 3, 5, 5, 90 >$	4007.4	701.7
$< 3, 5, 5, 110 >$	7851.4	1205.1

number of hard constraints and the number of soft constraints were set at 3,5 and 5, respectively: $< 3, 5, 5, d >$. The results were similar and the number of constraint checks was also reduced in all cases.

6   Conclusions and Future Work

In this paper, we present a heuristic technique called *Hard and Soft Constraint Ordering Heuristic* (HASCOH) that can be applied to any *generate and test* or *backtracking-based* search algorithm to solve non-binary constraints satisfaction problems. This heuristic technique carries out a classification of hard and soft constraints in order to study the tightest hard constraints first and to obtain ever better solutions. In this way, inconsistencies can be found earlier and the number of constraint checks can be significantly reduced.

For future work, we are working on a combination of a constraint ordering heuristic with a variable ordering heuristic in order to manage efficiently more complex problems. Also, we are working on a distributed model for solving non-binary CSPs by means of autonomous agents so that the problem is partitioned in subproblems in order to study first the tightest subproblems.

References

[1] R. Barták, 'Constraint programming: In pursuit of the holy grail', *in Proceedings of WDS99 (invited lecture), Prague, June,* (1999).

[2] C. Bessière, P. Meseguer, E.C. Freuder, and J. Larrosa, 'On forward checking for non-binary constraint satisfaction', *Artifical Intelligence,* 205–224, (2002).

[3] J.R. Bitner and Reingold E.M., 'Backtracking programming techniques', *Communications of the ACM 18,* 651–655, (1975).

[4] R. Dechter and I. Meiri, 'Experimental evaluation of preprocessing algorithms for constraints satisfaction problems', *Artificial Intelligence,* **68**, 211–241, (1994).

[5] E. Freuder, 'A sufficient condition for backtrack-free search', *Journal of the ACM,* **29**, 24–32, (1982).

[6] D. Frost and R. Dechter, 'Look-ahead value orderings for constraint satisfaction problems', *In Proc. of IJCAI-95,* 572–578, (1995).

[7] P.A. Geelen, 'Dual viewpoint heuristic for binary constraint satisfaction problems', *In proceeding of European Conference of Artificial Intelligence (ECAI'92),* 31–35, (1992).

[8] I.P. Gent, E. MacIntyre, P. Prosser, and T Walsh, 'The constrainedness of arc consistency', *Principles and Practice of Constraint Programming,* 327–340, (1997).

[9] R.M. Haralick and Elliot G.L., 'Increasing tree search efficiency for constraint satisfaction problems', *Artificial Intelligence,* **14**, 263–313, (1980).

[10] V. Kumar, 'Depthfirst search', *In Encyclopedia of Artificial Intelligence,* **2**, 1004–1005, (1987).

[11] V. Kumar, 'Algorithms for constraint satisfaction problems: a survey', *Artificial Intelligence Magazine,* **1**, 32–44, (1992).

[12] N. Sadeh and M.S. Fox, 'Variable and value ordering heuristics for activity-based jobshop scheduling', *In proc. of Fourth International Conference on Expert Systems in Production and Operations Management,* 134–144, (1990).

[13] M.A. Salido and F. Barber, 'A polynomial algorithm for continuous non-binary disjunctive CSPs: extended DLRs', *Knowledge-Based Systems,* **16**, 277–285, (2003).

[14] E. Tsang, *Foundation of Constraint Satisfaction,* Academic Press, 1993.

[15] R. Wallace and E. Freuder, 'Ordering heuristics for arc consistency algorithms', *In Proc. of Ninth Canad. Conf. on A.I.,* 163–169, (1992).

Lightweight MAC Algorithms

M.R.C. van Dongen (dongen@cs.ucc.ie)
Cork Constraint Computation Centre
Computer Science Department
University College Cork

Abstract

Arc-consistency algorithms are the workhorse of backtrackers that Maintain Arc-Consistency (MAC). This paper provides experimental evidence that, despite common belief to the contrary, it is not always necessary for a good arc-consistency algorithm to have an optimal worst case time-complexity. To sacrifice this optimality allows MAC solvers that (1) do not need additional data structures during search, (2) have an excellent average time-complexity, and (3) have a space-complexity that improves significantly on that of MAC solvers that do have optimal arc-consistency components. Results are presented from an experimental comparison between MAC-2001, MAC-3_d and related algorithms. MAC-2001 has an arc-consistency component with an optimal worst case time-complexity, whereas MAC-3_d has not. MAC-2001 requires additional data structures during search, whereas MAC-3_d does not. MAC-3_d has a space-complexity of $\mathcal{O}(e + nd)$, where n is the number of variables, d the maximum domain size, and e the number of constraints. We demonstrate that MAC-2001's space-complexity is $\mathcal{O}(ed\min(n, d))$. MAC-2001 required about 35% more average solution time than MAC-3_d for easy and hard random problems and MAC-3_d was the quickest algorithm to solve 23 out of 25 real-world problems, and was only marginally slower for the remaining 2. This indicates that lightweight algorithms like MAC-3_d are promising, especially if checks are cheap and memory is scarce.

1 Introduction

Arc-consistency algorithms significantly reduce the size of the search space of Constraint Satisfaction Problems (CSPs) at low costs. They are the workhorse of backtrackers that Maintain Arc-Consistency during search (MAC [14]).

Currently, there seems to be a shared belief in the constraint satisfaction community that, to be efficient, arc-consistency algorithms need an *optimal* worst case time-complexity [1, 3, 10, 20]. MAC algorithms like MAC-2001 that have an optimal worst case time-complexity require a space-complexity of at least $\mathcal{O}(ed)$ for creating data structures to remember their support-checks. We shall prove that MAC-2001's space-complexity is $\mathcal{O}(ed\min(n, d))$ because it has to *maintain* these additional data structures. As usual, n is the number of variables in the CSP, d is the maximum domain size of the variables and e is the number of constraints. We shall present an example illustrating that worst case scenarios for MAC-2001's space-complexity occur for easy problems that allow a backtrack free search.

We shall provide strong evidence to support the claim that arc-consistency algorithms do not always need an optimal worst case time-complexity. We shall experimentally compare five MAC algorithms. The first algorithm is MAC-2001 [3]. MAC-2001's arc-consistency component has an optimal $\mathcal{O}(ed^2)$ worst case time-complexity. The second and third algorithm are MAC-3 and MAC-3_d [11, 15, 16]. The fourth algorithm is new. It is called MAC-3_p. It lies in between MAC-3 and MAC-3_d. MAC-3, MAC-3_d and MAC-3_p have a better $\mathcal{O}(e + nd)$ space-complexity than MAC-2001 but their arc-consistency components have a non-optimal $\mathcal{O}(ed^3)$ worst case time-complexity. The fifth algorithm is also new. It is called MAC-2001_p. It is to MAC-2001 what MAC-3_p is to MAC-3. Finally, we shall introduce notation to compactly describe ordering heuristics.

For random and real-world problems and for as far as support-checks are concerned MAC-2001_p and MAC-2001 were, not surprisingly, by far the better algorithms. For any fixed arc-heuristic and for random problems where checks are cheap MAC-3, MAC-3_p and MAC-3_d were *all* better in clock on the wall time than MAC-2001 and MAC-2001_p, with MAC-3_d the best of all. MAC-2001_p required about 21% more time on average than MAC-3_d, whereas MAC-2001 required about 35% more time. MAC-3_d was the quickest algorithm for 23 out of 25 real-world problems. It was only marginally slower for the remaining two problems.

This paper is the first to report about AC-3_d and search. It is the first to report about MAC-3 based algorithms with a $\mathcal{O}(e+nd)$ space-complexity that perform significantly better than MAC-2001 for easy *and* hard problems. Our result about MAC-2001's $\mathcal{O}(ed\min(n,d))$ space-complexity is also a first. It points out a weakness of MAC searchers that do not repeat checks.

The results presented in this paper are important because of the following. Since the introduction of Mohr and Henderson's AC-4 [13], most work in arc-consistency research has been focusing on the design of better algorithms that do not re-discover (do not repeat checks). This focused research is justified by the observation that, as checks become more and more expensive, there will always be a point beyond which algorithms that do repeat will become slower than those that do not and will remain so from then on. However, there are many cases where checks are cheap and it is only possible to avoid re-discoveries at the price of a large additional bookkeeping. To forsake the bookkeeping at the expense of having to re-discover may improve search if checks are cheap *and* if problems become large.

The remainder of this paper is organised as follows. Section 2 provides an introduction to constraint satisfaction. Section 3 is an introduction to some notation to describe selection heuristics. Section 4 describes related work. Section 5 provides a detailed description of the algorithms under consideration and contains a proof that MAC-2001's space-complexity is $\mathcal{O}(ed\min(n,d))$. Section 6 presents our experimental results. Conclusions are presented in Section 7.

2 Constraint Satisfaction

A binary *constraint* C_{xy} between variables x and y is a subset of the cartesian product of the domains $D(x)$ of x and $D(y)$ of y. Value $v \in D(x)$ is *supported* by $w \in D(y)$ if $(v, w) \in C_{xy}$ and $w \in D(y)$ is supported by $v \in D(x)$ if $(v, w) \in C_{xy}$. Finally, variable x is said to *support* $w \in D(y)$ if there is a $v \in D(x)$ supporting $w \in D(y)$.

A *Constraint Satisfaction Problem* (CSP) is a tuple (X, D, C), where X is a set of variables, $D(\cdot)$ is a function mapping each $x \in X$ to its non-empty domain, and C is a set of constraints between variables in subsets of X. We shall only consider CSPs whose constraints are binary. CSP (X, D, C) is called *arc-consistent* if its domains are non-empty and for each $C_{xy} \in C$ it is true that every $v \in D(x)$ is supported by y and that every $w \in D(y)$ is supported by x. A *support-check* (consistency-check) is a test to find out if two values support each other.

The *tightness* of C_{xy} is defined as $1 - |C_{xy}| / |D(x) \times D(y)|$, where $\cdot \times \cdot$ denotes cartesian product. The *density* of a CSP is defined as $2e/(n^2 - n)$, for $n > 1$.

The *(directed) constraint graph* of CSP (X, D, C) is the (directed) graph whose nodes are given by X and whose arcs are given by $\cup_{C_{xy} \in C} \{(x, y), (y, x)\}$. The *degree* of $x \in X$ is the number of neighbours of x in the constraint graph of that CSP.

To transform a CSP to its arc-consistent equivalent does not remove solutions and usually significantly reduces the search space. To detect an arc-inconsistency in a problem provides a cheap proofs of its "global" unsatisfiability [11]. The detection of an arc-inconsistency provides a justification to backtrack. Arc-consistency can be established within an assymptotic worst case time-complexity which is polynomial in the size of the CSP [12]. The overhead of maintaining arc-consistency during search backtrack search significantly improves the average time-complexity of backtracking algorithms [14]. MAC is a backtracker that maintains arc-consistency during search. MAC-i uses arc-consistency algorithm AC-i to maintain arc-consistency.

The following notation is not standard but will turn out useful. Let $\delta_o(x)$ be the original degree of x, let $\delta_c(x)$ be the current degree of x, let $k(x) = |D(x)|$, and let $\#(x)$ be a *unique* number which is associated with x. We will assume that $\#(x) \leq \#(y)$ if and only if x is lexicographically less than or equal to y.

3 Operators for Selection Heuristics

In this section we shall introduce notation to describe and "compose" variable and arc selection heuristics. The reader not interested in the nitty gritty details of such heuristics may wish to skip this section and return to it later. Motivation, a more detailed presentation, and more examples may be found in [17, Chapter 3].

It is recalled that a relation on set T is called a *quasi-order* on T if it is reflexive and transitive. A relation, $\prec$, on T is called *linear* if $v \prec w \vee w \prec v$ for all $v, w \in T$. Linear quasi-orders may allow for "ties," i.e. they may allow for situations where $v \prec w \wedge w \prec v \wedge v \neq w$. A quasi-order $\preceq$ is called a *partial order* if $v \preceq w \wedge w \preceq v \implies v = w$ for all $v, w \in T$. An *order* (also called a *linear order*) is a partial order that is also a linear quasi-order. An order $\preceq$ *prefers* v to w if and only if $v \preceq w$.

The *composition* of order $\preceq_2$ and linear quasi-order $\preceq_1$ is denoted $\preceq_2 \bullet \preceq_1$. It is the unique order on T which is defined as follows:

$$v \preceq_2 \bullet \preceq_1 w \iff (v \preceq_1 w \wedge \neg w \preceq_1 v) \vee (v \preceq_1 w \wedge w \preceq_1 v \wedge v \preceq_2 w).$$

In words, $\preceq_2 \bullet \preceq_1$ is the selection heuristic that uses $\preceq_1$ and "breaks ties" using $\preceq_2$. Composition associates to the left, i.e. $\preceq_3 \bullet \preceq_2 \bullet \preceq_1$ is equal to $(\preceq_3 \bullet \preceq_2) \bullet \preceq_1$.

Let $\preceq$ be a linear quasi-order on T, and let $f :: Y \mapsto T$ be a function. Then $\otimes_{\preceq}^f$ is the unique linear quasi-order on Y which is defined as follows:

$$v \otimes_{\preceq}^f w \iff f(v) \preceq f(w), \qquad \text{for all } v, w \in Y.$$

Finally, let $\pi_i((v_1, \ldots, v_n)) = v_i$ for $1 \leq i \leq n$.

We now need no more notation. For example, the minimum domain size heuristic with a lexicographical tie breaker is given by $\otimes_{\preceq}^{\#} \bullet \otimes_{\leq}^k$, the ordering on the maximum original degree with a lexicographical tie breaker by $\otimes_{\preceq}^{\#} \bullet \otimes_{\geq}^{\delta_o}$, the *Brelaz heuristic* (cf. [7]) with a lexicographical tie breaker by $\otimes_{\preceq}^{\#} \bullet \otimes_{\geq}^{\delta_c} \bullet \otimes_{\leq}^k$, and $\otimes_{\preceq}^{\# \circ \pi_2} \bullet \otimes_{\preceq}^{\# \circ \pi_1}$ is the lexicographical arc-heuristic. As usual, $\cdot \circ \cdot$ denotes function composition.

4 Related Literature

In 1977, Mackworth presented an arc-consistency algorithm called AC-3 [11]. AC-3 has a $\mathcal{O}(ed^3)$ worst case time-complexity [12]. AC-3 has a $\mathcal{O}(e + nd)$ space-complexity. AC-3 cannot remember all its support-checks. AC-3 uses *arc-heuristics* to repeatedly select and remove an arc, (x, y), from a data structure called a *queue* (a set, really) and to use the constraint between x and y to *revise* the domain of x. Here, to revise the domain of x using the constraint between x and y means to remove the values from $D(x)$ that are not supported by y. AC-3's arc-heuristics determine the constraint that will be used for the next support-check. Besides these arc-heuristics there are also *domain-heuristics*. These heuristics, when given the constraint that will be used for the next support-check, determine the values that will be used for the next support-check. The interested reader is referred to [11, 12] for further information about AC-3.

Wallace and Freuder pointed out that arc-heuristics can influence the efficiency of arc-consistency algorithms [19]. Similar observations were made by Gent *et al.* [8]. A recent study of arc-heuristics was carried out by le Coutre *et al.* [9]. Despite these findings only a few authors describe the heuristics that were used for their experiments. To facilitate ease of replication all information to repeat experiments should be described in full and should also include information about arc-heuristics.

Bessière and Régin presented AC-2001 [3], which is based on AC-3 (see also [20] for a similar algorithm). AC-2001 revises one domain at a time. The main difference between AC-3 and AC-2001 is that AC-2001 uses a lexicographical domain-heuristic and that for each variable x, for each $v \in D(x)$ and each constraint between x and another variable y it remembers the last support for $v \in D(x)$ with y so as to avoid repeating checks that were used before to find support for $v \in D(x)$ with y. AC-2001 has an optimal upper bound of $\mathcal{O}(ed^2)$ for its worst case time-complexity and its space-complexity is $\mathcal{O}(ed)$. AC-2001 behaves well on average. It was observed that AC-3 is a good alternative for stand alone arc-consistency if checks are cheap and CSPs are under-constrained but that AC-3 is very slow for over-constrained CSPs and CSPs in the phase transition [2, 3].

We made similar observations in experimental comparisons between AC-7, AC-2001 and AC-3_d, which is a cross-breed between Mackworth's AC-3 and Gaschnig's DEE [5, 11, 15]. We did *not* consider search. The only difference between AC-3 and AC-3_d is that AC-3_d sometimes takes two arcs from the queue and simultaneously revises *two* domains with a *double-support* domain-heuristic. A double-support heuristic is one that prefers checks between two values each of whose support statuses are unknown. For two-variable CSPs the double-support heuristic is optimal and requires about half the checks that are needed by a lexicographical heuristic if the domain sizes of the variables are about equal and sufficiently large [16]. AC-3_d and MAC-3_d have a low $\mathcal{O}(e + nd)$ space-complexity. AC-3_d was promising for stand alone arc-consistency.

5 Description of MAC-3 Based Algorithms

5.1 MAC-3_d and MAC-3_p

AC-3_d is a cross-breed between AC-3 and DEE [5, 11, 15]. Pseudo-code for AC-3_d is depicted in Figure 1. The "foreach $s \in S$ do *statement*" construct assigns the members in S to s from small to big and carries out *statement* after each assignment. The only difference between AC-3 and AC-3_d is that AC-3_d sometimes takes two arcs out of the queue and *simultaneously* revises *two* domains with Algorithm $\mathcal{D}$. Pseudo code for $\mathcal{D}$ is depicted in Figure 2. $\mathcal{D}$ uses a *double-support* domain-heuristic, i.e. a heuristic that prefers double-support checks. The idea behind this approach is that successful double-support checks lead to two supports at the price of a single support-check. For two-variable CSPs and in terms of saving checks $\mathcal{D}$ is optimal. It is about twice as efficient on average as a lexicographical heuristic [16]. The constants *unsupported*, *single*, and *double* that are used in $\mathcal{D}$ are pairwise different and smaller than the values in the domains of the variables. The function *revise* in AC-3_d is defined in [11].

AC-3_p is a "poor man's" version of AC-3_d; It is not as efficient but easier to implement. It can be obtained from AC-3_d by replacing the call to $\mathcal{D}$ in the 7th line of AC-3_d by "$revise(x, y, change_x)$ and $revise(y, x, change_y)$." The difference between AC-3_p and AC-3_d is AC-3_d's double-support heuristic.

$\mathcal{D}$'s space-complexity is $\mathcal{O}(d)$. In $\mathcal{D}$ the *row-support* are the values in $D(x)$ that are supported by y and the *column-support* are the values in $D(y)$ that are supported by x. It easy to prove that $\mathcal{D}$ correctly computes its row-support. To prove that it also correctly computes its column-support is not much more difficult. The proof relies on the fact that after establishing row-support any c that is not yet known to be supported can only be supported by an $r \in D(x)$ such that $rkind[r] = double \land rsupp[r] < c$.

AC-3_d and AC-3_p inherit their $\mathcal{O}(ed^3)$ worst case time-complexity and $\mathcal{O}(e + nd)$ space-complexity from AC-3. MAC-3_d (MAC-3_p) is implemented by replacing AC-3 in MAC-3 by AC-3_d (AC-3_p). The space-complexity of MAC-3_d and MAC-3_p is equal to $\mathcal{O}(e + nd)$.

```
function AC-3_d( X ) : Bool;
    Q := { ( x, y ) ∈ X² :  x and y are neighbours };
    while Q ≠ ∅ do begin
        select and remove any arc ( x, y ) from Q;
        if ( y, x ) is also in Q then begin
            remove ( y, x ) from Q;
            if not D(x, y, change_x, change_y) then
                return false;
            else begin
                if change_x then
                    Q := Q ∪ { ( z, x ) :  z ≠ y, z is a neighbour of x };
                if change_y then
                    Q := Q ∪ { ( z, y ) :  z ≠ x, z is a neighbour of y };
            end
        end
        else if not revise(x, y, change_x) then
            return false;
        else if change_x then
            Q := Q ∪ { ( z, x ) :  z ≠ y, z is a neighbour of x };
    end;
    return true;
end;
```

Figure 1: The AC-3$_d$ Algorithm.

```
function D(x, y, var change_x, var change_y) : Bool;
begin
    change_x := false;
    change_y := false;
    foreach c ∈ D(y) do
        csupp[c] := unsupported;
    /* Compute row-support. */
    foreach r ∈ D(x) do begin
        rkind[r] := unsupported;
        rsupp[r] := unsupported;
        if ∃c ∈ D(y) s.t. csupp[c] = unsupported and c supports r then begin
            rsupp[r] := first such value c;
            csupp[rsupp[r]] := r;
            rkind[r] := double;
        end
        else if ∃c ∈ D(y) s.t. csupp[c] ≠ unsupported and c supports r then begin
            rsupp[r] := first such value c;
            rkind[r] := single;
        end
        else begin
            D(x) := D(x) \ { r };
            change_x := true;
        end;
    end;
    /* Complete column-support. */
    foreach c ∈ D(y) s.t. csupp[c] = unsupported do
        if ∄r ∈ D(x) s.t. rsupp[r] < c and rkind[r] = double and r supports c then begin
            D(y) := D(y) \ { c };
            change_y := true;
        end;
    return D(x) ≠ ∅;
end;
```

Figure 2: Algorithm D.

5.2   MAC-2001 and MAC-2001$_p$

Pseudo-code for an arc-based version of AC-2001 and the *revise*-2001 algorithm upon which it depends is depicted in Figures 3 and 4. For the purpose of the presentation of

```
                                          function revise-2001( x, y, var change ): Bool;
                                          begin
function AC-2001( X ): Bool;                 change := false;
begin                                        foreach r ∈ D(x) do
   Q := { ( x, y ) ∈ X² :  x and y are neighbours };      if last[x][r][y] ∉ D(y) then
   while Q ≠ ∅ do begin                          if ∃c ∈ D(y) s.t. c > last[x][r][y]
     select and remove any arc ( x, y ) from Q;          and c supports r then
     if not revise-2001(x, y, change_x) then         last[x][r][y] := the first such value c;
        return false;                           else begin
     else if change_x then                         D(x) := D(x) \ { r };
        Q := Q ∪ { ( z, x ) :  z ≠ y, z is a neighbour of x };      change := true;
   end;                                          end;
   return true;                              return D(x) ≠ ∅;
end;                                       end;
```

Figure 3: The AC-2001 Algorithm.   Figure 4: Algorithm *revise*-2001.

AC-2001 it is assumed that the values in the domains are ordered from small to big. For each variable x, for each value $v \in D(x)$, and for each neighbour y of x it is assumed that $last[x][v][y]$ is initialised to some value that is smaller than the values in $D(y)$.

AC-2001 finds support for $v \in D(x)$ with y by checking against the values in $D(y)$ from small to large. It uses a counter $last[x][v][y]$ to record the last check that was carried out to find support for $v \in D(x)$ with y. Seeking support for $v \in D(x)$ this allows it to save checks by not considering $w \in D(y)$ such that $w \leq last[x][v][y]$.

MAC-2001 requires additional data structures during search. It maintains the counter $last[x][v][y]$ to remember the last support for $v \in D(x)$ with $D(y)$. The space-complexity of $last$ is $\mathcal{O}(ed)$ [3]. It seems to have gone unnoticed so far that MAC-2001 has a $\mathcal{O}(ed \min(n, d))$ space-complexity. The reason for this space-complexity is that MAC-2001 has to *maintain* the data structure $last$. This only seems to be possible using one or a combination of the following two methods:

1. Save all relevant counters once before AC-2001. Upon backtracking these counters have to be restored. This requires a $\mathcal{O}(ned)$ space-complexity because $\mathcal{O}(ed)$ data structures may have to be saved n times.

2. Save each counter before the assignment to $last[x][v][y]$ in *revise*-2001 and count the number of changes, c, that were carried out. Upon backtracking, restore the c counters in the reverse order. This comes at a space-complexity of $\mathcal{O}(ed^2)$ because each of the $2ed$ counters may have to be saved $\mathcal{O}(d)$ times.

Therefore, MAC-2001's space-complexity is $\mathcal{O}(ed \min(n, d))$. Christian Bessière (private communication) implemented MAC-2001 using Method 2.

The consequences of MAC-2001's space requirements can be prohibitive. For example, without loss of generality we may assume a lexicographical value ordering. Let $n = d > 1$ and consider the binary CSP where all variables should be pairwise different. Finally, assume that Method 2 is used for MAC-2001 (Method 1 will lead to a similar result). Note that the "first" solution can be found with a backtrack free search. Also note that in the first solution i is assigned to the i-th variable. We shall see that MAC-2001 will require a lot of space to solve the given CSP.

Just before the assignment of i to the i-th variable we have the following. For each variable x, for each variable $y \neq x$, and for each $v \in D(x) = \{i, \dots, n\}$ we have $last[x][v][y] = \min(\{i, \dots, n\} \setminus \{v\})$. To make the CSP arc-consistent after the assignment of i to the i-th current variable, (only) the value i has to be removed from the domains of the future variables. Unfortunately, for each of the remaining $n - i$ future variables x, for each of the remaining $n - i$ values $v \in D(x) \setminus \{i\}$, and for each of the remaining $n - i - 1$ future variables $y \neq x$, i was the last known support for $v \in D(x)$ with y. This means that $(n - i)^2 \times (n - i - 1)$ counters must be saved and incremented during the AC-2001 call following the assignment of i to the i-th variable. In total, MAC-2001 has to save $\sum_{i=1}^{n}(n - i)^2 \times (n - i - 1)$, i.e. $(n - 2) \times (n - 1) \times n \times (3n - 1)/12$ counters. For $n = d = 500$, MAC-2001 will require space for at least $15,521,020,750$ counters and this may not be available on every machine. Sometimes MAC algorithms that do not re-discover *do* require a lot of space, even for deciding relatively small CSPs that allow a backtrack free search.

The last thing that remains to be done in this section is to describe AC-2001$_p$. This algorithm is to AC-2001 what AC-3$_p$ is to AC-3. If its arc-heuristic selects (x, y) from the queue and if (y, x) is also in the queue then it will remove both and use (at most) two calls to *revise*-2001 to revise the domains of x and y.

6 Experimental Results

6.1 Implementation Details

All implementations were based on our own implementation of MAC-3$_d$ and all used the same basic data structures that were used by MAC-3$_d$. The implementations of MAC-2001 and MAC-2001$_p$ were arc-based. This allowed us to evaluate the algorithms for different arc-heuristics. Previously, we used Christian Bessière's variable based implementation of MAC-2001 [17]. However, Bessière's implementation came with only one arc-heuristic and it was about 17% slower than our own implementation.

All solvers were real-full-look-ahead solvers. To ensure that they visited the same nodes in the search tree they were equipped with the same dom/deg variable ordering heuristic, which using the notation introduced in Section 3 is given by $\otimes_{\leq}^{\#} \bullet \otimes_{\leq}^{k/\delta_o}$. We considered three arc-heuristics called *lex*, *rlex*, and *comp*, which are defined as:

$$lex = \otimes_{\leq}^{\#o\pi_2} \bullet \otimes_{\leq}^{\#o\pi_1},$$

$$rlex = \otimes_{\leq}^{\#o\pi_1} \bullet \otimes_{\leq}^{\#o\pi_2}, \quad \text{and}$$

$$comp = \otimes_{\leq}^{\#o\pi_2} \bullet \otimes_{\geq}^{\delta_c o\pi_2} \bullet \otimes_{\leq}^{ko\pi_2} \bullet \otimes_{\leq}^{\#o\pi_1} \bullet \otimes_{\geq}^{\delta_c o\pi_1} \bullet \otimes_{\leq}^{ko\pi_1}.$$

The queue was implemented as a directed graph G. This data structure contains a $\mathcal{O}(n)$ linked list N to represent the nodes of G that have an incoming arc: $N = \{x : \exists y \text{ s.t. } (x, y) \in G\}$. The data structure also contains a $\mathcal{O}(n)$ array that contains a linked lists for each member of N to represent the other ends of the arcs. The total size of these linked lists does not exceed $\mathcal{O}(e)$. This brings the space-complexity for our queue representation to $\mathcal{O}(e)$. With this implementation selecting the best arc with respect to *lex* takes $\mathcal{O}(1)$ time, whereas selecting the best arc with respect to *rlex* and *comp* takes $\mathcal{O}(n)$ time. We did not use a $\mathcal{O}(n \times n)$ lookup table to quickly find out if a certain arc was in the queue. With such a table the space-complexity of MAC-3, MAC-3$_p$ and MAC-3$_d$ would have increased from $\mathcal{O}(e + nd)$ to $\mathcal{O}(n \max(n, d))$.

6.2 Random Problems

Random problems were generated for $15 \leq n = d \leq 30$. We shall refer to the class of problems for a given combination of $n = d$ as the problem class with *size n*. The problems were generated as follows. For each problem size and each combination (C, T) of average density C and uniform tightness T in $\{ (i/20, j/20) : 1 \leq i, j \leq 19 \}$ we generated 50 random CSPs. Next we computed the average number of checks and the average time that was required for deciding the satisfiability of each problem using MAC search. All problems were run to completion. Frost *et al.*'s model B [6] random problem generator was used to generate the problems (http://www.lirmm.fr/~bessiere/generator.html).

The test was carried out in parallel on 50 identical machines. All machines were Intel Pentium III machines, running SuSe Linux 8.0, having 125 MB of RAM, having a 256 KB cach size, and running at a clock speed of about 930 MHz. Between pairs of machines there were small (less than 1%) variations in clock speed. Each machine was given a unique identifier in the range from 1 through 50. For each machine random problems were generated for each combination of density and tightness. The CSP generator on a particular machine was started with the seed given by 1000 times the machine's identifier. No swapping occurred. The total time for our comparison is equivalent to more than 100 days of computation on a single machine.

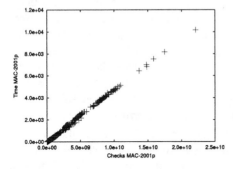
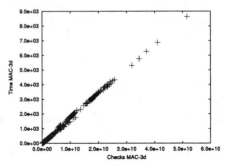

Figure 5: Size 30: Scatter plot of time of MAC-2001$_p$ with *comp* for first solution vs. average number of checks.

Figure 6: Size 30: Scatter plot of time of MAC-3$_d$ with *comp* for first solution vs. average number of checks.

Figures 5 and 6 depict scatter plots of the time required by MAC-2001$_p$ and MAC-3$_d$ both equipped with a *comp* heuristic versus the number of checks that they required to find the first solution for problem size 30. Both figures suggest that the solution time linearly depends on the number of checks. A similar linear relationship between the solution time and the number of checks was observed for all algorithms, for all heuristics, and *all* problem sizes. Note that the figures demonstrate that *many* problems were

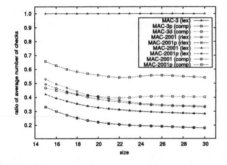 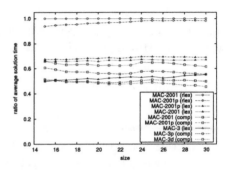

Figure 7: Ratio of average number of checks vs. problem size for random problems and search. For each size the average number of checks is divided by the average number of checks required by MAC-3 with the *lex* arc-heuristic.

Figure 8: Ratio of average solution time vs. problem size for random problems and search. For each size the average time is divided by the average time required by MAC-2001 with the *rlex* arc-heuristic.

difficult and took tens of minutes to hours to complete.

We also observed linear relationships between the average solution times of MAC-3_d and MAC-2001_p and between their average number of checks. A multi parameter regression analysis demonstrated that this linear dependency is very significant [18]. It should not come as a complete surprise that the average solution time of a given algorithm more or less linearly depends on its average number of checks. However, it is not at all clear why there should also be a linear dependency between the average solution times of two algorithms and between their average number of checks. Note that it follows from transitivity and from the different kinds of linear dependencies that were observed before (checks of MAC-2001_p versus time of MAC-2001_p, checks of MAC-3_d versus time of MAC-3_d, checks of MAC-2001_p versus checks of MAC-3_d, and time of MAC-2001_p versus time of MAC-3_d) that, for example, the average number of checks required by MAC-3_d also linearly depends on the average solution time of MAC-2001_p and vice versa. These observations deserve further investigation.

Figure 7 depicts the ratio between the average number of checks on the one hand and the average number of MAC-3 with a *lex* arc-heuristic on the other for problem sizes 15–30 and different combinations of algorithms and arc-heuristics. Similarly, Figure 8 depicts the ratio between the average solution time and the average solution time of MAC-2001 with an *rlex* arc-heuristic. The order from top to bottom in which the algorithms and heuristics are listed in the legends of the figures corresponds to the height of their graphs for problem size 30. It is difficult to see but what seem to be two lines at the bottom of Figure 7 are two pairs of lines. The pair at the bottom corresponds to MAC-2001 and MAC-2001_p with a *comp* heuristic. The other pair corresponds to MAC-2001 and MAC-2001_p with a *lex* heuristic. As the problem size increases the lines for MAC-2001 and MAC-2001_p with an *rlex* heuristic also seem to converge. MAC-2001_p and MAC-2001 with a *comp* heuristic are the best for saving checks.

For problem size 30 the average solution time of MAC-2001_p was about 36.289 seconds, that of MAC-2001 was about 40.294 seconds, and that of MAC-3_d was about 29.910 seconds. On average and over all problems MAC-2001_p required about 21% more time than MAC-3_d, whereas MAC-2001 required about 35% more time.

As a rule and given any of the algorithms under consideration the heuristic *comp* was better than *lex* which, in its turn, was better than *rlex* both for checks and time. For all three heuristics and for saving time MAC-2001 and MAC-2001_p are never better on average than MAC-3, MAC-3_p and MAC-3_d. MAC-3 with *lex* requires about 5 times more checks on average than MAC-2001 and MAC-2001_p with *comp* but solves more quickly on average. MAC-3's lack of intelligence for constraint propagation does not seem to hinder it at all when checks are cheap. MAC-3 performed even better with *comp*. Our findings about MAC-3_d are consistent with our previous work [15, 17]. The results about MAC-2001 and MAC-3 are in contrast with other results from the literature [3, 10]. However, this should be no reason for dismissing our results. Our testing was thorough and fair and ours is the most comprehensive comparison that we know of.

For random problems and for clock on the wall time the best algorithm was MAC-3_d with a *comp* heuristic. MAC-3_p also with *comp* was a good second. MAC-3_d's double-support heuristic allows it to improve on MAC-3_p. MAC-2001_p, the best heavy-weight algorithm, required about 21% more time on average than MAC-3_d.

6.3 Real-World Problems

The real-world problems came from the CELAR suite [4]. We did not consider optimisation but only considered satisfiability. We considered all 25 problems from the suite. These problems are given by RLFAP 1–11 and GRAPH 1–14. Space requirements only allow a detailed presentation of results for a few of these problems. To facilitate comparison, detailed results are presented in Table 1 for the same problems that were considered in [3]. Complete results from a similar comparison may be found in [18]. For every problem the solution time was averaged over 50 runs. Checks were implemented as function calls and were more expensive than for the random problems.

The column "R/G" in Table 1 describes the problems. An "R" in this column stands for RLFAP and a "G" stands for GRAPH. For each problem the least number of checks and the least average time recorded for that problem for all arc-heuristics is printed in **bold face**. For each of the remaining heuristics the least average number of checks and least average time is printed *italicised*.

The results for MAC-2001 with *comp* are similar to [3, Table 2]. For MAC-3 and *comp* they are significantly better. Bessière and Régin's MAC-3 always requires more checks and for RLFAP 11 it requires almost 14 times more checks.

For these problems, where checks are more expensive, MAC-3's uncontrolled spending of checks makes it lose out in time against MAC-2001 and MAC-2001_p. MAC-3_d recorded the least number of checks for 12 out of the 25 problems. However, on average MAC-2001 and MAC-2001_p were the best when it comes to saving checks. MAC-2001_p and MAC-2001 recorded the best time for RLFAP 11 and for GRAPH 9 and for GRAPH 6 (results for GRAPH 6 are not listed in Table 1). However, whereas MAC-3 became less competitive because checks became more expensive, MAC-3_d still recorded the best solution time for the remaining three problems in Table 1 *and*

Algorithm	R/G	Checks			Time		
		lex	*rlex*	*comp*	*lex*	*rlex*	*comp*
MAC-3	R 1	4.238e+06	4.021e+06	4.165e+06	0.307	0.389	0.396
MAC-3$_p$	R 1	4.002e+06	4.017e+06	3.641e+06	0.281	0.323	0.323
MAC-3$_d$	R 1	2.681e+06	2.721e+06	1.924e+06	**0.249**	*0.296*	*0.277*
MAC-2001	R 1	*1.850e+06*	1.854e+06	1.778e+06	0.290	0.394	0.381
MAC-2001$_p$	R 1	1.861e+06	*1.852e+06*	**1.776e+06**	0.294	0.338	0.348
MAC-3	R 11	2.895e+08	1.563e+08	5.643e+07	20.480	13.055	5.162
MAC-3$_p$	R 11	2.129e+08	1.419e+08	4.361e+07	14.690	11.271	3.921
MAC-3$_d$	R 11	1.713e+08	1.154e+08	3.081e+07	13.670	10.610	3.584
MAC-2001	R 11	3.545e+07	*2.775e+07*	1.041e+07	11.057	9.130	3.799
MAC-2001$_p$	R 11	*3.480e+07*	2.903e+07	**1.037e+07**	*9.730*	*8.651*	**3.332**
MAC-3	G 9	4.423e+06	4.506e+06	3.889e+06	0.339	0.435	0.395
MAC-3$_p$	G 9	4.336e+06	4.504e+06	3.594e+06	0.325	0.369	0.345
MAC-3$_d$	G 9	3.308e+06	3.465e+06	2.178e+06	**0.299**	*0.346*	*0.305*
MAC-2001	G 9	1.866e+06	*1.870e+06*	1.795e+06	0.317	0.420	0.393
MAC-2001$_p$	G 9	*1.865e+06*	1.871e+06	**1.792e+06**	0.326	0.365	0.370
MAC-3	G 10	8.252e+06	8.305e+06	5.682e+06	0.616	0.742	0.585
MAC-3$_p$	G 10	8.076e+06	8.578e+06	5.506e+06	0.589	0.715	0.538
MAC-3$_d$	G 10	7.020e+06	7.493e+06	4.299e+06	0.557	0.686	0.498
MAC-2001	G 10	2.689e+06	*2.682e+06*	2.353e+06	**0.465**	0.599	0.521
MAC-2001$_p$	G 10	*2.671e+06*	2.740e+06	**2.332e+06**	0.468	*0.583*	*0.497*
MAC-3	G 14	3.892e+06	3.942e+06	3.404e+06	0.298	0.379	0.340
MAC-3$_p$	G 14	3.826e+06	3.940e+06	3.102e+06	0.286	0.322	0.299
MAC-3$_d$	G 14	2.865e+06	2.976e+06	1.744e+06	*0.258*	*0.295*	**0.253**
MAC-2001	G 14	*1.651e+06*	*1.651e+06*	**1.590e+06**	0.270	0.356	0.331
MAC-2001$_p$	G 14	*1.651e+06*	1.652e+06	**1.590e+06**	0.277	0.308	0.314

Table 1: Average results for real-world problems.

for the 21 problems for which results are not listed. It shared the best solution time for GRAPH 6 with MAC-2001$_p$ and the best time with MAC-3$_p$ for five other problems. The results in Table 1 seem to suggest that *lex* is a good heuristic for MAC-3$_d$. However, this is not true. Out of the 23 problems for which MAC-3$_d$ recorded the best solution time it did so for *comp* for 17 problems. The differences between the solution times of MAC-3$_d$ and MAC-2001$_p$ are not very large. However, we believe it is fair to say that MAC-3$_d$ is better in solving this class of real-world problems more quickly than MAC-2001$_p$ and MAC-2001.

7 Conclusions and Recommendations

We compared five algorithms called MAC-2001, MAC-2001$_p$, MAC-3, MAC-3$_p$, and MAC-3$_d$. MAC-2001 and MAC-2001$_p$ have an arc-consistency component with an optimal worst case time-complexity. The remaining algorithms do not but they have the advantage of a $\mathcal{O}(e + nd)$ space-complexity. We demonstrated that MAC-2001's space-complexity is $\mathcal{O}(ed \min(n, d))$, which may be prohibitive even for CSPs that are relatively easy. We compared the algorithms for search and for three different arc-heuristics, called *lex*, *rlex*, and *comp*. We considered random problems where checks are cheap and real-world problems where checks are expensive. For the random problems our findings are that good arc-consistency algorithms do not need an optimal worst case time-complexity. *Our results suggest the opposite.* For any given arc-heuristic MAC-2001 and MAC-2001$_p$ always required fewer checks but more time than the others. MAC-3$_d$ with a *comp* arc-heuristic was the best combination for saving time. MAC-2001$_p$ required about 21% more time than MAC-3$_d$ and MAC-2001 required about 34% more. For the real-world problems MAC-2001 and MAC-2001$_p$ were again superior in saving checks but MAC-3$_d$ was better in solving quickly, albeit only marginally. Our results indicate that lightweights like MAC-3$_d$ are promising.

Acknowledgement Thanks to Christian Bessière for the use of his solver in an early stage of this work and for useful discussions, thanks to Rick Wallace, Chris Beck, Ken Brown and other members of 4C for early discussions, thanks to Christian van den Bosch for conducting the experiments, and to Gene Freuder for his support. This work has received support from Science Foundation Ireland under Grant 00/PI.1/C075.

References

[1] C. Bessière, E.C. Freuder, and J.-C. Régin. Using inference to reduce arc consistency computation. In C.S. Mellish, editor, *Proceedings of the Fourteenth International Joint Conference on Artificial Intelligence*, volume 1, pages 592–598, Montréal, Québec, Canada, 1995. Morgan Kaufmann Publishers.

[2] C. Bessière, E.G. Freuder, and J.-C. Régin. Using constraint metaknowledge to reduce arc consistency computation. *Artificial Intelligence*, 107(1):125–148, 1999.

[3] C. Bessière and J.-C. Régin. Refining the basic constraint propagation algorithm. In *Proceedings of the Seventeenth International Joint Conference on Artificial Intelligence*, pages 309–315, 2001.

[4] B. Cabon, S. De Givry, L. Lobjois, T. Schiex, and J.P. Warners. Radio link frequency assignment. *Journal of Constraints*, 4:79–89, 1999.

[5] J. Gaschnig. Experimental case studies of backtrack vs. Waltz-type vs. new algorithms for satisficing assignment problems. In *Proceeding of the 2nd Biennial Conference, Canadian Society for the Computational Studies of Intelligence*, pages 268–277, 1978.

[6] Ian Gent, Ewan MacIntyre, Patrick Prosser, Barbara Smith, and Toby Walsh. Random constraint satisfaction: Flaws and structure. *Journal of Constraints*, 6(4):345–372, 2001.

[7] I.P. Gent, MacIntyre E., P. Prosser, B.M. Smith, and T. Walsh. An empirical study of dynamic variable ordering heuristics for the constraint satisfaction problem. In

E.C. Freuder, editor, *Principles and Practice of Constraint Programming*, pages 179–193. Springer, 1996.

[8] I.P. Gent, E. MacIntyre, P. Prosser, P. Shaw, and T. Walsh. The constrainedness of arc consistency. In *Proceedings of the 3rd International Conference on Principles and Practice of Constraint Programming*, pages 327–340. Springer, 1997.

[9] C. Lecoutre, F. Boussemart, and F. Hemery. Au cœur de la consistance d'arc. In *Proceedings of JNPC'03 (Journées Nationales sur la résolution pratique de Problèmes NP-complets)*, 2003.

[10] C. Lecoutre, F. Boussemart, and F. Hemery. De AC3 à AC7. In *Proceedings of the 12th International French Speaking Conference on Logic and Constraint Programming*, pages 267–280, 2003.

[11] A.K. Mackworth. Consistency in networks of relations. *Artificial Intelligence*, 8:99–118, 1977.

[12] A.K. Mackworth and E.C. Freuder. The complexity of some polynomial network consistency algorithms for constraint satisfaction problems. *Artificial Intelligence*, 25(1):65–73, 1985.

[13] R. Mohr and T. Henderson. Arc and path consistency revisited. *Artificial Intelligence*, 28:225–233, 1986.

[14] D. Sabin and E.C. Freuder. Contradicting conventional wisdom in constraint satisfaction. In A.G. Cohn, editor, *Proceedings of the 11th European Conference on Artificial Intelligence*, pages 125–129. John Wiley and Sons, 1994.

[15] M.R.C. van Dongen. AC-3$_d$ an efficient arc-consistency algorithm with a low space-complexity. In P. Van Hentenryck, editor, *Proceedings of the 8th International Conference on Principles and Practice of Constraint Programming*, volume 2470 of *Lecture notes in Computer Science*, pages 755–760. Springer, 2002.

[16] M.R.C. van Dongen. Domain-heuristics for arc-consistency algorithms. In B. O'Sullivan, editor, *Recent Advances in Constraints*, volume 2627 of *Lecture Notes in Artificial Intelligence*, pages 61–75. Springer, 2003.

[17] M.R.C. van Dongen. Lightweight arc-consistency algorithms. Technical Report TR-01-2003, Cork Constraint Computation Centre, January 2003.

[18] M.R.C. van Dongen. Lightweight MAC algorithms. Technical Report TR-02-2003, Cork Constraint Computation Centre, April 2003.

[19] R.J. Wallace and E.C. Freuder. Ordering heuristics for arc consistency algorithms. In *AI/GI/VI '92*, pages 163–169, Vancouver, British Columbia, Canada, 1992.

[20] Y. Zhang and R.H.C. Yap. Making AC-3 an optimal algorithm. In *Proceedings of the Seventeenth International Joint Conference on Artificial Intelligence*, pages 316–321, 2001.

SESSION 3:

SPATIO-TEMPORAL REASONING AND MACHINE LEARNING

SPARQS: Automatic Reasoning in Qualitative Space

Baher A. El-Geresy

School of Computing, University of Glamorgan

Treforest, Wales, UK

Alia I. Abdelmoty

Department of Computer Science

Cardiff University,

Cardiff, Wales, UK

Abstract

In this paper the design and implementation of a general qualitative spatial reasoning engine (SPARQS) is presented. Qualitative treatment of information in large spatial databases is used to complement the quantitative approaches to managing those systems, in particular, it is used for the automatic derivation of implicit spatial relationships and in maintaining the integrity of the database. To be of practical use, composition tables of spatial relationships between different types of objects need to be developed and integrated in those systems. The automatic derivation of such tables is considered to be a major challenge to current reasoning approaches. In this paper, this issue is addressed and a new approach to the automatic derivation of composition tables is presented. The method is founded on a sound set-theoretical approach for the representation and reasoning over randomly shaped objects in space. A reasoning engine tool, SPARQS, has been implemented to demonstrate the validity of the approach. The engine is composed of a basic graphical interface where composition tables between the most common types of spatial objects is built. An advanced interface is also provided, where users are able to describe shapes of arbitrary complexity and to derive the composition of chosen spatial relationships. Examples of the application of the method using different objects and different types of spatial relationships is presented and new composition tables are built using the reasoning engine.

1 Introduction

Qualitative Spatial Representation and Reasoning (QSRR) is an active field of AI research where formalisms for encoding and manipulating qualitative spatial knowledge are studied[10]. A main aim of these techniques is the provision of tools to enhance the derivation and retrieval of implicit knowledge in large spatial databases typically used in applications such as, Geographic Information Systems (GIS), medical and biological databases and Computer Aided Design, Manufacture and Process Planning (CAD/CAM/CAPP). Such application domains are characterised by handling very large sets of entities, relationships and constraints and their manipulation usually involve substantial computational costs. The ability to handle a certain level of indeterminacy makes QSRR techniques attractive in those domains. The goal is for such techniques to complement and enhance the traditional, usually computationally expensive, geometrical methods, especially when precise information are neither available nor needed. A simple example in a GIS is the derivation of the fact that the location of Peterhouse College is in the UK, from the facts that it is located in Cambridge and Cambridge is in the UK, without needing to execute a polygon-in-polygon geometric computation. Applications of QSRR include, qualitative spatial scene specification and scene feasibility problems, checking the similarity and consistency of data sets, integrating different spatial sets, and in initial pruning of search spaces in spatial query processing. Research is also ongoing for incorporating QSRR in the definition and implementation of spatial query languages. However, the qualitative approach has obvious limitations where useful characteristics of spatial objects such as shape and size are not used. Also, its application becomes limited when exact positions and tolerance constraints are considered. Hence, it can be argued that both the quantitative and qualitative approaches have complementary areas of strength and that any system which can combine the two paradigms in a way which uses their strength would be an effective platform for a range of novel and conventional applications. One approach to utilising QSRR in such systems is by the automatic development of composition or transitivity tables between different types of spatial objects. Reasoning can then be transformed into a simple process of table look-up to be invoked when needed. Several works have addressed this problem previously, and some composition tables between simple objects have been reported. These approaches are generally limited and applicable only in simple constrained domains. The problem is, however, recognised as a major challenge to automatic theorem provers [3, 25], and no general solution has yet been found.

In this paper, a new approach is proposed for the automatic reasoning of spatial relationships and the automatic building of composition tables. The approach is novel as composition tables between object of any type and complexity can be derived. The proposed method is implemented using java in the SPARQS reasoning engine tool. The engine is used to validate the method and demonstrate its generality. The paper is structured as follows. Section 2 outlines the representation approach in topological spaces. In section 3, the reasoning method is presented and applied over topological relations between different types of objects. The reasoning engine is described in section 4, and the process of building composition tables is also explained. Discussions and conclusions are given in section 5 and new composition tables between different object types are presented in the appendix.

2 The Formalism

This section addresses the problem of qualitative representation of objects with random spatial complexity and their topological relationships. The reasoning formalism is then presented, consisting of a) general constraints to govern the spatial relationships between objects in space, and b) general rules to propagate relationships between those objects. Both the constraints and the rules are based on a uniform representation of the topology of the objects, their embedding space and the representation of the relationships between them.

2.1 The General Representation Approach

Objects of interest and their embedding space are divided into components according to a required resolution. The connectivity of those components is explicitly represented. Spatial relations are represented by the intersection of object components [1] in a similar fashion to that described in [17] but with no restriction on object components to consist only of two parts (boundary and interior).

The topology of the object and the embedding space can then be described by a matrix whose elements represent the connectivity relations between its components. This matrix shall be denoted *adjacency matrix*. In the decomposition strategy, the complement of the object in question shall be considered to be infinite, and the suffix 0, e.g. (x_0) is used to represent this component.

Hence, the topology of a space S containing an object x is defined using the following equation.

$$x = \bigcup_{i=1}^{n} x_i \tag{1}$$

$$S_x = x \cup x_0 \tag{2}$$

where S_x is used to denote the space associated with object x.

In figure 1 different possible decompositions of a simple convex polygon and its embedding space is shown along with their adjacency matrices. In 1 (a), the object is represented by two components, a linear component x_1 and an areal component x_2 and the rest of the space is represented by an infinite areal component x_0 representing the surrounding area. In 1(d), only one areal component is used to represent the polygon. Both representations are valid and may be used in different contexts. Different decomposition strategies for the objects and their embedding spaces can be used according to the precision of the relations required and the specific application considered. The higher the resolution used (or the finer the components of the space and the objects), the higher the precision of the resulting set of relations in the domain considered.

The fact that two components are connected is represented by a (1) in the adjacency matrix and by a (0) otherwise. Since connectivity is a symmetric relation, the resulting matrix will be symmetric around the diagonal. Hence, only half the matrix is sufficient for the representation of the object's topology and the matrix can be collapsed to the structure in figure 1(c) and (f).

Semi-bounded areas of the embedding space can also be represented (as virtual components) if needed. For example, figure 2(a) shows a possible decomposition of a concave shaped object and its embedding

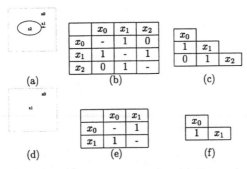

Figure 1: (a), (d) Possible decompositions of a simple convex polygon and its embedding space. (b), (e) Adjacency matrices corresponding to the two shapes in (a) and (d) respectively. (c), (f) Half the symmetric adjacency matrix is sufficient to capture the object representation.

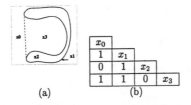

Figure 2: (a) Using virtual components to represent semi-bounded components in space. (b) Adjacency matrix for the shape in (a).

space. In 2(b) the adjacency matrix for its components is presented. The object is represented by two components a linear component x_1 and an areal component x_2 and the rest of its embedding space is represented by a finite areal component x_3 (representing the virtual enclosure) and infinite areal component x_0 representing the surrounding area.

2.1.1 The Underlying Representation of Spatial Relations

In this section, the representation of the topological relations through the intersection of their components is adopted and generalized for objects of arbitrary complexity.

Distinction of topological relations is dependent on the strategy used in the decomposition of the objects and their related spaces. For example, in figure 3 different relationships between two objects x and y are shown, where in 3(a) x is outside y and in 3(b) x is inside y. Object y is decomposed into two components y_1 and y_2 and the rest of the space associated with y is decomposed into two components: y_3 representing the enclosure and y_0 representing the rest of the space. Note that it is the identification of the (virtual) component y_3 that makes the distinction between the two relationships in the figure. The complete set of spatial relationships are identified by combinatorial intersection of the components of one space with those of the other space.

If $R(x, y)$ is a relation of interest between objects x and y, and X and Y are the spaces associated with the objects respectively such that m is the number of components in X and l is the number of components in Y, then a spatial relation $R(x, y)$ can be represented by one instance of the following equation:

$$R(x, y) = X \cap Y$$

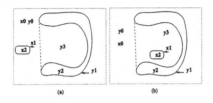

Figure 3: Different qualitative spatial relationships can be distinguished by identifying the appropriate components of the objects and the space.

	y_0	y_1	y_2	y_3
x_0	1	1	1	1
x_1	1	0	0	0
x_2	1	0	0	0

(a)

	y_0	y_1	y_2	y_3
x_0	1	1	1	1
x_1	0	0	0	1
x_2	0	0	0	1

(b)

Figure 4: The corresponding **intersection matrices** for the relationships in figure 3 respectively.

$$= \left(\bigcup_{i=1}^{m} x_i \right) \cap \left(\bigcup_{j=1}^{l} y_j \right)$$

$$= (x_1 \cap y_1, \cdots, x_1 \cap y_l, x_2 \cap y_1, \cdots, x_m \cap y_l)$$

The intersection $x_i \cap y_j$ can be an empty or a non-empty intersection. The above set of intersections shall be represented by an intersection matrix, as follows,

$$R(x,y) = \begin{array}{c|c|c|c|c} & y_0 & y_1 & y_2 & \cdots \\ \hline x_0 & & & & \\ \hline x_1 & & & & \\ \hline x_2 & & & & \\ \hline \vdots & & & & \end{array}$$

For example, the intersection matrices corresponding to the spatial relationships in figure 3 are shown in figure 4. The components x_1 and x_2 have a non-empty intersection with y_0 in 4(a) and with y_3 in 4(b). Different combinations in the intersection matrix can represent different qualitative relations. The set of valid or sound spatial relationships between objects is dependent on the particular domain studied.

2.2 The General Reasoning Formalism

The reasoning approach consists of: a) general constraints to govern the spatial relationships between objects in space, and b) general rules to propagate relationships between the objects.

2.2.1 General Constraints

The intersection matrix is in fact a set of constraints whose values identifies specific spatial relationships. The process of spatial reasoning can be defined as the process of propagating the constraints of two spatial relations (for example, $R_1(A, B)$ and $R_2(B, C)$), to derive a new set of constraints between objects. The derived constraints can then be mapped to a specific spatial relation (i.e. the relation $R_3(A, C)$).

A subset of the set of constraints defining all possible spatial relations are general and applicable to any relationship between any objects. These general constraints are a consequence of the initial assumptions used in the definition of the object and space topology. The two general constraints are:

1. Every unbounded (infinite) component of one space must intersect with at least one unbounded (infinite) component of the other space.

2. Every component from one space must intersect with at least one component from the other space.

2.2.2 General Reasoning Rules

Composition of spatial relations is the process through which the possible relationship(s) between two object x and z is derived given two relationships: R_1 between x and y and R_2 between y and z. Two general reasoning rules for the propagation of intersection constraints are presented. The rules are characterized by the ability to reason over spatial relationships between objects of arbitrary complexity in any space dimension. These rules allow for the automatic derivation of the composition (transitivity) tables between any spatial shapes.

Reasoning Rules

Composition of spatial relations using the *intersection* representation approach is based on the transitive property of the subset relations. In what follows the following subset notation is used. If x' is a set of components (set of point-sets) $\{x_1, \cdots, x_{m'}\}$ in a space X, and y_j is a component in space Y, then $\sqsubseteq$ denotes the following subset relationship.

- $y_j \sqsubseteq x'$ denotes the subset relationship such that: $\forall x_i \in x' (y_j \cap x_i \neq \phi) \wedge y_j \cap (X - x_1 - x_2 \cdots - x_m) = \phi$ where $i = 1, \cdots m'$. Intuitively, this symbol indicates that the component y_j intersects with every set in the collection x' and does not intersect with any set outside of x'.

If x_i, y_j and z_k are components of objects x, y and z respectively, then if there is a non-empty intersection between x_i and y_j, and y_j is a subset of z_k, then it can be concluded that there is also a non-empty intersection between x_i and z_k.

$$(x_i \cap y_j \neq \phi) \wedge (y_j \subseteq z_k) \rightarrow (x_i \cap z_k \neq \phi)$$

This relation can be generalized in the following two rules. The rules describe the propagation of intersections between the components of objects and their related spaces involved in the spatial composition.

Rule 1: Propagation of Non-Empty Intersections

Let $x' = \{x_1, x_2, \cdots, x_{m'}\}$ be a subset of the set of components of space X whose total number of components is m and $m' \leq m$; $x' \subseteq X$. Let $z' = \{z_1, z_2, \cdots, z_{n'}\}$ be a subset of the set of components of space Z whose total number of components is n and $n' \leq n$; $z' \subseteq Z$. If y_j is a component of space Y, the following is a governing rule of interaction for the three spaces X, Y and Z.

$$
\begin{aligned}
(x' \sqsupseteq y_j) \quad &\wedge \quad (y_j \sqsubseteq z') \\
&\rightarrow \quad (x' \cap z' \neq \phi) \\
&\equiv \quad (x_1 \cap z_1 \neq \phi \vee \cdots \vee x_1 \cap z_{n'} \neq \phi) \\
&\qquad \wedge (x_2 \cap z_1 \neq \phi \vee \cdots \vee x_2 \cap z_{n'} \neq \phi) \\
&\qquad \wedge \cdots \\
&\qquad \wedge (x_{m'} \cap z_1 \neq \phi \vee \cdots \vee x_{m'} \cap z_{n'} \neq \phi)
\end{aligned}
$$

The above rule states that if the component y_j in space Y has a positive intersection with every component from the sets x' and z', then each component of the set x' must intersect with at least one component of the set z' and vice versa.

The constraint $x_i \cap z_1 \neq \phi \vee x_i \cap z_2 \neq \phi \cdots \vee x_i \cap z_{n'} \neq \phi$ can be expressed in the intersection matrix by a label, for example the label a_r ($r = 1$ or 2) in the following matrix indicates $x_1 \cap (z_2 \cup z_4) \neq \phi$ (x_1 has a positive intersection with z_2, or with z_4 or with both). A $-$ in the matrix indicates that the intersection is either positive or negative.

	z_1	z_2	z_3	z_4	$\cdots$	z_n
x_1	$-$	a_1	$-$	a_2		$-$

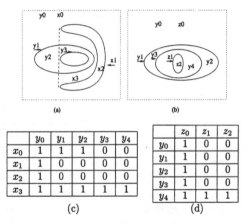

(a)   (b)

	y_0	y_1	y_2	y_3	y_4
x_0	1	1	1	0	0
x_1	1	0	0	0	0
x_2	1	0	0	0	0
x_3	1	1	1	1	1

(c)

	z_0	z_1	z_2
y_0	1	0	0
y_1	1	0	0
y_2	1	0	0
y_3	1	0	0
y_4	1	1	1

(d)

Figure 5: (a) and (b) Spatial relationships between non-simple objects x, y and z. (c) and (d) Corresponding intersection matrices.

Rule 1 represents the propagation of non-empty intersections of components in space. A different version of the rule for the propagation of empty intersections can be stated as follows.

Rule 2: Propagation of Empty Intersections

Let $z' = \{z_1, z_2, \cdots, z_{n'}\}$ be a subset of the set of components of space Z whose total number of components is n and $n' < n$; $z' \subset Z$. Let $y' = \{y_1, y_2, \cdots, y_{l'}\}$ be a subset of the set of components of space Y whose total number of components is l and $l' < l$; $y' \subset Y$. Let x_i be a component of the space X. Then the following is a governing rule for the spaces X, Y and Z.

$$(x_i \sqsubseteq y') \quad \wedge \quad (y' \sqsubseteq z')$$
$$\rightarrow \quad (x_i \cap (Z - z_1 - z_2 \cdots - z_{n'}) = \phi)$$

Remark: if $n' = n$, i.e. x_i may intersect with every element in Z, or if $m' = m$, i.e. z_k may intersect with every element in X, or if $l' = l$, i.e. x_i (or z_k) may intersect with every element in Y, then no empty intersections can be propagated for x_i or z_k. Rules 1 and 2 are the two general rules for propagating empty and non-empty intersections of components of spaces.

Note that in both rules the intermediate object (y) and its space components plays the main role in the propagation of intersections. The first rule is applied a number of times equal to the number of components of the space of the intermediate object. Hence, the composition of spatial relations becomes a tractable problem which can be performed in a defined limited number of steps.

2.3   Example 1: Propagation of Definite Relations

The example in figure 5 is used for demonstrating the composition of relations using non-simple spatial objects. Figure 5(a) shows the relationship between a concave polygon x and a polygon with a hole y and 5(b) shows the relationship between object y and a simple polygon z where z touches the the hole in y. The intersection matrices corresponding to the two relationships are also shown.

The reasoning rules are used to propagate the intersections between the components of objects x and z as follows. From rule 1 we have,

- y_0 intersections:

$$\{x_0, x_1, x_2, x_3\} \sqsupseteq y_0 \quad \wedge \quad y_0 \sqsubseteq \{z_0\}$$
$$\rightarrow \quad x_0 \cap z_0 \neq \phi \wedge x_1 \cap z_0 \neq \phi$$
$$\wedge \quad x_2 \cap z_0 \neq \phi \wedge x_3 \cap z_0 \neq \phi$$

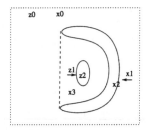

Figure 6: Resulting definite relation from the composition of the relations in figure 5.

- y_1 intersections:

$$\{x_0, x_3\} \sqsupseteq y_1 \land y_1 \sqsubseteq \{z_0\} \rightarrow x_0 \cap z_0 \neq \phi \land x_3 \cap z_0 \neq \phi$$

- y_2 intersections:

$$\{x_0, x_3\} \sqsupseteq y_2 \land y_2 \sqsubseteq \{z_0\} \rightarrow x_0 \cap z_0 \neq \phi \land x_3 \cap z_0 \neq \phi$$

- y_3 intersections:

$$\{x_3\} \sqsupseteq y_3 \land y_3 \sqsubseteq \{z_0\} \rightarrow x_3 \cap z_0 \neq \phi$$

- y_4 intersections:

$$\{x_3\} \sqsupseteq y_4 \land y_4 \sqsubseteq \{z_0, z_1, z_2\} \rightarrow x_3 \cap z_0 \neq \phi \land x_3 \cap z_1 \neq \phi \land x_3 \cap z_2 \neq \phi$$

Refining the above constraints, we get the following intersection matrix.

	z_0	z_1	z_2
x_0	1	0	0
x_1	1	0	0
x_2	1	0	0
x_3	1	1	1

The resulting matrix corresponds to one possible relationship between x and z as shown in figure 6.

2.4   Example 2: Propagation of Indefinite Relations

The example in figure 7 is used for demonstrating the composition of relations using non-simple spatial objects, resulting in a set of possible relationships between objects x and z. The figure shows example relationships and the corresponding intersection matrices, between regions with indeterminate boundaries x and y and z as defined in [7]. The problem of representing vague regions have been addressed in various research works previously [28]. In [28] a set of 44 possible relations is defined between the two region with broad boundaries. The following is an example of how the reasoning rules are applied to derive the composition of two example relations.

The reasoning rules are used to propagate the intersections between the components of objects x and z as follows. From rule 1 we have,

- y_1 intersections:

$$\{x_1, x_2\} \sqsupseteq y_1 \quad \land \quad y_1 \sqsubseteq \{z_1\}$$
$$\rightarrow \quad x_1 \cap z_1 \neq \phi \land x_2 \cap z_1 \neq \phi$$

- y_2 intersections:

$$\{x_1, x_2\} \sqsupseteq y_2 \quad \land \quad y_2 \sqsubseteq \{z_2, z_0\}$$
$$\rightarrow \quad x_1 \cap (z_2 \cup z_0) \neq \phi \land x_2 \cap (z_2 \cup z_0) \neq \phi$$

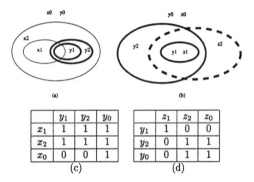

Figure 7: (a) and (b) Spatial relationships between vague regions x, y and z. (c) and (d) Corresponding intersection matrices.

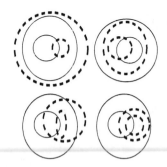

Figure 8: Possible configurations for the composition in figure 7.

- y_0 intersections:

$$\{x_1, x_2, x_0\} \sqsupseteq y_0 \quad \wedge \quad y_0 \sqsubseteq \{z_2, z_0\}$$
$$\rightarrow \quad x_1 \cap (z_2 \cup z_0) \neq \phi \wedge x_2 \cap (z_2 \cup z_0) \neq \phi$$
$$\wedge \quad x_0 \cap (z_2 \cup z_0) \neq \phi$$

Refining the above constraints, we get the following intersection matrix.

	z_1	z_2	z_0
x_1	1	a_1,c_1	a_2,d_1
x_2	1	b_1,c_2	b_2,d_2
x_0	0	?	1

Where a_1 and a_2 represent the constraint $x_1 \cap (z_2 \vee z_0) = 1$ and b_1 and b_2 represent the constraint $x_2 \cap (z_2 \vee z_0) = 1$, c_1 and c_2 represent the constraint $z_2 \cap (x_1 \vee x_2) = 1$ and d_1 and d_2 represent the constraint $z_0 \cap (x_1 \vee x_2) = 1$ and the ? represents $(1 \vee 0)$. The result matrix corresponds to one of four possible relationships between x and z, namely numbers 21, 22, 23 and 25, as shown in figure 8.

3 SPARQS: The Reasoning Engine

To demonstrate the validity of the proposed approach, a reasoning engine has been designed and implemented using java. The interface to the program, named SPARQS (SPAtial Reasoning in Qualitative Space) consists of two parts. A basic interface is provided, where the topology of some common spatial object shapes are predefined, as shown in figure 9(a). Users are able to choose object types from a

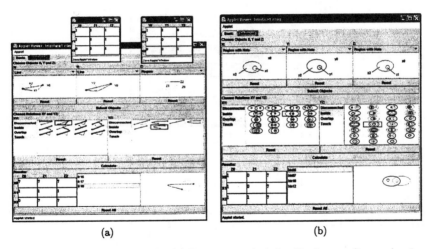

Figure 9: The basic interface in SPARQS. (a) Composition of relationships between lines and region. (b) Composition of relationships between regions with holes.

menu of available ones, namely, points, line, simple region, region with indeterminate boundaries and concave regions. Users are then offered a selection of possible topological spatial relationships between the chosen object types, Sets of relationships are shown graphically and categorised using a coarse classification scheme under four headings, namely, disjoint, inside, overlap and touch to enhance the usability of the interface. The reasoning rules are applied to propagate the intersection matrices and produce the result matrix. The constraints in the matrix are then matched to the set of possible relationships and all the ones satisfying the constraints are displayed in the result window, as shown in figure 9(a) . The program is flexible where the input spatial relationships can be changed and resubmitted and the result re-calculated, as shown in figure 9(b).

A preliminary implementation of an advanced interface is also provided as shown in figure 10. Users are able to fill in adjacency and intersection matrices, which are subsequently used by the system to derive the resulting relationships. Some validation checks are done on the input matrices, e.g. to reject matrices that violate the general constraints described earlier, where no rows or columns in the matrix are allowed to contain only zeros. The result constraint matrix is therefore dependent on the validity of the input shapes and relations. Enhancement to the interface may be possible, where a more guided approach to input, possibly using sketch-based techniques, can be utilised to ensure valid entries.

The engine has been used to derive new composition tables between all the combination of objects defined in the basic interface, e.g. between simple regions, concave regions and regions with indeterminate boundaries, etc.

4 Comparison with Related Work

The main advantage of the method proposed above is its uniformity. The same methodology is used for the definition of simple, complex, composite regions, as well as regions with indeterminate boundaries. The method is also adaptable, where different levels of representation can be devised by hiding or revealing the details of objects as required. The method is therefore well adapted for use as a basis for a spatial reasoning formalism.

Representing complex regions has been addressed in many works. In [11, 10], Cohn et al extended a logic-based formalism to handle concave regions, and regions with holes (doughnut shapes). New axioms and theories had to be devised to define the new shapes. The main drawback of this approach is its

Figure 10: The advanced interface in SPARQS. Users specify the adjacency and intersection matrices. The example in the figure corresponds to the Example 1 above.

complexity, as new, possibly considerable, extensions of the formalism have to be devised with every new shape considered.

In [17, 16], Egenhofer et al used point-set topology to define simple regions, using three components, boundary, interior and exterior. The method proposed here deviates from their work in one important respect which has far-reaching implications. The constraint on the object components has been relaxed to be any possible set of components which satisfies the main assumptions behind the formalism. The notions of boundaries, interiors and exteriors were dropped and the notion of object and space components is used instead. Other methods were devised in [15] to define regions with holes, through the definition of spatial relationships between simple regions and no extension for the method was proposed for the definition of irregular or concave regions.

The work of Clementini and De Felice [7] follows closely the method of Egenhofer, and provides a definition for regions with holes using boundaries, interiors and exteriors. Their method inherits the same limitations of [17]. In another work [8], Clementini et al addressed the issue of defining composite regions for use in spatial query languages, by defining explicit relationships between all the components in the object, in the same way, regions with holes were defined in [15].

In [6], Clementini et al proposed a method of representing unique topological relationships between two composite regions (composed from simple regions without holes) as a set of rules which use only binary topological relationships at component level to decide the topological relationship between complex objects at higher level. The work of Nguyen et al [23] follows a similar approach to the above, but generalises the rules for connected composite objects with or without holes.

Coenen and Pepijin [9] proposed an ontology for objects and relationships in spatio-temporal domains. They assumed the space to consist of sets of points and used set-theoretic notions to define objects in that space. Their approach is distinctive from the above where space is considered to be discrete, not continuous. The method was used to define a general "object" and quantitative identifiers are used to qualify the object properties. Extending the method for distinguishing between different types of regions was not proposed.

Vague regions or regions with undetermined boundaries were studied in [12, 7, 4, 18, 20, 27]. Only simple convex regions with no holes were considered and the undetermined boundary was represented by a surrounding ring [12, 7]. Approaches to spatial reasoning in the literature can generally be classified into a) approaches using *transitive propagation* and b) approaches using *theorem proving*.

- Transitive propagation: In this approach the transitive property of some spatial relations is utilised to carry out the required reasoning. This applies to the *order relations*, such as before, after and $(<, =, >)$ (for example, $a < b \land b < c \rightarrow a < c$), and to subset relations such as contain and inside (for example, $inside(A, B) \land inside(B, C) \rightarrow inside(A, C)$ and $east(A, B) \land east(B, C) \rightarrow east(A, C)$).

Transitive property of the subset relations was employed by Egenhofer [14] for reasoning over topological relationships. Transitive property of the order relations has been utilised by Mukerjee & Joe [22], Guesgen [19], Lee & Hsu [21] and Papadias & Sellis [24].

Although order relations can be utilised in reasoning over point-shaped objects, they cannot be directly applied when the actual object shapes and proximity of objects are considered.

- Theorem proving (elimination): Here, reasoning is carried out by checking every relation in the full set of *sound* relations in the domain to see whether it is a valid consequence of the composition considered (theorems to be proved) and eliminating the ones which are not consistent with the composition [13].

  Bennett [2] have proposed a propositional calculus for the derivation of the composition of topological relations between simple regions using this method. However, checking each relation in the composition table to prove or eliminate is not possible in general cases and is considered a challenge for theorem provers [26, 5].

In general limitation of the methods in the above two approaches can be summarised as follows:

- Spatial reasoning is studied only between objects of similar types, e.g. between two lines or two simple areas. Spatial relations exist between objects of any type and it is limiting to consider the composition of only specific object shapes.

- Spatial reasoning was carried out only between objects with the same dimension as the space they are embedded in, e.g. between two lines in 1D, between two regions in 2D, etc.

- Spatial reasoning is studied mainly between simple object shapes or objects with controlled complexity, for example, regions with holes treated as concentric simple regions. None of the methods in the literature have been presented for spatial reasoning between objects with arbitrary complexity.

The method proposed here is simple and general - only two rules are used to derive composition between objects of random complexity and is applicable to different types of spatial relations.

5 Conclusions

In this paper, a general approach to qualitative representation and reasoning has been presented. The method is simple and is based on a uniform representation of objects and spatial relationships. Objects are decomposed into representative components and their topology described in an adjacency matrix. The set of sound topological relations between objects are represented by the interaction of the object components. The approach is general where composition of spatial relations can be applied between objects of random dimension and complexity. An implementation of the method is also presented to demonstrate its validity and generality. Using the reasoning engine, SPARQS, several new composition tables were built between common spatial object types, viz, points, lines, polygons, concave polygons and regions with holes. The engine also includes a more flexible interface where manual input of adjacency and intersection matrices can be used to derive the composition of other random object shapes. The automatic derivation of composition tables presents an important step towards the realisation of a general qualitative reasoning engine which can be utilised in large spatial databases.

References

[1] El-Geresy B.A. and Abdelmoty A.I. Order in Space: A General Formalism for Spatial Reasoning. *Int. J. on Artificial Intelligence Tools*, 6(4):423–450, 1997.

[2] B. Bennett. Spatial Reasoning with Propositional Logics. In *Principles of Knowledge Representation and Reasoning (KR94)*, pages 51–62. Morgan Kaufmann, 1994.

[3] B. Bennett, A. Isli, and A. Cohn. When does a composition table provide a complete and tractable proof procedure for a relational constraint language, 1997.

[4] I. Bloch. Fuzzy Relative Position between Objects in Image Processing: a Morphological Approach. *IEEE Transactions on Pattern Analysis and Machine Intelligence*, 21(7):657–664, 1999.

[5] A.G.P. Brown and F.P. Coenen. Spatial reasoning: improving computational efficiency. *Automation in Construction*, 9(4):361–36, 2000.

[6] A. Clementini and P. Di Felice. A Model for Representing Topological Relationships Between Complex Gemetric Features in Spatial Databases. *Information Sciences*, 3:149–178, 1995.

[7] E. Clementini and P. Di Felice. An Algebraic Model for Spatial Objects with Indeterminate Boundaries. In P.A. Burrough and A.U. Frank, editors, *Geographic Objects with Indeterminate Boundaries, GISDATA*, pages 155–169. Taylor & Francis, 1996.

[8] E. Clementini, P. Di Felice, and G. Califano. Composite Regions in Topological Queries. *Information Systems*, 20(7):579–594, 1995.

[9] F.P. Coenen and V. Pepijn. A generic ontology for spatial reasoning. In *Research and Development in Expert Systems XV, proc. of ES'98*, pages 44–57. Springer Verlag, 1998.

[10] A G Cohn and S M Hazarika. Qualitative spatial representation and reasoning: An overview. *Fundamenta Informaticae*, 46(1-2):1–29, 2001.

[11] A.G. Cohn, B. Bennett, J. Gooday, and N.M. Gotts. Qualitative Spatial Representation and Reasoning with the Region Connection Calculus. *Geoinformatica*, 1(3):1–42, 1997.

[12] A.G. Cohn and N.M. Gotts. The "Egg-Yolk" Representation of Regions with Indeterminate Boundaries. In P.A. Burrough and A.U. Frank, editors, *Geographic Objects with Indeterminate Boundaries, GISDATA*, pages 171–187. Taylor & Francis, 1996.

[13] A.G. Cohn, D.A. Randell, Z. Cui, and B. Bennet. Qualitative Spatial Reasoning and Representation. In P. Carrete and M.G. Singh, editors, *Qualitative Reasoning and Decision Technologies*, pages 513–522, 1993.

[14] M.J. Egenhofer. Deriving the composition of Binary Topological Relations. *Journal of Visual Languages and Computing*, 5:133–149, 1994.

[15] M.J. Egenhofer, E. Clementini, and Di Felicem P. Topological Relations Between Regions With Holes. *Int. J. Geographic Information Systems*, 8(2):129–142, 1994.

[16] M.J. Egenhofer and R.D. Franzosa. PointSet Topological Spatial Relations. *Int. J. Geographic Information Systems*, 5(2):161–174, 1991.

[17] M.J. Egenhofer and J.R. Herring. A Mathematical Framework for the Definition of Topological Relationships. In *Proceedings of the 4th international Symposium on Spatial Data Handling*, volume 2, pages 803–13, 1990.

[18] H.W. Guesgen and J. Albrech. Imprecise reasoning in geographic information systems. *Fuzzy Sets and Systems*, 113(1):121–131, 2000.

[19] Guesgen, H.W. Spatial reasoning based on allen's temporal logic. Technical Report TR-89-049, International Computer Science Institute, Berkeley, California, 1989.

[20] F. Karbou. An interval approach to fuzzy surroundedness and fuzzy spatial relations. In *19th International Conference of the North American Fuzzy Information Processing Society*, 2000.

[21] S-Y Lee and F-J Hsu. Picture Algebra for Spatial Reasoning of Iconic Images Represented in 2D C-string. *Pattern Recognition*, 12:425–435, 1991.

[22] A. Mukerjee and G. Joe. A Qualitative Model for Space. In *Proceeding of the 8th National Conference on Artificial Intelligence, AAAI, 1990*, pages 721–727, 1990.

[23] V.H. Nguyen, C. Parent, and S. Spaccapietra. Complex Regions in Topological Queries. In *Proceeding of the Internation Conference on Spatial Information Theory COSIT'97*, volume LNCS 1329, pages 175–192. Springer Verlag, 1997.

[24] D. Papadias and T. Sellis. Spatial reasoning using symbolic arrays. In *Theories and Methods of Spatio-Temporal Reasoning in Geographic Space*, LNCS 716, pages 153–161. Springer Verlag, 1992.

[25] D. Randell and M. Wikowski. Building Large Composition Tables via Axiomatic Theories. In *Principles of Knowledge Representation and Reasoning: Proceedings of the Eighth International Conference (KR-2002)*, pages 26–35. AAAI Press, 2002.

[26] D.A. Randell, A.G. Cohn, and Z. Cui. Computing Transitivity Tables: A Challenge for Automated Theorem Provers. In *Proceedings of CADE 11*, Lecture Notes In Computer Science, 1992.

[27] K. Sridharan and H.E. Stephanou. Fuzzy distances for proximity characterization under uncertainty. *Fuzzy Sets and Systems*, 103(3):427–434, 1999.

[28] M.F. Worboys and E. Clementini. Integration of imperfect spatial information. *Journal of Visual Languages and Computing*, 12:61–80, 2001.

Incorporating Reactive Learning Behaviour into a Mini-robot Platform

Mark Elshaw, Debra Lewis and Stefan Wermter

School of Computing and Technology, Centre for Hybrid Intelligent
Systems, University of Sunderland, St Peter's Way, Sunderland
SR6 0DD, United Kingdom
[Mark.Elshaw][Stefan.Wermter]@sunderland.ac.uk
www.his.sunderland.ac.uk

Abstract

In the Neuro-robotics Lab of the Centre for Hybrid Intelligent
Systems we have organised various challenging undergraduate
student projects using Mindstorm, Khepera and PeopleBot robots. In
this paper we will describe a particularly interesting undergraduate
student project involving the introduction of intelligent behaviour
onto a mini-robot platform. In the past robots were mainly hard-
coded to perform actions that limited their adaptability to their
environment. As a response to this problem there has been
considerable interest in producing robots that can learn. By
developing a fly-catcher robot scenario using a mini-robot platform it
was possible to consider the incorporation of learned intelligent
behaviour for navigation and the use of object recognition. In doing
so neural network learning was incorporated into a mini-robot. This
research offers a restricted insight for robot users into issues
associated with intelligent goal-directed learning on mini-robots that
are also applicable to those using more sophisticated robots including
our work on the MirrorBot (Biomimetic multimodal learning in a
mirror neuron-based robot) project.

1. Introduction

The Neuro-robotics Lab in the Centre for Hybrid Intelligent Systems at the
University of Sunderland has a wide selection of sophisticated intelligent robots
within its purpose built laboratory including two large PeopleBot robots,
mindstorms, Kephera etc. One important component of our work is to organise
challenging undergraduate student projects using these robots. This has proved
very successful in the past with projects on the association of language with robot
actions on the PeopleBot, navigation on an interactive Khepera, neural network
based object manipulations using the Khepera, vision processing on the PeopleBot
for landmark navigation and language recognition and creation on a PeopleBot
tour-guide robot (http://www.his.sunderland.ac.uk/Robots_frame.html). In this
paper we will describe a particularly interesting undergraduate student project by

Debra Lewis using a mindstorm robot. In nature fly-catching animals may have restricted computational resources and this motivated our interest to try to model a fly-catcher as a small mini-robot. These insights include real-time processing, efficient programming techniques, multi-modal inputs, image processing and incorporating learned behaviour.

This paper considers the introduction of intelligent learned behaviour on a mini-robot platform to perform the functions of navigation and recognition. This system combines readings from the two modalities vision and touch to navigate around an environment, performs object recognition and captures an object in real-time. Despite the very restrictive nature of a mini-robot such as the mindstorm robot that was used in this case intelligent learning behaviour was incorporated into the system. This involved the introduction of a neural network to perform navigation and the use of object recognition. Although there is considerable research into mini-robots, goal-directed learning has previously had little impact.

The mindstorm robot platform is very basic. It contains a RCX Microcomputer, LEGO elements, motors, light and touch sensors, and an infrared transmitter [1]. The RCX is an autonomous microprocessor that is programmable using the computer language Not Quite C [2]. Once programmed the RCX takes simple inputs from the environment based on sensor readings, processes the data and then produces the appropriate output by typically manipulating the motor directions [3, 4, 5]. Although these robots are restricted in the number of sensors that can be put on the robot and the memory space (6k) to download programs, they are suitable for modelling simple intelligent learning behaviour to perform actions autonomously. The Not Quite C programming language is based on 'C', but it is very limited in comparison. It is only possible to use 32 global and 16 local integer variables. Hence, Not Quite C is not able to provide the complex algorithms and real-valued functions that are typically associated with machine learning.

The add-on accessory set for vision contains a basic digital camera and basic software for object recognition. The Vision Command Set offers possibilities to have the robot perform actions based on what it sees. However, this set does lack sophisticated support algorithms typically required for object recognition. Further, although the mindstorm robot software and the Vision Command software are designed to work together, they are clearly distinct with the mindstorm software working autonomously on the robot and Vision Command through the PC.

In order to examine the suitability for including learned behaviour on a restricted mini-robot platform a fly-catcher scenario was devised. The scenario involved putting the robot into an environment and having it look for an object, known as the fly. If the robot could not see its prey it moved around until it achieved line-of-sight. Once the fly was observed the fly-catcher was required to go to it, grab it and then relocate the fly. This paper includes an examination of intelligent robot systems, a description of the intelligent navigation and object recognition approaches used on the fly-catcher robot and finally a discussion of the fly-catcher robot's overall performance. By doing so we are also able to consider the use of neural learning in goal-directed behaviour, which gives us certain insight for use in our research on the MirrorBot project. This project uses the mirror-neuron theory of Rizzolatti and Arbib, 1998 [6] who found that neurons located in the F5 area of a primate's brain were activated by both the performance of the action and its observation. It is argued that the recognition of motor actions comes from the presence of a goal and so the motor system does not solely control movement but also performs goal-directed behaviour [7]. The notion of goal-directed neural behaviour could have a significant impact on learning robots as it offers an approach for robot learning through imitation and multi-modal information fusion in a biologically inspired manner.

2. Intelligent Robot Systems

In the past robots such as the Honda robot required hard-coding of all behaviour and so could not learn and adapt to changes in their environment [8]. To overcome the need for hard-coded robots researchers are examining intelligent learning in robots. Robot learning according to Araújo and Barreto (2001) [9] is a challenging domain due to its complexity, restrictions on the amount of training data available and the real-time decision-making. Below is an examination of a few examples of robotic learning systems that have been developed.

For instance, in our research [10, 11] using the MIRA[1] PeopleBot robot as part of the MirrorBot project we developed a modular self-organising model that controls robot actions using language instruction. The MirrorBot project examines perceptual processes using models of cortical assemblies and mirror neurons to explore the emergence of semantic representations of actions and concepts in a neural robot. In this context we focused on how language instructions for actions were modelled in a self-organising memory. In particular it focused on the neurocognitive clustering of actions based on the part of the body that performs the action and regional modularity for language areas in the brain. This approach used actual sensor readings from the robot to represent low level semantic features of the actions as the input to the neural network and also as the basis for the robot's behaviour.

Furthermore, Calabretta et al. (1998) [12] examined an intelligent approach for control of a robot to perform litter collection. This approach broke down behaviour into sub-elements that match diverse neural modules as an implementation of evolutionary adaptive procedures. Three different architectures were considered for litter collection: a feedforward network, a hardwired modular architecture which allowed the required behaviour to be controlled by different neural modules, and finally the duplication-based modular architecture where the modules were not hardwired but added during the evolutionary process. It was found that the architectures with modules outperformed those with a basic network structure. For the hardwired modular architecture the evolved individuals always developed a single module to control the left motor, the pick-up process and used two competing neural modules for the right motor. For the duplication-based modular approach the evolved individuals used both neural modules to control the left

---

[1] MIRA is the robot used in the MirrorBot Project and MIRA stands for MIrror neuron Robot Agent.

motor, the right motor, the pick-up procedure and the release process.

Kazer and Sharkey (2001) [13] developed a model of how the hippocampus combines memory and anxiety to produce novelty detection in a robot. In the network structure layers CA3 and CA1 depicted the same regions in the hippocampus. The network weights linked these layers by performing Hebbian learning. Categorising input vectors as novel or familiar identified the amount of anxiety. The novelty/familiarity categorisation relied on activation, which was dependant on inhibition. The model was found to offer a direct association between anxiety and Hebbian-learning models of hippocampal learning.

A learning robot was devised by Pérez-Uribe (2001) [14] that used a trial-and-error learning approach. The computerised systems used the temporal-difference approach to learn to predict by using reinforcement learning. Pérez-Uribe (2001) [14] used a neural model in the learning robot that decided between three possible actions: perceive a pattern while moving left; perceive a pattern while moving right; and perceive no pattern. Once the correct selection was made the operator pushing a button gave rewards. Such an approach is of interest as it offers an opportunity for robot learning through human teaching.

Demiris (2002) [15] devised an architecture to achieve robot learning through imitation using behaviour and forward models. The behaviour model was given information on the current state and the goal and produced the required motor commands. The forward model then created the expected next state based on the output from the behaviour model. The predicted state was compared with the actual state of the demonstrator to produce an error signal. The error signal was used to create a confidence value to establish the confidence by which a particular behaviour was identified. The approach used two simulated robots, the demonstrator and the imitator. The demonstrator robot was observed by the imitator robot performing a single action or a series of actions and then required to predict what was being performed from a stored set of actions or action orders. As the demonstrator performed the action or series of actions the confidence in certain actions or series of actions reduced as it became less likely that they were being performed and the confidence in the final prediction increased. This therefore gave the robot the ability to imitate the demonstrators and understand what was being performed.

3.   Reactive Fly-Catcher Mini-robot System

In order to perform the actions outlined in our scenario the robot received binary inputs from two touch sensors on the front of the robot and one at the back. Using readings produced by these sensors the conditions of the motors were altered based on learned behaviour. Furthermore the fly-catcher used object recognition to locate the fly and capture it. A photograph of the fly-catcher robot and the fly prey is given in Figure 1.

3.1   Neural Network for Intelligent Navigation Behaviour

It was decided to use a neural network for navigation control on the fly-catcher robot as this learning technique has proved successful for navigation in more sophisticated robots and it gives us a chance to consider the viability of the technique for use on a mini-robot. Given the restrictions imposed by the mindstorm robot platform the selection of the most appropriate neural network to perform this task in an autonomous manner was critical. Two basic architectures were considered the self-organising map (SOM) and the back-propagation multi-layer perception (MLP).

The SOM consists of two layers, an input layer and output layer, and is an unsupervised training approach [16]. Such a network learns by creating a topological representation of the critical characteristics of the input through a pattern of active and inactive units. Although having a SOM on an autonomous robot would enable it to investigate its environment it is likely that this would require a connected PC for a mini-robot to perform the computations required and so the mini-robot would no longer be autonomous.

It was decided to produce the intelligent navigation behaviour using the supervised learning approach of the multi-layer perceptron (MLP). A supervised approach involves training the network using both the inputs and the required outputs. McClelland and Rumelhart (1986) [17] pioneered the MLP, which combines processing neurons into at least three layers, the input layer, the middle hidden layer and output layer. Figure 2 provides a typical representation of a MLP network.

Figure 1. The fly-catcher robot and its fly prey.

260

The learning rule typically used for the multi-layer neural network is the back-propagation rule that allows the network to learn to classify. This rule creates the output of the network compares this with the required output and by propagating the error back through the network alters the weights to reduce the error [18].

The connections between sensors (three inputs) and motors (two outputs) and the two neurons in the hidden layer of the navigation MLP are shown in Figure 3. It can be seen from Table 1 that the input units received values from the touch sensors to indicate if the robot is blocked (1 if blocked, 0 if not blocked). The robot learned the direction that the motors need to take to avoid the obstacle, which is represented by +1, 0 or −1 (+1 forward, 0 turn off motor and −1 move back). For instance, when the left front sensor was pressed, the required action would turn the robot to the right by turning off the left motor and have the right motor reverse. This would have the output representation of 0, -1. The network was trained using the 8 possible input and output combinations in Table 2.

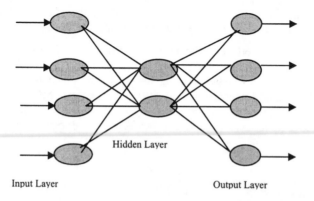

Figure 2. The multi-layer perceptron network architecture.

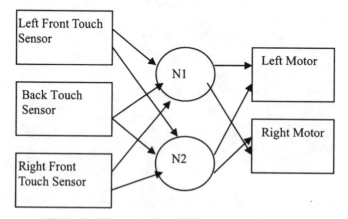

Figure 3. The navigation MLP network structure.

Input			Output	
Sensor Front left	Sensor Back	Sensor Front right	Motor Left	Motor Right
1	0	0	0	-1
0	1	0	1	1
0	0	1	-1	0

Table 1. Input representation for intelligent navigation.

Input			Output	
Sensor Front left	Sensor Back	Sensor Front right	Motor Left	Motor Right
1	0	0	0	-1
0	1	0	1	1
0	0	1	-1	0
1	0	1	-1	-1
1	1	0	0	1
0	1	1	1	0
1	1	1	0	0
0	0	0	1	1

Table 2. The 8 possible inputs and output combinations for intelligent navigation.

3.2 Object Recognition using a Mini-robot

Intelligent robot vision and object recognition is an area of active research, which has allowed some new and novel approaches for analysing what is seen by the robot camera. A vision processing based robot by Nehmzow (1999) [19] used a SOM to cluster vision data from a camera in an autonomous manner to differentiate between images that included boxes and those that did not. By using the SOM to process the robot's sensory signals, distinct sensory perceptions were mapped onto clear areas of the network, with close perceptual patterns clustering together in an area. Of the camera images that contained boxes, 70% were correctly identified as containing boxes and of those without boxes 60% were classified correctly.

Furthermore, Weber and Wermter (2003) [20] in our Neuro-robotics Lab produced a vision system based on an associator neural network to localise an object within the visual field. The model was used to direct the MIRA robot so it altered the pan and tilt of its camera to centralise the object. The neural architecture used "what" and 'where' pathways. The 'what' pathway used two areas: input and a two-layer hidden area. The lower layer of the hidden area gained bottom-up connections from the input. The upper layer of the hidden layer received the output of the lower layer neurons. After it received this initial input, it updated its activations using its previous activations. Furthermore, input came from the connected area of the "where" pathway. The "where" neurons via recurrent weights were fully connected and also received inputs from the highest layer of the 'what' network.

Wilson and Mitchell (2000) [21] developed an artificial retina that detected high contrast objects in the line of vision and relayed this information to the host processor. The retina broke down the image into smaller subsections to help analyse the line of vision. Moreover, Cipolla (1995) [22] developed a robot that included 'stereo' vision in a robot that learned by experience by attaching two independent cameras.

Roy and Pentland (2002) [23] developed a robotic system called CELL that could learn shape and colour words that incorporated object recognition. Object recognition was achieved by taking multiple two-dimensional images of the object from different positions that collectively form the model of that object. Histograms of features were derived from the object models that represented them. Shape was determined by locating the boundary pixels of the object in the image. The use of multidimensional histograms to represent shape allowed the comparison of different objects. This enabled a comparison of the two-dimensional histograms that represent the objects from specific viewpoints. Out of the 15 two-dimensional histograms from the viewpoints the 4 closest for the two objects were taken and the difference summed.

In order to identify the fly, the fly-catcher mini-robot used the Vision Command set to perform colour recognition. By using this software to capture pictures at up to 30 frames per second on a 352 x 288 resolution camera the fly-catcher robot could recognise pre-defined colours. Once received, inputs from the camera are passed into the recognition software on the PC, the Vision Command set sends messages via the infrared tower to the RCX stating whether the desired colour was recognised. Based on this colour recognition the Not Quite C programmed RCX produced the appropriate motor commands. The mindstorm colour recognition package used a process that compared the RGB values for the predefined colour with the RGB value of the main colour of the object it encounters. The Vision Command software divided the visual field into various regions and so was able to detect where in the visual field the fly was and so used this information to move towards it.

Although the camera and recognition software added new functionality to a mindstorm robot, it does have two main limitations. By using RGB values lighting played a critical part in what colour the robot was actually looking for and whether it recognised the colour under different conditions. Running vision with the navigation approach caused the navigation and vision software to 'fight' for control of the motors and so produced the situation where the motors were being turned on and off continuously. To overcome the first limitation efforts were made to keep the lighting in the environment constant. Furthermore, it became necessary to allow the vision or navigation function currently in control of the motors to temporarily suspend the other until that function had finished with the motor output, then pass control back to the other by use of a semaphore system.

The fly-catcher determined whether to close its gripper on the recognised fly and relocate to a new position by using a light sensor on its front. If the fly was in the correct position the light sensor's value passed a certain threshold and so the fly-catcher performed the appropriate behaviour.

When testing the navigation multi-layer perceptron using artificially created inputs off the robot it was found that the network did produce values close enough to the required output values that a thresholding approach could be incorporated in the robot. This thresholding approach stated that if the output was greater than +0.5 the motor moves forward, if it was below −0.5 it was reversed and between −0.5 and +0.5 the motor was turned off.

Once the trained reactive behaviour was incorporated in the fly-catcher, this robot and the fly were repeatedly placed into the environment at different locations. This was done to establish how well it would perform the task of navigation and object recognition under diverse circumstances. The environment was completely white, with a base 180cm by 120 cm and 60 cm high walls around the edge of the base. In order to test the navigation behaviour, block shaped obstacles of different colours to the fly were positioned in the environment. Despite the white colouring of the environment causing the reflection of the fly on the wall and block obstacles, the simple navigation behaviour of the robot enabled it to navigate round the environment and move into a position to recognise the fly in 80% of the test cases. Figure 4 shows the fly-catcher robot looking for its prey.

Furthermore, when the robot recognised the fly and repositioned itself to the front of the fly, it was able to take hold of the fly and move it from the capture site 100% of time. However, when the robot came at the fly from a different angle in only 50% of the cases did the robot grasp the fly and move it from the capture site. Table 3 provides a summary of these results.

Flies navigated to and recognised correctly	Percentage of recognised flies captured if approached from front	Percentage of recognised flies capture if approached from side
80%	100%	50%

Table 3. Performance of the fly-catcher robot.

Despite the many limitations associated with mini-robots like the mindstorm robot and its programming language Not Quite C, it was possible to overcome these to produce simple intelligent behaviour. We were able to incorporate learned behaviour using a multi-layer perceptron neural network and performed object recognition. By using this simple reactive behaviour the robot was able to navigate round an environment, avoid obstacles, recognise its prey, grasp it and take it to a new location.

It might be argued that it is possible to use much more sophisticated platforms that have a large amount of hard disk space and memory, and can be programmed using a powerful programming language straight away. However, they have a much longer learning curve and may not offer the ease of use of the mini-robot considered here. Although the level of intelligent behaviour possible with mini-robots is limited they do give a valuable insight and introduction into the problems of incorporating learning and reactive behaviour on robots especially at the level of student projects. As seen in this paper such a robot can draw attention to issues such as lighting conditions for object recognition, the conflicts that can occur when trying to combine inputs from different modalities, gripper manipulation and learning approaches for producing complex reactive behaviour. In particular, this research has shown the use of neural learning in goal-directed behaviour on robots to encourage research into more sophisticated goal-directed behaviour on robots.

4. Conclusion

In conclusion, as part of an undergraduate project learning behaviour was introduced into a mini-robot based on a fly-catcher scenario to perform navigation and object behaviour. By doing so it was possible to consider the introduction of learned behaviour on a mini-robot. Although, such a robot does offer many limitations it is still possible to achieve good performance by using a multi-layer perceptron for navigation and colour recognition to identify the robots prey. Furthermore, many of the issues brought out from examination of this type of robot are applicable to more sophisticated ones. It is our belief that some of the findings on the mindstorm will aid our research into more sophisticated robot goal-directed behaviour on the larger PeopleBot robot for the MirrorBot project in a restricted but useful way.

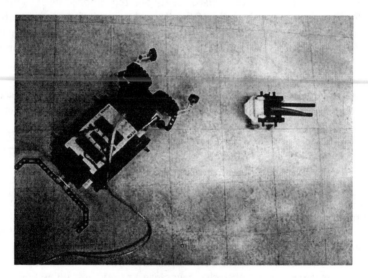

Figure 4. The fly-catcher robot looking for its prey.

Acknowledgements

This work is related and partially funded by the MirrorBot project supported by the EU in the FET-IST programme under grant IST- 2001-35282. We would like to thank the following members of the Centre for Hybrid Intelligent Systems for their help with this paper Sheila Garfield, John Murray and Cornelius Weber. In particular we would like to thank Harry Erwin and Christo Panchev for their assistance with the final year projects in the Neuro-robotics Lab.

References

1. Baum, D. Dave Baum's Definitive Guide to Lego Mindstorms, Apress, 2000.
2. Baum, D., Gasperi, M., Hempel, R. & Villa, L. Extreme mindstorm: advanced guide to LEGO mindstorm. Apress, 2000.
3. Nagata, J. Lego Mindstorms idea book, Starch Press, 2001.
4. Penfold, R. More Advanced Robotics with Lego Mindstorms. Bernard Babani (Publishing) Ltd, 2000.
5. Sato, J. Jim Sato's Lego mindstorms: The master's technique. Starch Press, 2001.
6. Rizzolatti G. & Arbib, M. Language within our grasp. Trends in Neuroscience, 1998; 21: 188-194.
7. Umilta, M. Kohler, E. Gallese, V., Fogassi, L. Fadiga, L., Keysers, C. & Rizzolatti, G. I know what you are doing: A neurophysical study. Neuron, 2001; 31:31.
8. Schaal, S. Is imitation learning the route to humanoid robots. Trends in Cognitive Science, 1999; 3(6): 233-242.
9. Araújo, A. & Barrato, G. A self-organizing context-based approach to the tracking of multiple robot trajectories. International Journal of Computer Research, 2001; 10(2): 139-179.
10. Elshaw M., Wermter S. & Watt P. Self-organisation of language instruction for robot action. Proceedings of the International Joint Conference on Neural Networks. Oregon, USA, July 2003.
11. Wermter S. & Elshaw M. Learning robot actions based on self-organising language memory. Neural Networks, 2003, 16(5-6): 661-669.
12. Calabretta, R., Nolfi, S., Parisi, D. & Wagner, P. Emergence of functional modularity in robots. In Proceedings of Artificial Life VI, Los Angeles, Editors C. Adami, R. Belew, H. Kitano and C. Taylor, MIT Press, 1998.
13. Kazer, J. & Sharkey, A. The role of memory, anxiety and Hebbian learning in hippocampal function: Novel explorations in computational neuroscience and robotics. In Emergent Neural Computational Architectures based on Neuroscience, Editors S. Wermter, J. Austin, and D. Willshaw, Springer-Verlag, Heidelberg, Germany, 2001, pp. 507-521.
14. Pérez-Uribe, A. Using a time-delay actor-critic neural architecture with dopamine-like reinforcement signal for learning in autonomous robots, In Emergent Neural Computational Architectures based on Neuroscience, Editors S. Wermter, J. Austin, and Willshaw, D., Springer-Verlag, Heidelberg, Germany, 2001, pp. 522-533.
15. Demiris, Y. Biologically inspired robot imitation mechanisms and their application as models of mirror neurons. Proceedings of the EPSRC/BBSRC International Workshop on Biological Inspired Robotics Bristol 14-16 August, 2002.
16. Kohonen, T. Self-organizing maps. Springer Verlag, Heidelberg, Germany, 1997.
17. McClelland, J. & Rumelhart, D. Mechanisms of sentence processing: assigning roles to constituents of sentences. Parallel Distributed Processing: Explorations in the Microstructure of Cognition Vol.2, MIT Press, Cambridge MA, 1986, pp. 272-325.

18. Beale, R. & Jackson, T. Neural computing an introduction. IOP Ltd, 1990, pp. 39-128.

19. Nehmzow, U. Meaning through clustering by self-organisation of spatial and temporal information. Computation for Metaphors, Analogy and Agents, Editor C. Nehaniv, Springer-Verlag, Heidelberg, Germany, 1999, pp. 209-299.

20. Weber C. & Wermter S. Object localisation using laterally connected "What" and "Where" associator networks. Proceedings of the International Conference on Artificial Neural Networks, Istanbul, Turkey, pp. 813-820, 2003.

21. Wilson, J. & Mitchell, R. Object detecting artificial retina. Kybernetes: The International Journal of Systems and Cybernetics, 2002; 29(1): 31-52.

22. Cipolla, R., Hollinghurst, N., Gee, A. & Dowland, R. Computer vision in interactive robotics. Assembly Automation, 1996, 16(1): 18-24.

23. Roy, D. & Pentland, A. Learning words from sights and sounds: A computational model. Cognitive Science, 2002; 26(1), 113-146.

An Approach to Instance Reduction in Supervised Learning

Ireneusz Czarnowski and Piotr Jędrzejowicz

Department of Information Systems

Gdynia Maritime University

Morska 83, 81-225 Gdynia, Poland

irek, pj@am.gdynia.pl

Abstract

The paper proposes a set of simple heuristic algorithms for instance reduction problem. Proposed algorithms can be used to increase efficiency of supervised learning. A reduced training set consisting of selected instances is used as an input for the machine-learning algorithm. This may result in reducing time needed for learning or increasing learning quality or both. The paper presents a collection of four algorithms, which are used to reduce the size of a training set. The algorithms are based on calculating for each instance in the original training set the value of its similarity coefficient. Values of the coefficient are used to group instances into clusters. Out of each cluster only a limited number of instances is selected to form a reduced training set. One of the proposed algorithms uses population-learning algorithm for selection of instances. The approach has been validated by means of computational experiment.

1 Introduction

As it has been observed in [20], in the supervised learning, a machine-learning algorithm is shown a training set, which is a collection of training examples called instances. Each instance has an input vector and an output value. After learning from the training set, the learning algorithm is presented with additional input vectors, and the algorithm must generalize, that is to decide what the output value should be.

It is well known that in order to avoid excessive storage and time complexity, and possibly, to improve generalization accuracy by avoiding noise and overfitting it is often necessary to reduce original training set by removing some instances before learning phase or to modify the instances using a new representation.

In the instance reduction approach a subset S of instances to keep from the original training set T can be obtained using incremental, decremental and batch search. An incremental search begins with an empty subset S and adds an instance to S if it fulfills some criteria (see for example [17]). The decremental search begins with $S = T$, and then searches for instances to remove from S (see for example [6, 20]). Finally, in a batch search mode, all instances are evaluated using some removal criteria. Then all those that do meet these criteria are removed in a single step (see for example [20]).

The paper proposes a set of simple heuristic algorithms denoted respectively IRA 1 - IRA 4 (IRA - Instance Reduction Algorithm), which belong to the batch search mode class.

The proposed algorithms are used to reduce the size of training set while maintaining or even improving ganeralization accuracy. The approaches involves the following steps:

- Calculating for each instance from the original training set the value of its similarity coefficient.

- Grouping instances into clusters consisting of instances with identical values of this coefficient.

- Selecting the representation of instances for each cluster and removing remaining instances, thus producing the reduced training set. For selecting instances four others methods are used.

Section 2 of the paper introduces the proposed similarity coefficient and presents a formal description of algorithms. Section 3 gives details of the computational experiment design. Section 4 discusses computational experiment results. Section 5 includes conclusions and suggestions for future research.

2   Instance Reduction Algorithm

This section presents a collection of heuristic algorithms IRA 1-IRA 4 used to decide whether an instance should be kept or removed from the training set. Instance Reduction Algorithms aim at removing a number of instances from the original training set T and thus producing reduced training set S. Let N denote the number of instances in T and n-the number of attributes. Total length of each instance (i.e. training example) is equal to $n+1$, where element numbered $n+1$ contains the output value. Let also $X = \{x_{ij}\}$ ($i = 1, \ldots, N, j = 1, \ldots, n+1$) denote a matrix of $n+1$ columns and N rows containing values of all instances from T.

Each of the proposed algorithms groups instances from input set T into clusters with identical value of similarity coefficient. The similarity coefficient is used to indication similar instances and to decide which instances are closest to set S.

2.1   IRA 1

The idea behind the first of the instance reduction algorithms has been suggested in the earlier paper of the authors [5]. The IRA 1 involves the following steps:

Stage 1. Transform X normalizing value of each x_{ij} into interval $[0, 1]$ and then rounding it to the nearest integer, that is 0 or 1.

Stage 2. Calculate for each instance from the original training set the value of its similarity coefficient I_i:

$$I_i = \sum_{j=1}^{n+1} x_{ij} s_j, i = 1, \ldots, N, \tag{1}$$

where:

$$s_j = \sum_{i=1}^{N} x_{ij}, j = 1, \ldots, n + 1. \tag{2}$$

Stage 3. Map input vectors (i.e. rows from X) into t clusters denoted as Y_v, $v = 1, \ldots, t$. Each cluster contains input vectors with identical value of the similarity coefficient I_i, where t is a number of different values of I_i.

Stage 4. Set value of the representation level K, which denotes the maximum number of input vectors to be retained in each of t clusters defined in Stage 3. Value of K is set arbitrarily by the user.

Stage 5. Select input vectors to be retained in each cluster. Let y_v denote a number of input vectors in cluster v, $v = 1, \ldots, t$. Then the following rules for selecting input vectors are applied:

- If $y_v \leq K$ then $S = S \cup Y_v$.

- If $y_v > K$ then the order of input vector in Y_v is randomized and the cluster partitioned into $q = \frac{y_v}{K}$ subsets denoted as D_{vj}, $j = 1, \ldots, q$. Generalization accuracy of each subset denoted as A_{vj} is calculated using the so called *leave-(q-1)-out test* with $X' = X - Y_v + D_{vj}$ as a training set. Subset of input vectors from cluster v maximizing value of A_{vj} is kept to store in the reduced training set.

2.2 IRA 2

IRA 2 uses two additional parameters - "precision" and "multiple". The first one determines the number of digits after the decimal point. The "multiple" determines rounding of the similarity coefficient.

The IRA 2 algorithm proceeds as follows:

Stage 1. Set value of the representation level K, which denotes the maximum number of input vectors to be retained in each clusters.

Stage 2. Set values of precision $pr = 0$ and multiple $ml = 1$.

Stage 3. Transform X normalizing value of each x_{ij} into interval $[0, 1]$.

Stage 4. Round x_{ij} to the nearest value of 0 or 1 with precision pr of digits after the decimal point.

Stage 5. Calculate for each instance from the original training set the value of its similarity coefficient I_i.

Stage 6. Round I_i up to the nearest multiple of ml.

Stage 7. Map instances (i.e. rows from X) into t clusters denoted as Y_v, $v = 1, \ldots, t$. Each cluster contains instances with identical value of the similarity coefficient I_i, where t is a number of different values of I_i.

Stage 8. Select instances to be retained in each cluster. Let y_v denote a number of input vectors in cluster v, $v = 1, \ldots, t$. Then the following rules for selecting instances are applied:

- If $y_v \leq K$ then $S = S \cup Y_v$.

- If $y_v > K$ and $K = 1$ then the order of instances in Y_v is randomized. Generalization accuracy of each instance in Y_v is calculated using the so called *leave-one-out test*. An instance from cluster v maximizing the generalization accuracy is kept in the reduced training set.

- If $y_v > K$ and $K > 1$ then set pr to 1 and then for instances in Y_v and for several values of ml (i.e. $ml = \{10, 20, 30\}$) repeat steps 4 - 8 calculating new values of similarity coefficient and creating q subsets denoted as D_{vj}, $j = 1, \ldots, q$, until number of elements of each subset is at least equal to K. Generalization accuracy of each subset denoted as A_{vj} is calculated using the so called *leave-(q-1)-out test* with $X' = X - Y_v + D_{vj}$ as a training set. Subset of instances from cluster v maximizing the value of A_{vj} is kept in the reduced training set.

2.3 IRA 3

IRA 3 is based on using the population-learning algorithm (PLA) for the selection of instances. Steps 1 - 4 in IRA 3 are identical as in IRA 1 but Step 5 is different:

Step 5. Select instances to be retained in each cluster:

- If $y_v \leq K$ and $K > 1$ then $S = S \cup Y_v$.

- If $y_v > K$ and $K = 1$ then $S = S \cup \{x_v\}$, where x_v is a selected reference instance from the cluster Y_v, where the distance $d(x^v, \mu^v) = \sqrt{\sum_{i=1}^{n} (x_i^v - \mu_i^v)^2}$ is minimal and $\mu^v = \frac{1}{y_v} \sum_{j=1}^{y_v} x_v$ is the mean vector of the cluster Y_v.

- If $y_v > K$ and $K > 1$ then $S = S \cup \{x_j^v\}$, where x_j^v $(j = 1, \ldots, K)$ are reference instances from the cluster Y_v selected by applying the PLA algorithm.

PLA for IRA 3. The population learning algorithms, introduced in [11], handle population of individuals, which represent coded solutions of the considered problem. Initially, a massive population of individuals, known as the initial population, is generated. The number of individuals in the initial population should be sufficient to represent adequately the whole space of feasible solutions. Sufficient number of individuals relates to the need of, possibly, covering the neighborhood of all of the local optima. Adequate representation of these neighborhoods is related to the need of assuring that the improvement process, originated at the initial stage, should be effective enough to carry at least some individuals to the highest stages of learning. The number of individuals for the particular PLA implementation is usually set at the fine-tuning phase.

Generating the initial population could be simply based on some random mechanism assuring the required representation of the whole feasible solution space. Once the initial population has been generated, individuals enter the first learning stage. It involves applying some, possibly basic and elementary, improvement schemes or conducting simple learning sessions. The improved individuals are then evaluated and better ones pass to the subsequent stage. A strategy of selecting better or more promising individuals must be defined and duly applied. At the following stages the whole cycle is repeated. Individuals are subject to improvement and learning, either individually or through information exchange, and the selected ones are again promoted to a higher stage with the remaining ones droppedout from the process. At the final stage the remaining individuals are reviewed with a view to selecting a solution to the problem at hand.

The PLA algorithm implemented for selection of reference instances maps instances x_v from Y_v into K subset D_{vj}, where the sum of the squared Euclidean distances between each instances x_v and the mean vector μ^j of the subset D_{vj} is minimal.

Vectors with minimal distance to the mean vector in subset are selected as K reference vectors. This selection method can be associated with one of the clustering technique known as k-means algorithm [13].

The representation of a solution p is coded as $(K + y_v)$-element vector, where the first K positions define how many elements from y_v are contained in K-subset, the next y_v positions represent input vector number from Y_v.

If P denotes population of individuals and M denotes size of population, where $P = \{p_1, p_2, \ldots, p_M\}$, then fitness of an individual p can by evaluated as:

$$J(p) = \sum_{j=1}^{K} \sum_{z \in T} \left\| p[z] - \mu^j \right\|^2, \qquad (3)$$

where

$$T = \begin{cases} (K, K + p[j]] & if \quad j = 1, \\ (K + \sum_{i=1}^{j-1} p[i], K + \sum_{i=1}^{j} p[i]] & otherwise, \end{cases}$$

and $p[z]$ denotes instance number, which there is in one of K subsets, and μ^j denotes the mean vector of the subset j.

The remaining assumptions for the PLA implementation include:

- An initial population is generated randomly.

- Four improvements methods are used (random local search, PMX crossover [16], local search, tabu search [7, 8]).

- There is a common selection criterion for all stages. At each stage, individuals with fitness below the current average are rejected.

The learning/improvement procedures require some additional comments.

The first procedure, random local search modifies an individual changing position randomly selected element (i.e. instance number) in an individual. If the fitness function value has improvement then the change is accepted.

The second improvement procedure involves PMX crossover between an individual and another randomly selected one. The crossover produces an offspring of two individuals, which are eveluated. The best of individual is retained. If the fitness function value has not improved, then the local search procedure is run.

The local search procedure modifies an individual by changing position randomly selected element within an individual. This element, representing instance number, is allocated to subset, where Euclidean distance to the mean vector is minimal. If the fitness function value of an individual has improved, them the change is accepted.

The fourth improvement procedure is based on tabu search algorithm [7, 8]. In first step is selected a element $p[i]$ $(i = K + 1, \ldots, y_v)$ within an individual. If selected element there isn't on list containing moves that at current stage are not allowed, then position this element within an individual is changed. If the fitness function value of an individual has improved, then the change is accepted. If an individual has not improved, then change position is repeated for two neighbors elements of $p[i]$. If in no case the individual has not improved, then $p[i]$ is added to list of tabu active moves and by s iterations positions for $p[i]$ and neighbors can't be changed. The parameter s is known as tabu tenure.

The implemented procedure can be run by c iterations. The both parameters, c and s have to be set by the user.

2.4   IRA 4

IRA 4 is identical to IRA 3 except that for selection of reference instances the PLA with real numbers representation is used. Others assumptions of the PLA implementation include:

- A solution p is a sequence of real numbers representing the K reference instances.

- The length of an individual is elements, where the first n positions represent the n dimensions of the first reference vector, the next n positions represent those of the second reference vector, and so on. These vectors are denoted as $m(j)$, $j = 1, \ldots, K$.

- An initial population is generated randomly.

- Three improvement methods are used (mutation, arithmetic crossover, Cauchy mutation).

- The fitness of an individual p is defined as follows:

$$J(p) = \sum_{j=1}^{K} \sum_{z \in D_{vj}} \|x^{vz} - m(j)\|. \tag{4}$$

- There is a common selection criterion for all stages. At each stage, individuals with fitness below the current average are rejected.

3 Experiments

To validate the proposed IRA it has been decided to use generalization accuracy as a criterion. A set of artificial neural networks (ANN) was used as learning machines. The machines were presented with the reduced sets of instances during the supervised learning stage and the results were compared with those obtained without reducing the respective training sets.

To train artificial neural networks an implementation of the population learning algorithm, was used. Neural network trained using PLA is further on referred to as PLAANN. Possibility of applying population learning algorithms to train ANN has been investigated in earlier papers of the authors [1, 2, 3, 4]. In order to increase efficiency of the approach it has been decided to use the parallel computing environment based on PVM (Parallel Virtual Machine). This allows for running parallel learning processes or groups of such processes and thus speeding up training of neural networks.

The experiment involved five datasets from UCI Machine Learning Repository [15] which are Wisconsin breast cancer, Cleveland heart disease, credit approval and thyroid disease. Additional problem is a customer intelligence in banking provided under the EUNITE World Competition 2002 [18]. All the above problems require classification based on input vectors with both - continuous and binary attributes.

Diagnosis of breast cancer involves classifying a tumor as either benign or malignant based on cell descriptions gathered by microscopic examination. Breast cancer databases was obtained from Dr. William H. Wolberg, University of Wisconsin Hospitals, Madison [14]. It includes 699 examples, 9 inputs and 2 outputs each.

Cleveland heart disease problem involves predicting heart disease, that is deciding whether at least one of four major vessels is reduced in diameter by more than 50%. The binary decision is made based on personal data. The data set includes 303 examples with 13 inputs and 2 outputs.

Credit card approval involves predicting the approval or rejection of a credit card to a customer. The data set consists of 690 examples with 15 inputs and two outputs with a good mix of attributes.

Thyroid disease problem involves predicting to determine whether a patient referred to the clinic hypothyroid. Therefore three classes are built: normal (not hypothyroid), hyperfunction and subnormal functioning. Because 92 percent of the patients are not hyperthyroid a good classifier must be significant better than 92%. The original data set consists of 3772 instances in training set with 21 inputs and three outputs.

The customer intelligence in banking problem requires classifying bank customers as either active or non-active. The data set consists of 12000 instances with 36 attributes each.

All ANN used during the experiment have had the MLP structure with 3 layers - input, hidden and output. Number of neurons in layers 1, 2 and 3, respectively, has been set to the following values:

- Wisconsin breast cancer - 9, 9 and 1.

- Cleveland heart disease - 13, 13 and 1.

- Credit approval - 15, 15 and 1.

- Thyroid disease - 21, 21 and 3.

- Customer intelligence in banking (CI) - 36, 15 and 1.

The range of weights has been set to $[-10, 10]$ and the sigmoid activation (transfer) function has had the sigmoid gain value set to 1.0.

4 Computational Experiment Results

Instance reduction algorithms proposed in Section 2 have been used to generate training sets for all considered problems. For each problem five reduced instance sets have been generated with the representation levels set, respectively, to 1, 2, 3, 4, and 10.

In the computational experiment "*10 cross-validation*" approach was used. Each dataset was divided into 10 partitions and each reduction technique was given a training set T consisting of 9 of the partitions, from which it reduced a subset S. The ANN was trained using only the instances in S. Ten such trials were run for each dataset with each reduction algorithm, using a different one partitions as the test set for each trial. This methodology is described in [20].

Percentage of training examples retained for each training set is shown in Table 1. Applying IRA has clearly resulted in a substantial reduction of training set sizes as compared with original data sets.

The PLAANN classifier has been run 20 times for each representation level (i.e. 1, 2, 3, 4 and 10) and for each training set created by IRA 1-IRA 4. Characteristics of thus obtained classifications averaged over 20 runs are shown in Table 2.

The column "*Original set*" in Table 2 shows results obtained by applying the PLAANN to the original, non-reduced training set using the "*10 cross-validation*" approach.

Overall performance of PLAANN classifier seems quite satisfactory. It is also clear that increasing inspiration level leads to better performance in terms of classifier quality at a cost of higher requirement in terms of computation time. For problems: credit, heart and breast the PLAANN learned on reduced

Table 1: Average percentage of training examples retained by IRA 1 - IRA 4

Problem	$K = 1$	$K = 2$	$K = 3$	$K = 4$	$K = 10$
Credit	28%	41%	49%	55%	69%
Heart	34%	39%	47%	55%	67%
Breast	37%	55%	57%	63%	81%
CI	1%	1%	2%	3%	5%
Thyroid	9%	14%	15%	18%	30%

training set gives accuracy of classification comparable to accuracy on non-reduced set. However the training time is decreased average from 160s to 25s.

It might be worth noting that in case of the Customer Intelligence problem PLAANN applied to original set of instances has not been able to find any satisfactory solution in reasonable time and in fact classification process has been stopped. Accuracy of classification obtained with original set was 58%. However the PLAANN trainied on reduced set guarantees accuracy better then 80% already after 120s of computation time.

For the thyroid problem with original training set the PLAANN gives accuracy of classification at the level of about 92%, which is a standard performance. Accuracy of classification for the discussed problem has grown substantially with the reduction of the original dataset size.

Comparison of the proposed IRAs with other approaches to instance reduction is shown in Table 3.

The column "Retained" in Table 3 shows what percent of the original training set has been retained by the respective reduction algorithm. All the results, except these produced by the proposed IRA, were reported in [20]. Acronyms used in Table 3 stand for k Nearest Neighbour (kNN), Condensed Nearest Neighbour (CNN), Selective Nearest Neighbour (SNN), Instance Based (IB) and Decremental Reduction Optimization Procedure (DROP).

As is shown in Table 3 the results achieved on reduced training set produced by IRA in more then one case are better in comparisons with all of other reduction algorithms and especially then kNN method that is accept as reference method. For all variants of IRA only level of reduction instances isn't significantly higher then for other methods.

For the Customer Intelligence problem, that is shown in Table 2, the results have another dependence, where the input training set is reduced significantly along with increasing of accuracy.

Generally the bests performances are achieved by classifiers learned on training set created by IRA 3 and IRA 4. In major cases the IRA 4 gives better

Table 2: Average accuracy (%) of PLAANN results in the classification experiment

Reduction method	Problem	$K = 1$	$K = 2$	$K = 3$	$K = 4$	$K = 10$	*Original set*
	Heart	74.00	78.00	73.80	79.87	82.70	85.70
	Credit	85.34	81.36	79.61	78.31	85.10	88.10
IRA1	Breast	93.04	93.45	93.45	93.68	95.84	96.6
	CI	67.44	68.57	68.63	69.45	71.80	58.70
	Thyroid	93.45	93.98	94.57	94.71	95.69	93.10
	Heart	74.00	76.89	77.12	80.04	83.15	85.70
	Credit	85.34	83.33	84.56	83.45	85.87	88.10
IRA2	Breast	93.04	93.68	94.07	94.21	94.81	96.60
	CI	67.44	72.40	75.80	75.31	76.48	58.70
	Thyroid	93.45	93.45	94.68	94.50	94.68	93.10
	Heart	76.00	77.89	79.20	81.32	84.33	85.70
	Credit	80.10	86.50	86.50	87.20	87.28	88.10
IRA3	Breast	93.80	94.15	94.87	94.92	96,20	96.60
	CI	70.00	75.30	77.00	79.50	80.50	58.70
	Thyroid	93.45	94.20	94.10	94.80	96.60	93.10
	Heart	76.00	76.70	78.12	81.45	83.73	85.70
	Credit	80.10	86.54	86.90	87.10	88.10	88.10
IRA4	Breast	93.80	94.20	94.71	95.10	96.15	96.60
	CI	70.00	74.45	79.80	80.50	83.40	58.70
	Thyroid	93.45	96.50	97.00	98.21	98.48	93.10

Table 3: Performance comparison of different instance reduction algorithms

Algorithm	Breast		Heart		Credit	
	Accuracy	Retained	Accuracy	Retained	Accuracy	Retained
IRA1 $K = 1$	93.04%	37.34%	74.00%	33.66%	85.34%	28.38%
IRA1 $K = 10$	95.84%	81.00%	82.70%	67.00%	85.10%	69.00%
IRA2 $K = 10$	94.81%	81.00%	83.15%	67.00%	85.87%	69.00%
IRA3 $K = 1$	93.80%	37.34%	76.00%	33.66%	80.10%	28.38%
IRA3 $K = 10$	96.20%	81.00%	84.33%	67.00%	87.28%	69.00%
IRA4 $K = 10$	96.15%	81.00%	83.73%	67.00%	88.10%	69.00%
kNN	96.28%	100.00%	81.19%	100.00%	84.78%	100.00%
CNN	95.71%	7.09%	73.95%	30.84%	77.68%	24.22%
SNN	93.85%	8.35%	76.25%	33.88%	81.31%	28.38%
IB2	95.71%	7.09%	73.96%	30.29%	78.26%	24.15%
IB3	96.57%	3.47%	81.16%	11.11%	85.22%	4.78%
DROP3	96.14%	3.58%	80.84%	12.76%	83.91%	5.96%

solution but the both methods show the good property for work with large data sets.

Computational experiment has been carried on a SGI Challenge R4400 workstation with 12 processors. A number of slave workers used by the master varied in different runs from 5 to 15 and in each were been chosen randomly. The size of the initial population in the IRA 3 implementation of the PLA was set to 100. A maximum number of repetitions for each learning/improvement procedure was set to 500 and the parameter s for tabu search algorithm was set to 20. In the IRA4 implementation the respective parameters were set to 50 for the initial population size and 500 for the number of repetitions.

5 Conclusions

Main contribution of the paper is proposing and provisionally validating a simple heuristic instance reduction algorithms, which can be used to increase efficiency of the supervised learning. Computational experiment results support authors' claim that reducing training set size still preserves basic features of the analyzed data. The approach extends a range of available instance reduction algorithms. Moreover, it is shown that the proposed algorithm can be, for some problems, competitive in comparison with the existing techniques.

Properties of the proposed algorithm should be, however, further studied with a view of finding an efficient procedure of selecting a combination of instances to be retained from a cluster of instances with identical similarity coefficient.

Another direction of research should focus on establishing decision rules for finding a representation level suitable for each cluster allowing different representation levels for different clusters.

References

[1] Czarnowski, I. & Jędrzejowicz, P. An Approach to Artificial Neural Network Training. In: Max Bramer, Alun Preece and Franc Coenen (eds.) Research and Development in Intelligent Systems XIX, Springer, 2002, 149-162

[2] Czarnowski, I. & Jędrzejowicz, P. Application of the Parallel Population Learning Algorithm to Training Feed-forward ANN. In: P. Sincak et all (eds.) Inteligent Technologies. Theory and Applications. IOS Press, Amsterdam, 2002, 10-16

[3] Czarnowski, I. & Jędrzejowicz, P. Population Learning Metaheuristic for Neural Network Training. Proceedings of the Sixth International Conference on Neural Networks and Soft Computing (ICNNSC), Zakopane, 2002

[4] Czarnowski, I., Jędrzejowicz, P., Ratajczak, E. Population Learning Algorithm - Example Implementations and Experiments. Proceedings of the Fourth Metaheuristics International Conference, Porto, 2001, 607-612

[5] Czarnowski, I. & Jędrzejowicz, P. An Instance Reduction Algorithm for Supervised Learning. In: M.A. Klopotek, S.T. Wierzchoń and K.Trojanowski (eds.) Intelligent Information Processing and Web Mining, Springer, Berlin, 2003, 241-250

[6] Gates, G.W. The Reduced Nearest Neighbour Rule. IEEE Transactions on Information Theory, IT-18-3, 1972, 431-433

[7] Glover, F. Tabu Search - Part I. ORSA Journal of Computing 1, 1990, 190-206

[8] Glover, F. Tabu Search - Part II. ORSA Journal of Computing 2, 1990, 4-32

[9] Gómez-Ballester, E., Micó, L., Oncina, J. A Fast Approximated k-Median Algorithm. Structural, Syntactic and Statistical Pattern Recognition, Lecture Notes in Computer Science, Vol. 2396. Springer Verlag, Berlin, 2002, 684-690

[10] Grudziński, K. & Duch, W. SBL-PM: Simple Algorithm for Selection of Reference Instances in Similarity Based Methods. Proceedings of the Intelligent Information Systems, Bystra, Poland, 2000, 99-107

[11] Jędrzejowicz, P. Social Learning Algorithm as a Tool for Solving Some Difficult Scheduling Problems. Foundation of Computing and Decision Sciences (24), 1999, 51-66

[12] Li, J., Dong, G., Ramamohanarao, K. Instance-based Classification by Emerging Patterns. Proceedings of the Fourth European Conference on Principles and Practice of Knowledge Discovery in Database. Lyon, France, 2000, 191-200

[13] Likas, A., Vlassis, N., Verbeek, J.J. The Global k-Means Clustering Algorithm. Pattern Recognition 36(2), 2003

[14] Mangasarian, O.L. & Wolberg, W.H. Cancer Diagnosis Via Linear Programming. SIAM News, 23(5), 1990, 1-18

[15] Merz, C.J. & Murphy, P.M. UCI Repository of Machine Learning Databases [http://www.ics.uci.edu/~ mlearn/MLRepository.html]. Irvine, CA: University of California, Department of Information and Computer Science, 1998

[16] Michalewicz, Z. Genetic Algorithms + Data Structures = Evolution Programs. 3rd edn. Springer-Verlag, Berlin Heidelberg New York, 1996

[17] Salzberg, S. A Nearest Hyperrectangle Learning Method. Machine Learning, 6, 1991, 277-309

[18] The European Network of Excellence on Intelligent Technologies for Smart Adaptive Systems (EUNITE) - EUNITE World competition in domain of Intelligent Technologies - http://neuron.tuke.sk/competition2/

[19] Tomek, I. An Experiment with the Edited Nearest-Neighbour Rule. IEEE Transactions no Systems, Man, and Cybernetics, 6-6, 1976, 448-452

[20] Wilson, D. R. & Martinez, T. R. Reduction Techniques for Instance-based Learning Algorithm. Machine Learning, Kluwer Academic Publishers, Boston, 33-3, 2000, 257-286

SESSION 4:

KNOWLEDGE ORGANISATION, REPRESENTATION, V&V AND REFINEMENT

Optimal Decision Explanation by Extracting Regularity Patterns

Concha Bielza
Juan A. Fernández del Pozo
Decision Analysis Group, Technical University of Madrid
Campus de Montegancedo, Boadilla del Monte, 28660 Madrid, Spain

Peter Lucas
Institute for Computing and Information Sciences, University of Nijmegen
Toernooiveld 1, 6525 ED Nijmegen, The Netherlands

Abstract

When solving decision-making problems with modern graphical models like influence diagrams, we obtain the decision tables with optimal decision alternatives. For real-life clinical problems, these tables are often extremely large, hindering the understanding of the reasons behind their content. *KBM2L* lists are new structures that simultaneously minimise memory storage space of these tables, and search for a better knowledge organisation. In this paper, we study the application of *KBM2L* lists in finding and thoroughly studying the optimal treatments for gastric non-Hodgkin lymphoma. This is a difficult clinical problem, mainly because of the uncertainties involved. The resultant lists provide high-level explanations of optimal treatments for the disease, and are also able to find relationships between groups of variables and treatments.

1 Introduction

An *influence diagram* (ID) is a modern decision-theoretic formalism, nowadays frequently adopted as a basis for the construction of decision-support systems (DSS), and used to structure and solve decision-making problems [1]. It consists of a graph structure, which is directed and acyclic, and probabilities and utilities modelling the uncertainties and preferences that come with the problem concerned. The result of solving, or evaluating as is the technical term, an ID are *decision tables* containing the optimal decision alternatives. Thus, for every decision, there is an associated decision table with the best alternative, i.e. the alternative with the maximum expected utility, for every combination of variables. The evaluation algorithm determines which these variables are.

For some medical problems, usually problems that involve difficult trade-offs between benefits and risks of a treatment, doctors may use decision tables to determine the best recommendations in treating patients. However, medical doctors may find it difficult to accept such recommendations if they do not understand the reasons behind the table content. Questions a medical doctor is likely to ask are then: "why is the proposed decision optimal?", and "what are the implicit rules underlying the modelled decision problem?" Answering these questions can be seen as providing *explanations* to medical decisions; these may provide new insights into the problem, and, as a knowledge synthesis, may also serve to validate a system.

Considering that the table sizes are exponential in the number of variables, finding explanations is a hard task, also from a purely computational viewpoint. Turning the huge tables into more compact tables will bring out memory savings. If the resulting compact tables offer insight into the original tables, then finding explanations and optimising the storage space of the decision tables are to some extent the same problem.

In [2], we introduced *KBM2L* lists to address this problem. Finding explanations is a goal pursued by a number of disciplines such as knowledge-based systems and machine learning. Thus, our approach bears some resemblance to techniques for knowledge extraction such as used in the construction of tree-based classifiers [3], oblivious read-once decision graphs [4], and rough sets [5], and to the identification of relevant nodes for each decision node in an ID [6, 7]. As explained in detail in [2], the *KBM2L* method tries to reorganise a knowledge structure by a global search for good, representative candidates. At the start of the algorithm there are already correctly classified cases represented in table form, which may be interpreted as representing types of patients, and we try to extract reasons underlying this classification. Unlike the typical situation in machine learning, these cases are unique as they correspond to configurations of variables in the original ID. Note that our method is applied after the ID has been solved, whereas most of the work on the ID framework concerns operations on the graph structure before evaluating the ID [6].

In order to investigate the usefulness of this method within a medical setting, an ID regarding the treatment of *non-Hodgkin lymphoma of the stomach*, abbreviated to *gastric NHL*, previously developed by one of the authors in collaboration with expert clinical oncologists, was chosen as an experimental vehicle [8]. This is a realistic clinical model, reflecting the current scientific evidence in medical literature about this disorder. It can be used to determine the optimal treatment for individual patients with gastric NHL. A treatment consists of the prescription of either or not antibiotics, followed by curative or palliative surgery, or no surgery at all, and finally by a combination of chemotherapy, radiotherapy, or none of these two. The probabilistic part of the model, a Bayesian network, can be used independently to predict prognosis and to generate patient-specific risk profiles. The model exceeds common prognostic models based on logistic regression, as it is part of a DSS that can answer many different clinical questions.

In this paper, we analyse this ID with the aim of extracting patterns from it; these are then used to explain the optimal treatment alternatives that can be generated by evaluating the diagram. The paper is organised as follows. Section 2 reviews the technique of *KBM2L* lists. Section 3 summarises the structure and content of the gastric NHL model. Section 4 discusses the results of applying *KBM2L* lists to the NHL model. Section 5 finishes off with some conclusions. This paper is an extended version of [9].

2 Using *KBM2L* lists for explanation purposes

2.1 Basic concepts

A decision table that is obtained by evaluating an ID comprises two parts. The first part is the set of all variable configurations, which can be indexed assuming an order, natural or conventional, in the values of their discrete domains. The second part is the table content, namely, the optimal alternative determined by the ID for each configuration. As variables in the clinical field are usually patient attributes, the term *attributes* will be used in the following instead of 'variables'.

Attributes can be arranged in different orders always maintaining the same information. A *base* is a vector whose elements are the attributes in a specific order. Given a base, an *index* is a vector whose elements are the base attribute values, interpreted as the coordinates with respect to that base. A fixed order in the set of attributes and in each discrete domain allows us to consider a decision table as a multidimensional matrix.

We can map this multidimensional matrix to a linear array or list in a way similar to sequential memory allocation in computers [10]. Given a cell of the table with index $\mathbf{c} = (c_0, c_1, \ldots, c_n)$, we define $f : \mathbb{R}^{n+1} \to \mathbb{R}$, such that

$$f(c_0, c_1, ..., c_n) = c_0 \prod_{i=1}^{n} D_i + c_1 \prod_{i=2}^{n} D_i + \cdots + c_n = q \tag{1}$$

where q is the $\mathbf{c}$-offset with respect to the first element of the table in a given base, D_i denotes the cardinality of the i-th attribute domain for $i = 0, 1, \ldots, n$, and $w_i = \prod_{j=i+1}^{n} D_j = w_{i+1} D_{i+1}$ is called its *weight*, for $i = 0, 1, \ldots, n - 1$ and $w_n = 1$. Either in index-notation or in offset-notation, all the table values can be accessed using equation (1).

In order to shorten the list obtained from the decision table, we look at the cell content, i.e. the optimal alternatives. It is quite common to find sets of *consecutive* cells leading to the *same* optimal alternative or content, as the optimal decisions present some level of knowledge granularity. Then, much in the way as sparse matrices are managed, the new compact list will only store one index (or equivalently its offset) per set. We will choose its last index (offset). This last index together with the shared optimal alternative, representing a set of records or cases, is called *item*. The shorter resulting list composed of items is called a *KBM2L* list, which stands for a Multidimensional Matrix whose content is a Knowledge Base (a more general structure than a decision table), that is transformed into a List [2].

An item is denoted by $\langle$*index* or *offset, alternative*|, where the $\langle$ symbol reflects that the item offsets increase monotonously, and the | symbol reflects granularity. For example, the fragment of the list in offset notation $(p - 1, y)\langle(p, x)\langle \ldots \langle(p+q, x)\langle(p+q+1, z)$, with x, y, z three different optimal alternatives has length $q+3$. However, the fragment collapses to $\langle p-1, y|\langle q, x|\langle q+1, z|$ in a *KBM2L* list with length 3.

2.2 Explanations

In index notation, which is closely related to the attributes, let us consider the set of indices an item represents. Since the indices are ordered, this set will range from an index I_{inf} to I_{sup}, corresponding to the extreme cases of the item. This set has two parts. The first part is the index *fixed* part: the common components of all the item cases. The second part, complementary to the first part, is the *variable* part: the cases do not share the same values. Both parts can be derived from the indices I_{inf} and I_{sup}; the fixed part is obtained by taking the logical AND: $I_{\text{inf}} \wedge I_{\text{sup}}$.

These concepts open up automatic reasoning explanation possibilities. The fact that the respective attributes in the fixed part take equal values, somehow *explains* why the optimal alternative is also equal throughout the item. Hence, the set of attributes of the fixed part can be interpreted as the optimal alternative explanation. In the variable part, the attributes are not relevant in deciding the best action to be taken.

2.3 Implementation

We have implemented a construction process of a *KBM2L* list from a decision table. The process starts with an empty list, i.e., with an item representing the complete absence of knowledge. The use of different bases maintains the same table knowledge but changes the granularity or data organisation and perhaps, the memory requirements to store the final list of items. Our aim is to get a base that minimises the number of items, bringing up the knowledge grains. This is a combinatorial optimisation problem, which is *NP*-hard, searching for solutions in the space of the possible permutations of attributes (the domains order being fixed). During the search, the computation of the new storage space that each base requires and copying the information from one *KBM2L* to another in a different base may be too time-consuming or even intractable.

In [2], we provide efficient heuristics to solve all these problems. To guide the search for a good base, a genetic and a variable neighbourhood algorithm have been implemented and tested. Also, some learning heuristics allow for reorganising and fast and/or partially copying complex lists. Moreover, the search space may be reduced by discarding candidates for better bases. This is carried out via a procedure which infers whether a given list is inferior to the present one.

3 The gastric non-Hodgkin lymphoma diagram

Primary gastric non-Hodgkin lymphoma is a relatively rare disorder, accounting for about 5% of gastric tumours. This disorder is caused by a chronic infection with the bacterium *Helicobacter pylori* [11]. It is as yet not completely clear which factors influence the prognosis of patients with this disease. The rare nature of the disease makes it difficult to collect data of sufficient numbers of patients which can be used to determine these factors. What is clear, however, is

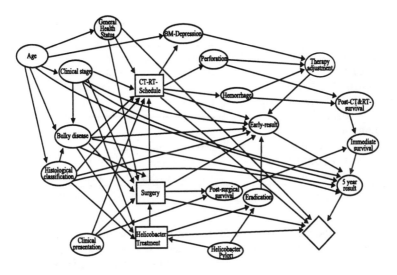

Figure 1: Influence diagram for the treatment of gastric NHL

that some form of decision support is needed to assist clinicians in the treatment of these patients. Models that have been used for that purpose in the past, are normally only capable of predicting the prognosis of the disease, but cannot be used to select treatment.

To overcome these limitations, the last author with the help of two oncologists constructed a number of influence diagrams [8]. These models are only meant to be used for patients with histologically confirmed gastric NHL. We have taken the most complex version with 3 decision nodes for this study, which will be briefly reviewed in the following. The first of the decision nodes, HELICOBACTER-TREATMENT (HT), corresponds to the decision to prescribe antibiotics against H. pylori. The second decision concerns carrying out SURGERY (S), i.e. the total or partial resection of the stomach. Its alternatives are: curative, i.e. complete removal of the locoregional tumour mass, palliative, i.e. incomplete removal, or none. The last decision, CT-RT-SCHEDULE (CTRTS), concerns the selection of chemotherapy (Chemo), radiotherapy (Radio), chemotherapy followed by iceberg radiotherapy (Ch.Next.Rad), and none.

The influence-diagram model is depicted in Fig. 1. It consists of 17 chance nodes (ellipses), one value node (diamond), three decision nodes (rectangles), 42 arcs, 8,282 probability entries where the biggest table has 3,840 entries, and an initial table for the value node of size 144. Nodes to the left of the decision nodes (see Fig. 1) concern pretreatment information; those to the right of decision nodes are posttreatment nodes. The attributes required for the reading of the next section are shown in Table 1.

The diagram structure was determined from the known causal relationships and the probabilistic (in)dependencies found in the literature. Probabilities

Table 1: Attributes and values	
Attributes	**Values**
HELICOBACTER-TREATMENT (HT)	No, Yes
SURGERY (S)	None, Curative, Palliative
CT-RT-SCHEDULE (CTRTS)	None, Radio, Chemo, Ch.Next.Rad
GENERAL-HEALTH-STATUS (GHS)	Poor, Average, Good
CLINICAL-STAGE (CS)	I, II1, II2, III, IV
BULKY-DISEASE (BD)	Yes, No
HISTOLOGICAL-CLASSIFICATION (HC)	Low.Grade, High.Grade
HELICOBACTER-PYLORI (HP)	Absent, Present
CLINICAL-PRESENTATION (CP)	None, Hemorrhage, Perforation, Obstruction

were elicited with the aid of logical and qualitative probabilistic relationships against which the numerical assessments were checked. For the two largest conditional probability tables associated with EARLY-RESULT and 5-YEAR-RESULT, a special additive model was used to ease the assessment.

A Bayesian network was obtained from the ID by converting the decision nodes into chance nodes [12]. Thus, the accuracy of the assessments was tested by comparing prior and posterior marginal probability distributions of this network with frequency data provided by literature and from clinical experience. Also, a database with 137 patients was employed to assess the model's accuracy, and in addition a new joint probability distribution was learnt from the database and its prior marginal probabilities were compared with those of the original network.

Utility elicitation, from the patient's perspective, was carried out using two methods: direct scaling and the reference gamble. In the first method, the possible clinical outcomes are assessed directly using a linear numerical scale. The second method is based on gambles or choices between lotteries making the assessment in probabilistic terms in an indirect fashion. Standard reference texts describe these methods [13]. Several utility functions were obtained and refined by examining the performance of the system as regards the optimal treatments proposed for some typical patients. Finally, a clinically faithful utility function was obtained.

Although the development of a decision-theoretic model like this is complex and time-consuming, also facing the computational difficulties in the evaluation stage [14], such models have been shown to be very useful. They can be applied to yield prognostic information about a specific patient, given particular patient characteristics and, perhaps, therapeutic decisions. They can be applied to determine the optimal treatment. Moreover, reasoning in the reverse direction, assuming that the final results of the treatment are known, the models can be used to generate probabilistic profiles that fit these final results. Obviously, all these capabilities are valuable in guiding the clinical decision-making process. However, understanding the treatment advice generated by a DSS for the whole patient population is not so straightforward. Clinicians would benefit from having clear and concise explanations of the results of the system, which would justify these results and help them understand. In addition, this would yield an alternative way for validating a system.

A preliminary evaluation of the gastric NHL model's accuracy had already been accomplished by means of a double blinded clinical study. The present research, where we use KBM2L lists to better understand the treatment basis of the gastric NHL model, complements this earlier study. The excellent results obtained for another medical problem have encouraged us to study the gastric NHL diagram [15].

4 Results

Evaluation of the ID yielded three decision tables, each containing the optimal treatment for each combination of attributes in the tables. The first table concerning the HT decision, depends on 4 attributes: CS, BD, HC and HP. Using the attributes in this order, i.e. using the base (CS, BD, HC, HP), we built a *KBM2L* list. It had 17 items covering the whole set of 40 cases; 32 cases corresponded with HT = No, organised in 9 items; 8 cases were associated with HT = Yes, grouped into 8 items.

The second table, for the S decision, has 7 attributes. The previous decision HT and two new attributes (GHS and CP) add to this attribute set. The base (GHS, HT, CS, BD, HC, HP, CP) led to a *KBM2L* list with 385 items, covering the whole set of 960 cases. The distribution of these items was: 193 were associated with S = None (663 cases), and 192 with S = Curative (297 cases).

The last table, for the CTRTS decision, has 8 attributes. The *KBM2L* list built with respect to the base (GHS, S, HT, CS, BD, HC, HP, CP) consisted of 678 items covering the whole set of 2,880 cases. There were 164 items with CTRTS = None (490 cases), 188 with CTRTS = Radio (862 cases), 280 with CTRTS = Chemo (1404 cases) and 46 with CTRTS = Ch.Next.Rad (124 cases).

This information may be suitably displayed with the aid of the spectrum charts we have designed for the *KBM2L* lists, see the top Fig. 2. These spectra show the unidimensional memory layout and the case grouping into items depending on the base. They show the cases ordered by the offset (X-axis) where treatments with the same optimal alternative have obtained the same colour. A spectrum is a visualisation tool for (high) multidimensional data. Every color block represents an item. We can see graphically the sensitivity of the data faced with the context and explore patterns on data.

Next, we applied our variable neighbourhood algorithm to each *KBM2L* list to improve the current bases. Improved lists for each decision node are shown in the bottom Fig. 2. For HT, S, and CTRTS, the CPU times were 2.5, 164, and 2238.3 seconds, respectively, and 12, 78, and 168 base changes were required.

Next, we sequentially chained the three tables associated with the previous lists to produce a single global table with the complete knowledge. First, the HT table is propagated throughout the S table, and the rows not matching those

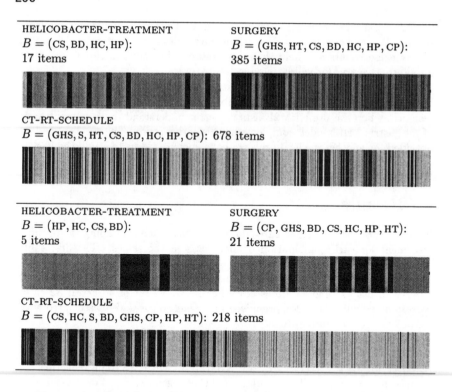

HELICOBACTER-TREATMENT
$B = (\text{CS}, \text{BD}, \text{HC}, \text{HP})$:
17 items

SURGERY
$B = (\text{GHS}, \text{HT}, \text{CS}, \text{BD}, \text{HC}, \text{HP}, \text{CP})$:
385 items

CT-RT-SCHEDULE
$B = (\text{GHS}, \text{S}, \text{HT}, \text{CS}, \text{BD}, \text{HC}, \text{HP}, \text{CP})$: 678 items

HELICOBACTER-TREATMENT
$B = (\text{HP}, \text{HC}, \text{CS}, \text{BD})$:
5 items

SURGERY
$B = (\text{CP}, \text{GHS}, \text{BD}, \text{CS}, \text{HC}, \text{HP}, \text{HT})$:
21 items

CT-RT-SCHEDULE
$B = (\text{CS}, \text{HC}, \text{S}, \text{BD}, \text{GHS}, \text{CP}, \text{HP}, \text{HT})$: 218 items

Figure 2: Non-optimised *(above)* and optimised *(below)* KBM2L spectra for the tables

of the HT table are marked. Second, the S table is then propagated throughout the CTRTS table. Both the rows that do not match those of the S table and the non-optimal rows are marked. All the marked rows are removed from the final table. The final table included 6 attributes because HT, S, CTRTS form the new combined optimal alternatives.

As a result, the base is $B_0 = (\text{BD}, \text{HP}, \text{GHS}, \text{CS}, \text{CP}, \text{HC})$ and its *KBM2L* list has 340 items. Note that in this global table, we have more possible decisions than in the simpler lists related to the individual treatments, i.e. up to $2 \cdot 3 \cdot 4 = 24$, although only 13 are obtained. Palliative surgery is not applied or some other combinations either. The information of this *KBM2L* is shown in Table 2.

Taking into account the cardinality of each attribute domain, the number of possible combinations is 480. Therefore, the knowledge represented by the 340 items seems to be considerably fragmented, and there are therefore reasons for optimisation. Again, after 107 base changes, run in 273.5 seconds, we get a shorter list and refine the knowledge about the decisive attributes. The list has 195 items, a sizeable improvement (a reduction of 42.6%). The optimal base is $B_{final} = (\text{HP}, \text{HC}, \text{CP}, \text{CS}, \text{BD}, \text{GHS})$. The item distribution is shown in Table 2.

Table 2: Optimising the global table

Optimal (HT,S,CTRTS) alternative	#Cases	#Items in B_0	#Items in B_{final}
(No,None,None)	21	12	7
(No,None,Radio)	68	44	31
(No,None,Chemo)	179	88	40
(No,Curative,None)	48	41	26
(No,Curative,Radio)	45	44	34
(No,Curative,Chemo)	19	11	13
(No,Curative,Ch.Next.Rad)	4	4	4
(Yes,None,None)	3	3	1
(Yes,None,Radio)	34	34	13
(Yes,None,Chemo)	27	27	9
(Yes,Curative,None)	22	22	10
(Yes,Curative,Radio)	7	7	6
(Yes,Curative,Chemo)	3	3	1

B_0: 340 items

B_{final}: 195 items

Figure 3: Non-optimised and optimised spectra for the global table

Fig. 3 shows the two spectra associated with B_0 and B_{final}.

Table 3 presents a portion of the optimal *KBM2L* list; we will next consider some of the more noteworthy items. The fixed part of each item, i.e. its explanation, is shown in bold face. This list can be read as representing 195 rules (items) indicating, in the consequent, the optimal global policy as a function of the key attributes. The further to the left the attribute is, the more important it becomes (a higher weight with respect to the base, see equation (1)).

Consider rule 80, (HT = No, S = Curative, CTRTS = Chemo), in comparison to rule 81, (HT = No, S = Curative, CTRTS = Ch.Next.Rad). Both rules include only one case since their variable parts are empty. The patient state GHS has values 'Average' and 'Good', respectively, which explains the difference between the two rules. The reason is that if a patient's health status is good, a more aggressive treatment can be selected. The difference between rule 125, (HT = No, S = Curative, CTRTS = Chemo), and rule 127, (HT = Yes, S = Curative,

Table 3: The optimal *KBM2L* list

# Item	Description	Size
0	⟨*HP*: **Absent**, *HC*: **Low.Grade**, *CP*: **None**, *CS*: II1, *BD*: No, *GHS*: Good, (*HT*: No, *S*: None, *CTRTS*: Radio)|	12
1	⟨*HP*: **Absent**, *HC*: **Low.Grade**, *CP*: **None**, *CS*: **II2**, *BD*: **Yes**, *GHS*: Average, (*HT*: No, *S*: None, *CTRTS*: Chemo)|	2
...	...	
80	⟨*HP*: **Absent**, *HC*: **High.Grade**, *CP*: **Perforation**, *CS*: **IV**, *BD*: **No**, *GHS*: **Average**, (*HT*: No, *S*: Curative, *CTRTS*: Chemo)|	1
81	⟨*HP*: **Absent**, *HC*: **High.Grade**, *CP*: **Perforation**, *CS*: **IV**, *BD*: **No**, *GHS*: **Good**, (*HT*: No, *S*: Curative, *CTRTS*: Ch.Next.Rad)|	1
...	...	
125	⟨*HP*: **Present**, *HC*: **Low.Grade**, *CP*: **Perforation**, *CS*:**III**, *BD*: **No**, *GHS*: Good, (*HT*: No, *S*: Curative, *CTRTS*: Chemo)|	3
126	⟨*HP*: **Present**, *HC*: **Low.Grade**, *CP*: **Perforation**, *CS*:**IV**, *BD*: **Yes**, *GHS*: Good, (*HT*: Yes, *S*: None, *CTRTS*: None)|	3
127	⟨*HP*: **Present**, *HC*: **Low.Grade**, *CP*: **Perforation**, *CS*: **IV**, *BD*: **No**, *GHS*: Good, (*HT*: Yes, *S*: Curative, *CTRTS*: Chemo)|	3
128	⟨*HP*: **Present**, *HC*: **Low.Grade**, *CP*: **Obstruction**, *CS*: **I**, *BD*: **Yes**, *GHS*: **Poor**, (*HT*: Yes, *S*: Curative, *CTRTS*: None)|	1
...	...	
193	⟨*HP*: **Present**, *HC*: **High.Grade**, *CP*: **Obstruction**, *CS*: **II2**, *BD*: **No**, *GHS*: **Poor**, (*HT*: No, *S*: Curative, *CTRTS*: None)|	1
194	⟨*HP*: **Present**, *HC*: **High.Grade**, *CP*: **Obstruction**, *CS*: IV, *BD*: No, *GHS*: Good, (*HT*: No, *S*: None, *CTRTS*: Chemo)|	14

CTRTS = Chemo), can be explained by noting that the clinical stage (CS) of the disease is different for both items. Clearly the system has decided that the treatment for the most advanced stage of the disease (CS = IV) for the slowly progressing low-grade version of gastric NHL should be more agressive than for the less advanced stage (CS = III), where both disease stages are essentially incurable. This is obviously a choice that might be open to debate amongst oncologists.

Clinician may be not only interested in comparing rules but also in finding out under which circumstances a treatment is applied. Consider, for example, treatment $T \equiv (\text{HT} = \text{No}, \text{S} = \text{Curative}, \text{CTRTS} = \text{Ch.Next.Rad})$, which belongs to 4 items as shown in Table 2, including the already mentioned item 81. Focusing on this treatment, a new base organisation is sought distinguishing only a pair of possible treatments T and $\neg T$. The resultant base is now (GHS, HC, CP, BD, CS, HP), with only 3 items (lengths 456, 4 and 20, respectively). Note that attribute GHS has gained in importance. The cases associated with T are now grouped into *one* item and the resulting explanation is GHS = Good, HC = High.Grade, CP = Perforation, BD = No.

5 Conclusions

The regularity patterns regarding optimal treatments which can be distinguished in decision tables not only depend on the problem concerned, but also on their internal organisation. A good organisation of such tables reduces the memory required to store them, but, more importantly in a medical setting, it also finds out which key attributes are able to explain the treatment suggestions. This certainly appeared to be the case with the gastric NHL model.

During the refinement of an ID, medical experts involved in the construction process may study whether the generated explanations for the optimal treatment suggestions agree with their own knowledge. Based on these insights, parts of a diagram may then be improved.

In the near future, our research will be directed towards implementing a method for performing sensitivity analysis within our framework.

Acknowledgments. Research supported by Ministry of Science and Technology, Project DPI2001-3731.

References

[1] Shachter, R.D.: Evaluating Influence Diagrams. Operations Research **34** 6 (1986) 871-882

[2] Fernández del Pozo, J.A., Bielza, C., Gómez, M.: A List-Based Compact Representation for Large Decision Tables Management. European Journal of Operational Research (2003) *to appear*

[3] Duda, R.O., Hart, P.E., Stork, D.G.: Pattern Classification. 2nd edition. Wiley, New York (2001)

[4] Kohavi, R.: Bottom-Up Induction of Oblivious Read-Once Decision Graphs. In: Bergadano, F., De Raedt, L. (eds.): Machine Learning: ECML-94. Lecture Notes in Computer Science, Vol. 784. Springer-Verlag, Berlin (1994) 154-169

[5] Pawlak, Z.: Rough Set Approach to Knowledge-Based Decision Support. European Journal of Operational Research **99** (1997) 48-57

[6] Lauritzen, S., Nilsson, D.: Representing and Solving Decision Problems with Limited Information. Management Science **47** 9 (2001) 1235-1251

[7] Vomlelová, M., Jensen, F.V.: An Extension of Lazy Evaluation for Influence Diagrams Avoiding Redundant Variables in the Potentials. In: Gámez, J.A., Salmerón, A. (eds.): Proc. of the 1st European Workshop on Probabilistic Graphical Models, University of Castilla-LaMancha, Spain (2002) 186-193

[8] Lucas, P., Boot, H., Taal, B.: Computer-Based Decision-Support in the Management of Primary Gastric non-Hodgkin Lymphoma. Methods of Information in Medicine **37** (1998) 206-219

[9] Bielza, C., Fernández del Pozo, J.A., Lucas, P.: Finding and Explaining Optimal Treatments. In: Dojat, M., Keravnou, E., Barahona, P. (eds.): Artificial Intelligence in Medicine, Proc. 9th Conference on Artificial Intelligence in Medicine in Europe, AIME 2003. Lecture Notes in Computer Science, Springer *to appear*

[10] Knuth, D.E.: The Art of Computer Programming, Vol. 1: Fundamental Algorithms. Addison-Wesley, Reading (1968)

[11] Eidt, S., Stolte, M., Fishcer, R.: Helicobacter Pylori Gastritis and Primary Gastric non-Hodgkin's Lymphoma. Journal of Clinical Pathology **47** (1994) 436-439

[12] Cooper G.F.: A Method for Using Belief Networks as Influence Diagrams. In: Proceedings of the Workshop on Uncertainty in Artificial Intelligence, Minneapolis, Minnesota, (1988) 55-63

[13] Farquhar, P.H.: Utility Assessment Methods. Management Science **30** (1984) 1283-1300

[14] Bielza, C., Gómez, M., Ríos-Insua, S., Fernández del Pozo, J.A.: Structural, Elicitation and Computational Issues Faced when Solving Complex Decision Making Problems with Influence Diagrams. Computers & Operations Research **27** 7-8 (2000) 725-740

[15] Fernández del Pozo, J.A., Bielza, C., Gómez, M.: Knowledge Organisation in a Neonatal Jaundice Decision Support System. In: Crespo, J., Maojo, V., Martín, F. (eds.): Medical Data Analysis. Lecture Notes in Computer Science, Vol. 2199. Springer-Verlag, Berlin (2001) 88-94

Model-based Planning in Physical domains using SetGraphs*

Max Garagnani

Department of Computing, The Open University

Milton Keynes, UK

Abstract

This paper proposes a non-propositional representation framework for planning in physical domains. Physical planning problems involve identifying a correct sequence (plan) of object manipulations, transformations and spatial rearrangements to achieve an assigned goal. The problem of the *ramification* of action effects causes most current (propositional) planning languages to have inefficient encodings of physical domains. A simpler and more efficient representation is proposed, in which actions, goals and world state are modelled using 'setGraphs'. A setGraph is an abstract data-structure able to capture *implicitly* the structural and topological *constraints* of a physical domain. Despite being *model-based*, the representation also allows the use of *types* and propositional furmulae to specify additional domain constraints. Experimental results obtained with a specific implementation of the representation indicate significant improvements in performance in all of the domains considered.

1 Introduction

Research in AI and cognitive psychology has since long demonstrated that the type of problem *representation* adopted plays a fundamental role in determining the difficulty of problem solving [4][5], and has identified at least two main types of approaches: a so-called *model-based* (or analogical) representation, and a *propositional* (or Fregean, or sentential) representation [7]. In a model-based representation, facts are represented using a data structure which is, to a significant extent, *isomorphic* to (i.e., a model of) the *semantics* of the problem domain. By contrast, propositional representations (e.g., predicate calculus, modal logic) are *syntactical* descriptions whose structure has no bearing to the structure and semantics of the represented state of affairs [6].

Throughout their history, AI planning domain-description languages have encoded *all* aspects of a problem (and, in particular, *spatial* and *topological* relations) using exclusively propositional representations (e.g., STRIPS, ADL, PDDL [2]). These languages require even the most basic physical *constraints* of the world (such as the fact that an object cannot be simultaneously in two places) to be declared and/or dealt with *explicitly*. In such representations, taking into account the *ramifications* of the effects of an action in domains

*This work was partially supported by the UK Engineering and Physical Sciences Research Council, grant no. GR/R53432/01.

that involve moving and transforming (possibly large) sets of objects – subject to various constraints, physical properties and spatial relations – leads to significant computational-workload overheads.

In spite of various recent extensions in the expressive power of domain-modelling languages (e.g., see [2]), the possibility of using model-based representations to improve planning performance has been left almost completely unexplored. This lack of attention may be attributed to the fact that analogical representations tend to be less expressive and more domain-specific than propositional ones. Nevertheless, although more general, propositional representations are much less efficient, as they lack a semantic (or heuristic) guidance, necessary to effectively navigate large search spaces [6].

The overall aim of this work is to investigate new and expressive domain-modelling formalisms in which the basic, common-sense physical constraints of the world are *implicitly* and effectively encoded in the problem representation. In particular, this paper proposes an abstract representation in which the state of the world is described as a 'setGraph', a data-structure designed specifically to capture the structural and topological constraints of a domain. Although model-based, the abstract character of the representation and its capability to make use of propositional descriptions endow the model with sufficient generality and expressive power to encode a large class of problems.

In the proposed representation, a domain is described through basic concepts of graph and set theory. A computational implementation of the model is, therefore, quite straightforward. Nevertheless, it should be clarified that this paper is not concerned with the definition of a specific language for the computational encoding of the proposed representation.[1] Indeed, the description of the model is kept intentionally abstract and intuitive, in order to avoid any low-level, syntactical details which could commit the representation to a particular language or paradigm.

The rest of the paper is organised as follows: Section 2 identifies more precisely the class of physical domains considered; Section 3 describes the abstract structure of a setGraph, while Section 4 illustrates the meaning of *action* in it and some of its formal properties. Experimental results obtained with a prototype planner implementing an instance of the abstract model are reported in Section 5. Section 6 contains a brief survey of the related literature, and Section 7 concludes by discussing advantages, limitations and possible extensions.

2 Move and Change

In the mid seventies, Hayes and Simon [4] analyzed the performance of subjects solving various 'isomorphs' of the Tower of Hanoi (ToH) problem. These isomorphs used different 'cover stories' but always involved a problem space *identical* to that of a three-disk ToH problem. The rules for state transformation were also identical in number, relevance, and restrictiveness to those of the

---

[1] The syntax of a domain-description language developed for a particular instance of this representation was proposed in [3].

ToH problem. In spite of the structural identity of the domains, the subjects

> "exhibited large and systematic differences in the relative difficulty that they experienced with two broad classes of isomorphs. These two classes have been labeled *Move* [...] and *Change* problems, respectively [...], on the basis of whether successive problem transformations require moving an object from one spatial location to another, or changing some properties of an object that remains at a fixed location" [5, pp.249-250]

Following the classification proposed by Hayes and Simon, '*move*' domains are defined here as problems involving the *rearrangement* – subject to a set of *constraints* – of a finite number of mobile objects over a finite set of possible locations. By contrast, '*change*' domains are characterised by a set of *stationary* objects that can change some of their properties (subject to a set of constraints) while remaining at fixed locations. These two classes can be thought of as representing the two extremes of a *continuum* of planning domains, in which change of state and movement are present in various degrees. The Tower of Hanoi is a prototypical example of the class of move domains, as it does not contain any change component. Other classical domains that can be included in this category are Blocksworld (BW), Eight-puzzle, Briefcase, Robot world, Gripper, and Logistics. By contrast, the "Monster Change" problem (see Appendix A), one of the ToH isomorphs that Hayes and Simon used in their experiments, can be taken as a prototype of the class of change domains. Another example of a typical change domain is the *Homeowner* domain [11].

The following sections describe a *unified* representation for move and change domains based on 'setGraphs'. The two main ideas motivating the use of set-Graphs are the following: (1) a model-based formalism allows a more efficient representation of *any* move problem; and (2) all change problems can be reformulated as *equivalent* move problems. This allows a single and more *efficient* formalism for planning in any domain that falls within the move-change continuum. Point (2) is discussed in Section 4.2, while point (1) is supported by experimental evidence (see Section 5). First of all, however, it is necessary to clarify some of the terms and concepts used throughout the discussion.

2.1   Terminology

The definitions of the concepts of mobile and stationary objects are quite intuitive: an object is 'mobile' if the set of possible actions allows changing its 'location' (i.e., the *place* in which the object lies – see below), and 'stationary' otherwise. A similar definition has been proposed by Long and Fox: "A mobile object is defined to be one that can make a self-propelled transition from being situated in one location to being situated in another location" [9].

Intuitively, a 'location' can be thought of as a *qualitatively* distinct area of space (containing a set of – mobile or stationary – objects). However, one can define a location simply as a type of possibly mobile object that can be *associ-*

ated with a set of objects. Hence, locations are not necessarily stationary.[2] The locations between which a location-object can move can be seen, in turn, as (higher-level) locations. In summary, the representation can be simply limited to *stationary* and *mobile* objects that may be allowed to contain (or be associated with)[3] other objects. Objects that *are* allowed to contain other objects will be called *places*. *Stationary* places represent 'fixed' locations.

For example, consider the Blocksworld domain. Here, each block can be considered a mobile object, able to 'contain' other objects, namely, the block(s) lying on top of it. The predicate On(x,y) can be seen as specifying the location of object x (i.e., the content of *place y*). The 'Table' object can be thought of as a (stationary) place, able to contain blocks. A block can be moved from stack to stack subject to the requirements (*constraints*) that the block itself and its destination (another block) are both 'empty' (i.e., clear).

As illustrated by the previous example, a physical domain can be subject to several (qualitative or quantitative) constraints, which restrict the movement and transformation of the objects and determine the topology and properties of the domain. For example, given two places "a" and "b", the transition of a mobile object from "a" to "b" may be subject to the existence of a specific relationship (a 'road') between them, or to the number of objects already in "b" being less than a certain value.

Finally, the concepts of 'mobile' and 'stationary' objects should not be confused with those of *dynamic* and *static* objects. Dynamic objects may change their *properties* (value of their attributes) and relations during plan execution, whereas *static* objects cannot. In this respect, stationary objects can be dynamic. In the Grid domain, for example, the state of a (stationary) location does not change as the result of the arrival or departure of an 'agent', but it does change (from 'locked' to 'unlocked') if the agent uses an appropriate 'key'.

3 SetGraphs

In the proposed paradigm of representation, the current state of the world is modelled by a *setGraph*, defined as follows:

Definition 3.1 A *setGraph* is a pair $\langle P, R \rangle$, where P is a finite set of *setNodes*, and R is a finite set of *edges*. N is a 'setNode' *iff* it satisfies one of the two following conditions:

1) $N = \emptyset$

2) $\forall x \in N$, x is a setNode

An 'edge' consists of a pair (x, y), where x, y can be any two of the setNodes appearing in P.

---

[2]Note that if a location 'A' moves, all objects in A move with it, but the location *of the objects* (their 'container') remains 'A'.

[3]The significance of the different use of the term 'contain' *vs.* 'associated-with' is clarified in Section 3.

SetNodes and edges may be assigned (not necessarily unique) labels. According to the definition, setNodes are 'nested' sets of (possibly labelled) empty sets, with no limit on the level of nesting. SetNodes and edges can be of different *types* (or sorts), and have different pre-defined structure and behaviour. The specification of setNode and edge properties corresponds to the imposition of further constraints on the problem. In particular, the different types of setNodes and edges are organized in two separate *hierarchies*, in which the properties of a type are inherited by all of its instances and sub-types. SetNode types are further divided into two separate hierarchies, namely, a *place* hierarchy and an *object* hierarchy. SetNodes that are instances of place types will be allowed to contain other setNodes (of select types), whereas instances of object types are *necessarily empty* setNodes (i.e, unable to contain other setNodes)[4].

For example, consider a 'Ferry' domain with three cars ("A", "B" and "C"), one ferry ("Ferry") and two locations ("Port1" and "Port2") between which the ferry can sail. The initial state {(at-ferry Port1) (at A Port1) (at B Port1) (on C Ferry)} can be encoded as a setGraph $\alpha = \langle P_1, R_1 \rangle$, where:

$$P_1 = \{ \text{Port1}\{A\{ \}, B\{ \}, F\{ \}\}, \text{Ferry}\{C\{ \}\}, \text{Port2}\{ \} \}$$
$$R_1 = \{ (\text{Port1}, \text{Port2}), (\text{Port2}, \text{Port1}), (F, \text{Ferry}) \}$$

P_1 contains all the setNodes (objects or places) of the domain. A, B, C and F will have been declared as *objects* (i.e., necessarily empty setNodes) of two types: 'car' (instances A, B, C) and 'ferry_symbol' (instance F). The domain will also have two types of *place* ('port' and 'ferry_place', with instances 'Port1', 'Port2' and 'Ferry', respectively). Finally, the type constraints imposed should allow a 'port' place to contain any type of *object* but no places, and a 'ferry_place' to contain ($\leq k$) objects of type 'car'.

In R_1, two (unlabelled) edges are used to represent a (bi-directional) relationship between the two ports. The edge (F,Ferry) encodes an *association* between the ferry-symbol 'F' and the ferry-place 'Ferry'. The setNode 'F' is a symbolic representation of the 'Ferry' place, and metaphorically contains the set of cars currently on board. Figure 1 depicts a graphical representation of setGraph α, where places are depicted as dashed ellipses and edges as arrows, bi-directional arrows are arcs, and small circles indicate objects.

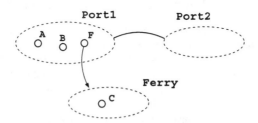

Figure 1: Graphical representation of setGraph $\alpha = \langle P_1, R_1 \rangle$

---

[4]This does not prevent setNodes from being able to be *associated* to other setNodes.

4 Dynamics of a SetGraph

The possible transformations of a setGraph have been assumed to follow two general, intuitive rules: (1) any setNode can be moved from any (setNode) place to any other place (subject to the specific constraints of the domain); and (2) when a setNode is moved, all edges connecting it to other setNodes remain attached to it, and all setNodes contained in it move with it, while the rest of the state remains unchanged (default persistence).

These rules capture the properties of many physical domains, in which a 'structured' set of places and connecting edges form an underlying *static data structure* that cannot be affected by the possible actions. However, in principle, edges between objects and places could be modified by some of the possible actions of the domain. For example, in a hypothetical *'Road maintenance'* domain, 'off-road' connections between different places could be dynamically *created* or *removed* during plan execution, in order to allow the workers to have access to different locations (and resources) during different phases of the work. In order to model these dynamics, the representation should allow the definition of a set of *primitive* transformations which can modify the underlying structure of the setGraph by adding and removing to/from it edges and setNodes. This type of transformations involves *non-conservative* changes of the setGraph, i.e., actions which do not preserve the initial number of setNodes and edges. These dynamics would appear to be particularly relevant for modelling *production* and *consumption* of resources.

In this paper we concentrate on the representation of actions involving only *conservative* changes; however, the formalism can be easily extended to include such 'lower-level', primitive setGraph transformations.

In many domains, the two general conservative rules introduced earlier are not sufficient to prevent the generation of incorrect moves. For example, in the Ferry domain, a car currently in 'Port1' could be moved directly to 'Port2' (or vice versa). In order to prevent undesirable moves, the legal transformations of a setGraph will be allowed to be defined through a set of domain-specific *action schemata*.

4.1 Syntax and Semantics of Action Schemata

An action schema (or *operator*) specifies a transformation of a sub-part of a setGraph. It consists of *preconditions* (specifying the situation required to hold in the relevant elements before the action is executed) and *effects* (describing the changes that its application produces on the elements identified).

The preconditions of an operator will be expressed simply as a *typed* set-Graph, in which places, objects and edges are identified by their sort[5]. This allows the schema to be generally applicable in different situations. In addition, the preconditions may be augmented with a set of (qualitative or quantitative) *constraints* on the properties of the elements involved (expressed using a *propositional* formalism).

---

[5]The use of specific instances in an action should still be permitted, though.

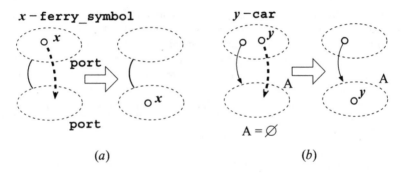

Figure 2: Ferry domain: *(a)Sail* and *(b)Board* operators

The effects of the action application on the current state will be described here using both *procedural* representations (indicating *which* setNodes are being moved to which places) and *declarative* representations (specifying the *resulting* situation in the relevant places after the action application). For example, Figures 2.(*a*) and 2.(*b*) depict, respectively, the '*Board*' and '*Sail*' operators for the Ferry domain (see also Figure 1). The left- and right-hand sides of each schema represent, respectively, preconditions and (declarative) effects of the actions. Notice that *all* places, edges and nodes appearing in the preconditions are in a *bijective* mapping with those in the effects. Thicker, dashed arrows in the preconditions are procedural representations indicating which setNode(s) should be moved and where. Constraints on the types and properties of setNodes can be specified in the the preconditions using *parameters*. For example, in the *Board* action schema, object '*y*' must be an instance of type '*car*', and place '*A*' must be empty. In addition, notice the use of type names (e.g., 'port') to require, where appropriate, the presence of specific types of places.

An action schema can be applied in the current state (setGraph) S when both of the following conditions are met:

(*i*) all places, objects and edges present in the preconditions *match* (i.e., can be bound to) *distinct* elements of S which are arranged in identical topological structures (same 'pattern' of places, edges and objects);

(*ii*) for the chosen bindings, all the specified constraints are satisfied, and each of the setNodes being moved matches the type of setNodes that its destination place is allowed to contain.

The definition of '*match*' is as follows: two types match *iff* one is a sub-type of the other; two instances match *iff* they have the same label; an instance x and a type T match *iff* x is an instance of T (or of any of T's sub-types). A place (specified in an action preconditions) containing n setNodes matches any place (of the appropriate type) containing *at least* n setNodes (of the appropriate type). Matching edges must connect setNodes that match.

The *goal* of a problem will be specified simply as a (possibly typed) setGraph, allowed to contain both specific instances and typed elements, but no constraints. Given a setGraph S, the conditions for the achievement of a goal G are analogous to the requirements described in (i) for action application.

For example, it is easy to see that all elements in the preconditions of the *Sail* operator can be mapped to corresponding (distinct) elements of the setGraph shown in Figure 1, as all elements in the preconditions match corresponding (distinct) elements of the state. Note that the second part of condition (ii) is required because the destination place of an action precondition could be bound to an instance (in the state) which has *restrictions* on the type of its contents. The following example illustrates this situation.

Example 4.1 One way to represent the ToH domain using setNodes consists of considering every disk as a place allowed to contain up to one disk (place) of a smaller size. The 'peg' type can be represented as a place able to contain up to one disk of *any* size. The smallest disk can be represented as a place which is not allowed to contain any type of places. In the case of three disks, these constraints can be imposed using the following hierarchy of place types:

$$\text{Small}\{\ \} \prec \text{Medium}\{\text{Small}\} \prec \text{Large}\{\text{Medium}\} \prec \text{Peg}\{\text{Large}\} \prec \text{PLACE} \quad (4.1)$$

where '$x \prec y$' means that type x is subtype of y, and '$type_1\ \{type_2\}$' means that places of type '$type_1$' can only contain instances (of places) matching '$type_2$'.[6] The type 'PLACE' is the root of the place-type hierarchy.

Using (4.1) as a basis, it is possible to describe the legal movements of the disks using only one operator. Figure 3.(a) depicts the initial state for a ToH problem with three disks (places) labelled 'S', 'M' and 'L' and three pegs ('P1', 'P2', 'P3'). 'S' is an instance of the type 'Small', 'M' of 'Medium', and 'L' of 'Large'. The three peg-places are instances of 'Peg'. Figure 3.(b) represents the *Move* action schema.

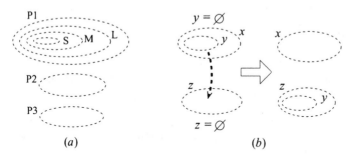

Figure 3: Tower of Hanoi domain: (a) initial state; (b) *Move* operator

To see why condition (ii) is needed, consider the preconditions of the *Move* operator. The type of the places x, y and z, unspecified, is assumed by default to be the most general (i.e., 'PLACE'). Hence, disk y and its destination place z (a disk or a peg) can be bound to (match) *any* pair of distinct places which

---

[6]Note that an instance of a type matches all of its *super*-types. Hence, for example, a 'Small' disk can be contained also in 'Large' and 'Peg' places.

are currently empty (clear). However, in order to prevent a larger disk from being moved into a smaller one (and avoid writing a distinct operator for each possible legal move), it is necessary to introduce the second part of condition (*ii*), which brings into the picture the constraints (imposed by formula 4.1) on which types of disks can be contained in which types of places. For example, according to (4.1), disk 'L', an instance of 'Large' place, does not match the *type* of places allowed in 'M' or in 'S'.

4.2 Movement and State Transformation

In any physical domain containing move and change elements, an object can be characterised by its *spatial location* and by a set of attribute-value associations that determine its current *state* (e.g., type, color, temperature, size, etc.). Any of such properties, in general, can be affected by an action. Hence, the proposed paradigm should be able to represent them and to encode their possible transformations. It is immediate to see how the abstract structure of setGraph and the action schemata can be used to represent and plan the *movement* of objects (i.e., the change of spatial location).[7] If the number of possible states that an object can be in is finite, then also *state* changes can be easily represented using setGraphs. In fact, given an object x with k possible states $\{s_1, \ldots, s_k\}$, it is possible to build a setGraph having k places $\{p_1, \ldots, p_k\}$ distinct from the other existing setNodes. A new setNode x', situated in place p_j and linked to x, will encode the fact that object x is currently in state s_j. A state change $s_j \rightarrow s_i$ will be represented by *moving* x' from place p_j to place p_i. Legal movements can be specified by appropriate action schemata, according to the domain-specific constraints.

The following Lemma and Proposition present more formal properties of the expressiveness of a setGraph representation:

Lemma 4.2 Given a finite domain U with k objects $U = \{o_1, \ldots, o_k\}$, any n-ary relation $P \subseteq U^n$ having cardinality l can be represented as a setGraph containing $(k + l)$ setNodes and nl edges.

Proof Every object $o_j \in U$ can be represented by a distinct setNode s_j. Each of the 'l' relational instances $(x_1, \ldots, x_n) \in P$ can be represented as an additional setNode s_{k+i} with n edges linking it to the setNodes that correspond to the objects $x_1, \ldots, x_n$. Hence, the lemma follows immediately.

Proposition 4.2 If *non-conservative* changes are permitted, setGraph domain descriptions are *at least* as expressive as STRIPS domain descriptions.

Proof In order to prove the thesis, it will be sufficient to show that any state and operations that can be specified in STRIPS can also be encoded using the setGraph formalism. In STRIPS, a state is a collection of relational instances. From lemma 4.2, it follows that any STRIPS state can be encoded as a set-

---

[7]Indeed, the next section shows that this leads to more efficient planning.

Graph. In addition, each (ground) STRIPS operator consists of a 'Precondition' list, 'Add' list and 'Delete' list, each containing a conjunction of propositions (i.e., relational instances). Again, from lemma 4.2 it follows that any Precondition list can be encoded as a setGraph and used as preconditions in the left-hand side of a setGraph action-schema definition. Finally, in order to encode the addition and deletion of relational instances to/from the state as specified by the Add and Delete lists, it is sufficient to extend the setGraphs with a set of primitive, non-conservative transformations (as discussed in the previous section) that allow edges and setNodes to be dynamically added to and removed from a setGraph.   Q.E.D.

5   Experimental Results

In order to assess the capability of the proposed representation to encode physical domains effectively efficiently, various domains (including Logistics, BW, Briefcase, Rocket, ToH, Eight-puzzle, Miconic, Gripper and Robot, taken from the set of benchmarks used in the International Planning Competitions and planning literature) were translated into setGraph based representations. A prototype planner was developed, which implements a '*Cartesian*' restriction of the general representation proposed. In particular, the specific instance implemented does not allow the use of edges, but permits places and objects to be assigned identical labels to encode place-object 'associations'. In addition, places are allowed to have an internal structure consisting of a matrix (or vector) of adjacent sub-places. In other words, a place can be either a *set* of objects, or a one- or two-dimensional *array* of 'cells', each one allowed to contain up to *one string* (representing an object). In spite of the restricted expressiveness, this simpler, 'diagrammatic' version still contains most of the fundamental characteristics of the general model proposed, and allows a first assessment of the validity of its basic premises without requiring unnecessary (and possibly futile) implementation effort.

A subset of the domains listed above (namely, Eight-puzzle, Miconic, BW, Briefcase and Gripper) was re-formulated for this representation, and used to carry out an initial set of experiments. The BW encoding used in the experiments and a possible problem instance are reported in Figure 4. In order to compare the performance of the new planning representation with respect to that of a standard propositional languages, two planners were actually built, identical in all aspects except for the *representation* which they adopted. The first planner (named 'PMP', Pattern-Matching Planner) describes and solves problems using the representation just introduced, while the second planner (called 'PP', Propositional Planner) relies on the classical propositional STRIPS formalism (with types). Both planners were implemented using the same programming language (Java), adopted exactly the same search method (blind, breadth-first, forward search), and were run on the same machine. In addition, each of the five domains used for the tests was described so as to present exactly the same *search space* in each of the two representations. The

```
(define (domain Blocksworld)
  (:ObjectTypes block table)
  (:PlaceTypes stack [object::1])
  (:action PutOn
     :parameters (x - block y - object)
     :pre (stack {x | _ } stack {y | _ })
     :post (stack {_ | _ } stack {y | x })
  )
)

(define (problem Sussman)
  (:domain Blocksworld)
  (:Objects A B C - block T - table)
  (:Places s1 s2 s3 - stack)
  (:init s1 [T | A | C | _ | _ ]
         s2 [T | B | _ | _ | _ ]
         s3 [T | _ | _ | _ | _ ] )
  (:goal stack {C | B | A} )
)
```

Figure 4: Blocksworld domain description and 'Sussman' problem instance

results obtained showed a superior performance of PMP on *all* of the domains, and on *all* of the problem instances. The speed-up factor varied from a minimum of two to as much as *ninety* times faster. For reasons of space, we report in Table 1 only the values obtained with the Gripper domain (the complete set of results and the details of the domain-description language adopted are discussed in [3]). The speed-up demonstrated is a result of the ability of the representation to (*i*) *implicitly* capture the basic, common-sense physical and topological constraints of the domain, and hence perform efficient *updates* of the current state (avoiding the ramification problem), and to (*ii*) *organize* in appropriate data structures the relevant entities of the domain, allowing more efficient look-up operations.

Table 1: Time (s.) for Gripper problems ('*m-n*' ≡ *m* balls in room 'A' and *n* balls in room 'B').

	1-0	2-0	2-1	3-0	2-2	3-1	4-0	4-1
PP	0.0	0.3	5.1	31.4	166.8	862.1	1866.4	> 16 *hours*
PMP	0.0	0.0	0.4	1.1	2.8	12.8	26.2	354.3

6 Related Work

An object-centred domain-description language (OCL_h) has been recently proposed by Liu and McCluskey in [8], based on the idea of modelling a domain as a set of objects subject to various constraints. However, OCL_h is fully sentential; consequently, some of the constraints which would be *implicit* in a setGraph still have to be explicitly declared in OCL_h (e.g., the fact that if an agent holds an object of a certain (different) type, the location of the object must coincide with that of the agent).

The work of Long and Fox [9] on the structure of planning domains and Generic Types of objects is also relevant in this context. Long and Fox have developed domain analysis techniques which allow the *automatic* detection of 'generic types' of objects (such as mobiles and 'portables') in a domain, given its purely propositional description. In essence, the physical domains considered here can be seen as combining the three abstract classes of 'transportation', 'transformation' and 'construction' domains identified by Long and Fox.

Another relevant approach is that of Cesta and Oddi [1], in which planning is seen as the problem of deciding the behavior of a dynamic domain described as a set of state variables subject to constraints. The (propositional) domain-description language proposed (DDL.1) is related to the approach taken in this paper, as it allows the description of a semantic model representing the domain as a set of possible *state changes*.

An early example of integration of model-based and sentential representations is the hybrid system of Myers and Konolige [10], who proposed a formal framework for combining analogical and deductive reasoning. In their system, operators invoked by inference rules of a sentential module (based on a logical first-order predicate language) manipulated analogical ('diagrammatic') structures which represented the state of the world. This and other related approaches falling within the area of diagrammatic reasoning [6] are particularly pertinent to the specific implementation of setGraphs used in the experiments. However, none of them appears to formulate an abstract model for encoding and solving domains within a planning framework, or to compare experimentally the *computational* efficiency of analogical and propositional representations on a given set of (planning) problems, as it has been done in the present work.

7 Discussion

The main contribution of this paper consists of having introduced a new representation tool (the setGraph) and proposed a new, model-based planning paradigm based on it, in which many of the constraints of the real-world are implicitly, effectively and naturally encoded in the domain description.

The main advantages of a setGraph representation with respect to a sentential planning formalism are that: (1) it is more efficient; (2) it is simpler, more abstract and intuitive, and (3) it better supports common-sense reasoning about action. In addition, despite being model based, the formalism is at least as expressive as any STRIPS-like propositional language (assuming that non-conservative actions are allowed). Furthermore, many 'abstract' (i.e., non-physical) domains are *isomorphic* to physical problems, and can be represented and solved using setGraphs. In particular, Fox and Long's domain analyisis techniques [9] can be used for *automatically* detecting the inherent structure of a domain from its purely propositional description, and to reveal the presence of generic types of objects even when the domain engineer is unaware of them.

In addition to offering better performance in physical domains, the representation is simpler, less error-prone and of easier use for the domain engineer. Various forms of common-sense reasoning are also better supported. For example, setGraphs facilitate heuristic-extraction, abstraction, and learning. Consider, for example, the process of macro-operator learning. The high number of possible combinations that a purely propositional, unstructured encoding involves makes this process complex and inefficient. However, sets of places and edges can be very efficiently compared and 'matched', in search of the occurrence of the same topological structure ('pattern').

One of the main limitations of the formalism is that representing state-change requires the number of possible states of an object to be *finite*. This prevents the use of numerical attributes which vary on infinite domains. In order to overcome this limitation, the representation should be extended so that objects (setNodes) can be associated to *numerical* values. This would allow the representation of mathematical functions and of other aspects of the physical world, such as time and continuous resources. Finally, the representation of uncertainty also needs to be addressed. A possible approach to this issue might be to adopt Myers and Konolige's idea of *sets* of analogical models for representing uncertainty and incomplete information [10].

In summary, the advantages of the proposed representation and its potential benefits in terms of performance motivate further investigation on setGraph and model-based planning formalisms, and on their use in *conjunction* with propositional and numerical descriptions. This paper lays the foundations for future developments in this direction.

References

[1] A. Cesta and A. Oddi. DDL.1: A formal description of a constraint representation language for physical domains. In M. Ghallab and A. Milani, editors, *New Directions in AI Planning*, pages 341–352. IOS Press (Amsterdam), 1996. (Proceedings of the 3rd European Workshop on Planning (EWSP95), Assisi, Italy, September 1995).

[2] M. Fox and D. Long. PDDL2.1: An extension to PDDL for expressing temporal planning domains. *Journal of Artificial Intelligence Research – Special issue on the 3rd International Planning Competition*, 2003. (forthcoming).

308

[3] M. Garagnani and Y. Ding. Model-based planning for object-rearrangement problems. In *Proceedings of the International Conference on Automated Planning and Scheduling (ICAPS-03) - Workshop on PDDL*, pages 49–58, 2003.

[4] J.R. Hayes and H.A. Simon. Psychological differences among problem isomorphs. In N.J. Castellan, D.B. Pisoni, and G.R. Potts, editors, *Cognitive theory*. Erlbaum, 1977.

[5] K. Kotovsky, J.R. Hayes, and H.A. Simon. Why Are Some Problems Hard? Evidence from Tower of Hanoi. *Cognitive Psychology*, 17:248–294, 1985.

[6] Z. Kulpa. Diagrammatic representation and reasoning. *Machine GRAPHICS & VISION*, 3(1/2):77–103, 1994.

[7] J.H. Larkin and H.A. Simon. Why a diagram is (sometimes) worth ten thousands words. *Cognitive Science*, 11:65–99, 1987.

[8] D. Liu and T.L. McCluskey. The OCL Language Manual, Version 1.2. Technical report, Department of Computing and Mathematical Sciences, University of Huddersfield (UK), 2000.

[9] D. Long and M. Fox. Automatic synthesis and use of generic types in planning. In S. Chien, S. Kambhampati, and C.A. Knoblock, editors, *Proceedings of the 5th International Conference on AI Planning and Scheduling Systems (AIPS'00)*, pages 196–205, Breckenridge, CO, April 2000. AAAI Press.

[10] K. Myers and K. Konolige. Reasoning with analogical representations. In B. Nebel, C. Rich, and W. Swartout, editors, *Principles of Knowledge Representation and Reasoning: Proceedings of the Third International Conference (KR92)*, pages 189–200. Morgan Kaufmann Publishers Inc., San Mateo, CA, 1992.

[11] E.P.D. Pednault. Synthesizing plans that contain actions with context-dependent effects. *Computational Intelligence*, 4(4):356–372, 1988.

Appendix A - Monster Change Problem (from [5])

In the Monster Change problem, three extra-terrestrial monsters are holding three crystal globes. Both monsters and globes come in exactly three sizes with no other permitted: small, medium and large. The small monster holds the medium-size globe; the medium-size monster holds the large globe; and the large monster holds the small globe. Each monster can change the globe that it is holding by shrinking it or expanding it, subject to the following constraints: (1) only one globe may be changed at a time; (2) if two globes have the same size, only the globe held by the larger monster may be changed; and (3) a globe may not be changed to the same size as the globe of a larger monster. The problem is to shrink and expand the globes so that each monster has a globe proportionate to its own size.

Quality Checking of Medical Guidelines through Logical Abduction

Peter Lucas

Institute for Computing and Information Sciences
University of Nijmegen, Toernooiveld 1
6525 ED Nijmegen, The Netherlands
E-mail: peterl@cs.kun.nl

Abstract

Formal methods have been used in the past for the verification of the correctness of formalised versions of medical guidelines. In this paper a second possible application of the use of formal methods is proposed: checking whether a guideline conforms to global medical quality requirements. It is argued that this allows spotting design errors in medical guidelines, which is seen as a useful application for formal methods in medicine. However, this type of verification may require medical knowledge currently not available within the guidelines, i.e. medical background knowledge. In this paper, we propose a method for checking the quality of a treatment for a disorder, based on the theory of abductive diagnosis. We also examine the medical background knowledge required to be able to quality check a guideline. The method is illustrated by the formal analysis of an actual guideline for the management of diabetes mellitus type 2.

1 Introduction

There has been significant progress in the life sciences over the last couple of decades, yielding results, for example in molecular biology and human genetics, which are now gradually reshaping the face of medicine. One consequence of this is now becoming apparent: medicine is becoming more and more complicated at an astonishing rate. On the one hand, the number of different patient management options has risen considerably, whereas, on the other hand, health-care authorities increasingly expect that medical doctors take decisions balancing benefits for the patient against financial costs. The latter will only happen if medical doctors are offered appropriate support in their decision-making process.

A first step into this direction was taken by the medical profession itself by understanding the need of basing clinical decision-making more and more on sound scientific evidence; this trend has become known as *evidence-based medicine* [14, 17]. In practice, evidence-based medicine implies that general practitioners and medical specialists in particular areas are increasingly involved in the development of guidelines, aimed at promoting standards of medical care. Guidelines are documents offering a detailed description of steps that must be taken by health-care professionals in managing a disease in a patient to avoid substandard practices or outcomes. Modern guidelines are based on scientific evidence derived from good-quality studies reported in medical journals, rather than on consensus among medical doctors as was the case just a few years ago.

Some researchers in artificial intelligence (AI) have picked up on these developments, and are involved in the design of computer-oriented languages, tools and systems that support the design and deployment of medical guidelines. Examples are PROforma [3, 4], Asbru [15] and GLIF [11]; these languages and their associated tools have been evolving since the 1990s, a process that is now gaining momentum due to the increased interest in guidelines within the medical community. AI researchers see guidelines as good real-world examples of highly structured, systematic documents that are amenable to formalisation.

What the research efforts mentioned above have in common is that medical guidelines are taken as a start and are subsequently translated, sometimes only partially, into a guideline-representation language, so that they can be executed as a program, or at least in principle. Once a guideline has been represented in this way, the resulting program-like representation may also be used as a basis to investigate properties of the original guideline. In some cases, researchers have gone one step further and used logical methods to analyse guidelines [4, 10]. These approaches offer potentially useful ways to exploit formal methods in the context of medical guidelines. However, so far AI researchers have had difficulty in achieving medically relevant results, i.e. the sort of results that could act as input to the improvement of medical guidelines. This is not surprising as the development of medical guidelines is done in a relatively thorough fashion by a team of expert clinicians and guideline developers; even though the resulting documents are in natural language, they rarely contain obvious flaws. The 'flaws' that researchers have been able to identify are typical for natural language text; whether they are also typical for guidelines as such is questionable. Examples of detected 'flaws' in the text include ambiguities (e.g. use of the term 'clinical jaundice' in conjunction with 'jaundice', intended to mean the same thing) and incompleteness (e.g. 'rapid increase in blood glucose levels', where the adjective 'rapid' is not precisely defined) [10]; this likely only indicates that the guideline developers choose to refrain from detail. This approach of translating the text of a guideline into a formal language, and then using tools for the formal analysis of the formal representation is therefore not without problems. We call this the *object-level* approach.

Another approach is to abstract from the actual guideline text and to ask the question what general medical quality criteria need to be fulfilled by the guideline. For example, one would expect that a good-quality medical guideline regarding treatment of a disorder would preclude the prescription of redundant drugs, or advise against the prescription of treatment that is less effective than some alternative. Carrying out such checks could be valuable, in particular during the process of *designing* medical guidelines. This is called the *meta-level* approach.

In this paper, we propose a meta-level approach to quality checking of medical guidelines, based on the theory of *abductive diagnosis* [1, 8, 9, 12]. We also examine the medical background knowledge required to be able to quality check a guideline. Instead of using one of the guideline-representation languages, we explore the use of temporal logic for these purposes, as this allows us to abstract from unnecessary detail, and this language is compatible with program logics, i.e. the interpretation of guidelines as programs. The usefulness of the method is studied by analysing the official guideline on diabetes mellitus type 2 management currently in use by the Dutch general practitioners.

The paper is organised as follows. In the next section, we start by explaining what medical guidelines are and what purpose they serve in the health-care; in addition, the role formal methods have played so far in checking medical guidelines is described. In Section 3 a method for formalising guidelines and checking them against design decisions based on abductive diagnosis is described. The guideline on the management of diabetes mellitus type 2 that has been used in the case study is given attention to in Section 4. The analysis of this guideline using the method described in Section 3 can be found in Section 5. Finally, Section 6 discusses what has been achieved, offers further motivation on the usefulness of the developed method in comparison to other methods, and suggests some future plans for research.

2 Medical Guidelines

A medical guideline is a structured document, containing detailed advice on the management of a particular disorder or group of disorders, aimed at health-care professionals. As modern guidelines are based on scientific evidence, they contain information about the quality of the evidence on which particular statements are based; e.g. statements at the highest recommendation level are usually obtained from randomised clinical trials [17].

The design of a medical guidelines is far from easy. Firstly, the gathering and classification of the scientific evidence underlying and justifying the recommendations mentioned in a guideline is time consuming, and requires considerable expertise in the medical field concerned. Secondly, medical guidelines are very detailed, and making sure that all the information contained in the guideline is complete for the guideline's purpose, and based on sound medical principles is hard work. An example of a tiny portion of a guideline is shown in Figure 1; it is part of the guideline for general practitioners about the treatment of diabetes mellitus 2. This guideline fragment is used in this paper as a running example.

One way to use formal methods in the context of guidelines is to automatically verify whether a medical guideline fulfils particular properties, such as whether it complies with quality *indicators* as proposed by health-care professionals [10]. For example, using particular patient assumptions such as that after treatment the levels of a substance are dangerously high or low, it is possible to check whether this situation does or does not violate the guideline. However, verifying the effects of treatment as well as examining whether a de-

- Step 1: diet

- Step 2: if Quetelet Index (QI) ≤ 24, prescribe a sulfonylurea drug; otherwise, prescribe a biguanide drug

- Step 3: combine a sulfonylurea drug and biguanide (replace one of these by a α-glucosidase inhibitor if side-effects occur)

- Step 4: one of the following:

    - oral antidiabetics and insulin

    - only insulin

Figure 1: Tiny fragment of a clinical guideline on the management of diabetes mellitus type 2. If one of the steps $k = 1, 2, 3$ is ineffective, the management moves to step $k + 1$.

Table 1: Used temporal operators; t stands for a time instance.

Notation	Informal meaning	Formal meaning
$H\varphi$	φ has always been true in the past	$t \models H\varphi \Leftrightarrow \forall t' < t : t' \models \varphi$
$G\varphi$	φ is true at all future times	$t \models G\varphi \Leftrightarrow \forall t' > t : t' \models \varphi$

veloped medical guideline complies with global criteria, such as that it avoids the prescription of redundant drugs, or the request of tests that are superfluous, is difficult to impossible if only the guideline text is available.

Thus, the capability to check whether a guideline fulfils particular medical objectives may require the availability of more medical knowledge than is actually specified in a medical guideline. How much additional knowledge is required may vary from guideline to guideline. In the development of the theory below it is assumed that at least some medical background knowledge is required; the extent and the purpose of that background knowledge is subsequently established using a real medical guideline. The development and evaluation of a formal method that supports this process is the topic of the remainder of the paper.

3   Formalisation of Good Practice Medicine

Medical guidelines regarding a disorder usually contain particular sections dealing with the diagnosis, treatment and follow-up of a disorder. In this study, we restrict ourselves to the treatment part, although similar principles may apply to the other parts of a guideline.

3.1 Using Temporal Logic

As medical management is a time-oriented process, diagnostic and treatment actions described in guidelines are performed in a temporal setting. It has been shown previously that the step-wise, possibly iterative, execution of a guideline, such as the example in Figure 1, can be described precisely by means of temporal logic [10]. This is a modal logic, where relationships between worlds in the usual possible-world semantics of modal logic is understood as time order, i.e. formulae are interpreted in a *temporal frame* $\mathcal{F} = (\mathbb{T}, <, I)$, where $\mathbb{T}$ is the set of intervals or time points, $<$ a time ordering, and I an interpretation of the language elements with respect to $\mathbb{T}$ and $<$. Modal operators added to the language of first-order logic include $\circ$, where $\circ\varphi$ has the operational meaning of an execution step, followed by execution of program part φ, formally: **step**; φ.

In this paper, we abstract from such detailed execution semantics of guidelines, and use more abstract temporal operators. The language of standard logic, with equality and unique names assumption, is therefore augmented with the operators G, H, P and F, where the temporal semantics of the first two operators is defined in Table 1. The last two operators are simply defined in terms of the first two operators:

$\vDash P\varphi \leftrightarrow \neg H\neg\varphi$ (somewhere in the past)

$\vDash F\varphi \leftrightarrow \neg G\neg\varphi$ (somewhere in the future)

This logic offers the right abstraction level to cope with the nature of the temporal knowledge in medical guidelines required for our purposes. However, more fine-grained temporal operators can be added if needed.

In addition it is necessary to specify additional axioms that indicate that progression in time is *linear* (there are other axiomatisations possible, such as branching time, see [16]). The most important of these are:

(1) *Transitivity*: $\vDash FF\varphi \rightarrow F\varphi$

(2) *Backward linearity*: $\vDash (P\varphi \wedge P\psi) \rightarrow (P(\varphi \wedge \psi) \vee P(\varphi \wedge P\psi) \vee P(P\varphi \wedge \psi))$

(3) *Forward linearity*: $\vDash (F\varphi \wedge F\psi) \rightarrow (F(\varphi \wedge \psi) \vee F(\varphi \wedge F\psi) \vee F(F\varphi \wedge \psi))$

Transitivity ensures that we can move along the time axis from the past into the future; backward and forward linearity ensure that the time axis does not branch. Consider, for example, axiom (3), which says that if there exists a time t when φ is true, and a time t' when ψ holds, then there are three possibilities: φ and ψ hold at the same time, or at some time in the future φ and further away in the future ψ hold; the meaning of the last disjunct is similar. Other useful axioms concern the boundedness of time; assuming that time has no beginning and no end, gives rise to the following axioms: $\vDash H\varphi \rightarrow P\varphi$ and $\vDash G\varphi \rightarrow F\varphi$.

3.2 Application to Medical Knowledge

It is assumed that two types of knowledge are involved in detecting the violation of good medical practice:

- Knowledge concerning the (patho)physiological mechanisms underlying the disease, and the way treatment influences these mechanisms. The knowledge involved could be causal in nature, and is an example of *object-knowledge*.

- Knowledge concerning good practice in treatment selection; this is *meta-knowledge*.

Below we present some ideas on how such knowledge may be formalised using temporal logic (cf. [7] for earlier work).

We are interested in the prescription of drugs, taking into account their mode of action. Abstracting from the dynamics of their pharmacokinetics, this can be formalised in logic as follows:

$$(\mathsf{G}\, d \wedge r) \rightarrow \mathsf{G}(m_1 \wedge \cdots \wedge m_n)$$

where d is the name of a drug or possibly of a group of drugs indicated by a predicate symbol (e.g. $\mathrm{SU}(x)$, where x is universally quantified and 'SU' stands for sulfonylurea drugs, such as Tolbutamid), r is a (possibly negative or empty) *requirement* for the drug to take effect, and m_k is a mode of action, such as decrease of release of glucose from the liver, which holds at all future times.

The modes of action m_k can be combined, together with an *intention* n (achieving normoglycaemia, i.e. normal blood glucose levels, for example), a particular patient *condition* c, and *requirements* r_j for the modes of action to be effective:

$$(\mathsf{G}m_{i_1} \wedge \cdots \wedge \mathsf{G}m_{i_m} \wedge r_1 \wedge \cdots \wedge r_p \wedge \mathsf{H}c) \rightarrow \mathsf{G}n$$

Good practice medicine can then be formalised as follows. Let $\mathcal{B}$ be background knowledge, $T \subseteq \{d_1, \ldots, d_p\}$ be a set of drugs, C a collection of patient conditions, R a collection of requirements, and N a collection of intentions which the physician has to achieve. A set of drugs T is a *treatment* according to the theory of abductive reasoning if [12]:

(1) $\mathcal{B} \cup \mathsf{G}T \cup C \cup R \nvDash \bot$ (the drugs do not have contradictory effects), and

(2) $\mathcal{B} \cup \mathsf{G}T \cup C \cup R \vDash N$ (the drugs handle all the patient problems intended to be managed)

If in addition to (1) and (2) condition

(3) $O_\varphi(T)$ holds, where O_φ is a meta-predicate standing for an optimality criterion or combination of optimality criteria φ, then the treatment is said to be *in accordance with good-practice medicine*.

A typical example of this is subset minimality $O_\subset$:

$$O_\subset(T) \equiv \forall T' \subset T : T' \text{ is not a treatment according to (1) and (2)}$$

i.e. the minimum number of effective drugs are being prescribed. For example, if $\{d_1, d_2, d_3\}$ is a treatment that satisfies condition (3) in addition to (1) and (2), then the subsets $\{d_1, d_2\}$, $\{d_2, d_3\}$, $\{d_1\}$, and so on, do not satisfy conditions (1) and (2). In the context of abductive reasoning, subset minimality is often used in order to distinguish between various solutions; it is also referred to in literature as *Occam's razor*. Another definition of the meta-predicate O_φ is in terms of minimal cost O_c:

$$O_c(T) \equiv \forall T', \text{with } T' \text{ a treatment: } c(T') \geq c(T)$$

where $c(T) = \sum_{d \in T} cost(d)$; combining the two definitions also makes sense. For example, one could come up with a definition of $O_{C,c}$ that among two subset-minimal treatments selects the one that is the cheapest in financial or ethical sense.

4 Management of Diabetes Mellitus Type 2

An analysis of the medical guideline on diabetes mellitus type 2 was carried out as a case study. An additional aim was to identify the kind of background knowledge required in order to determine the global quality of the guideline, and so the guideline itself was only formalised so far as required to investigate the usefulness of the theory of quality checking introduced above.

4.1 Initial Analysis

It is well known that diabetes type 2 is a very complicated disease: various metabolic control mechanisms are deranged and many different organ systems, such as the cardiovascular and renal system, may be affected by the disorder. Here we focus on the derangement of glucose metabolism in diabetic patients, and even that is nontrivial. To support non-expert medical doctors in the management of this complicated disease in patients, access to a guideline is really essential.

One would expect that as this disorder is so complicated, the diabetes mellitus type 2 guideline is also complicated. This, however, is not the case, as may already be apparent from the guideline fragment shown in Figure 1. This already indicates that much of the knowledge concerning diabetes mellitus type 2 is missing from the guideline, and that without this background knowledge it will be impossible to spot the sort of flaws we are after. Hence, the conclusion is that a deeper analysis is required; the results of such an analysis are discussed next.

4.2 Diabetes Type 2 Background Knowledge

Figure 2 summarises the most important mechanisms and drugs involved in the control of the blood level of glucose. The protein hormone insulin, which is produced by the *B cells* in the Langerhans islets of the *pancreas*, has the following major effects:

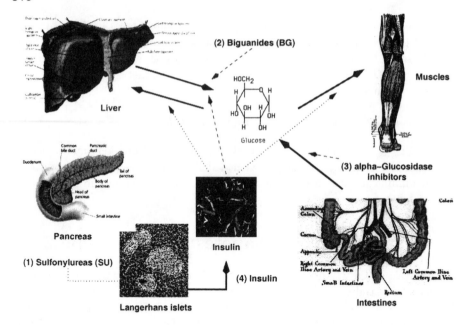

Figure 2: Summary of drugs and mechanisms controlling the blood level of glucose; − − →: inhibition, ·······→: stimulation.

- it increases the uptake of glucose by the liver, where it is stored as glycogen, and inhibits the release of glucose from the liver;

- it increases the uptake of glucose by insulin-dependent tissues, such as muscle and adipose tissue.

At some stage in the natural history of diabetes mellitus type 2, the level of glucose in the blood is too high (hyperglycaemia) due to decreased production of insulin by the B cells. A popular hypothesis explaining this phenomenon is that target cells have become insulin resistant, which with a delay causes the production of insulin by the B cells to raise. After some time, the B cells become exhausted, and they are no longer capable of meeting the demands for insulin. As a consequence, hyperglycaemia develops.

Treatment of diabetes type 2 consists of:

- Use of *sulfonylurea* (SU) drugs, such as tolbutamid. These drugs stimulate the B cells in producing more insulin, and if the cells are not completely exhausted, the hyperglycaemia can thus be reverted to normoglycaemia (normal blood glucose levels).

- Use of *biguanides* (BG), such as metformin. These drugs inhibit the release of glucose from the liver.

- Use of *α-glucosidase inhibitors*. These drugs inhibit (or delay) the absorption of glucose from the intestines.

- Injection of *insulin*. This is the ultimate, causal treatment.

As insulin can only be administered by injection, in contrast to the other drugs which are normally taken orally, doctors prefer to delay prescribing insulin as long as possible. Thus, the treatment part of the diabetes type 2 guideline mentions that one should start with prescribing oral antidiabetics (SU or BG, cf. Figure 1). Two of these can also be combined if taking only one has insufficient glucose-level lowering effect. If treatment is still unsatisfactory, the guideline suggests to: (1) either add insulin, or (2) stop with the oral antidiabetics entirely and to start with insulin.

From a medical point of view, advice (1) above is somewhat curious. Since the oral antidiabetics are no longer effective, the conclusion must be that the B cells are exhausted. Under these circumstances, it does not make a lot of sense to prescribe an SU drug. Prescription of a BG (or α-glucosidase inhibitor) is still justified, as by adding such an oral antidiabetic to insulin, the number of necessary injections can be reduced from twice a day to once a day. Finally, when on insulin treatment, patients run the risk of getting hypoglycaemia, which can be seen as a side effect of insulin not mentioned explicitly in the guideline.

In the remainder of the paper, we will carry out an analysis of the diabetes mellitus type 2 guideline adopting the method described in Section 3 to demonstrate its usefulness.

5 Formalisation of the Diabetes Mellitus 2 Quality Check

The formal analysis of the guideline consists of two steps: first the necessary background knowledge, identified in the previous section, is formalised using temporal logic. Subsequently, this knowledge is explored to formally examine the quality of the guideline.

5.1 Formalisation of Background Knowledge

The background knowledge concerning the (patho)physiology of the glucose metabolism as summarised above is formalised using temporal logic, and kept as simple as possible. The specification is denoted by $\mathcal{B}_{DM2}$:

$$\text{G Drug}(insulin) \rightarrow \text{G}\,(uptake(liver, glucose) = up \,\wedge$$
$$uptake(peripheral\text{-}tissues, glucose) = up)$$

$$\text{G}(uptake(liver, glucose) = up \rightarrow release(liver, glucose) = down)$$

$$(\text{G Drug}(\text{SU}) \wedge \neg capacity(B\text{-}cells, insulin) = exhausted) \rightarrow$$
$$\text{G}\,secretion(B\text{-}cells, insulin) = up$$

$$\text{G Drug}(\text{BG}) \rightarrow \text{G}\,release(liver, glucose) = down$$

$$(\text{G}\,secretion(B\text{-}cell, insulin) = up \,\wedge$$

$$capacity(\textit{B-cells, insulin}) = subnormal \wedge$$
$$QI \le 27 \wedge \mathrm{H}\,\mathrm{Condition}(hyperglycaemia))$$
$$\rightarrow \mathrm{G}\,\mathrm{Condition}(normoglycaemia)$$

$$(\mathrm{G}\textit{release}(\textit{liver, glucose}) = down \wedge$$
$$capacity(\textit{B-cells, insulin}) = subnormal \wedge$$
$$QI > 27 \wedge \mathrm{H}\,\mathrm{Condition}(hyperglycaemia))$$
$$\rightarrow \mathrm{G}\,\mathrm{Condition}(normoglycaemia)$$

$$((\mathrm{G}\textit{release}(\textit{liver, glucose}) = down \vee$$
$$\mathrm{G}\textit{uptake}(\textit{peripheral-tissues, glucose}) = up) \wedge$$
$$capacity(\textit{B-cells, insulin}) = nearly\text{-}exhausted \wedge$$
$$\mathrm{G}\textit{secretion}(\textit{B-cells, insulin}) = up \wedge$$
$$\mathrm{H}\,\mathrm{Condition}(hyperglycaemia))$$
$$\rightarrow \mathrm{G}\,\mathrm{Condition}(normoglycaemia)$$

$$(\mathrm{G}\textit{uptake}(\textit{liver, glucose}) = up \wedge$$
$$\mathrm{G}\textit{uptake}(\textit{peripheral-tissues, glucose}) = up) \wedge$$
$$capacity(\textit{B-cells, insulin}) = exhausted \wedge$$
$$\mathrm{H}\mathrm{Condition}(hyperglycaemia))$$
$$\rightarrow \mathrm{G}(\mathrm{Condition}(normoglycaemia) \vee \mathrm{Condition}(hypoglycaemia))$$

$$(\mathrm{Condition}(normoglycaemia) \oplus \mathrm{Condition}(hypoglycaemia)$$
$$\oplus \mathrm{Condition}(hyperglycaemia))$$

where $\oplus$ stands for the exclusive OR. Note that when the B-cells are exhausted, increased uptake of glucose by the tissues may not only result in normoglycaemia but also in hypoglycaemia (something not mentioned in the guideline).

5.2 Quality Check

Subsequently, the consequences of various treatment options were examined using the method introduced above. Hypothetical patients are considered, and treatment is selected according to the guideline fragments given in Figure 1:

- Consider a patient with hyperglycaemia due to nearly exhausted B-cells:

$$\mathcal{B}_{\mathrm{DM2}} \cup \mathrm{G}\,T \cup \{capacity(\textit{B-cells, insulin}) = nearly\text{-}exhausted\} \cup$$
$$\{\mathrm{HCondition}(hyperglycaemia)\} \models \mathrm{GCondition}(normoglycaemia)$$

holds for $T = \{\mathrm{Drug(SU)}, \mathrm{Drug(BG)}\}$, which also satisfies the minimality condition $O_{\mathrm{C}}(T)$.

- Prescription of treatment $T = \{\mathrm{Drug(SU)}, \mathrm{Drug(BG)}, \mathrm{Drug(insulin)}\}$ for a patient with exhausted B-cells, as is suggested by the guideline, yields:

$$\mathcal{B}_{\mathrm{DM2}} \cup \mathrm{G}\,T \cup \{capacity(\textit{B-cells, insulin}) = exhausted\} \cup$$
$$\{\mathrm{HCondition}(hyperglycaemia)\} \models$$
$$\mathrm{G}(\mathrm{Condition}(normoglycaemia) \vee \mathrm{Condition}(hypoglycaemia))$$

In the last case, it appears that it is possible that a patient develops hypogly-caemia due to treatment; if this possibility is excluded, then the minimality condition $O_C(T)$, and also $O_{C,c}(T)$, do not hold. In either case, good practice medicine is violated, which is to prescribe as few drugs as possible, taking into account costs and side-effects of drugs. Here, three drugs are prescribed whereas only two should have been prescribed (BG and insulin, assuming that insulin alone is too costly), and the possible occurrence of hypoglycaemia should have been prevented. This shows that the method is indeed useful in the setting of guideline-quality checking, as both identified problems are medically relevant, and need to be redressed in future versions of the guideline.

6 Discussion

In this paper, we have developed a basis for a theory of quality-checking of medical guidelines, based on the idea that the quality of a guideline design is for the largest part based on its compliance with specific treatment aims and global requirements. To this purpose, use was made of the theory of abduc-tive, diagnostic reasoning, i.e. we proposed to diagnose potential problems with a guideline using logical abduction [1, 8, 9, 12], even though in the example guideline the mentioned treatment was scrutinised. What was diagnosed were problems in the relationship between medical knowledge, suggested treatment actions in the guideline text and treatment effects; this is different from tra-ditional abductive diagnosis, where observed findings are explained in terms of diagnostic hypotheses [9]. To our knowledge it is the first time that the structure of abductive diagnosis has been used in this particular fashion. We think that this approach to quality checking can be practically useful in the development of medical guidelines, as it helps designers to make an explicit distinction between object-knowledge and meta-knowledge, with various levels of detail, and an abductive reasoning system may then assist in finding flaws.

It also became apparent that guideline quality checks may require adding a significant amount of medical knowledge to the guideline knowledge already available. This knowledge may be specified in an abstract fashion, and thus compared to the detailed specification of a medical guideline required for its automated execution, the volume of knowledge to be added may be moderate. Nonetheless, much of this knowledge is not available within an actual guideline, and is therefore genuine background knowledge. Collecting this background knowledge in designing a guideline may be problematic despite the fact that guideline development teams normally include expert physicians in the field concerned: this background knowledge can only be elicited at the cost of some additional effort in the guideline development process.

There are also other ways in which the physiological background knowl-edge could have been represented. For example, using qualitative reasoning approaches, such as qualitative differential equations as proposed in the the-ory of qualitative simulation by Kuipers [5, 6], or using the qualitative process theory (QPT) by Forbus [2] could have been considered, as these approaches also allow one to abstract from the numerical detail. Our choice was dictated by the wish to remain close to the program semantics attached to formalised guidelines, which is based on temporal logic [10]. Combining formal verification with the approach to quality checking of guidelines developed in this paper is then possible.

So far, we have not made use of automated means to check the quality of a guideline design. As both object- and meta-knowledge can be represented in a language offered by standard theorem provers, partial automation of the process is possible in principle. This is something we wish to investigate in the future; in particular, an interactive theorem prover like KIV [13] may enable us to actually quality check medical guidelines. This would then complement the earlier work on object-level verification of medical guidelines using KIV [10].

References

[1] Console L, Theseider Dupré D, and Torasso P. On the relationship between abduction and deduction, Journal of Logic and Computation 1991; 1(5): 661–690.

[2] Forbus KD. Qualitative process theory. Artificial Intelligence 1984; 24: 85–168.

[3] Fox J, Johns N, Lyons C, Rahmanzadeh A, Thomson R, and Wilson P. PROforma: a general technology for clinical decision support systems. Computer Methods and Programs in Biomedicine 1997; 54: 59–67.

[4] Fox J, and Das S. Safe and Sound: Artificial Intelligence in Hazardous Applications. Cambridge: MIT Press (jointly published with the American Association of Artificial Intelligence), 2000.

[5] Kuipers BJ. Qualitative simulation. Artificial Intelligence 1986; 29: 289–388.

[6] Kuipers BJ. Qualitative Reasoning. The MIT Press, Cambridge, Massachusetts, 1994.

[7] Lucas PJF. Logic engineering in medicine. The Knowledge Engineering Review 1995; 10(2): 153–179.

[8] Lucas PJF. Symbolic diagnosis and its formalisation. The Knowledge Engineering Review 1997; 12(2): 109–146.

[9] Lucas PJF. Analysis of notions of diagnosis. Artificial Intelligence 1998; 105(1–2): 293–341.

[10] Marcos M, Balser M, Ten Teije A, and Van Harmelen F. From informal knowledge to formal logic: a realistic case study in medical protocols. Proceedings of the 12th EKAW-2002, 2002.

[11] Ohno-Machado L, Gennari J, Murphy S, et al. Guideline Interchange Format: a model for representing guidelines. Journal of the American Medical Informatics Association 1998; 5(4): 357–372.

[12] Poole D. A methodology for using a default and abductive reasoning system. International Journal of Intelligent Systems 1990, 5(5), 521–548.

[13] Reif W. The KIV Approach to Software Verification. In: M. Broy and S. Jähnichen (eds.), KORSO: Methods, Languages, and Tools for the Construction of Correct Software. Lecture Notes in Computer Science, Volume 1009, Springer-Verlag, Berlin, 1995.

[14] Sackett DL, Richardson WS, Rosenberg W, and Brian R. Evidence Based Medicine–How to Practice and Teach EBM. Haynes Churchill Livingstone, 1996.

[15] Shahar Y, Miksch S, and Johnson P. The Asgaard project: a task-specific framework for the application and critiquing of time-oriented clinical guidelines. Artificial Intelligence in Medicine 1998; 14: 29–51.

[16] Turner R. Logics for Artificial Intelligence. Ellis Horwood, Chichester, 1985.

[17] Woolf SH. Evidence-based medicine and practice guidelines: an overview. Cancer Control 2000; 7(4): 362–367.

Constraint Relaxation Techniques to Aid the Reuse of Knowledge Bases and Problem Solvers

Tomas Nordlander[1], Ken Brown[2], and Derek Sleeman[1]

[1]Department of Computing Science, University of Aberdeen, Scotland, UK
{tnordlan, sleeman}@csd.abdn.ac.uk
[2]Cork Constraint Computation Centre, Department of Computer Science,
University College Cork, Ireland
k.brown@cs.ucc.ie

Abstract: Effective re-use of knowledge bases requires the identification of plausible combinations of both problem solvers and knowledge bases, which can be an expensive task. Can we identify impossible combinations quickly? The capabilities of combinations can be represented using constraints, and we propose using constraint relaxation to help eliminate impossible combinations. If a relaxed constraint representation of a combination is inconsistent then we know that the original combination is inconsistent as well. We examine different relaxation strategies based on constraint graph properties, and we show that removing constraints of low tightness is an efficient strategy which is also simple to implement.

1. Introduction

The MUSKRAT (Multistrategy Knowledge Refinement and Acquisition Toolbox) framework aims to unify problem solving, knowledge acquisition and knowledge-base refinement in a single computational framework [1]. Given a set of Knowledge Bases (KBs) and Problem Solvers (PSs), the MUSKRAT-Advisor [2] investigates whether the available KBs will fulfil the requirements of the selected PS for a given problem. The Advisor informs the user if the available KBs are sufficient. Our research addresses the problem of checking whether combinations of existing KBs could be reused with the selected PS. We propose to represent the KBs and PSs as Constraint Satisfaction Problems (CSPs), which can be combined to produce composite CSPs. If a combined CSP is solvable, then the original combination of KBs with the selected PS could be used to solve the given problem; if the resultant CSP is inconsistent, then the combination cannot be used. Identifying a suitable combination thus requires examining a series of CSPs, and rejecting insolvable ones until we find one with a solution. Proving CSPs insolvable can be a lengthy process; we would like to find a way to do this quickly. The method we propose here is to relax a CSP, and if we can prove that the relaxed version is insolvable then we know that the original CSP does not have a solution either. However, if the relaxed CSP has a solution, then the original CSP represents a *plausible* combination. To test this proposal, we investigate different relaxation strategies for binary CSPs and test them on randomly generated problems. We suggest that removing constraints with low tightness is an effective method for identifying insolvable combinations. Thus this paper reports a contribution to the challenging problem of Knowledge Reuse as it presents an aid based on Constraint Programming to enable a quick identification of inconsistent combinations.

2. Background

This work is supported by the Advanced Knowledge Technologies (AKT) Interdisciplinary Research Collaboration, which focuses on six challenges to ease substantial bottlenecks in the engineering and management of knowledge; reuse of knowledge is one of those challenges [3]. Current work in reuse has resulted in systems where a number of components have been reused, including ontologies, problem-solving methods (PSMs), and knowledge bases (KBs) [3]. The use of cases in Case Based Reasoning is a related activity [4].

2.1 Reusing Knowledge Based Systems

One of the main goals of the Knowledge Based System (KBS) community is to build new systems out of existing Problem Solvers (say Problem Solving Methods) and existing Knowledge Bases. At an early stage the Knowledge Engineering sub-area identified a range of Problem Solving Methods, which they argued covered the whole range of problem solving and included methods for Classification and Diagnosis through to Planning (so-called synthesis tasks) [5]. An early but powerful example of reuse of a PSM was the use of the EMYCIN shell with a variety of domain-specific knowledge bases [6]. More recently, systems like PROTÉGÉ have provided an option to write KBs in a standardised format like OKBC [7]. This then takes the goal of building new Knowledge-Based Systems (KBSs) one step further. A possible approach is to take the required KB and PSM and to produce manually, initially, a series of mappings, which will make the 2 components "comparable" [7], and thus to develop a new KBS from pre-existing components.

We have chosen to work with the domain of scheduling, mainly because the constraint community has been successful in addressing real world problems in this area. Also, we argue that the nature of scheduling problems are very close to CSPs, hence it would be relatively easy to transform PSs and KBs in this domain. We will now consider an example of a mobile phone manufacturer to understand our notion of KB and PS reuse. The manufacturer has two factories, three suppliers and two delivery companies to transport phones to wholesalers around the world (Figure 1).

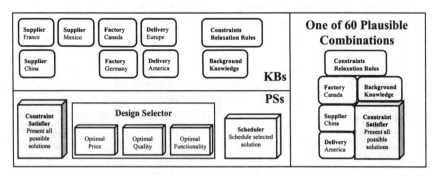

Figure 1. Combining KBs with selected PS

Along with the domain-specific KBs, the system also consists of background knowledge (e.g., ISO 9001, Safety Standards), and constraint relaxation rules to identify those constraints, which the system is allowed to relax (e.g. accept a screen with a maximum of 64 colours instead of 4096). This toy example has 5 PSs and 7 KBs (for each of the factories, suppliers, and delivery companies) to combine as well as the obligatory KBs about background knowledge and constraint relaxation rules (See Figure 1). To solve a task one needs to have: 1 Problem Solvers (out of 5), 1 supplier (out of 3), 1 factory (out of 2), 1 delivery company (out of 2), background knowledge and constraint relaxation. Since the number of possible combination is 60 (5*3*2*2*1*1=60), we would like to eliminate some of the insolvable combinations quickly, leaving a couple of plausible combinations, which need to be evaluated thoroughly. Let us assume that the manufacturer would like, if possible, to reuse knowledge to answer questions such as: Can we manufacture, within the guidelines of ISO 9001 and European safety standards (CE), a mobile phone with a 4096 colour screen, not heavier then 100g and have it delivered to the American market within 6 months?

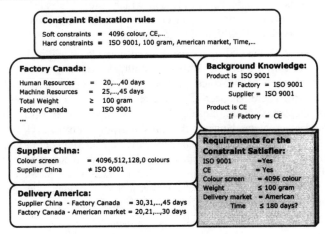

Figure 2. One of 60 Plausible Combinations

Figure 2 illustrates one candidate combination, as well as the requirements for the selected problem solver. With the knowledge and problem solving requirements in Figure 2 we can demonstrate that the combination is inconsistent, as one of the requirements given to the PS, viz., ISO 9001 certified, our background knowledge states that to make a phone certified, both the manufacture and the part supplier need to be ISO 9001 certified. Figure 2 shows that only the factory is certified hence the combination is inconsistent.

White & Sleeman [1] discussed the creation of Meta Problem Solvers, which check if combinations of KBs with a PS, represented as a CSP, are plausible. However, this approach was unable to verify if any discarded combination contained a solution. As noted earlier, we propose to use constraint programming as our PSM and to represent combination of KBs and PSs as CSPs. We will show that some of our strategies can not only identify insolvable combinations quickly, but also verify that their related CSPs do not have any solutions.

2.2 CSP

Constraint Satisfaction techniques attempt to find solutions to constrained combinatorial decision problems [8, 9], and there are a number of efficient toolkits and languages available (e.g. [10, 11]). The definition of a constraint satisfaction problem (CSP) is:

- a set of variables $X = \{ X_1, ..., X_n \}$,
- for each variable X_i, a finite set D_i of possible values (its domain), and
- a set of constraints $C_{<j>} \subseteq D_{j1} \times D_{j2} \times ... \times D_{jt}$, restricting the values that subsets of the variables can take simultaneously.

A solution to a CSP is an assignment of a value from its domain to every variable, in such a way that all constraints are satisfied. The main CSP solution technique interleaves consistency enforcement [12], in which infeasible values are removed from the problem, with various enhancements of backtracking search. The same approach also serves to identify insolvable problems.

The approach of relaxing CSPs has received considerable attention [13-15], but has focused on changing the CSP to introduce solutions. Relaxing problems is also a common technique in mathematical programming, e.g. to obtain better bounds in optimisation [16]. There has been extensive research on randomly generated CSPs [13, 17], which show a phase transition between solvable and insolvable problems, with the hardest problems being at the transition point. Problem classes in these CSPs can be described by a tuple $<n,m,c,t>$, where n is the number of variables and m is the number of values in each domain, c is the number of constraints, and t is the number of forbidden tuples in each constraint (a measure of problem tightness). Much of this research concentrates on binary CSPs, in which each constraint is defined over a pair of variables. Any CSP with finite domains can be modelled by a CSP with only binary constraints [8, 18].

3. Empirical Studies

The aim of relaxing CSPs is to produce new CSPs, which are easier to prove inconsistent. It is not obvious that relaxing an insoluble CSP will produce an easier problem. In fact, phase transition research (e.g. [19]) seems to indicate the opposite when the original CSP is inconsistent – as constraints become more loose, or the connectivity of the problems become more sparse, the time to prove inconsistency for random problems increases. If our approach is to work, we need to identify suitable relaxation strategies, which avoid the increase in solution time. In this section, we describe a series of experiments designed to test whether our approach is practical and to identify suitable relaxation strategies. For this paper, we limit the experiments to randomly generated binary CSPs, with a view to extending the results to real world problems. First we will describe the software, and then present the experiments. For the experiments, we generate a set of random problems, prove them inconsistent by search, and then apply various relaxation strategies and measure the reduction in search effort. The experiments are divided into three groups according to the distribution of the random problems.

3.1 CSP-Suite

The CSP-Suite [20] used in these experiments is written in SICStus Prolog [11] and consists of Generating, Relaxing, and Solving modules (Figure 3).

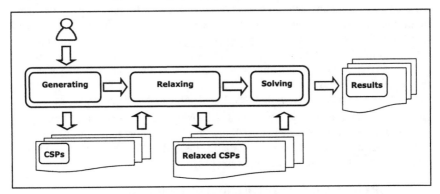

Figure 3. The CSP-Suite

The *Generating* module creates random binary CSPs. Our random CSPs are slightly different from most reported in the literature. We want to find local properties of a problem which indicate how to relax it, so rather than have every constraint in a problem with the same tightness, we instead allow the tightness to vary. This also produces random CSPs which are closer to real world problems. The tightness of individual constraints in our problems will be uniformly, normally, or exponentially distributed. Thus, for different tightness distributions we use different ways to describe the tightness tuple. The uniform problem classes have 5-tuples $<n,m,c,[t_\mu,r]>$, where t_μ is the average number of forbidden tuples, with the number for each constraint selected uniformly at random from the range $[t_\mu-r, t_\mu+r]$. The normal problem classes introduce standard deviation (sd) in our tightness tuple; $<n,m,c,[t_\mu,sd,r]>$. The standard deviation parameter controls the width of the bell curve. The exponential distribution requires a somewhat different notation: $<n,m,c,[t_m,stp,r]>$, where t_m (tightness middle) shows the middle of the distribution range, which is *not* the same as average distribution. The parameter *stp* has an effect on the steepness of the exponential probability curve. Even though only a positive exponential distribution has been tested in this paper (many low tightness constraints that decay exponentially to few high tightness constraints), it is also possible to generate a negative exponential tightness distribution. First we create a skeleton graph by successively adding nodes, then we randomly add constraints until we reach "c", then take each constraint in turn, decide how many tuples it should forbid, and then randomly remove that number of tuples.

The *Relaxing* module generates relaxed CSPs from original CSPs by removing a specified number of constraints according to nine different strategies. Random Removal simply chooses the constraints randomly. Greedy Search considers each constraint in turn, removing it, solving the relaxed CSP, and replacing the constraint. It then selects the constraint whose removal gave the best performance improvement, removes it, and repeats the whole process on the resulting CSP. Greedy Ordering uses the first iteration of Greedy Search to generate an ordering list for all constraints then removes constraints in the order suggested. Node Degree selects constraints in ascending or descending order of the degree of their associated variables in the constraint graph. Isolate Node selects high or low degree nodes and removes a series of constraints incident on those nodes (i.e. it tries to remove variables from the problem). Tightness removes constraints in ascending or descending order of their tightness. Note that the two Greedy strategies would not be applicable in our eventual framework, since they must solve many CSPs each time. They are useful here as reference points showing what might be achievable. We also used the results of the Greedy search to analyse the properties of the most profitable removed constraints, and from that developed some of the other strategies.

The *Solving* module simply solves the CSPs using the finite domain library [21], and records search effort each time. Since the library does not report constraint checks, we use the resumption statistic instead. We have confirmed that resumptions correlate well with CPU time [22].

3.2 CSPs with Uniformly Distributed Tightness

First, we consider problems with a uniform distribution of tightness. In Figure 4, for the problem class <20,10,133, [65, 15]>, we show the resumption profit achieved (i.e. how much easier it is to solve the relaxed CSP compared to the original) by each strategy, removing up to 60 constraints each time. The problem class is in the over-constrained region, and in all cases we considered, remained over-constrained even after removing the constraints. The graph shows that removing low-tightness constraints is the most profitable of the applicable strategies, for this problem class. We assume that although such constraints are easy to satisfy, they are likely to be redundant when showing there is no solution, since they rule out so few combinations, and thus they introduce many extra branches into the search tree for no benefit.

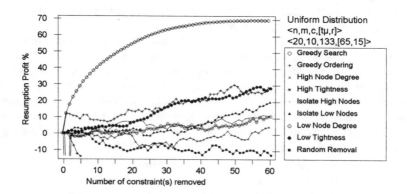

Figure 4. Relaxation Strategies when removing up to 60 constraints

We then concentrate on the Low Tightness strategy, and Figure 5 illustrates its effect on 4 different problem classes. Whilst the graph shows a negative result for the <20,10,133,[45,15]> curve, the others are positive. In the best case we can create relaxed CSPs that are up to 45% easier to solve than the original CSPs, still without introducing a solution. The graphs suggest that the Low Tightness Removal strategy works better on CSPs with high tightness and wide distribution.

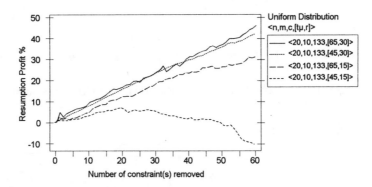

Figure 5. Low Tightness Removal Strategy when removing 60 constraints

As discussed at the start of section 3, strategy (1), randomly removing constraints from a randomly generated inconsistent CSP, is likely to make it harder to prove inconsistency. Does the same effect happen for Low Tightness Removal? I.e., is there a point at which removing constraints is no longer profitable? In Figure 6 we plot the search effort against the number of constraints in problems obtained by relaxing an original problem using Low Tightness Removal, and we include Random Removal for comparison. We start with a particular problem class on the right-hand side of the curve, remove constraints according to each strategy, and solve the new problem after each removal. In three cases, we avoid any significant hardness peak with the Low Tightness strategy, and for the fourth a peak appears only after removing approximately 40 constraints. That peak is further to the left than for Random Removal, and the peak normally coincides with the solubility transition. Figure 7 shows the transition curves, and we can see that in four cases, the transition point for Low Tightness Removal appears later (further left) than for Random Removal. This gives us some confidence that we can use our relaxation strategy reliably without introducing new solutions.

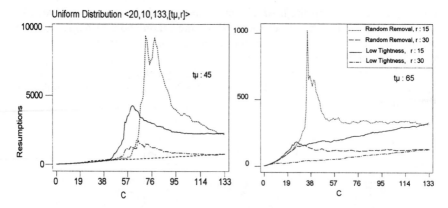

Figure 6. Search effort for Random Removal vs. Low Tightness Removal

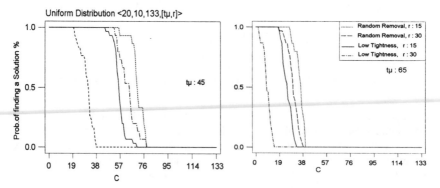

Figure 7. Transition phase for Random Removal vs. Low Tightness Removal

3.3 CSPs with Normally and Exponentially Distributed Tightness

We now repeat the experiments on problems with normally distributed tightness (Figures 8 to 11) and with exponentially distributed tightness (Figures 12 to 15). Although the graphs suggest that the results of the low tightness strategy are slightly better for CSPs with a uniformly distributed tightness that have a high average and a wide distribution range, it is evident from figures 8 &12 that low tightness is still the best strategy for all distributions.

There are only two differences in the results for these distributions when compared to Uniform. Firstly, as seen in figure 10, there are only two cases instead of three where we can avoid any significant hardness peak when relaxing using the Low Tightness strategy. Secondly, when we compare the Random curves (Figure 10 & 14) we notice that the hardness peak is not only a bit wider but also slightly higher than the uniform distribution graphs in section 3.2. Still, for all cases, the transition point for low tightness is later than for random (see Figures 11 & 15), which leaves us with some confidence that we can use our relaxation strategy reliably without introducing new solutions even when the tightness is exponentially distributed.

Note that the reason that we use a different standard deviation (*sd*) for problem classes with a different range is to obtain an equal bell-shaped distribution form for all our problem classes (Figure 9-11). Additionally, in order to achieve a similar exponential decay for the problem classes with different range values we use a different steepness (*stp*) (Figure 13-15).

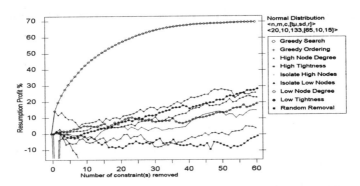

Figure 8. Relaxation Strategies when removing up to 60 constraints

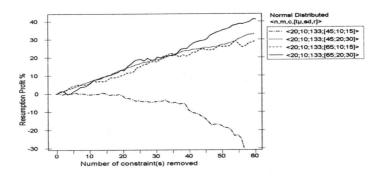

Figure 9. Low Tightness Removal Strategy when removing 60 constraints

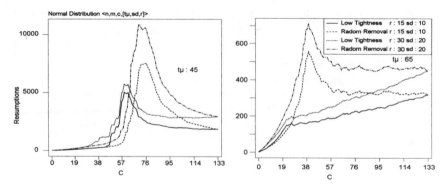

Figure 10. Search effort for Random Removal vs. Low Tightness Removal

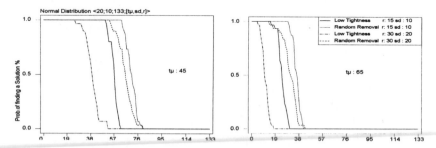

Figure 11. Transition phase for Random Removal vs. Low Tightness Removal

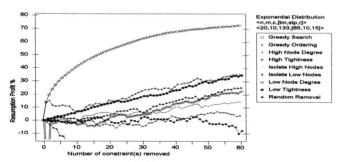

Figure 12. Relaxation Strategies when removing up to 60 constraints

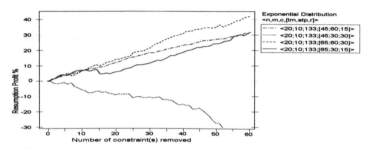

Figure 13. Low Tightness Removal Strategy when removing 60 constraints

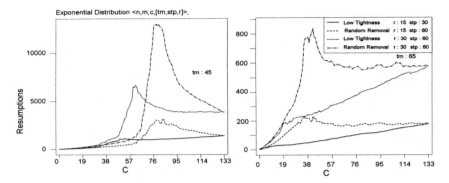

Figure 14. Search effort for Random Removal vs. Low Tightness Removal

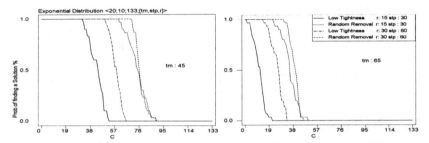

Figure 15. Transition phase for Random Removal vs. Low Tightness Removal

4. Future Work

In this paper, we have tested the effectiveness of constraint relaxation for quickly identifying inconsistent random CSPs with uniform, normal and exponential tightness distributions. Our original aim was to apply this technique to the problem of knowledge base reuse. Therefore, the main focus of future work will be on extending this approach to more realistic CSPs. We will focus on scheduling problems. These are likely to involve non-binary and global constraints, and constraint graphs with particular properties (e.g. [23]). We will also carry out investigations into theoretical CSP concepts, including higher consistency levels and problem hardness. One of our primary objectives was to detect combination of problem solvers (PSs) and knowledge bases (KBs), which are inconsistent. So we plan to take combination of PS and KBs and systematically explore the effect of relaxing one or more constraints. Thus when a new task, is encountered we will search the case-base for the nearest case(s) and perform the actions which these cases(s) suggest. We hope this approach will quickly and efficient lead us to detecting consistent and inconsistent PS-KBs combinations. As a related activity, we plan to also investigate scheduling ontologies [24, 25], to help characterise problems in terms of specific domain entities and relationships. We hope these studies will help us to further understand the problem of KB reuse, this being one of our original aims.

5. Summary

This paper has briefly discussed reuse of KBs and PSs, and described our method to alleviate part of this challenging issue. We propose to represent each KB and each PS as a Constraint Satisfaction Problem (CSP), which can be combined to obtain larger CSPs. In parallel to this theoretical discussion, we have conducted experiments on creating and relaxing binary CSPs with 9 different relaxation strategies. We have shown that our idea of relaxing CSPs can be useful for detecting inconsistency. In particular, we have shown that the simple strategy of removing constraints of low tightness is effective, and reduces the time to detect inconsistency. We will apply these results to determine whether combinations of KBs and a PS are plausible when reusing knowledge-based components for real world problems.

6. Acknowledgements

This work is supported under the EPSRC's grant number GR/N15764 and the Advanced Knowledge Technologies Interdisciplinary Research Collaboration, which comprises the Universities of Aberdeen, Edinburgh, Sheffield, Southampton and the Open University. We thank Mats Carlsson at SICTStus for helpful discussions about resumption, constraint checks and search effort.

7. References

1. White, S. & Sleeman, D., A Constraint-Based Approach to the Description & Detection of Fitness-for-Purpose, *ETAI*, vol. 4, pp. 155-183, 2000.
2. White, S. & Sleeman, D., Providing Advice on the Acquisition and Reuse of Knowledge Bases in Problem Solving, 11th Banff Knowledge Acquisition Workshop. SRDG Publications, Calgary Canada, 1998, pp. 21.
3. AKT, Reuse Knowledge, [WWW], Available from: http://www.aktors.org/publications/reuse/, [Accessed 1 June 2003].
4. Kolodner, J., *Case-Based Reasoning*. San Mateo, CA: Morgan Kaufmann, 1993.
5. Hayes-Roth, F., Waterman, D. & Lenat, D., *Building Expert Systems*. London: Addison-Wesley, 1983.
6. Bennett, J. & Engelmore, R., Experience using EMYCIN. In Rule-Based Expert Systems, in *Experience using EMYCIN. In Rule-Based Expert Systems*, B. Buchanan and E. Shortliffe, Eds. London: Addison-Wesley, 1983, pp. 314-328.
7. Gennari, J. H., Musen, M. A., Fergerson, R., et al., The Evolution of Protégé: An Environment for Knowledge-Based Systems Development., *International Journal of Human-Computer Studies*, vol. 58, pp. 89-123, 2003.
8. Barták, R., Online Guide to Constraint Programming, [WWW], Available from: http://kti.ms.mff.cuni.cz/~bartak/constraints/binary.html, [Accessed March 2003 1998].
9. Tsang, E., Foundations of Constraint Satisfaction. London & San Diego: Academic Press, 1993.
10. ILOG Solver, 5.3 ed. Paris: ILOG Inc., http://www.ilog.com/, 2003

11. SICStus Prolog, 3.9.1 ed. Kista: Swedish Institute of Computer Science, http://www.sics.se/sicstus/, 2001
12. Freuder, E., Synthesizing constraint expressions, CACM, 1978, pp. 958-966.
13. Freuder, E. & Wallace, R., Partial Constraint Satisfaction, *Artificial Intelligence*, vol. 58, pp. 2170, 1992.
14. Bistarelli, S., Montanari, U. & Rossi, F., Constraint Solving over Semi-rings, IJCAI'95, 1995, pp. 624--630.
15. Schiex, T., Fargier, H. & Verfaillie, G., Valued Constraint Satisfaction Problems: hard and easy problems, IJCAI'95, 1995, pp. 631-637.
16. Hooker, J., Logic-based methods for optimization : combining optimization and constraint satisfaction. New York, 2000, pp. 209.
17. MacIntyre, E., Prosser, P., Smith, B., et al., Random Constraint Satisfaction: Theory meets Practice, CP-98, 1998, pp. 325-339.
18. Bacchus, F., Chen, X., Beek, P. v., et al., Binary vs. non-binary constraints, *Artificial Intelligence*, vol. 140, pp. 1-37, 2002.
19. Prosser, P., Binary constraint satisfaction problems: Some are harder than others, Proceedings ECAI-94 (11th European Conference on Artificial Intelligence), 1994, pp. 95-99.
20. CSP-Suite, 1.90 ed. Aberdeen: University of Aberdeen, http://www.csd.abdn.ac.uk/~tnordlan/Proglog%20programs, 2002
21. SICStus, Constraint Logic Programming over Finite Domains, in *SICStus Prolog User's Manual*, vol. Release 3.9.1, R. 3.9.1, Ed. Kista: Intelligent Systems Laboratory Swedish Institute of Computer Science, 2002, pp. 345-381.
22. Nordlander, T., First Year Report, Aberdeen University, 2002.
23. Walsh, T., Search on high degree graphs, IJCAI-2001, 2001, pp. 266-274.
24. Rajpathak, D., Motta, E. & Roy, R., The Generic Task Ontology For Scheduling Applications, International Conference on Artificial Intelligence, Las Vegas, 2001.
25. Smith, S. F. & Becker, M. A., An Ontology for Constructing Scheduling Systems, *AAAI Symposium on Ontological Engineering*, Mars 1997.

SESSION 5:

MULTI-AGENT SYSTEMS AND RECOMMENDER SYSTEMS

Adaptive Brokering in Agent-Mediated Electronic Commerce

Timothy J Norman, Derek H Sleeman, Nial Chapman*

Dept of Computing Science, University of Aberdeen

Aberdeen UK

{tnorman,sleeman}@csd.abdn.ac.uk, n.chapman@jkna.com

Abstract

In this paper we advocate an approach that extends models of trust and reputation to take into account the competence of agents. The argument is that such an approach will lead to more reliable agent-mediated electronic commerce environments than those in which agents are simply considered to have cooperated or defected. If there is a mismatch between the advertised and actual competence of an agent and the agent fails to complete a task as a consequence of this mismatch, then the description of this agent's competence should be refined in addition to any loss in reputation. Consequently, this agent is less likely to be employed for an inappropriate task in the future. Two models of adaptive brokering are presented in this paper that illustrate the use of refinement techniques in developing effective brokering mechanisms for agent-mediated electronic commerce.

1 Introduction

In both managed and open agent-mediated electronic commerce environments trust in and reputation of agents are important issues. For example, in a managed auction house it is important for the participants to trust in the integrity of the auctioneer. This trust is typically based on the reputation of the institution that the auctioneer represents. In traditional marketplaces, or auction houses, it is common to maintain that reputation, at least in part, by requiring all goods offered for sale to be given over to that institution for inspection prior to them being offered for sale. However, in electronic commerce environments such controls are rarely possible — the agent operating as a broker must assess the reliability, quality of service and other aspects of a potential service provider on the basis of past encounters. For example, a service provider that has consistently provided a reliable service of a specific type in the past, as reported by consumers of that service, may be considered to have a good reputation for the delivery of that specific service. This is an instance of the more general problem of modelling the reliability of an agent with respect to a specific task (or problem solving activity) and hence how trustworthy that agent is [1]. The more frequently an agent fails to deliver on its agreements, the

---

*Currently Director of JKNA E-Business Solutions Ltd.

more likely that it will be considered untrustworthy and the less likely it will be employed in the future. It is this that provides the context of the research reported in this paper. We argue, however, that existing models of reputation and trust in multi-agent systems are inadequate, principally because they do not address the important question of modifying a model of the competence of an agent as a result of past encounters.

Schillo *et al.* [7], for instance, investigate the use of learning in the generation of a model of the trustworthiness of agents within electronic commerce scenarios. The question addressed is that, given there are a number of agents offering the same or equivalent services, which agent is the most trustworthy on the basis of past experience. All other things being equal, the most trustworthy agent should be the best choice. In determining the trustworthiness of an agent, evidence is taken from experience (past encounters with that agent) and the testimonies of others. This idea of using both evidence from past encounters and recommendations from others [5] has been further studied in the context of trust and reputation in multi-agent systems. Yu and Singh [9] present a decentralised reputation system based on an acquaintance model to help in the identification of appropriate witnesses, and on Dempster-Shafer theory for combining evidence. Sabater and Sierra [6] extend this use of combining evidence and social (or acquaintance) networks by representing the trustworthiness of an agent in more than one dimension. A seller agent could, for example, be judged on the basis of whether it can be trusted to deliver on time, or whether it can be trusted not to over-charge for the service concerned. In all of these models of trust and reputation, all failures are assumed to be due to the agent being either *unwilling* or *unable* to perform the task concerned; i.e. no distinction is made between defection and a lack of competence. The question is reduced to: which agents is least likely to fail in this encounter?

In contrast, we would like to assume, for the sake of this discussion, that all failures are due to the agent being *unable* to complete the agreed task rather than unwilling; i.e. agents always cooperate, but fail due to circumstances outside of their control. We then focus on a different aspect of the same problem: which agent is most competent at this task? Consider an agent that represents a wholesaler of some commodity to clients within a supply chain; e.g. supplying bananas to supermarkets. Suppose that this agent has signed a contract to supply some quantity of the commodity within a specific deadline, and suppose that the deadline is passed and the delivery has not arrived. Is it appropriate to simply record this as a failure and modifying a representation of the reputation of this supplier? Certainly, but it may also be reasonable to determine the cause of this failure, thus increasing the likelihood of there being fewer future problems of this kind with respect to this supplier. Suppose that the supplier can meet the quantity required, but needed additional time in this instance to complete the delivery. According to the model proposed by Sabater and Sierra [6], this will be recorded as a failure to meet the deadline (a more fine-grained analysis of the agent's past performance than that possible in models such as that proposed by Yu and Singh [9]). There is, however, an alternative. Suppose that the broker records the fact that the delivery time required for this quantity of bananas was, perhaps, an underestimate. If, over a number of encounters, this problem occurs with some regularity for this agent under similar circumstances, it may be better to refine the model of the tasks that this agent can competently perform.

Evidence from such encounters should be recorded, so that appropriate modifications to a representation of the competence of this supplier may be made. This may be done by, for example, changing the constraints on delivery time for this supplier, commodity pair (see section 2). If a broker is able to adapt its models of the competencies of agents in this way, it will be able to develop a more accurate picture of the services available from agents, and provide a more reliable service to its customers.

We advocate an approach that extends models of trust and reputation to take into account the *competence* of agents. The argument is that such an approach will lead to more reliable agent-mediated electronic commerce environments than those in which simple cooperate/defect level information is recorded, but it should be noted that the work reported in this paper is complementary to these existing models of trust and reputation. In this paper we present two simple mechanisms whereby a broker may use the minimum of information of successes and failures in service delivery to adapt its models of the competencies of agents, and use supply chain scenarios to illustrate them (see section 2.1). In the first model, learning techniques are employed to enable the broker to adapt competence models through experience (section 3). In the second model, we investigate a simple mechanism whereby the broker and supplier may agree on a modification to the model of the competence of that supplier (section 4). Before these mechanisms are discussed, however, we present the broker-based multi-agent architecture that provides the context of this research.

2   A broker-based architecture

In this paper, we make a number of simplifying assumptions. First, we assume that there is a single broker that provides the service of putting together a coalition of agents that can, together, complete the task set by an agent. The use of a single broker introduces a single point of failure for the system and a potential bottleneck. An alternative solution would be to have a number of agents that provide this brokering service (or even allow any agent to take on the role of a broker) and introduce a mechanism whereby information about the reputation and competence of agents within the community to be propagated through social connections [6, 9]. In this work we are not concerned about how information on the reputation or the competence of an agent is shared within a community. Our focus is on the recognition of a conflict between the advertised competence of an agent and its perceived performance, and the resolution of this conflict. For this reason, the use of a single broker in this analysis is a reasonable simplifying assumption.

Second, as discussed in the introduction, we assume that if an agent has advertised a competence, then it is willing to perform this problem-solving activity for any other agent within the system at any time. This has been done to simplify the interaction between the broker and potential suppliers so that the broker makes a local decision on which agents to involve in the completion of a task. We do not, for example, use the Contract Net or any other contracting mechanism for the distribution of tasks. This is because we are interested primarily in the identification and resolution of conflicts between advertised and perceived competence, and not in the use of auction mechanisms.

Further, we use a simple model of agents' competencies. Each competence is modelled in terms of the competence type, and constraints on its inputs and outputs. For example, an agent may advertise that it is competent at providing a transportation service. The set of constraints on the inputs to a competence, CI_j, are the preconditions of the competence. For example, the agent providing a transportation service may have a maximum weight for each unit, which would correspond to the capacity of the largest truck in the fleet available to that delivery company. The set of constraints on the outputs of the competence, CO_j, are the postconditions of the competence. For example, the agent providing the transportation service may constrain the time at which the task may be expected to complete.

The process of completing a task is assumed to be coordinated by the broker in the following stages: advertising, problem specification, the production of a solution to the problem (a plan of action), the coordination of task execution, and the resolution of any conflicts between advertised competence and observed behaviour.

Service providers advertise their competencies to the broker. These adverts consist of the competence type, constraints on the inputs to and on the outputs from the competence as described above.

Agents that wish to have a problem solved — e.g. a service delivered — submit a request to the broker in the form of a task description, T, and a set of constraints, S which the solution must satisfy. For example, the task may be to have bananas delivered and the constraints may include the quantity, quality and deadline by which they must be received. This constitutes the problem to be solved by the broker.

The broker may then construct a plan to solve this problem with the information it has about agents' competencies. Let us assume that the task, T, can be solved by the application of a series of processes applied to the intermediate results produced. The plan is, therefore, an ordered set of problem-solving activities:

$$T : PS_1 [CI_1, CO_1] \rightarrow PS_2 [CI_2, CO_2] \rightarrow \ldots \rightarrow PS_N [CI_N, CO_N]$$

Here, the task, T, is shown as having been refined into a total ordering of problem solving activities, $PS_1 \ldots PS_N$, each with input, $CI_1 \ldots CI_N$, and output, $CO_1 \ldots CO_N$, constraints. In general, however, this may be a partial ordering of problem solving activities, and hence some may be executed in parallel. Furthermore, we have assumed that only a single plan would be generated, but the approach could easily be extended to deal with a solution tree.

During the planning phase only the competence information is available to the broker; i.e. the $PS_j[CI_j, CO_j]$ terms in the example given the previous section. This information is used during the planning stage to make predictions about the outputs that will be generated during execution, and hence enable the construction of a plan. The actual outputs, $O_1 \ldots O_N$ shown below, only become available during execution. For example, the output generated by problem solver PS_1 on completion of this operation is shown below as O_1.

$$T : PS_1[CI_1, CO_1] \rightarrow O_1 \rightsquigarrow PS_2[CI_2, CO_2] \rightarrow O_2 \rightsquigarrow \ldots$$
$$\ldots \rightarrow PS_N[CI_N, CO_N] \rightarrow O_N$$

This, typically distributed, execution of the plan for solving task, T, provides the broker with information about how the agents assigned problem solving activities performed. This provides useful information for the broker to check and possibly refine its model of agents' competencies.

During execution the broker acts as a co-ordinator. That is the broker will pass I_j, or O_{j-1}, to PS_j and will check that this satisfies the constraints, CI_j. Similarly the output O_j will be checked against CO_j and passed to the next agent if the tests are satisfied. However, we wish to investigate the situation where an agent's observed behaviour does not match its advertised competence. There are two cases that we consider. The first is where the inputs, I_j, to agent PS_j satisfy the constraints specified in the competence description, but the outputs O_j do not. Here, the agent does not appear as competent as had been thought and the competence description may need to be *specialised*. The second is where the the inputs to the agent do not satisfy the constraints specified in the competence description and the outputs do. In this case it appears that the agent is more competent that its descriptions suggest, and so these may need to be *generalised*.

The agent execution framework being used here also provides the opportunity to experiment with agents to see if they are indeed more competent than their descriptors suggest. Suppose PS_j provides the expected output when provided with I_j (O_{j-1}), then this input can be modified say to include a wider range of values or an object suggested by background knowledge. So for instance suppose PS_2 executed satisfactorily with an input value of 6, then we might try values 5 and then 7, if both were successful, and 4 and 8 were unsuccessful, then the associated input constant 6 would be replaced by the range 5-7. Alternatively, if PS_3 operated satisfactorily with one of its values being "apple" then background knowledge might suggest we try "banana", "orange" etc, and if they were both successful then the competencies would be rewritten to include the descriptor "fruit".

Failure within the execution phase of this process may lead the broker to refine its model of the competencies of specific agents within the coalition. Note, however, that there may be many causes of failure during the execution of a plan: a resource upon which the agent depends becomes unavailable, the completion of the problem solving activity has a 'likelihood of success' associated with it, and so on. As we have seen, failures that are of interest here are those in which there is a mismatch between the expected and actual outputs of a problem solving activity.

In discussing the execution phase of the process, the sorts of discrepancies which we might encounter were outlined. These can be summarised as agents being unable to do some of the tasks which would be expected of them given the description of their competencies; in a certain sense these agents are *incompetent* and their descriptions need to be specialised to exclude the tasks that the broker now knows they are unable to do. The other situation identified is where the agents are able to do a wider range of tasks than suggested by their descriptors and so their descriptors need to be generalised to include these additional situations. (In a sense these agents are being *modest* about their capabilities.) These situations (some more difficult to detect than others) provide case-based evidence for possible revision, or refinement, of the broker's model of an agent's competence.

In the following sections we discuss in detail two strategies through which a broker may refine its model of the competencies of agents, so that it may develop and maintain a more accurate picture of the tasks that agents can perform. In the first model presented, the focus is exclusively on the use of refinement techniques by the broker to modify its model of agent competencies from experience (see section 3). This is then extended into a model that takes into account both the refinement of agent competencies and the agents' reputation (see section 4). Before describing these mechanisms in more detail, however, we present a couple of supply-chain-like scenarios for the purposes of illustration — these being the scenarios in which the implementation of these adaptive brokering mechanisms have been tested.

2.1 Two Scenarios

In this supply chain scenario the task set by the customer is for the broker to arrange delivery of a quantity of bananas by some deadline. This customer agent is assumed to be a representative of an organisation such as a supermarket, and supplier agents are assumed to represent banana wholesalers. The transportation agents are representatives of haulage firms who provide the transportation of goods from suppliers to customers. The broker agent, as discussed above, coordinates the completion of the task set by the customer (see figure 1).

The broker will construct a plan (in this case the planning task is rather trivial) by choosing a supplier and transportation agent that can carry out the task within the constraints provided. The plan will be executed, the supplier and transporter informed, and the bananas will, if all goes well, be delivered to the customer.

The first participating agent is the customer agent: the representative of a supermarket that is attempting to purchase bananas. Let us assume that the

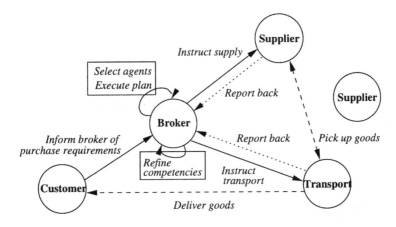

Figure 1: A supply chain scenario.

customer agent may specify three constraints on the performance of the task of banana supply: the number of pallets of bananas required, the unit cost of supply (this includes the purchase price plus delivery costs) and the deadline to be met. Note that in this paper we are not concerned with the negotiation of a contract to supply; we assume that if the combination of these constraints as specified by the customer cannot be met, the broker simply reports failure. In a complete solution to this type of scenario there will be trade-offs to consider between cost and delivery time, for example, that would require some form of bartering between the customer and broker.

There are two types of service provider in this scenario: banana suppliers and transportation service providers. Banana suppliers advertise their competencies in terms of the minimum and maximum number of pallets of bananas that they can supply within a specific period of time and to a specific unit cost. Each supplier can advertise a number of instances of this competence type: for example, one supplier may advertise that it can supply up to 50 pallets within one day at £20 per pallet, and it can also supply between 50 and 200 pallets within three days at £19 per pallet. Transportation service providers advertise their competencies in terms of the number of pallets that they can deliver, the time required for delivery and the delivery cost (for the sake of simplicity we ignore distance). For example, one delivery agent may advertise that it can deliver up to 60 pallets within one day for £5 per pallet, and that it can deliver up to 60 pallets within two days for £3 per pallet.

The second scenario considered concerns the management of the production of vehicle suspension. The task set by the customer is for the broker to arrange the delivery of the necessary parts to make the suspension for a vehicle that has certain characteristics. The customer is assumed to be a representative of an organisation such as a car manufacturer. The supplier agents are representatives of shock absorber suppliers or spring suppliers (the two main components of a suspension system). The broker, as discussed above, coordinates the completion of the task set by the customer.

In this scenario the customer will submit a request for suspension to the suspension broker indicating the type of vehicle required (off-road or on-road), the weight of the vehicle and the type of performance required (high performance or normal performance). The broker uses knowledge of suspension systems to then make a decision on the type of shock absorber and spring that is required. With this information and information on the competencies of shock absorber and spring suppliers, it arranges for the supply of these parts. If all goes well the required parts will be gathered and the suspension system built to the customers requirements.

3 Adapting Competence Models by Experience

The first strategy is for the broker to use refinement techniques, after every encounter, to develop an accurate picture of the competencies of agents. The broker agent holds a view of each of the agent's competencies in a table. It uses these values to determine which agent it will choose to perform a task — which agent it considers, at the present time, to be most suited to the task. If there are two or more suitable agents the broker selects one to ensure fair distribution of task instances. Following task execution, the model of that agent's competence may be revised.

Following the receipt of an order to supply bananas, the broker searches for supplier/transport agent combinations that can meet the criteria specified. Furthermore, for the sake of this investigation, we allow the broker to consider supplier/transport agent combinations where their combined constraints do not meet those specified by the customer. The following two types of case are then considered as information on which to refine the model of an agent's competence: when an agent fails to meet its advertised competence, and when an agent succeeds in fulfilling a task that is outside its advertised competence.

Let us suppose that the supplier and transport agents provide accurate information about unit cost and delivery time; i.e. the only variable that is to be considered here is the number of pallets of bananas that a supplier can supply and a transport agent can deliver. In the following we denote the number of pallets of bananas that the customer requires as n. We denote the minimum and maximum number of pallets that an agent, i, has advertised that it may supply/transport under competence c as c^i_{min} and c^i_{max} respectively, where i is a supplier, $i \in S$, or a transport agent, $i \in T$. We also denote the set of all supplier agents' competencies as C^S and the set of all transport agents' competencies as C^T. Now, we can define the set of all competencies for suppliers and transport agents such that the number of pallets of bananas required is either met by that competence or exceeds the competence by some δ; these are denoted by C^S_δ and C^T_δ respectively. The definition of C^S_δ is as follows, and C^T_δ is defined in a similar way. $C^S_\delta = \{c^s \in C^S \text{ s.t. } c^s_{min} - \delta \leq n \leq c^s_{max} + \delta\}$

In selecting a set of candidate supplier/transport agent pairs, we first create those pairs such that the advertised competence satisfies the required number of pallets of bananas for at least one of the agents involved; i.e. the task is outside the advertised competence of at most one of the agents involved. The degree to which the task may be outside the advertised competence of an agent can be varied by varying δ. We define the set of pairs of competencies P_{δ_s, δ_t} that meet the cost and time criteria exactly and meet the constraint on the number of pallets within δ_s for the supplier and δ_t for the transport agent with the aid of a predicate function that checks cost and time constraints, costAndTime(): $P_{\delta_s, \delta_t} = \{(c^s, c^t) \text{ s.t. } c^s \in C_{\delta_s}^S, \ c^t \in C_{\delta_t}^T, \text{ costAndTime}(c^s, c^t)\}$. Now, the set of pairs of agents that are candidates for the task concerned with a variation of δ is candidates $= (P_{0,\delta} \cup P_{\delta,0})$

The actual pair employed will be selected according to the number of times each agent has been selected to ensure that tasks are fairly distributed among all able supplier and transport agents. If there is a tie (i.e. more than one pair has been employed an equal number of times) a winner is selected at random. Let the pair that is actually selected be denoted by (c^s, c^t).

Following the execution of these tasks the broker checks whether the output of each subtask (supply and delivery) meets the criteria specified in the task set by the customer. The competence of one of the participant agents is then refined if one of the following conditions are met:

- If c^s succeeds and $(c^s, c^t) \in P_{\delta,0} \setminus P_{0,0}$; i.e., the supplier succeeded in satisfying a constraint that is outside its advertised competence. In this case, competence c^s is generalised.

- If c^s fails and $(c^s, c^t) \in P_{0,0}$; i.e., the supplier failed to satisfy its advertised competence. In this case, competence c^s is specialised.

- If c^t succeeds and $(c^s, c^t) \in P_{0,\delta} \setminus P_{0,0}$; i.e., the transport agent succeeded in satisfying a constraint that is outside its advertised competence. In this case, competence c^t is generalised.

- If c^t fails and $(c^s, c^t) \in P_{0,0}$; i.e., the transport agent failed to satisfy its advertised competence. In this case, competence c^t is specialised.

The learning techniques used in this system are well understood, and are basically extending a range of values to include an additional data point (i.e. generalisation), and refining a range to exclude a particular data point (i.e. specialisation). Additionally, in an earlier section we discussed replacing banana by the class fruit. This is generalisation against a predefined hierarchy. Details of appropriate algorithms capable of the specialisation and generalisation tasks discussed above are given in Mitchell [4]. These techniques have been used in the REFINER+ system which has the capability of inferring class descriptions from class-labelled instances; it can also suggest how overlaps between classes might be removed, Winter and Sleeman [8].

Perhaps the most important questions about the use of refinement techniques are determining how much to refine the failing/successful agent and when to refine the failing/successful agent. In the case of a failing agent, the system will automatically refine the agent's competence by an amount that is determined by the extent of the failure. That is the algorithm applies a minimum specialisation. Indeed, it is generally a conservative algorithm and the generalisations which are applied are also minimal. Additionally, as presently implemented these learning actions are applied immediately after a "mismatch" is detected, and such refinements take place regardless of the agent's past behaviour record. In a real life situation it may not be fair, or indeed sensible, to adopt this approach.

The second question that should be asked is how much an agent should be refined (effectively punished or rewarded). The mechanism discussed here refines the competence description of an agent on the extent of the failure or success. An agent that fails a task by a small margin will have its value refined less than an agent that fails a task by a large margin. The converse is true with successful agents. However, there may be situations in which a normally successful agent fails a task by a very large margin, or a normally unsuccessful agent also fails a task again by a large margin. Should the successful agent be punished (have it value refined) as much as the unsuccessful agent or should the successful agent's past record be taken into account when determining the level of punishment?

These questions, and many more like these, are extremely important questions that must be addressed in the design of systems that employ techniques such as those discussed in this section. Rather than addressing these issues here, we investigate an extension to this model that moves toward a coherent model that distinguishes between defection and lack of competence.

4 Adapting Competence Models by Agreement

One of the principal limitations of the mechanism discussed in the previous section is that the model of an agent's competence recorded by the broker is not available to the supplier. A supplier advertises what it believes it can do, and then the broker, following the experience that it has with the supplier fulfilling requests, adapts its beliefs about the competence of that supplier. Furthermore, the broker uses simple episodic information on which to base any adaptations of an agent's competence; it may be more effective to obtain explanations for a failure from the supplier. Here, we extend the model discussed in section 3 to allow the supplier to have some input into how the broker deals with a possible mismatch between its model of the supplier's competence and its behaviour.

The broker records the reputation of suppliers, and under certain conditions (detailed below) it will seek the agreement of a supplier to revise the constraints on the services/task that the supplier has advertised. The broker does not use refinement techniques to directly modify its model of an agent's competence, but to create a revised competence description that is suggested to the supplier. It does, however, record the performance of the agents concerned on the basis of: (i) the number of times that the service type has been used by the agent (N); and (ii) the number of times that the agent has failed that particular service type (F). This provides the broker with an evaluation of the agent's performance $R = \frac{F}{N}$.

The broker agent uses R for two purposes. Firstly, to select an appropriate agent (the agent deemed to be the most appropriate at the present time) for the service based on the service records of all agents. Secondly, it uses R to trigger an attempt to gain the agreement of the supplier for it to revise the model of that supplier's competence. The broker operates as follows. When the broker decides that a task is to be performed, it obtains a list of all competencies that meet the requirements of the task within some δ as before: C_δ. The broker then selects a competence (and hence an agent to be delegated the task) on the basis of the following rules.[1] If the agent has never been used (N = 0), then use that agent (or select a random agent from all those that have not been used). This ensures that all agents in the system will be given the opportunity to carry out a service that they have advertised competence for. If there are no such agents, select the agent/competence pair with the lowest failures/attempts ratio, R. This ensures that the broker chooses the most suitable, and arguably, the most reliable agent. If there is more than one agent/competence pairs with a minimum R value, then the system will select the agent/competence pair from this set with the lowest number of invocations (minimum N), and then pick one at random in the case of a tie. This ensures that the system remains fair and doesn't favour one particular agent.

Following the execution of each task, the broker, as before, checks the output, and proceeds in the following manner. First, N = N + 1 for the selected agent/competence pair. If the agent succeeds and its competence, c, is in the set of competencies $C_\delta \setminus C_0$ — i.e., the supplier succeeded in satisfying a constraint that is outside its advertised competence — then the broker calculates a proposed generalisation and asks the supplier whether or not it agrees to this modification. If the supplier agrees, the broker refines competence c accordingly. If the supplier disagrees no action is taken. If the agent fails, then the broker will attempt to find an alternative agent to perform the task, and if $c \in C_0$ — i.e., the supplier failed to satisfy its advertised competence — then F = F + 1 for that agent/competence pair.

On completion of the transaction, the broker performs the following checks for each agent/competence pair that were involved in the transaction. If the new ratio, R, for that agent/competence pair is above some threshold, τ, the broker calculates a proposed specialisation and asks the supplier whether or not it agrees to this modification. If the supplier agrees, the broker refines the competence as specified, and F = N = 0 for this agent/competence pair.

The main advantages of this system are that the competence model held by the broker is transparent to the supplier agent concerned, and the selection

---

[1]There are many ways in which an agent may be selected given a set of candidate agents. A detailed discussion and analysis of different policies is, however, outside the scope of this paper. Here we present one reasonable strategy that takes into account the information available to the broker.

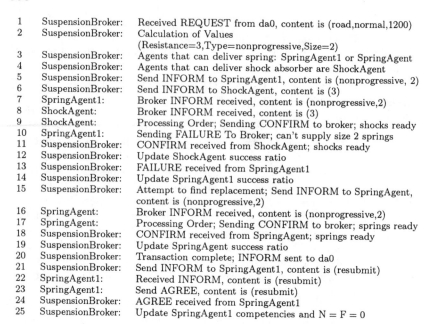

1	SuspensionBroker:	Received REQUEST from da0, content is (road,normal,1200)
2	SuspensionBroker:	Calculation of Values (Resistance=3,Type=nonprogressive,Size=2)
3	SuspensionBroker:	Agents that can deliver spring: SpringAgent1 or SpringAgent
4	SuspensionBroker:	Agents that can deliver shock absorber are ShockAgent
5	SuspensionBroker:	Send INFORM to SpringAgent1, content is (nonprogressive, 2)
6	SuspensionBroker:	Send INFORM to ShockAgent, content is (3)
7	SpringAgent1:	Broker INFORM received, content is (nonprogressive,2)
8	ShockAgent:	Broker INFORM received, content is (3)
9	ShockAgent:	Processing Order; Sending CONFIRM to broker; shocks ready
10	SpringAgent1:	Sending FAILURE To Broker; can't supply size 2 springs
11	SuspensionBroker:	CONFIRM received from ShockAgent; shocks ready
12	SuspensionBroker:	Update ShockAgent success ratio
13	SuspensionBroker:	FAILURE received from SpringAgent1
14	SuspensionBroker:	Update SpringAgent1 success ratio
15	SuspensionBroker:	Attempt to find replacement; Send INFORM to SpringAgent, content is (nonprogressive,2)
16	SpringAgent:	Broker INFORM received, content is (nonprogressive,2)
17	SpringAgent:	Processing Order; Sending CONFIRM to broker; springs ready
18	SuspensionBroker:	CONFIRM received from SpringAgent; springs ready
19	SuspensionBroker:	Update SpringAgent success ratio
20	SuspensionBroker:	Transaction complete; INFORM sent to da0
21	SuspensionBroker:	Send INFORM to SpringAgent1, content is (resubmit)
22	SpringAgent1:	Received INFORM, content is (resubmit)
23	SpringAgent1:	Send AGREE, content is (resubmit)
24	SuspensionBroker:	AGREE received from SpringAgent1
25	SuspensionBroker:	Update SpringAgent1 competencies and $N = F = 0$

Figure 2: Extracts from a simulation of the refinement-by-agreement broker.

strategy outlined above provides a fair distribution of tasks between registered agents. We now illustrate the operation of this broker using the second scenario introduced in section 2.1; extracts from the simulation are presented in figure 2.

Agent da0 initiates the procedure by submitting a request to the broker. As shown in figure 2, the broker has the choice of selecting two spring agents (line 3) both claiming to be capable of performing the task. The broker selects SpringAgent1 because both agents have the same R at this time, and N for this agent/competence pair is less than N for the other option. Unfortunately, SpringAgent1 is unable to complete the transaction (line 10) and so indicates this to the broker who then updates its success ratio (line 14). The broker then attempts to complete the transaction using the alternative spring agent (SpringAgent). This time the transaction can complete and confirmation is sent to the purchasing agent (line 20). Once the transaction has terminated the broker checks the success ratios of all agents and offers a chance to resubmit competencies to any agent that falls below a predetermined threshold value. As SpringAgent1 now falls below this value it is asked to resubmit (line 21). SpringAgent1 is programmed to agree to a resubmit request and so resubmits more realistic competencies (line 23). Its success ratio is reset giving the agent a clean slate albeit with lesser competency values. Note that agents may choose not to resubmit but then run the risk of holding on to a poor success ratio that may prevent them from being chosen for future tasks.

5 Discussion and Future Research

There are many issues that are worthy of discussion here including the need to investigate relaxing some of the assumptions discussed in section 2. However, here we focus on a couple of issues to do with the models presented in sections 3 and 4, because these lead to interesting areas for future research.

The first issue is concerned with how the reputation of an agent is determined. Here, we have assumed that reputation relates to a specific competence of an agent rather than the agent itself. Rather, the reputation of an agent, as perceived by the broker, should be determined by all its encounters with that agent. Thus, to produce an estimate of the reliability of an agent, the broker must take into account a number of episodic encounters with it over time. It is also important to consider issues of deception: the agent may use a strategy of revising its competency adverts in an attempt to hide past defections. This problem may occur in any reputation monitoring system. The sequence of encounters, defections, competency revisions, etc., does, however, provide a rich series of data through which the broker may assess the reliability of an agent. This assessment of reputation is, essentially, a summarisation problem, and it may, therefore, be worthwhile investigating summarisation techniques [3] in producing a solution.

In section 4 the broker gives a service provide agent a choice if it fails to satisfy an advertised competence: it must either agree to a revision of its competence or this failure will be treated as a defection. This is a reasonable stance for the broker to take, but the suggested revision of the competence description originates from the broker. The service provider may have further explanation regarding the cause of the failure that may inform the revision. A further extension to this model may, therefore, be for the recognition of a mismatch between the competence model and the perceived behaviour of the supplier to lead to a more complex dialogue between these two agents focused on determining the reason for failure: an inquiry.

6 Conclusion

In this paper two models of adaptive brokering have been presented: first, a broker that refines its model of agents' competencies on the basis of experience; and second, an extension to this model is explored with a view to showing how these techniques complement existing models of trust and reputation. There are two important advantages to incorporating these refinement techniques in agent-mediated electronic commerce. First, the recognition of a mismatch between and advertised competence and perceived behaviour and refining the model of this agent's competence may lead to fewer inappropriate allocations of tasks in future situations. Second, the investigation triggered by such a mismatch may lead to more accurate assessments of the reliability and hence the reputation of agents within multi-agent systems.

7 Acknowledgements

The initial implementation and evaluation of the adaptive brokering models discussed in this paper was performed by Nial Chapman while he was supported by a MTP EPSRC grant pursuing an MSc in Electronic Commerce Technology [2] at the University of Aberdeen: http://www.csd.abdn.ac.uk/ecommerce.

References

[1] C. Castelfranchi, and R. Falcone, Principles of trust for MAS: Cognitive anatomy, social importance, and quantification, **Proceedings of the Third International Conference on Multi-Agent Systems**, pp. 72–79, 1998.

[2] N. Chapman, **Refining Models of Agent Competencies**, MSc Thesis, University of Aberdeen, 2002.

[3] S. G. Sripada, E. Reiter, J. Hunter, J. Yu and I. Davy, Modelling the task of summarising time series data using KA techniques, in A. Macintosh, M. Moulton and A. Preece (eds), **Applications and Innovations in Intelligent Systems IX**, Springer, pp. 183-196, 2001.

[4] T. M. Mitchell. **Machine Learning**, McGraw-Hill, 1997.

[5] P. Resnick, R. Zeckhauser, E. Friedman and K. Kuwabara, Reputation systems: Facilitating trust in Internet interactions, **Communications of the ACM**, 43(12):45–48, 2000.

[6] J. Sabater and C. Sierra, Reputation and social network analysis in multi-agent systems, In **Proceedings of the First International Joint Conference on Autonomous Agents and Multi-Agent Systems**, pp. 475–482, 2002.

[7] M. Schillo, P. Funk and M. Rovatsos, Using trust for detecting deceitful agents in artificial societies, **International Journal of Applied Artificial Intelligence**, 14(8):825–848, 2000.

[8] M. Winter and D. Sleeman, REFINER+: An efficient system for detecting and removing inconsistencies in example sets, In M. A. Bramer, J. L. Nealon and R. Milne (eds.) **Research & Development in Expert Systems XII**, Information Press Ltd, pp. 115-132, 1995.

[9] B. Yu and M. P. Singh, Distributed reputation management for electronic commerce, **Computational Intelligence**, 18(4):535–549, 2002.

CONOISE: Agent-Based Formation of Virtual Organisations

Timothy J Norman, Alun Preece, Stuart Chalmers

Dept of Computing Science, University of Aberdeen

Aberdeen UK

{tnorman,apreece,schalmer}@csd.abdn.ac.uk

Nicholas R. Jennings, Michael Luck,
Viet D Dang, Thuc D Nguyen

Dept of Electronics and Computing Science, University of Southampton

Southampton UK

{nrj, mml, vdd00r, tdn01r}@ecs.soton.ac.uk

Vikas Deora, Jianhua Shao, W Alex Gray, Nick J Fiddian

Dept of Computer Science, Cardiff University

Cardiff, UK

{v.deora, j.shao, alex, nick}@cs.cf.ac.uk

Abstract

Virtual organisations (VOs) are composed of a number of individuals, departments or organisations each of which has a range of capabilities and resources at their disposal. These VOs are formed so that resources may be pooled and services combined with a view to the exploitation of a perceived market niche. However, in the modern commercial environment it is essential to respond rapidly to changes in the market to remain competitive. Thus, there is a need for robust, flexible systems to support the process of VO management. Within the CONOISE (www.conoise.org) project, agent-based models and techniques are being developed for the automated formation and maintenance of virtual organisations. In this paper we focus on a critical element of VO management: how an effective VO may be formed rapidly for a specified purpose.

1 Introduction

Virtual organisations (VOs) are composed of a number of autonomous entities (representing different individuals, departments and organisations) each of which has a range of problem solving capabilities and resources at their disposal. These entities co-exist and sometimes compete with one another in a ubiquitous virtual marketplace. Each entity attempts to attract the attention of potential customers by describing the cost and qualities of its services, with the goal of selling these services. Sometimes, however, one or more of the entities may realise there are potential benefits to be obtained from pooling resources: either with a competitor (to form a coalition) or with an entity with complementary expertise (to offer a new type of service). When this potential is recognised, the relevant entities go through a process of trying to form a new VO to exploit the perceived niche. Consider two examples. First, suppose that two relatively small airline companies with complementary routes agree to cooperate and coordinate their services so that they may offer flights, as a coalition, between a wider range of destinations, with a view to becoming more competitive in this market. Second, a streamed video content provider and a high bandwidth mobile service provider may agree to collaborate in the delivery of such content as a service to mobile devices — a new type of service. Given the independent nature of the entities involved, there are numerous reasons why the formation of a VO may fail. If it succeeds, however, the collection of independent entities will act as a single conceptual unit in the context of the proposed service (they may continue to retain their individual identity outside this context). In particular, the participants must cooperate and coordinate their activities in delivering the services of this newly formed organisation — the participants must have the ability to manage the VO effectively. In dynamic environments, however, the context may change at any time, such that the VO is no longer viable. It will then need to either disband or re-arrange itself into a new organisation that better fits the prevailing circumstances.

This automated formation and ongoing management of virtual organisations in open environments represents a major research challenge. A key objective in putting such organisations together is to ensure that they are both agile (able to adapt to changing circumstances) and resilient (able to achieve their objectives in a dynamic and uncertain environment). In such environments, the participants' behaviour will be informed by exploiting a number of diverse forms of information — advertisements (capabilities and reputations of individual agents), meta-data (schemas and ontologies) and information resources (databases and knowledge bases).

The CONOISE VO management model builds upon extant research results. In particular, we are exploiting those from two large-scale projects in the broad area of enterprise-wide business management systems: ADEPT [6] and KRAFT [13]. The ADEPT project was concerned with the flexible management (through automated negotiation) of business processes within a static organisational structure. The KRAFT project developed flexible models and techniques for information interchange. Both these projects contribute important elements to CONOISE, but the novel contribution of the CONOISE project is to provide a model of VO management that operates in a robust and resilient manner in complex electronic commerce scenarios. In this paper, we focus on the first element of a complete VO management system: VO formation. The formation of a virtual organisation within the CONOISE system is grounded on three key technologies: the decision-making mechanism of an individual agent, an auction mechanism for the allocation of contracts, and the representation of services. The contribution of this paper lies in the integration of these technologies to provide a solution to the problem of forming effective virtual organisations in complex, information rich environments.

Before the CONOISE solution to VO formation is discussed in detail (section 3), it is important to have a better understanding of the issues that must be considered in developing a computational model of VO formation and to present a specific scenario in which the ideas presented in this paper may be grounded (section 2). Following the detail on VO formation, we discuss avenues for future development by returning to the example introduced in section 2 and present our conclusions to this paper (section 4).

2 A VO Formation Scenario

In presenting an overall picture of the CONOISE VO management process, we will use a specific scenario. This scenario illustrates a number of important characteristics that must be taken into account in the development of an effective VO management system. First, there may be multiple services available from a number of agents representing independent organisations. Multiple agents may offer broadly similar services. The services themselves are described by multiple attributes; for example, price, quality, and delivery time. The services available may change over time: new services may become available, or agents may alter the way in which existing services are offered. Services may differ in terms of the number and heterogeneity of the tasks involved in the delivery of the service and their degree of interdependence, and the type and frequency of interactions between different customers while the service is being delivered. The agents involved in the system may also employ different policies for dealing with the uncertainty inherent in such a domain; for example, an agent may generate slack resources to limit the possibility of a loss in service to the customer, or it may employ rigorous coordination mechanisms to improve supply chain integration.

With these issues in mind, consider the following scenario. A user wants to purchase and receive a monthly movie subscription package on his PDA/phone, and a monthly news service. The user also wants a monthly package for his PDA/phone that includes 30 free text messages and at least 50 free minutes per month. This is a reasonably complex and realistic set of requirements that incorporates four types of service: movies, news, text messaging and a phone service. Within the scenario, a requirements agent, RA, represents this user. In addition to the agent representing the customer's requirements, there are a number of agents representing service providers (SP1–SPn). The services that these agents provide are captured as 'packages', which may represent quite complex offers (see section 3.2). Suppose that agent SP1 offers a number of packages containing news and movies services. The packages on offer may include, for example, news and movies services for one month at £30 per month, and the same service for six months at £25 per month.

Prior to the requirements agent, RA, initiating the process of VO formation, it is assumed that each service provider advertises the services that they offer — e.g. movies or text messaging — to a yellow pages agent (YP). This agent is consulted by the requirements agent and asked to recommend agents that

Service Provider	Movies (per month)	News (no. of daily updates)	Text (no. of free messages)	Phone (no. of free mins.)
SP1	10	24		
SP2		72		
SP3			120	30
SP4	5			30

Table 1: An Example Set of Available Packages

have advertised the ability to deliver movies, news, text messaging or phone services. Following the receipt of this information, the RA will distribute a call for bids to fulfill a specific set of requirements (see figure 1).

In this call for proposals the units movies, news, text messaging and the values associated will represent components in a package and the values and attributes of that package. The service provider agents must now decide whether and what to bid in response to this call. Suppose that there are four service provider agents contacted in this way — SP1–SP4 — and the packages on offer are those illustrated in table 1. Note that SP3 imposes a further constraint of the package that it offers: both the services stated in the package must be taken together. How these packages are constructed is not specified, but an individual service provider could have put a package together from its own resources or through the formation of a virtual organisation.

The requirements agent must, once the deadline for proposals to be submitted has passed, select some combination of services that best suits the needs of the user. An appropriate combination of services given these bids is to take the movies service offered by SP1 (note that this package may be split into its component services), the news service offered by SP2 and both text and phone services offered by SP3. Although the text messaging service requirement is not met, this represents the best choice given the circumstances. Thus, once proposal acceptances and rejections are sent to the agents that submitted bids, a virtual organisation is formed that involves RA, SP1, SP2 and SP3.

We will return to this scenario throughout the following section and then again in section 4 where VO maintenance is discussed as the principal focus of future development. However, at this point we present the detail of the CONOISE VO formation mechanism.

3   The Formation of a Virtual Organisation

As discussed in the introduction, the novelty of this research lies in the technologies being employed in the management of virtual organisations and their integration in a coherent VO management system. Here we focus on the first element of this integrated system: the formation of a VO. In developing a model of VO formation, there are a number of issues that must be taken into account including:

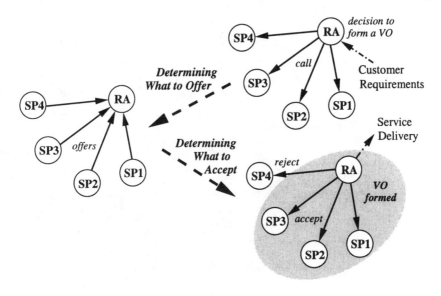

Figure 1: The agent decision making process.

- An agent that is considering whether to offer to join a VO must determine the conditions under which it is profitable for it to join (see section 3.1).

- An agent must be able to recognise circumstances in which it should initiate VO formation (see section 3.1).

- The agent that initiates the VO formation process must, given a number of offers, determine the best combination of business partners (see section 3.2).

- In the support of these decisions, rich descriptions of service quality are required to capture the extent to which services meet the expectations of consumers (see section 3.3).

3.1   Determining What to Offer

The purpose of a service provider agent is be able to create a bid in reply to a call for services, and decide how much resource it can, and more importantly, how much resource it *wants* to provide as a bid for the procurement of that service. Furthermore, any agent may, when considering what to offer, take on the role of the requirements agent in figure 1 and issue a call for bids if it identifies a shortfall in its existing resources available. Each agent must, therefore, be able to act as a contractor and supplier in any given situation.

To give such dual-purpose functionality, we have designed a Constraint Satisfaction Program (CSP) that models the decision making process the agent must take in such scenarios.

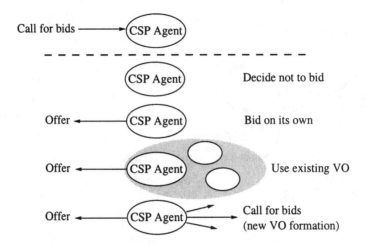

Figure 2: The agent decision making process.

Figure 2 shows one such scenario, where the agent acts as the supplier and receives a call for bids. It has the following possible responses: (i) It can decide *not* to bid for the service; (ii) It can bid using just its own resources; (iii) It can provide a bid from within an existing VO collaboration utilising the combined VO's resources; or (iv) It identifies a need for extra resources not available within the existing VO.

We can see that the last option represents the scenario where the agent becomes the contractor, and itself begins the process of issuing a call for bids to other agents in the environment.

The technique used to provide the decision making process is based on a cumulative scheduling CSP [3]. Usually, this is defined as the maximum allowable limit from a finite 'pool' of resource that *can* be used collectively by the agents at any given time [1]. We define our problem differently; rather than the agents taking resources from a communal resource, we have the agents contributing to the communal resource, and we define a *minimum* allowable limit so that the set of agents *must* provide this service *at least or above* the required threshold limit over the required time. If it is not possible, then we use the CSP to highlight the deficit and can then look to contracting-out for the provision of this shortfall.

To explain our cumulative scheduling based algorithm, we first define the problem. Given a set of n agents in a VO, each of whom can provide a specific finite amount of a resource R, $\{R_1..R_n\}$, a set of start times describing when the agent can begin providing each of the resources $\{S_1..S_n\}$ and a set of durations over which the resource is available $\{D_1..D_n\}$ we can say, for an agent $i \in \{1\ldots n\}$, that the function $\delta_i(t)$ evaluates to 1 if the current time t is within the agent's resource start and end time $(S_i < t \leq (S_i + D_i))$, and 0 otherwise. Then, an amount r of resource R is available over a time period

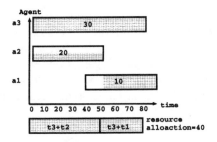

Figure 3: An example schedule.

$1..v$ iff $\forall t \in \{1..v\} \left(\sum_{i=1}^{n} R_i \delta_i(t)\right) \geq r$ In other words, the total sum of the resource provided by the set of agents with indices $\{1 \ldots n\}$ in a VO at any time between $1..t$ does not fall below the resource limit r specified. Using this representation means that we can also use constraints on the agent resource domains to represent existing commitments on those resources.

In our scenario, this helps us to model the decision making process as the agent can look at the existing partners in its VO, as well as its own resources and the existing commitments, and see whether it can accommodate the new allocation of resources asked of it. As an example, let us look at an agent a1 who is in a VO with two other agents a2,a3. All can provide a certain amount of bandwidth (10, 20 and 30 units respectively). Agent a1 is asked to provide a total bandwidth amount of 40 units (as described in the introduction) from time 0 to 80, so it uses the knowledge of the amount of resources contributed from the other agents in the VO (along with its own) to work out if this is possible. Figure 3 shows an example allocation. A total rate of 40 units is provided by a3 and a2 between 0 and 50, then a3 and a1 between 50 and 80. We can also add constraints on the resources available for each agent at each point in time to represent commitments under other contracts.

Of course there are many permutations that we can have in this resource allocation process. What we have described so far shows what the agent *can* do, but we also want to be able to model a utility that allows the agent to choose between competing viable allocations (i.e. decide what it *wants* to do).

We have implemented this utility using constraint reification, where each constraint on the domain of the resource has an associated value, 1 or 0, which depends on the success or failure of the constraint. For instance, using SICStus Prolog notation, X $\leq$ Y# <=> B states that if X is less than Y, the variable B is set to 1, otherwise it is set to 0. When the agents try to provide a new resource we take into account the current commitments of the agent (all the constraints currently posted against the resources) and we get a set of reified values for each commitment which we can then use to see which constraints are satisfiable alongside the new call for bids, and which ones 'fail', and so have a 0 value in their reification, that is, the resources cannot be allocated in the current situation. We can also highlight *where* the new bid is failing and identify the shortfall. Using this information, we also have a basis on which we can look at quality and pricing metrics (see section 3.3) for commitments in comparison to the new resource being bid for, and this therefore allows us to prioritise the commitments we have against any new ones that might arise. Before we discuss quality issues, however, we will address the problem of which offers the agent initiating VO formation should accept to create the best, or at least a satisfactory, VO.

3.2 Determining What to Accept

Since VOs do not have a rigid organisational framework, the selection of partners is one of the most important activities in the formation of the VO [12]. However, there are several requirements that need to be met by this process:

- The most suitable set of partners from those that are available should be selected. In this context, most suitable means the ones with lowest price bids. Note that the *price* here does not just mean the monetary value of the bids but may be a combined rating value, calculated from monetary value and other attributes of the goods/services offered by the partners (e.g. delivery time).

- The selection should occur within a computationally reasonable time frame so that the market niche can be exploited as it becomes available.

- The potential partner should be able to vary their bid depending on their involvement in the VO. Thus, for example, a partner may be willing to complete services more cheaply if it has a high degree of involvement in the VO (because the intrinsic costs can be depreciated over many instances). In contrast, if an agent has a comparatively small involvement then the unit cost may be much higher.

Given the open nature of the environment and the lack of a pre-ordained structure, we believe this creation process is best achieved using some form of marketplace structure (auction). This is because markets are a highly effective structure for allocating resources in situations in which there are many self-interested and autonomous stake-holders. There are, however, many different types of auction (see [15] for a classification) but in this work it was decided to adopt a *combinatorial auction* approach. A combinatorial auction is a sophisticated type of auction where multiple units of multiple (potentially inter-related) items are traded simultaneously. In a combinatorial auction, bidders may bid for arbitrary combinations of items. For example, a single bid may be for 5 movies, 24 news updates (per day) and 20 minutes of phone at a total price p per month. A more complicated bid may be for q_1 movies and q_2 news updates at price $30 * q_1 + 3 * q_2$ if $q_1 < 10$ and $q_2 < 24$, and at price $20 * q_1 + 2 * q_2$ if $q_1 \geq 10$ and $q_2 \geq 24$. This particular type of auction is suitable for this problem because the degree of flexibility in expressing offers allows the potential partners to vary their bid depending on their involvement in the VO.

However, the main disadvantages of combinatorial auctions stem from the lack of a compact and expressive bid representation and efficient clearing algorithms for determining the prices, quantities and trading partners as a function of the bids made. Without such algorithms, because of the computational complexity of the problem, there may be unacceptable delays for auctions that have only a medium number of participants. Thus, in the CONOISE context, a compact and expressive bid representation language and efficient clearing algorithms for combinatorial auctions have been developed [4].

Specifically, we developed a bid presentation language where the price of a package, $P_i(r_1, \ldots, r_m)$ is specified as: $\omega_i(t_1, \ldots, t_m) \cdot (\sum_{j=1}^{m} P_i^j(r_j))$, where P_i^j is the price function of agent i for item j, in the form of a piecewise linear curve (i.e. the function's graph is composed of many segments, each of which is linear), t_j is the segment number of P_i^j that r_j belongs to and ω_i is a function that expresses correlations between items in the set of segments.

More precisely, each piece-wise linear function P_i^j is composed of N_i^j linear segments, numbered from 1 to N_i^j. Each individual segment with segment number l, $1 \leq l \leq N_i^j$, is described by a starting quantity $s_{i,l}^j$ and an ending quantity $e_{i,l}^j$, a unit price $\pi_{i,l}^j$ and a fixed price $c_{i,l}^j$, with the meaning that: bidder i wants to trade any r units of item j, $s_{i,l}^j \leq r \leq e_{i,l}^j$ with the price $P = \pi_{i,l}^j \cdot r + c_{i,l}^j$.

Note that the segments are not required to be continuous; that is, $(s_{i,l+1}^j - e_{i,l}^j)$ may not equal 1. Also, for convenience, we call segment number 0 the segment in which the starting quantity, the ending quantity, the unit price and the fixed price are all equal to 0. Thus, the number of segments of P_i^j, including this special segment, will equal $N_i^j + 1$.

The correlation function ω_i has many potential uses in real-life scenarios. For example, suppose bidder i, selling 3 items (movies, text messages and phone calls), wants to express things like "I am willing to sell 100 minutes of phone calls per month and 50 text messages per month together with a price p, but not separately". Using our correlation function, this can be expressed by adding segments t_1 and t_2, which contain only 100 and 50, to the functions P_i^1 and P_i^2, respectively, then giving $\omega_i(t_1, t_2, t_3)$ a very small value, for every t_3, and giving $P_i^1(100)$ and $P_i^2(50)$ very big values. This way, the auctioneer will never choose to buy 100 minutes of phone calls or 50 text messages separately.

This means of representing bids is novel and superior to popular bid representations. Compared with other work in this area [5, 14] it is more expressive as it allows bidders to detail the correlation between separate items. Compared to XOR atomic proposition presentations, it is nearly as expressive but much more compact. Moreover, this case is important to consider because piecewise linear curves are commonly used in industrial trading applications [5] and any general curve can be approximated arbitrarily closely by a family of such functions [14].

Two sets of clearing algorithms have been developed: one with polynomial complexity and has been shown to produce a solution that is within a finite bound of the optimal, while the other is not polynomial but is guaranteed to produce the optimal allocation. In particular, the former uses a greedy approach, and has a running time of $O(n^2)$, where n is the number of bidders. The solution it produces is shown to be within a finite bound of the optimal, which is proportional to n and K^{m-1}, where m is the number of items and K is a small constant. On the other hand, the latter is guaranteed to produce the optimal allocation, and has a worst-case running time that is proportional to $mn \cdot (K'+1)^{mn}$, where K' is the upper bound on the number of segments of P_i^j. As these two sets of algorithms provide a trade-off between running time and optimality of solution, they provide the user with more flexibility. In cases where the running time is more crucial, the polynomial algorithms would be more appropriate, while in cases where optimality of the solution is more desirable, the optimal algorithms will be better suited.

3.3 Managing Quality of Delivery

In this section we describe the role of the Quality Agent (QA) in the CONOISE solution to the problem of VO management. The QA is responsible for collecting information related to the quality of the services offered by SPs, and to supply this information to the RA agent for it to use in the process of forming a VO. The information about quality of service (QoS) provides another basis for negotiation (in addition to the price), and thus is important to the process of VO formation.

There exist various interpretations of QoS in the literature and a large number of methods have been proposed for managing QoS in marketing, e-commerce and other systems [2, 9, 11, 16, 7]. While some qualities, such as network traffic and speed, may be monitored automatically, more subjective qualities, for example, frequency of news updates, require user preference information. Existing methods typically invite users to rate a service in absolute terms, e.g. *good, bad* or *7 out of 10*. Such quality ratings may not be very meaningful or can even be misleading in some cases, because the context within which the ratings are derived is not known.

In CONOISE, we attempt to address the problem by introducing a model for collecting and monitoring QoS relative to specific users or types of user. That is, we attempt to collect from service users (or their agents) QoS ratings as well as their expectations on QoS, so that we can measure how well a delivered service meets users' expectations. More specifically, let S be a service and $q_1, q_2, \cdots, q_n$ be a set of attributes with which we wish to monitor QoS for S. We collect the following from service users for each q_i of S: $\langle QE(q_i), QP(q_i), QR(q_i) \rangle$ where $QE(q_i)$ represents the QoS that the user expects from S with respect to q_i, $QP(q_i)$ the actual QoS of q_i perceived or experienced by the user after using S, and $QR(q_i)$ the rating that the user gives to S in terms of q_i. All three values are represented by real numbers in the range $[0, 1]$. For example, the quality of news update frequency may be rated by a user as $\langle QE(fr) = 0.65, QP(fr) = 0.76, QR(fr) = 0.85 \rangle$ indicating that an above average frequency was expected (0.65), the actual update delivered was more frequent (0.76) and, consequently,

Agent	SP1	SP2
A1	$< 0.9, 0.7, 0.5 >$	
A2	$< 0.4, 0.4, 0.6 >$	$< 0.4, 0.5, 0.9 >$
A3	$< 0.8, 0.6, 0.3 >$	
A4		$< 0.4, 0.5, 0.8 >$
A5	$< 0.9, 0.7, 0.5 >$	
A6	$< 0.9, 0.7, 0.6 >$	$< 0.9, 0.4, 0.2 >$

Table 2: A set of example quality ratings collected for SP1 and SP2.

the quality of service was considered to be good (0.85).

To combine QoS ratings collected from service users into an overall assessment of quality for a given service S, we perform two calculations: (i) combining individual ratings for each q_i of S into an aggregate rating, and (ii) combining the ratings for individual q_i's into an overall rating for S. Currently, we treat all quality attributes to be of equal importance and (ii) is derived by a simple average of the individual ratings. But it is possible to consider a weighted average so that the fact that some attributes are more significant than the others may be taken into account. The combination of individual ratings depends on the quality assessment request, R, received by the QA. If R specifies no quality expectation on q_i, then $Q(q_i) = \sum_{j=1}^{k} w_j \times QR_j(q_i)$. This is equivalent to the majority of existing approaches to quality calculation; the overall rating for q_i is a weighted sum of individual ratings, and the weights are used to allow factors such as trust to be taken into account [16]. If R specifies a quality expectation $E(q_i) = \alpha \in [0, 1]$ on q_i: (the quality expectation on q_i is α), then $Q(q_i) = \sum_{j=1}^{m} w_j \times QR_j'(q_i)$ Here, $QR_j'(q_i)$ is a rating whose corresponding expectation $QE_j'(q_i)$ is *compatible* with $E(q_i) = \alpha$. In this paper, we use a simple criteria for determining whether the two are compatible: $QE_j'(q_i)$ and $E(q_i) = \alpha$ are compatible if $|QE_j'(q_i) - \alpha| \leq \delta$, where δ is a constant. However, more complex forms of compatibility test are possible, for example, by specifying quality expectations as ranges and by allowing fuzzy matching between $QE_j'(q_i)$ and $E(q_i) = \alpha$. Further discussion on these issues are beyond the scope of this paper.

We now illustrate our quality model and assessment by considering the scenario given in section 2. Suppose that we have six agents (A1–A6) who have used the news services provided by SP1 and SP2. Each agent is then asked to rate the services in terms of news update frequency. Table 2 shows the ratings collected.

In this example, the users of SP1 have high expectations, but do not receive what they expect. Users of SP2, on the other hand, do not have high expectations but are generally satisfied with the service. It is this difference in expectation that QA exploits in assessing QoS for services. Suppose that QA is asked to assess QoS for SP1 and SP2 in terms of news update frequency, fr, given $E(fr)$ not specified, $E(fr) = 0.5$ and $E(fr) = 0, 8$, respectively. Assuming that we have $\delta = 0.1$, the result of calculation is: (i) when $E(\text{fr})$ not specified, QoS of SP1 is 0.50 and QoS of SP2 is 0.63; (ii) when $E(\text{fr}) = 0.5$, QoS of SP1 is 0.60 and QoS of SP2 is 0.85; and (iii) when $E(\text{fr}) = 0, 8$, QoS of SP1 is 0.50 and QoS of SP2 is 0.20. The quality ratings for SP1 and SP2 can, therefore, vary with respect to expectation. This is in contrast to more conventional approaches to quality calculations that do not consider user expectations (equivalent to $E(q_i)$ not specified), our method gives a more meaningful rating for a service on a case-by-case basis.

Finally, it is worth mentioning that although $QP(q_i)$, the quality perceived by the user, is not used in quality calculation at the moment, it can play an important role in deriving more accurate quality assessment. For example, by monitoring the relationship between $QR(q_i)$ and $|QE(q_i) - QP(q_i)|$ over a period of time with sufficient rating data, we can determine whether a particular agent has been "harsh" in rating services. By factoring such knowledge into quality calculations, we can deliver more accurate QoS assessment for the RA agent.

4 Conclusions and Future Development

In this paper, we have focussed our attention of VO formation. However, once formed, a VO must be managed effectively, and, possibly, restructured if new opportunities are identified or problems encountered. Returning to the scenario introduced in section 2, suppose that a new service provider, SP5, enters the environment offering a text messaging service with 200 free messages per month. This opportunity may have been recognised by the RA by monitoring new package advertisements, or by SP5 approaching the manager of the existing VO. If such an opportunity is recognised by RA it may consider re-negotiating the contracts that bind this VO together.

Suppose that RA attempts to re-negotiate with SP3 for just phone calls, and take the text messaging service provided by SP5. However, SP3's deal has a constraint that says both phone calls and text-messaging services must be taken together as a package. RA may then decide to seek an alternative provider of phone calls (in this case SP4). (There may, of course, be penalties to pay for withdrawing from the contract with SP3, and such factors must be taken into account when RA considers restructuring the VO.) As a result of this restructuring, SP3 ceases to be a member of the VO, but two new suppliers — SP4 and SP5 — become involved. It is not only opportunities in the form of new service packages becoming available that the manager of a VO (in this example RA) must take into account. Problems may occur that may force the restructuring of the VO; for example, SP2 may withdraw its news service. This issue of VO restructuring through bi-lateral negotiation is an important focus of interest in the CONOISE project [10], but it is outside the scope of this paper.

One important issue not considered here relates to issues of trust and reputation. Whenever interactions take place between different agents, trust and reputation take on particular significance, especially in the context of virtual organisations in which agents must rely on each other to ensure coherent and effective behaviour. Though some work has been done in this area, the focus on VOs has been limited, with the majority adopting the stance of assuming complete trust, and avoiding the issue. However, as has been recognised [8], questions of deception and fraud in communication and interaction, of assurance and reputation, and of risk and confidence, are critical, especially where interactions take place with new partners. In future work, we will seek to understand the requirements for trust and reputation and evaluate existing models with regard to identifying the specific needs of VOs. Among the potential mechanisms for trust and reputation are centralised reputation systems currently used in the context of marketplaces, and personalised reputation systems in social networks, both of which will be explored.

In conclusion, a flexible mechanism for the formation of VOs has been presented in this paper that combines constraint solving, market clearing and quality modelling techniques. This model has a number of significant advantages. First, through quality modelling and the use of expressive representations of service packages, the CONOISE system may be deployed in realistic electronic commerce scenarios. Second, through the use of state-of-the art market clearing algorithms, VOs formed by the CONOISE can be guaranteed to be within a finite bound of the optimal solution. Finally, taken in the context of the wider VO management process the VO formation mechanism presented in this paper represents a critical element of a flexible and robust solution to the problem of automating the management of virtual organisations.

References

[1] P. Baptiste, C. Le Pape and W. Nuijten, Constraint-based scheduling: Applying constraint programming to scheduling problems, **International Series in Operations Research and Management Science Volume 39**, 2001.

[2] M. Burgess, and W. A. Gray, and N. Fiddian, Establishing a taxanomy of quality for use in information filtering, **Proceedings of 19th British National Conference on Databases**, 2002.

[3] Y. Caseau and F. Laburthe, Cumulative scheduling with task intervals, **Logic Programing Proceedings of the 1996 Joint International Conference and Symposium on Logic Programming**, 363–377, 1996.

[4] V. D. Dang and N. R. Jennings, Polynomial algorithms for clearing multi-unit single-item and multi-unit combinatorial auctions, **Artificial Intelligence**, (to appear).

[5] M. Eso, S. Ghosh, J. Kalagnanam and L. Ladanyi, Bid evaluation in procurement auctions with piece-wise linear supply curves. **IBM Research Report RC 22219**, 2001.

[6] N. R. Jennings, P. Faratin, T. J. Norman, P. O'Brien, and B. Odgers Autonomous Agents for Business Process Management, **International Journal of Applied Artificial Intelligence**, 14(2):145-189, 2000.

[7] Y. W. Lee, D. M. Strong, B. K. Khan and R. Y. Wang, AIMQ: A methodology for information quality assessment, **Information and Management**, 40:133–146, 2002.

[8] M. Luck, P. McBurney and C. Preist, **Agent technology: Enabling next generation computing (a roadmap for agent based computing)**, AgentLink, 2003.

[9] L. Mui, A. Halberstadt and M. Mohtashemi, Notions of reputation in multi-agent systems: A review, **Proceedings of First International Joint Conference on Autonomous Agents and Multi-Agent Systems**, 2002.

[10] T. D. Nguyen and N. R. Jennings, A heuristic model for concurrent bilateral negotiations in incomplete information settings, **Proceedings of the Eighteenth International Joint Conference on Artificial Intelligence**, 2003.

[11] A. Parasuraman, V. A. Zeithaml and L. L. Berry, Reassessment of expectations as a comparison standard in measuring service quality: Implications for future research, **Journal of Marketing**, 58:201–230, 1994.

[12] S. A. Petersen and M. Gruninger, An agent-based model to support the formation of virtual enterprises, **International ICSC Symposium on Mobile Agents and Multi-agents in Virtual Organisations and E-Commerce**, 2000.

[13] A. D. Preece, K. Hui, A. Gray, P. Marti, T. Bench-Capon, D. Jones and Z. Cui, The KRAFT architecture for knowledge fusion and transformation, **Knowledge-Based Systems**, 13(2–3) 113–120, 2000.

[14] T. Sandholm and S. Suri, Market clearability, **Proceedings of The Seventeenth International Joint Conference on Artificial Intelligence**, 1145–1151, 2001.

[15] P. R. Wurman, Dynamic pricing in the virtual marketplace, **IEEE Internet Computing**, 5(2):36–42, 2001.

[16] B. Yu and M. Singh, Distributed reputation management for electronic commerce, **Proceedings of First International Conference on Autonomous Agents and Multi Agent Systems**, 2002.

I-SPY - Anonymous, Community-Based Personalization by Collaborative Meta-Search[*]

Barry Smyth[1,2], Jill Freyne[1], Maurice Coyle[1], Peter Briggs[1], and Evelyn Balfe[1]

[1] Smart Media Institute, University College Dublin,
Dublin, Ireland
[2] ChangingWorlds Ltd.
Trintech Building,
South County Business Park, Leopardstown,
Dublin, Ireland
{firstname.lastname}@ucd.ie

Abstract. Today's Web search engines often fail to satisfy the needs of their users, in part because search engines do not respond well to the vague queries of many users. One potentially promising solution involves the introduction of context into the search process as a means of elaborating vague queries. In this paper we describe and evaluate a novel approach to using context in Web search that adapts a generic search engine for the needs of a specialist community of users. This collaborative search method enjoys significant performance benefits and avoids the privacy and security concerns that are commonly associated with related personalization research.

1 Introduction

The *information overload* problem continues to frustrate Web users as they find it increasingly difficult to locate the right information at the right time, even with today's modern search engines. Many factors are responsible and certainly, the sheer quantity of information, and its growth rate, tax even the most advanced search engines. For example, various estimates indicate that even the largest search engines often cover only a fraction of the available information space [13]. However, this search engine coverage issue is just part of the problem, and indeed can be relieved by using meta-search methods [5, 18]. Perhaps a more pressing issue is the degree to which those pages that are covered can be accurately ranked relative to a given query. In particular, while search engines work very well for properly formulated queries, they come up short when presented with an average Web user's query, which contains only about 2 query terms [12]. The outcome is long lists of apparently relevant results, but with genuinely useful results (for the target user) few and far between. Furthermore these problems are exacerbated by the new generation of mobile Internet devices (eg. WAP

---

[*] The support of the Informatics Research Initiative of Enterprise Ireland is gratefully acknowledged

phones and PDAs)—their restricted input capabilities and limited screen real-estate mean that mobile users are even less likely to provide well formulated queries or tolerate long result-lists.

Generally speaking, recent advances have focused on ways to handle vague queries by improving existing page analysis, indexing and ranking methods. However, vagueness remains a significant problem: a query might include terms that identify the primary information target, but might exclude terms that usefully describe the search *context*. For example, a simple query for *"jaguar"* does not indicate whether the user is interested in cars or cats, and queries for *"Michael Jordan"* do not distinguish between the basketball star, the Berkeley professor, or the recently appointed chairperson of computer-services giant, EDS. Thus, many researchers have recently focused on ways to exploit context in Web search, either by explicitly establishing search context up-front or by implicitly inferring context as part of the search process (see also [11]).

We describe a novel, deceptively simple, yet powerful technique to exploit context during search (Section 3). This *collaborative search* method acts as a post-processing service for existing search engines that re-ranks results based on the learned preferences of a community of users; see also [19]. We describe its implementation in the I-SPY system (http://ispy.ucd.ie) and show how I-SPY achieves this level of personalization in an anonymous fashion, without storing individual user profiles, thus relieving many of the usual privacy issues associated with personalization techniques. In Section 4 we discuss the results of a preliminary live-user trial in which the collaborative search technique is found to enjoy improved result accuracy.

2 Background

The importance of context is well understood in Web search but where does context information come from and how can it be used? There are two basic options: either it can be *explicitly* provided by the user or search engine or it can be *implicitly* inferred from the local search environment; see [11] for a comprehensive review of the use of context in Web search.

2.1 Explicit Context Manipulation

There are two ways to capture explicit context; they are perhaps less interesting from an AI viewpoint, but are outlined here for completeness. Option one asks users to provide context terms as part of their search query. For example, Inquirus 2 [6] supplements a traditional keyword-based query with a context category; users select from a set of categories such as "research paper", "homepage" etc. It is a meta-search engine and uses the context categories to select which search engines to use to satisfy the user's query. The category can also be used for query modification (eg. a query for research papers on *"web search"* might be modified to include terms such as *"references"*). In related work [7] present techniques for automatically learning high-quality query modifications that are capable of improving search precision at reasonable levels of recall.

The second option for introducing context into Web search is to use a specialised search engine whose index has been designed to cover a restricted information domain (eg. www.invisibleweb.com, www.MP3.com, www.ireland.com etc), essentially fixing the context prior to searching. Some specialised search engines automatically maintain their indexes by using information extraction techniques to locate and index relevant content (see [10]). Good examples include CiteSeer [14], for searching scientific literature, and DEADLINER [9], for conference and workshop information. For example, CiteSeer crawls the Web looking for scientific articles in a variety of document formats (HTML, PDF, Postscript etc.) and builds an index that is well suited to literature searching.

2.2   Implicit Context Inference

Establishing the search context by asking users to provide context terms or by fixing the context through the use of a specialised search engine is clearly not a complete solution to the context problem. Whatever about their willingness to use specialised search engines for specialised searches, most users are fundamentally lazy and do not like having to include additional context terms as part of their query. But what if context could be automatically inferred? This question is being answered by a wide range of research focusing on different techniques for capturing different types of context. In fact two basic approaches have become popular depending on whether *external* or *local* context sources are exploited.

External Context Sources. Users rarely perform searches in isolation. It is much more likely that the search will be related to some other task that they are currently performing. Perhaps they are reading a Web page, replying to an email, or writing a document when they need to search for some associated piece of information. By taking advantage of a user's activity immediately prior to the search it may be possible to determine a suitable search context. This is the goal of systems such as Watson [4], the Remembrance Agent [17], and Letizia [15].

Watson and the Remembrance Agent provide just-in-time information access by deriving context from everyday application usage. For example, as a Watson user edits a document in Microsoft Word, or browses with Internet Explorer, Watson attempts to identify informative terms in the target document by using a heuristic term-weighting algorithm. If the user then searches with an explicit query, Watson modifies this query by adding these newly derived terms. Similarly, Letizia analyses the content of Web pages that the user is currently browsing, extracting informative keywords also using similar term-weighting heuristics, and proactively searches out from the current page for related pages. In this sense, Letizia is more of a browsing assistant than a search assistant but it does exploit context in a similar manner.

[8] describes a method that uses categories from the Open Directory Project (ODP) (www.dmoz.org) as a source of context to guide a topic-sensitive version

of PageRank [3]. Briefly, the URLs below each of the 16 top-level ODP categories are used to generate 16 PageRank vectors that are biased with respect to each category. These biased vectors are used to generate query-specific importance scores for ranking pages at query-time that are more accurate than generic PageRank scores. Similarly, for searches performed in context (eg. when a user performs a search by highlighting words in a Web page), context-sensitive PageRank scores can be computed based on the terms and topics in the region of the highlighted terms.

Local Context Sources. Local context analysis and relevance feedback techniques attempt to use the results of a search as the basis for context assessment. These methods analyse search results in order to extract useful context terms which can then be used to supplement the user's original query. Typically these context terms are those terms that are highly correlated in the initial search results. For example, the technique proposed by [16] extracts correlated terms from the top-ranking search results to focus context on the most relevant search results as opposed to the entire set.

This idea of using the local search context can be extended beyond a single search episode. Many users will perform a sequence of searches on a specific topic and their response to the results can provide valuable context information. Thus, by monitoring and tracking queries, results and user actions, it may be possible to model search context over an extended search session or even across multiple search sessions. For example [1] describes the SearchPad system which extracts context information, in the form of useful queries and promising result-lists, from multiple search sessions. Similarly, [2] describe the CASPER search engine for job advertisements, which maintains client-side user profiles that include job cases that users have liked and disliked in previous searches. These profiles are used to classify and re-rank the results of future searches based on features of jobs that users have preferred in the past.

3   Collaborative Search

Collaborative search is motivated by two key ideas. First, specialised search engines attract communities of users with similar information needs and so serve as a useful way to limit variations in search context. For example, a search field on a motoring Web site is likely to attract queries with a motoring theme, and queries like *"jaguar"* are more likely to relate to fast cars than wild cats. Second, by monitoring user selections for a query it is possible to build a model of query-page relevance based on the probability that a given page p_j will be selected by a user when returned as a result for query q_i.

The collaborative search approach combines both of these ideas in the form of a meta-search engine that analyses the patterns of queries, results and user selections from a given search interface. This approach has been fully implemented in the I-SPY search engine and will be detailed and evaluated in the following sections.

3.1 The I-SPY System Architecture

The I-SPY architecture is presented in Fig. 1. Each user query, q, is submitted to the base-level search engines (S_1 - S_n) after adapting q for each S_i using the appropriate adapter. Similarly, the result set, R_i, returned by a particular S_i is adapted for use by I-SPY to produce R_i', which can then be combined and re-ranked by I-SPY, just like a traditional meta-search engine. However, I-SPY's key innovation involves the capture of search histories and their use in ranking metrics that reflect user behaviours.

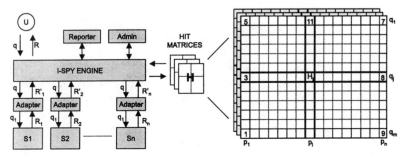

Fig. 1. The I-SPY system architecture.

The unique feature of I-SPY is its ability to personalize its search results for a particular community of users without relying on content-analysis techniques (eg. [2, 12]). To achieve this I-SPY borrows ideas from collaborative filtering research to profile the search experiences of users. Collaborative filtering methods represent user interests in terms of ratings (provided by the user, either implicitly or explicitly) over a set of items (eg. books, CDs, movies, etc.). Recommendations are made to a target user by selecting items from a set of users with correlated rating histories. Thus collaborative filtering operates by exploiting a graded mapping between users and items.

I-SPY exploits a similar relationship between queries and result pages (Web pages, images, audio files, video files etc.) represented as a *hit matrix* (see Fig. 1). It maintains a separate hit matrix for each search community and each element of the hit matrix, H_{ij}, contains a value v_{ij} (that is, $H_{ij} = v_{ij}$) to indicate that v_{ij} users have found page p_j relevant for query q_i. In other words, each time a user selects a page p_j for a query term q_i, I-SPY updates the hit matrix accordingly. For example, consider the situation in which an I-SPY search box is placed on the Web pages of a motoring Web site. This search box will be associated with a specific *search service* within I-SPY and as such is allocated its own hit matrix. The queries submitted through this search box, and results that are subsequently clicked, will be recorded in this particular hit matrix. In general, a single I-SPY deployment may service a number of separate search communities by maintaining separate hit matrices, performance permitting.

3.2 Collaborative Ranking

I-SPY's key innovation is its ability to exploit the hit matrix as a *direct* source of relevancy information; after all, its entries reflect concrete relevancy judgments by users with respect to query-page mappings. Most search engines, on the other hand, rely on *indirect* relevancy judgments based on overlaps between query and page terms, but I-SPY has access to the fact that, historically, v_{ij} users have selected page p_j when it is retrieved for query q_i. I-SPY uses this information in many ways, but in particular the relevance of a page p_j to query q_i is estimated by the probability that p_j will be selected for query q_i (see Equation 1).

$$Relevance(p_j, q_i) = \frac{H_{ij}}{\sum_{\forall j} H_{ij}} \qquad (1)$$

By way of an example, Figs. 2 and 3 show two screen-shots of the I-SPY system. Each presents part of the results page for a query by a computer science student for the *Occam* programming language; in this case a single query term, *Occam*, is used as shown. Fig. 2 shows the standard result-list returned before I-SPY has built up its hit table data and so the results are ordered using a standard meta-search ranking function, giving preference to results that are highly ranked by I-SPY's underlying search engines; in this case, Yahoo! and Splat!, although only Yahoo! results happen to be shown in the screenshots. Clearly the results presented are not so relevant. In fact none of first 4 results shown refer directly to the Occam programming language. For example, the first result is for a page entitled "*What is Occam's Razor?*" and relates to William of Occam's famous principle of choice; this result obtains a ranking score of 25% as indicated.

In contrast, Fig. 3 shows the results for the same query, but after I-SPY has been *trained* by a community of computer science students; see Section 4 for further details. The results are now ranked by I-SPY's relevance metric, as discussed above, rather than by the standard meta-search ranking function. The point is that this time the results are very different; all of the top 4 results are clearly relevant to the Occam programming language rather than other interpretations of the query. For example, the top ranking result, "*The Occam Archive*", has a relevance value of 34%. In other words, this page has been selected 34% of the times that *Occam* has been used as a query. Note that this page is assigned a score of only 11% by the standard meta-search ranking function and previously would have been ranked in 6th position.

3.3 Community Filtering

A key point to understand about this relevancy metric is that it is tuned to the preferences of a particular set of users - the community of I-SPY users - and the queries and pages that they tend to prefer. Deploy I-SPY on a motoring web site and its hit matrix will be populated with query terms and selected pages that are relevant to car fans. Over time the value-space of the relevancy metric will adapt to fit the appropriate query-page mappings that serve this target community. For

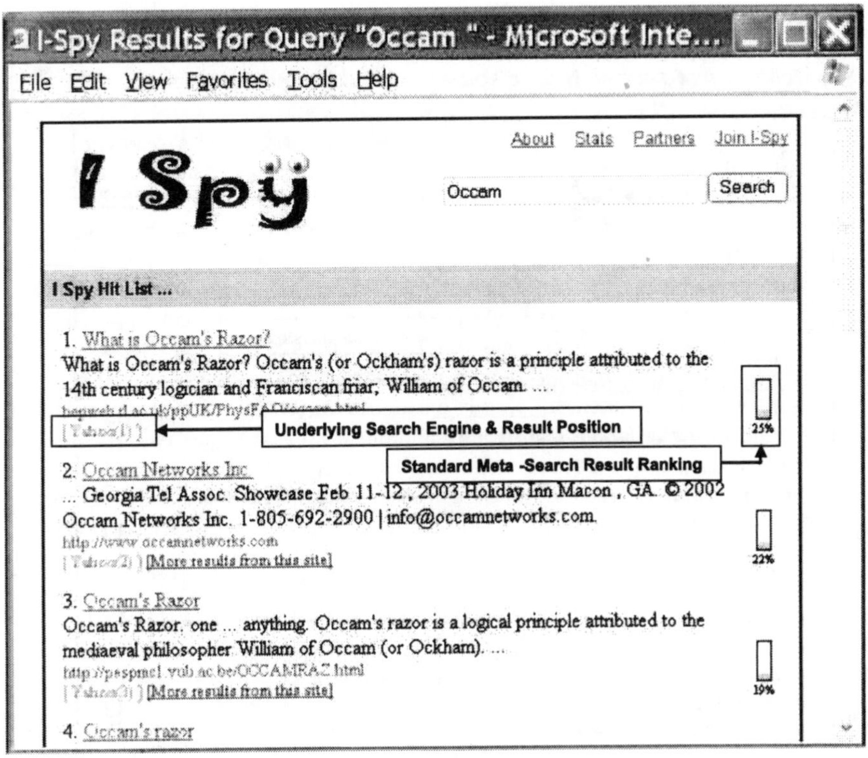

Fig. 2. I-SPY search results before training.

374

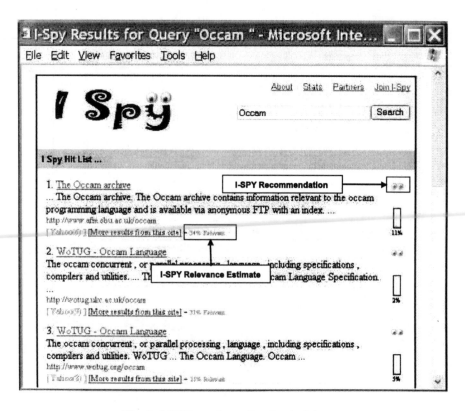

Fig. 3. I-SPY search results after training.

example, queries for *"jaguar"* will tend to result in the prioritisation of car sites because previously when users have submitted this query term they will have selected Jaguar car sites, ignoring the wild cat pages. The wild cat pages may still be returned but will be relegated to the bottom of the result-list.

In fact I-SPY can deploy multiple I-SPY search agents, each with its own separate hit table. Thus the central I-SPY engine can be used to service many different search services across a range of portals, for example, each one adapted for the needs of a particular user group through its associated hit matrix. Alternatively, different hit matrices could be associated with different regions of the same site to bias search with respect to different topics. For instance, above we reviewed work by [8] in which PageRank is biased with respect to different topic groups in an Internet directory (ODP). A similar strategy can be supported by I-SPY. Placing a search box on the *Programming Languages* directory page will naturally tend to capture queries from this domain. The behaviour of the users providing these queries will gradually adjust I-SPY's relevancy metric and ranking function in favour of Programming Languages pages.

I-SPY's administration module (see Figure 1) manages this functionality and also supports the potential for sharing or combining hit matrices when appropriate, as a way of kick-starting the tuning of a new search service, or of broadening the scope of the search bias; for example, a music site may benefit from an I-SPY search service that uses an initial hit matrix that is the combination of hit matrices that have been previously generated from related services such as an entertainment search service and a live concert search service.

4 Evaluation

In this section we describe the results of a preliminary evaluation of I-SPY, focusing on its ability to anticipate the needs of a community of users.

4.1 Methodology

For our evaluation it was appropriate to focus on a specific search domain. We chose that of programming languages and selected the names of 60 programming languages listed by Yahoo!. I-SPY was configured to query two underlying search engines, Yahoo! (which uses Google) and Splat!, and each of the 60 queries was submitted to I-SPY to obtain a set of results pages based on a standard meta-search ranking function. This produced 60 result-lists containing between 10 and 30 results and with a median of 27 results.

A group of 20 computer science students took part in the evaluation. These students were asked to analyse each result-list and select those results that appeared to be relevant, based on the summary result description returned by I-SPY (which is the summary description returned by Yahoo! and/or Splat!).

Next, a leave-one-out relevancy evaluation was performed. Each user in turn was designated the *test* user with the remaining 19 serving as *training* users. The relevancy results produced by the training users are used to populate I-SPY's hit

376

matrix and the results for each query were re-ranked using I-SPY's behavioural ranking metric. Next we counted the number of these results listed as relevant by the test user for different result-list size limits (k); here $k = 5..30$, and result-lists with fewer than k items did not contribute to the results for that list size. Finally, we also made the equivalent relevancy measurements by analysing the results produced by the untrained version of I-SPY (*Standard*), which uses the standard meta-search ranking metric and which serves as a benchmark. So for each query, and each test user, we have the number of relevant results returned by I-SPY and by Standard for various different result-list sizes.

4.2 Results

Figure 4(a) presents these results for I-SPY and the benchmark search engine, as a graph of the mean number of relevant pages across all 20 users and 60 queries, and for each result-list size. Clearly the results indicate that I-SPY's collaborative search technique has a positive impact in terms of the number of relevant items returned. For example, when the results are restricted to the top 5 we find that the benchmark only returns 3.16 relevant pages on average, compared with 4.8 pages for I-SPY's behavioural ranking metric; a relative increase for I-SPY of over 50%. Put another way: I-SPY can retrieve about 8 relevant results with result-list sizes of 10 items. To retrieve the same number of relevant items takes our benchmark system 20 items.

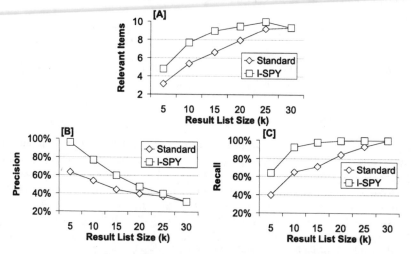

Fig. 4. Experimental results.

The I-SPY benefit is preserved across all result-list sizes although the relative benefit naturally decreases as the result-list increases to its maximum size of 30 items; at this size both engines retrieve the same number of relevant items since both have access to the same list of results and differ only in the way that they order them.

Fig. 4(B&C) present the corresponding precision and recall results. Briefly, the precision of a list of k results is the percentage of these k that are relevant, while the recall of a list of k results is the percentage of the relevant results that are among the k. Because of our experimental design these are really *bounded* versions of the standard precision and recall metrics and the measures for each engine will converge once a complete result-list is returned.

The results indicate a significant and consistent benefit for I-SPY over the standard meta-search benchmark. For example, for result-lists of 5 items, I-SPY achieves a precision of just over 96% compared to the standard meta-search precision of only 63%. Similarly, at the same list size, we find an average recall for I-SPY of 64% compared to just under 40% for the standard method. Indeed we see that I-SPY achieves 100% recall at just over 20 items; it takes the benchmark 30 items to achieve the same level of recall.

In summary, the above results indicate that I-SPY enjoys a clear advantage over the benchmark meta-search engine. Moreover, the fact that larger relative benefits are available at smaller result-list sizes is particularly interesting and useful. Users rarely sift through large result-lists even when they are returned and so the more relevant items that can be presented earlier on, the better; this is why it is important to evaluate precision and recall at different list sizes. In addition, these results indicate that I-SPY's technology is likely to be especially valuable in situations where large result-lists must be truncated for external reasons. This is commonly the case with mobile applications because of the limited screen-space of current mobile devices; many mobile devices are capable of displaying less than 5 items per screen.

5 Discussion

Finally, before concluding we discuss some further applications of collaborative search including its ability to guide query elaboration and page similarity predictions, as well as its use in multimedia retrieval domains. We also highlight some important issues that must be addressed if applicability is to be guaranteed across all domains.

5.1 Query Elaboration & Page Similarities

I-SPY's hit matrix can be used to estimate query term similarities and page similarities as well as query-page relevance. For example, the correlation between two hit matrix rows, corresponding to queries q_x and q_y, is a measure of the relationship between the relevancy of the different pages that have been selected for these queries. A strong positive correlation means that the same pages tend to be judged similarly for both queries. This indicates a potential relationship between q_x and q_y. Moreover, if q_x and q_y have a strong correlation, and a proper subset of q_x's relevant pages are found to be relevant for q_y then q_x might be a more general query than q_y. This type of information can be a valuable source of knowledge for query modification techniques that add related query terms (more specialised or generalised) to help cope with vague or under-specified queries.

Similarly, column correlations are used to compute result similarities as a way of automatically suggesting related pages to a user that may not have a direct similarity (in terms of term-overlap) to the specified query terms, and thus pages that would not be selected by the base-level search engines.

5.2 Multimedia Content

I-SPY's collaborative ranking, query elaboration and result similarity strategies can pay significant dividends in domains where traditional indexes are difficult or expensive to compile. For example, indexing non-textual content (music, graphics etc.) is expensive because of the lack of automatic indexing techniques. Consider an MP3 search engine and a preliminary index whereby individual MP3 files are manually indexed according to basic genre categories, with additional information (such as artist, album name, and title words) extracted by heuristic methods. Furthermore, assume that the Celine Dion song, "*My Heart Will Go On*" (the theme from the hit movie, Titanic) does not contain "*Titanic*" as a default index term, so searches on this term will fail to retrieve this result. For example, although Google is very good at retrieving songs by their title (as one would expect, since song titles are usually relatively unique) it fails to perform well when less specific queries are submitted; for instance, the above song is not returned in the top 100 results for the query "*Titanic*".

Occasionally a user will add "Celine Dion" to their failed "*Titanic*" query and get the above result. If they select it then I-SPY will log this in its hit table for the three query terms and, as a result, I-SPY now has the potential to suggest the above result in the future for the lone "*Titanic*" query. By taking advantage of these occasional query correlations I-SPY can effectively enhance the coverage, precision and recall of the underlying search engine irrespective of its content type or index completeness.

5.3 The Cold-Start Problem and Relevancy Biases

There are a number of important problems with collaborative search that need to be addressed in order to guarantee its full applicability across a broad range of search tasks. Perhaps the most important problem is the so-called *cold-start problem*, which refers to the fact that newly indexed Web pages will find it difficult to attract user attention since they will, by default, have a low relevancy score using I-SPY's metric and thus appear far down in result-lists, thus limiting their ability to attract the hits they may deserve for a given query. Essentially there is an in-built bias towards older pages.

There are a number of ways that this problem might be dealt with. One is to look at ways to normalise the relevancy of pages with respect to their *age*. For example, we might measure the age of a page by the time (or number of queries) since its first hit and amplify the relevancy of young pages relative to older pages.

Indeed there is another side to this problem. Just as new pages find it difficult to attract hits, so too older pages may find it too easy to attract hits. In the worst case scenario this could even bias I-SPY's result-lists towards pages that are likely to be out of date and thus less relevant to current users than they were to past users. Once again, biasing relevance towards new pages should help to cope with this problem.

Of course in general there are many factors that can and probably should be taken into account when ranking search results. We have focused primarily on I-SPY's relevancy factor, but other factors such as the age of a page and its meta-search ranking are also appropriate. As part of our future work we will explore how best to combine these factors to produce optimal result rankings. This may or may not involve a direct combination of the rankings. For example, one option is to present search results not as a single list of results, as is normally the case, but perhaps as two or more lists of results in order to emphasise the different qualities of the returned pages. For instance, in general only a subset of search results are likely to have non-zero I-SPY relevance scores (that is, a subset will have been selected in the past for the current query) and so it is practical to present the I-SPY results that do have relevancy scores as special recommendations (ranked by their relevancy) while presenting the remaining results separately, ranked by their meta-score. In turn a third list of new pages, ranked by meta-search score or relevancy, could also be separately presented.

6 Conclusions

Improving the accuracy of Web search engines by introducing context into the search process is an important and challenging research problem. In this paper we have described the I-SPY system which attempts to discover patterns in the activity of a community of searchers in order to determine general search context and prioritise search results accordingly. I-SPY can be used in collaboration with any underlying search engines, and builds a relevancy model based on the selection histories of its user community. This model can be used to re-rank search results based on the past selections of I-SPY users and we have shown that this approach can lead to significant improvements in overall search accuracy.

I-SPY's collaborative search method makes no strong assumptions about the form of the underlying search engines and is generally applicable across a range of content types. Its ranking metric is computationally efficient ($O(k)$ in the number of search results) and requires no additional parsing of result pages. Finally, its ability to personalize search results for the needs of a community is possible without the need to store individualised search histories; no individual user profiles are stored and no user identification is necessary. This has significant security and privacy advantages compared to many more traditional approaches to personalization.

References

1. K. Bharat. SearchPad: Explicit Capture of Search Context to Support Web Search. In *Proceedings of the Ninth International World-Wide Web Conference*, 2000.
2. K. Bradley, R. Rafter, and B. Smyth. Case-based User Profiling for Content Personalization. In O. Stock P. Brusilovsky and C. Strapparava, editors, *Proceedings of the International Conference on Adaptive Hypermedia and Adaptive Web-based Systems*, pages 62–72. Springer-Verlag, 2000.
3. S. Brin and L. Page. The Anatomy of A Large-Scale Web Search Engine. In *Proceedings of the Seventh International World-Wide Web Conference*, 2001.
4. J. Budzik and K. Hammond. User Interactions with Everyday Applications as Context for Just-In-Time Information Access. In *Proceedings International Conference on Intelligent User Interfaces*. ACM Press, 2000.
5. D. Dreilinger and A. Howe. Experiences with Selecting Search Engines Using Meta Search. *ACM Transactions on Information Systems*, 15(3):195–222, 1997.
6. E. Glover, S. Lawrence, M. D. Gordon, W. P. Birmingham, and C. Lee Giles. Web Search - Your Way. *Communications of the ACM*, 2000.
7. E. J. Glover, G. W. Flake, S. Lawrence, W. P. Birmingham, A. Kruger, C Lee Giles, and D. M Pennock. Improving Category Specific Web Search by Learning Query Modifications. In *Proceedings of the Symposium on Applications and the Internet (SAINT)*, pages 23–31. IEEE Computer Society, 2001.
8. T. H. Haveliwala. Topic-Sensitive PageRank. In *Proceedings of the World-Wide Web Conference*. ACM Press, 2002.
9. A. Kruger, C Lee Giles, F. Coetzee, E. Glover, G. Flake, S. Lawrence, and C. Omlin. Building a New Niche Search Engine. In *Proceedings of the Ninth International Conference on Information and Knowledge Management.*, 2000.
10. N. Kushmerick. Wrapper Induction for Information Extraction. In *Proceedings of the International Joint COnference on Artificial Intelligence*, pages 729–735. Morgan-Kaufmann, 1997.
11. S. Lawrence. Context in Web Search. *IEEE Data Engineering Bulletin*, 23(3):25–32, 2000.
12. S. Lawrence and C. Lee Giles. Context and Page Analysis for Improved Web Search. *IEEE Internet Computing*, July-August:38–46, 1998.
13. S. Lawrence and C. Lee Giles. Accessibility of Information on the Web. *Nature*, 400(6740):107–109, 1999.
14. S. Lawrence and C. Lee Giles. Searching the Web: General and Scientific Information Access. *IEEE Communications*, 37(1):116–122, 1999.
15. H. Lieberman. Letizia: An Agent That Assists Web Browsing". In C. Mellish, editor, *Proceedings of the International Joint Conference on Artificial Intelligence, IJCAI'95*, pages 924–929. Morgan Kaufman Publishers, 1995. Montreal, Canada.
16. M. Mitra, A. Singhal, and C. Buckley. Improving Automatic Query Expansion. In *Proceedings of ACM SIGIR*. ACM Press, 1998.
17. B. J. Rhodes and T. Starner. Remembrance Agent: A Continuously Running Automated Information Retrieval System. In *Proceedings of the First International Conference on the Practical Applications of Intelligent Agents and Multi-Agent Technologies.*, pages 487–495, 1996.
18. E. Selberg and O. Etzioni. The Meta-Crawler Architecture for Resource Aggregation on the Web. *IEEE Expert*, Jan-Feb:11–14, 1997.
19. B. Smyth, E. Balfe, P. Briggs, M. Coyle, and J. Freyne. Collaborative Web Search. In *Proceedings of the 18th International Joint Conference on Artificial Intelligence, IJCAI-03*. Morgan Kaufmann, 2003. Acapulco, Mexico.

Balancing User Satisfaction and Cognitive Load in Coverage-Optimised Retrieval

David McSherry

School of Computing and Information Engineering, University of Ulster, Coleraine BT52 1SA, Northern Ireland

Abstract

Coverage-optimised retrieval (CORE) is a new approach to retrieval in recommender systems which provides full *coverage* of the case library in the sense that for any case that is acceptable to the user, one of the recommended cases is at least as good in an objective sense and so also likely to be acceptable. Similarity to a target query representing the user's requirements is the weakest of several *preference* criteria according to which a given case may be considered at least as good as another in CORE. A basic premise in the approach is that the stronger the preference criterion on which a recommendation is based, the more likely it is to be acceptable to the user. However, the strength of the preference criterion must be balanced against the size of the retrieval set required to provide full coverage of the case library. We present a detailed analysis of retrieval in CORE that aims to increase our understanding of the trade-off between user satisfaction and cognitive load in the approach.

1 Introduction

An advantage of case-based reasoning (CBR) as an approach to product recommendation is that if none of the available products exactly matches the user's query, she can be shown the cases that are most *similar* to her query [1]. A basic premise in the approach is that one of the recommended cases may be acceptable to the user even though it fails to satisfy one or more of her requirements. However, several authors have questioned the assumption that the most similar product is the one that is most acceptable to the user [2,3,4]. For example, a case that satisfies only two of the user's requirements may be more similar than one that satisfies three of her requirements; or the most similar case may fail to satisfy a requirement that the user considers to be essential. The k-NN strategy of retrieving the k most similar cases, rather than a single case, only partially compensates for this limitation, as the number of cases that can be presented to the user is necessarily restricted in practice [4,5].

Thus the existence of a case in the case library that would be acceptable to the user does not guarantee that it will be retrieved. While retrieving every case in the case library is seldom feasible in practice, we argue that the next best thing is to ensure that for any case that is acceptable to the user, the retrieval set contains a case that is as at least as good in an objective sense and so also likely to be acceptable. This is the aim of a new approach to retrieval in recommender systems which we refer to as *coverage-optimised* retrieval (CORE) [6].

The CORE retrieval set provides full coverage of the case library in the sense that for any case that is acceptable to the user, one of the recommended cases is at least as good according to a given *preference* criterion. Similarity to the target query is the weakest of several preference criteria according to which a given case may be considered at least as good as another in CORE. A basic premise in the approach is that the stronger the preference criterion on which a recommendation is based, the more likely it is to be acceptable to the user. However, the size of the retrieval sets that a retrieval algorithm produces is an important factor in its ability to address the trade-off between user satisfaction and cognitive load to which Branting [5] refers. The strength of the preference criterion on which retrieval is based in CORE must therefore be balanced against the size of the retrieval set required to provide full coverage of the case library. Here we present a detailed analysis of retrieval in CORE that aims to increase our understanding of the trade-off between user satisfaction and cognitive load in the approach.

In Section 2, we examine four different preference criteria on which retrieval may be based in CORE. We also show that k-NN provides only limited coverage of the case library with respect to preference criteria that may be more predictive of user satisfaction than similarity to the target query. In Section 3, we describe how the retrieval set is constructed in CORE and examine factors that affect the trade-off between user satisfaction and cognitive load. Related work is discussed in Section 4 and our conclusions are presented in Section 5.

2 The CORE Preference Criteria

In this section, we examine four preference criteria that can be used to guide the retrieval process in CORE. We also present an empirical evaluation of the coverage provided by k-NN with respect to these preference criteria.

2.1 The Similarity Criterion

Similarity to a target query representing the requirements of the user is the standard preference criterion in CBR approaches to product recommendation [2]. The similarity of a given case C to a target query Q over a subset A_Q of the case attributes A is typically defined as:

$$Sim(C, Q) = \frac{\sum_{a \in A_Q} w_a sim_a(C, Q)}{\sum_{a \in A_Q} w_a} \qquad (1)$$

where for each $a \in A_Q$, w_a is a numeric weight representing the importance of a and $sim_a(C, Q)$ is a measure of the similarity of $\pi_a(C)$, the value of a in C, to $\pi_a(Q)$, the preferred value of a. The preference criterion we refer to as the *similarity* criterion is defined below in terms of this notation.

The Similarity Criterion. *In the context of a target query Q, a given case C_1 is at least as good as another case C_2 if $Sim(C_1, Q) \geq Sim(C_2, Q)$.*

In many e-commerce domains, one can identify attributes whose values most users would prefer to maximise (e.g. the amount of memory in a PC) or minimise (e.g. price). We will refer to these as *more-is-better* (MIB) and *less-is-better* (LIB) attributes respectively and assume that the value specified by the user is a preferred minimum in the case of a MIB attribute, or a preferred maximum in the case of a LIB attribute.

Often in practice, the local similarity measure for a MIB attribute assigns the highest possible similarity score to any case whose value for the attribute equals or exceeds the preferred minimum value [1,7,8]. However, the implication that all values that exceed the specified minimum are equally preferred is unrealistic. Another potential drawback is that the attribute's discriminating power may be reduced, particularly if the user chooses a "modest" value that is exceeded by the majority of cases in the case library.

We have similar reservations about local similarity measures that assign the highest possible similarity score to any case whose value for a LIB attribute is less than the preferred maximum. To address this issue, McSherry [3] proposes an approach to assessing the similarity of a given case with respect to MIB and LIB attributes which recognises that not all values which exceed a preferred minimum, or fall below a preferred maximum, are likely to be equally preferred. Accordingly, we use the following similarity measures for MIB attributes in our experiments:

$$sim_a(C, Q) = \frac{\pi_a(C) - \min(a)}{\max(a) - \min(a)} \tag{2}$$

where $\min(a)$ and $\max(a)$ are the minimum and maximum values of a in the case library. Also as proposed in [3], our similarity measure for LIB attributes is:

$$sim_a(C, Q) = \frac{\max(a) - \pi_a(C)}{\max(a) - \min(a)} \tag{3}$$

It is worth noting that we measure the similarity or *utility* of a given case with respect to a MIB or LIB attribute in a way that is independent of the user's query. As we shall see, however, preferred minimum and maximum values specified by the user play an important role in some of the CORE preference criteria.

2.2 The Compromise Criteria

Apart from similarity to the target query, another factor that is likely to influence the acceptability of a given case is the number of *compromises* it involves; that is, the number of attributes with respect to which it fails to satisfy the user's requirements. For example, a PC may satisfy the requirements of the user with respect to type and processor speed but not make or price. In terms of the attribute types discussed in Section 2.1, a product may fail to satisfy the requirements of the user in one or more of the following ways:

- Its value for a nominal attribute may not be the preferred value
- Its value for a MIB attribute may be less than the preferred minimum
- Its value for a LIB attribute may be greater than the preferred maximum

The above list can easily be extended to include other attribute types such as numeric attributes for which the user has in mind an ideal value and regards any departure from that value as a compromise [3]. For any case C and target query Q, we define:

$$compromises(C, Q) = \{a \in A_Q : \pi_a(C) \text{ fails to satisfy the user's requirements}\} \quad (4)$$

Thus $compromises(C, Q)$ is the set of attributes with respect to which C fails to satisfy the requirements of the user. As noted by Burkhard [2], compromises that the user may be prepared to make are often unrelated to the importance of the attributes in her query and cannot be predicted *a priori*. For example, even if the user considers price to be very important, she may be prepared to pay a little more than she intended for a product that meets her expectations with respect to other attributes. On the other hand, some of the user's requirements may in reality be hard constraints that she is not prepared to relax.

The preference criterion we refer to as the *weak* compromise criterion recognises the role of compromise in the acceptability of a recommended product. Specifically, it states that a given product is at least as good as another if it is at least as similar to the user's query and involves fewer compromises (or the same number of compromises).

The Weak Compromise Criterion. *In the context of a target query Q, a given case C_1 is at least as good as another case C_2 if $Sim(C_1, Q) \geq Sim(C_2, Q)$ and $|compromises(C_1, Q)| \leq |compromises(C_2, Q)|$.*

The weak compromise criterion is stronger than the similarity criterion and may therefore be more predictive of user satisfaction. Often, however, a user may be prepared to compromise only on certain attributes. In this case it is the *combination* of attributes in which a product differs from her query that matters, and not just the number of attributes [3]. This aspect of customer behaviour is recognised in the preference criterion we refer to as the *strong* compromise criterion.

The Strong Compromise Criterion. *In the context of a target query Q, a given case C_1 is at least as good as another case C_2 if $Sim(C_1, Q) \geq Sim(C_2, Q)$ and $compromises(C_1, Q) \subseteq compromises(C_2, Q)$.*

According to the strong compromise criterion, a given product is at least as good as another if it is at least as similar to the user's query and differs from her query in a subset of the attributes in which the other case differs from her query. This is obviously the stronger of our two compromise criteria. That is, if a given case is at least as good as another according to the strong compromise criterion, then it is at least as good according to the weak compromise criterion.

2.3 The Dominance Criterion

One of the strongest criteria according to which a user might be expected to consider a given product to be at least as good as another is that the first product is at least as good as the second with respect to *all* her stated requirements. We will refer to this as the *dominance* criterion.

The Dominance Criterion. *In the context of a target query Q, a given case C_1 is at least as good as another case C_2 if $sim_a(C_1, Q) \geq sim_a(C_2, Q)$ for all $a \in A_Q$.*

For example, if one PC has a faster processor and a lower price than another PC of the same make and type, then it is reasonable to expect a user who expresses her requirements in terms of these attributes to prefer the first PC.

Though not expressed in terms of compromise, the dominance criterion is in fact stronger than either of our two compromise criteria. Our proof of this important result relies on the assumption that:

$$sim_a(C, Q) = 1 \text{ if and only if } \pi_a(C) = \pi_a(Q) \qquad (5)$$

for any case C, query Q, and nominal attribute $a \in A_Q$. Because of the limitations of space, we also restrict our attention to the attribute types used in our experiments.

Theorem 1. *If C_1 is at least as good as C_2 according to the dominance criterion, then C_1 is at least as good as C_2 according to the strong compromise criterion.*

Proof. If C_1 is at least as good as C_2 according to the dominance criterion and $a \in A_Q$ is a MIB attribute such that $a \notin compromises(C_2, Q)$ then it follows from (2) that:

$$\pi_a(C_1) \geq \pi_a(C_2) \geq \pi_a(Q)$$

Thus $a \notin compromises(C_1, Q)$. Similarly, $a \notin compromises(C_1, Q)$ for any LIB attribute such that $a \notin compromises(C_2, Q)$. On the other hand, if $a \in A_Q$ is a nominal attribute such that $a \notin compromises(C_2, Q)$ then it follows from (5) that:

$$sim_a(C_1, Q) \geq sim_a(C_2, Q) = 1$$

and so $a \notin compromises(C_1, Q)$.

We have now established that $compromises(C_1, Q) \subseteq compromises(C_2, Q)$. Finally, it is clear that $Sim(C_1, Q) \geq Sim(C_2, Q)$ and so C_1 is at least as good as C_2 according to the strong compromise criterion as required.

2.4 Coverage in *k*-NN

In order of increasing strength, we will refer to our four preference criteria as P0 (the similarity criterion), P1 (the weak compromise criterion), P2 (the strong compromise criterion), and P3 (the dominance criterion). Below we formally define the concept of *coverage* with respect to a given preference criterion.

Definition 1. *We say that a given case C_2 is covered by a retrieval set RS with respect to a given preference criterion if $C_2 \in RS$ or there exists $C_1 \in RS$ such that C_1 is at least as good as C_2 according to the given preference criterion.*

The importance of coverage in this sense is that if an acceptable case that is not retrieved is covered by a retrieved case, then the retrieved case is also likely to be acceptable to the user. Another basic premise in our approach is that the likelihood of the retrieved case also being acceptable increases with the strength of the preference criterion with respect to which it covers the acceptable case. For example, if it covers the acceptable case only with respect to P0, this may not be enough to ensure that it is also acceptable. On the other hand, if it covers the acceptable case with respect to P3, then there is no attribute with respect to which it is less similar to the user's query.

Whether or not an excluded case is covered by the retrieval set for a given query depends on how the retrieval set is constructed and the preference criterion in terms of which coverage is defined. According to P0, the case that is most similar to the target query is at least as good as any other case. It follows that full coverage of the case library with respect to P0 is guaranteed in *k*-NN, since the retrieval set in this approach always includes the most similar case.

We now examine the levels of coverage provided by *k*-NN with respect to preference criteria P1, P2 and P3 for a recommender system in the PC domain. The case library contains the descriptions of 120 personal computers [9]. The attributes in the case library and weights assigned to them in our experiments are type (8), price (7), manufacturer (6), processor (5), speed (4), screen size (3), memory (2), and hard-disk size (1). Speed, screen size, memory, and hard-disk size are treated as MIB attributes in our experiments while price is treated as a LIB attribute. Our experimental design is based on a *leave-one-out* approach in which we temporarily remove each case from the case library and present its description as a query to the recommender system. For each query, we record the percentage of cases in the case library that are covered with respect to P1, P2 and P3 by the *k*-NN retrieval sets for $k = 1$ to 10. Average levels of coverage over all simulated queries are shown in Figure 1.

Though coverage with respect to P1 is very high for all retrieval-set sizes, it remains slightly less than 100% even for $k = 10$. This means that for at least one query there is a case that satisfies the user's requirements with respect to more attributes than any of the ten most similar cases. Though relatively low for small retrieval sets, coverage with respect to P2 increases with retrieval-set size to a maximum of 92% for $k = 10$. Even for $k = 10$, the *k*-NN retrieval set covers only 40% of cases on average with respect to P3, the strongest of our preference criteria.

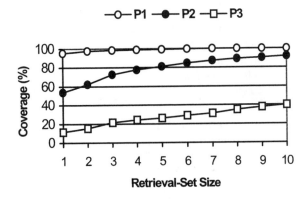

Figure 1. Coverage of the PC case library with respect to preference
criteria P1, P2 and P3 in k-NN

3 The CORE Retrieval Set

The aim in CORE is to construct a retrieval set of the smallest possible size that
provides full coverage of the case library with respect to a given preference
criterion. In this section, we describe how such a retrieval set is constructed and
examine factors that influence the size of the retrieval set required to provide full
coverage of the case library.

3.1 The Retrieval Process

In the algorithm outlined in Figure 2, Q is the target query and *Candidates* is a list
of candidate cases for addition to the retrieval set. CORE's assessment of whether
or not a given case is at least as good as another may be based on any of the
preference criteria P0-P3 described in Section 2. We assume that the candidate
cases, initially all cases in the case library, are sorted in order of non-increasing
similarity to the target query. We also assume that if C_1, C_2 are equally similar
cases such that C_1 is *better* that C_2 according to the given preference criterion, then
C_1 is listed before C_2 in *Candidates*.

Theorem 2. *The CORE retrieval set provides full coverage of the case library
with respect to the preference criterion on which retrieval is based. Moreover, no
smaller retrieval set can provide full coverage of the case library.*

Proof. A candidate case C_2 can fail to be included in the CORE retrieval set only
if there is already another case C_1 in the retrieval set which is such that C_1 is at
least as good as C_2. The proof that no smaller retrieval set can provide full
coverage of the case library relies on the *pigeon-hole* principle [10]. The details
are omitted because of the limitations of space.

```
algorithm CORE(Q, Candidates)
begin
    RetrievalSet ← φ
    while |Candidates| > 0 do
    begin
        C₁ ← first(Candidates)
        RetrievalSet ← {C₁} ∪ RetrievalSet
        covers(C₁) ← {C₁}
        for all C₂ ∈ rest(Candidates) do
        if C₁ is as at least as good as C₂
        then  covers(C₁) ← covers(C₁) ∪ {C₂}
        Candidates ← Candidates - covers(C₁)
    end
    return RetrievalSet
end
```

Figure 2. Algorithm for coverage-optimised retrieval

We will refer to the CORE algorithms in which retrieval is based on preference criteria P1, P2 and P3 as CORE-1, CORE-2 and CORE-3 respectively. It is worth noting that with P0 as the preference criterion, CORE is equivalent to 1-NN, and so CORE is in fact a generalisation of similarity-based retrieval.

3.2 Retrieval-Set Size

As we now show, the size of the CORE retrieval set depends on the strength of the preference criterion on which retrieval is based, the number of cases in the case library, and the length of the user's query.

Proposition 1. *The maximum possible size of the* CORE-1 *retrieval set for a given query Q is* $|A_Q| + 1$.

Proof. If the first case to be added to the CORE-1 retrieval set differs from Q in r attributes, then the next case to qualify can differ in at most $r - 1$ attributes, the next after that in at most $r - 2$ attributes, and so on. So the number of cases in the retrieval set can be at most $r + 1$. As $r \le |A_Q|$, it follows as required that the maximum possible size of the retrieval set is $|A_Q| + 1$.

Proposition 2. *The maximum possible size of the* CORE-2 *retrieval set for a given query Q is* $2^{|A_Q|}$.

Proof. The CORE-2 retrieval set contains at most one case for each subset of the attributes in A_Q. The result follows from the fact that a set with n elements has 2^n subsets.

The maximum possible size of the CORE-3 retrieval set depends on the number of values of each attribute in the target query and is not as easily determined. In practice, the CORE-1 and CORE-2 retrieval set are usually much smaller than their maximum possible sizes. For example, if the most similar case differs from the target query in only a single attribute, then the CORE-1 retrieval set can contain at most two cases.

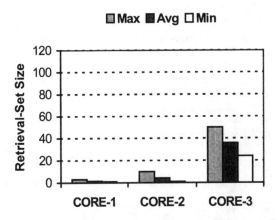

Figure 3. Size of the CORE retrieval set for full-length queries on the PC case library

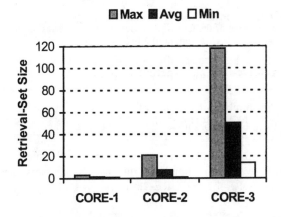

Figure 4. Size of the CORE retrieval set for full-length queries on the Travel case library

Figure 3 shows the maximum, average, and minimum sizes of CORE retrieval sets for full-length queries in another leave-one-out experiment on the PC case library. The results confirm our expectation that the number of cases required to provide full coverage of the case library in CORE-3 is much higher than in CORE-1 or CORE-2. Though unable to compete with CORE-1 in terms of coverage efficiency, CORE-2 has an average retrieval-set size of only 4.2, with 10 the maximum number of cases required to provide full coverage.

Figure 4 shows the results of a similar experiment on the Travel case library (*www.ai-cbr.org*) which contains over 1,000 holidays and their descriptions in terms of 8 attributes such as price, region, duration, and season. Of particular interest is the fact that the maximum size of the CORE-1 retrieval set (3 cases) remains unchanged on this much larger case library. In contrast, the maximum sizes of the CORE-2 and CORE-3 retrieval sets are more than double the corresponding results for the PC case library. It is worth noting, though, that the average size of the CORE-2 retrieval set has increased to only 7.5.

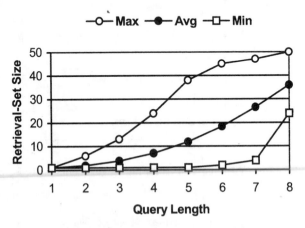

Figure 5. Size of the CORE-3 retrieval set for queries of increasing length on the PC case library

In a further leave-one-out experiment on the PC library, we generated all possible queries of length from 1 to 8 from the description of each left-out case. For example, the number of queries of length 3 is $^8C_3 = 56$. For each query length from 1 to 8, Figure 5 shows the maximum, average, and minimum size of the CORE-3 retrieval set. As might be expected, the average size of the retrieval set required to provide full coverage increases with query length. Average retrieval-set size was also found to increase with query length in similar experiments with CORE-1 and CORE-2.

3.3 Retrieval-Set Conformity

An interesting aspect of a retrieval algorithm's behavior, though not one that appears to have been considered in previous research, is how closely the retrieval sets it produces conform to those produced by *k*-NN. A simple measure of *conformity* is the percentage of cases retrieved for a given query that are also retrieved by *k*-NN. As the size of the CORE retrieval set cannot be predicted in advance, we measure its conformity relative to the k-NN retrieval set of the same size for the target query.

Definition 2. *The conformity of a given retrieval set RS for a target query Q is:*

$$conformity(RS) = \frac{|RS \cap S|}{|RS|} \times 100$$

where S is the k-NN retrieval set for Q with $k = |RS|$.

The fact that the CORE retrieval set always includes the case that is most similar to the target query ensures at least *some* conformity with k-NN. As we shall see, however, conformity of the CORE retrieval set may vary considerably with query length and the preference criterion on which retrieval is based.

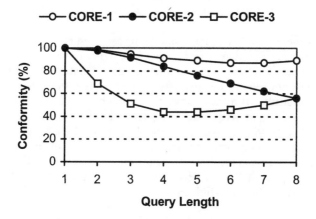

Figure 6. Conformity of the CORE retrieval set for queries of increasing length on the PC case library.

Figure 6 shows the average conformity of CORE retrieval sets for queries on the PC case library ranging in length from 1 to 8. Conformity with k-NN is high in both CORE-1 and CORE-2 for queries of length up to 4, and remains well above 80% for all query lengths in CORE-1. Although conformity decreases with query length in CORE-2, it is much higher than in CORE-3 for short queries, remaining above 75% until query length reaches 6.

It is interesting to note that conformity in CORE-3 is lowest for queries involving 4 or 5 attributes, but then increases to the extent that it equals the conformity of CORE-2 for full-length queries. A possible explanation is that a case may have low similarity to a query in which the majority of attributes are nominal and yet there may be no other case that is at least as good according to the dominance criterion because the first case has an unusually high value for a MIB attribute, or an unusually low price. Though unlikely to appear in the k-NN retrieval set, such a case must be included in the CORE-3 retrieval set to ensure that the case library is fully covered.

4 Related Work

Recent research on CBR approaches to product recommendation has highlighted a number of problems associated with similarity-based retrieval. As mentioned in the introduction, one problem is that the most similar case may not be the one that is most acceptable to the user [2,3,4]. A related issue is that the most similar cases also tend to be very similar to each other, with the result that the user may be offered a very limited choice [4,11]. More specifically, the retrieved cases may not be sufficiently representative of *compromises* that the user may be prepared to make [3]. For example, if all the recommended products are from a manufacturer that the user is not prepared to accept, then the system has failed to deliver a successful recommendation. While the user may be prepared to pay more for the manufacturer she prefers, none of the recommended products offers this compromise. As noted by Bridge and Ferguson [12], users may also have difficulty understanding why one product is recommended while another is not recommended.

Recently there has been considerable research interest in algorithms that combine measures of similarity and *diversity* in the retrieval process to achieve a better balance between these often conflicting characteristics of the retrieved cases [4,11]. Though not relying on diversity as a secondary measure of retrieval-set quality, CORE shares with these approaches the objectives of offering the user a better choice of alternatives and increasing the likelihood that one of the recommended cases will be acceptable. However, retrieval based on a combination of similarity and diversity measures makes it difficult to explain why a given case is recommended, whereas the reason for including a case in the CORE retrieval set can easily be explained. In CORE-1, for example, the reason is that there is no more similar case that satisfies as many of the user's requirements as the recommended case.

A potential problem faced by CORE and other algorithms that aim to offer the user a better choice of alternatives is that in many domains the user is not just seeking a single item that closely matches her query but would like to be informed of all items that are likely to be of interest [3,11]. Typically in such domains, the recommended items (e.g. jobs, rental apartments, bargain holidays) are available for a limited period or sought in competition with other users. A similar problem arises when the recommended items are books, films, or holiday destinations that the user has already read, seen, or visited. In recent work, we have shown how this issue can be addressed in an algorithm based on CORE-2 by providing the user with immediate access to cases for which a recommended case acts as a *representative* case [3].

Though similarly motivated by the need to support compromise more effectively, CORE has little in common with Burkhard's [2] "accumulation for acceptance" technique. For example, CORE-2 supports compromise by ensuring that all (minimal) compromises associated with the available products are represented in the retrieval set. Similarity continues to play an important role in the retrieval process, in that candidate cases for addition to the retrieval set are considered in order of decreasing similarity to the user's query.

In contrast to retrieval approaches in which some or all of the user's requirements are treated as hard constraints [13-15], there is no possibility of retrieval failure being caused by the absence of an exactly matching case in CORE. A case is eliminated in CORE only if one of the recommended cases is at least as good according to the preference criterion on which retrieval is based. The dominance criterion on which retrieval is based in CORE-3 is adapted from multi-criteria decision making, in which the elimination of "dominated" alternatives is a strategy sometimes used in the screening of decision alternatives [16]. The fact that the size of the retrieval set cannot be predicted in advance is a feature that CORE shares with *order-based retrieval* (OBR), in which the cases retrieved for a given query are the *maxima* in an order constructed from preferred values and other information elicited from the user [12]. However, there is no explicit notion of coverage in OBR, or ranking of the retrieved cases in order of similarity to the target query as in CORE.

5 Conclusions

Coverage-optimised retrieval (CORE) is a generalisation of similarity-based retrieval in recommender systems which ensures that the retrieval set for a target query provides full coverage of the case library with respect to a given preference criterion. That is, for any case that is acceptable to the user, the retrieval set is guaranteed to contain a case that is at least as good according to the given preference criterion, and so also likely to be acceptable. As might be expected, there is a trade-off between the strength of the preference criterion on which retrieval is based and the size of the retrieval set required to provide full coverage of the case library.

While the preference criterion in CORE-1 is weaker than in CORE-2, retrieval-set size tends to be much smaller in CORE-1. For full-length queries, the size of the CORE-1 retrieval set was never more than 3 in our experiments. The ability to provide full coverage of the case library with such a small set of cases may be a significant advantage when the number of cases that can be presented to the user is very limited, for example in Internet-enabled mobile phones [4].

More typically in practice, restrictions on retrieval-set size are less severe, and CORE-2 offers a good compromise between strength of preference criterion and retrieval-set size, with an average of only 7.5 cases required to provide full coverage for full-length queries on a case library containing over 1,000 cases. While the preference criterion in CORE-3 is stronger than in CORE-2, the retrieval set required to provide full coverage tends to be much larger in CORE-3, with an average retrieval-set size of 36 even for a relatively small case library.

References

1. Wilke, W., Lenz, M., Wess, S.: Intelligent Sales Support with CBR. In: Lenz, M., Bartsch-Spörl, B., Burkhard, H.-D., Wess, S. (eds) Case-Based Reasoning Technology. LNAI, Vol. 1400. Springer-Verlag, Berlin Heidelberg (1998) 91-113

2. Burkhard. H.-D.: Extending Some Concepts of CBR - Foundations of Case Retrieval Nets. In: Lenz, M. *et al.* (eds) Case-Based Reasoning Technology. LNAI, Vol. 1400. Springer-Verlag, Berlin Heidelberg (1998) 17-50

3. McSherry, D.: Similarity and Compromise. In: Ashley, K., Bridge, D. (eds) Case-Based Reasoning Research and Development. LNAI, Vol. 2689. Springer-Verlag, Berlin Heidelberg (2003) 291-305

4. Smyth, B., McClave, P.: Similarity vs. Diversity. In: Aha, D.W., Watson, I. (eds) Case-Based Reasoning Research and Development. LNAI, Vol. 2080. Springer-Verlag, Berlin Heidelberg (2001) 347-361

5. Branting, L.K..: Acquiring Customer Preferences from Return-Set Selections. In: Aha, D.W., Watson, I. (eds) Case-Based Reasoning Research and Development. LNAI, Vol. 2080. Springer-Verlag, Berlin Heidelberg (2001) 59-73

6. McSherry, D.: Coverage-Optimized Retrieval. Proceedings of the Eighteenth International Joint Conference on Artificial Intelligence, Acapulco, Mexico (2003) 1349-1350

7. Bergmann, R., Breen, S., Göker, M., Manago, M., Wess, S.: Developing Industrial Case-Based Reasoning Applications: The INRECA Methodology. Springer-Verlag, Berlin Heidelberg (1999)

8. Stahl, A.: Defining Similarity Measures: Top-Down vs. Bottom-Up. In: Craw, S., Preece, A. (eds) Advances in Case-Based Reasoning. LNAI, Vol. 2416. Springer-Verlag, Berlin Heidelberg (2002) 406-420

9. McGinty, L., Smyth, B.: Comparison-Based Recommendation. In: Craw, S., Preece, A. (eds) Advances in Case-Based Reasoning. LNAI, Vol. 2416. Springer-Verlag, Berlin Heidelberg (2002) 575-58

10. Epp, S.: Discrete Mathematics with Applications. PWS Publishing Company, Boston, MA (1995)

11. McSherry, D.: Diversity-Conscious Retrieval. In: Craw, S., Preece, A. (eds) Advances in Case-Based Reasoning. LNAI, Vol. 2416. Springer-Verlag, Berlin Heidelberg (2002) 219-233

12. Bridge, D., Ferguson, A.: An Expressive Query Language for Product Recommender Systems. Artificial Intelligence Review **18** (2002) 269-307

13. Bridge, D.: Towards Conversational Recommender Systems: a Dialogue Grammar Approach. In: Aha, D.W. (ed) Proceedings of the EWCBR-02 Workshop on Mixed-Initiative Case-Based Reasoning (2002) 9-22

14. Göker, M.H., Thompson, C.A.: Personalized Conversational Case-Based Recommendation. In: Blanzieri, E., Portinale, L. (eds) Advances in Case-Based Reasoning. LNAI, Vol. 1898. Springer-Verlag, Berlin Heidelberg (2000) 99-111

15. Ricci, F., Arslan, B., Mirzadeh, N., Venturini, A.: ITR: A Case-Based Travel Advisory System. In: Craw, S., Preece, A. (eds) Advances in Case-Based Reasoning. LNAI, Vol. 2416. Springer-Verlag, Berlin Heidelberg (2002) 613-627

16. Hong, I., Vogel, D.: Data and Model Management in a Generalised MCDM-DSS. Decision Sciences **22** (1991) 1-25

AUTHOR INDEX